KU-184-518

COMPLETE GUIDE TO CISM® CERTIFICATION

COMPLETE GUIDE TO CISM® CERTIFICATION

THOMAS R. PELTIER

JUSTIN PELTIER

Auerbach Publications is an imprint of the
Taylor & Francis Group, an informa business

Auerbach Publications
Taylor & Francis Group
6000 Broken Sound Parkway NW, Suite 300
Boca Raton, FL 33487-2742

Printed in the United States of America on acid-free paper
10 9 8 7 6 5 4 3 2 1

International Standard Book Number-10: 0-8493-5356-4 (Hardcover)
International Standard Book Number-13: 978-0-8493-5356-7 (Hardcover)

Library of Congress Cataloging-in-Publication Data

Peltier, Thomas R.
Complete guide to CISM certification / Thomas R. Peltier, Justin Peltier.
p. cm.
Includes bibliographical references and index.
ISBN 0-8493-5356-4 (alk. paper)
1. Electronic data processing personnel--Certification. 2. Computer security--Management--Examinations--Study guides. I. Peltier, Justin, II. Title.

QA76.3.P43 2006
005.8068--dc22 2006049913

Visit the Taylor & Francis Web site at
http://www.taylorandfrancis.com

and the Auerbach Web site at
http://www.auerbach-publications.com

Contents

Preface

The Certified Information Security Manager® (CISM®) certification program was developed by the Information Systems Audit and Controls Association (ISACA®). It has been designed specifically for experienced information security managers and those who have information security management responsibilities. The CISM® certification is for the person who manages, designs, oversees, or assesses an organization's information security program. The CISM® certification references international practices such as ISO guidelines, NIST guidelines, and others.

Certification has provided a positive effect on many careers as well as providing many benefits for employers. The Certified Information Security Manager is designed to provide executive management with assurance that those earning the designation have the required knowledge and ability to provide effective security management and consulting. The certification process examines the qualifications for the candidate in five functional areas (security governance, risk management, information security program management, information security management, and response management).

The CISM is not an entry-level certification, it is specifically developed for the information security professional who has acquired proven experience working on the "front lines." Information security individuals with five years or more experience managing the information security function of an enterprise or performing such duties will find the CISM most tailored to their knowledge and skills.

This book is the result of requests from attendees of our five-day exam preparation course. The book has been structured along the same lines as the class; each of the five key areas is discussed in detail. The reader is given the terms and concepts, along with discussions of their application. At the end of each key area, the reader is given a quiz on the materials just presented. At the end of the key area material, we have included a workbook to allow the reader to go back over the materials to reinforce the concepts presented. After the workbook, the reader is presented with a thirty-question final exam.

Preparing for an exam is hard work. The goal of this book is to present the reader with the knowledge and skills necessary to be successful.

About the Authors

Thomas R. Peltier is in his fifth decade in the field of computer technology. During this time he has shared his experiences with fellow professionals and because of this work he has been awarded the 1993 Computer Security Institute's (CSI) Lifetime Achievement Award. In 1999 the Information Systems Security Association (ISSA®) bestowed its Individual Contribution to the Profession Award on him and in 2001 he was inducted into the ISSA® Hall of Fame. Tom was also awarded the CSI Lifetime Emeritus Membership Award. Currently he is the president of Thomas R. Peltier Associates, LLC, which is an information security training firm. Prior to this he was director of policies and administration for the Netigy Corporation's Global Security Practice. Tom was the national director for consulting services for CyberSafe Corporation, and the corporate information protection coordinator for Detroit Edison. The security program at Detroit Edison was recognized for excellence in the field of computer and information security by winning the Computer Security Institute's Information Security Program of the Year for 1996. Previously Tom was the information security specialist for General Motors Corporation responsible for implementing an information security program for GM's worldwide activities.

Over the past decade, he has averaged five published articles a year on various computer and information security issues, including developing policies and procedures, disaster recovery planning, copyright compliance, virus management, and security controls. He has had published: *Policies, Standards, Guidelines and Procedures, Editions 1* and *2; Information Security Risk Analysis, Editions, 1* and *2; Information System Security Policies and Procedures: A Practitioners' Reference; The Complete Manual of Policies and Procedures for Data Security; How to Manage a Network Vulnerability Assessment;* and *Information Security Fundamentals*, and is the co-editor and contributing author for the CISSP® *Prep for Success Handbook*; and is a contributing author for the *Computer Security Handbook, Third* and *Fifth Editions* and *Data Security Management.*

Tom has been the technical advisor on a number of security films from Commonwealth Films. He is the past chairman of the Computer Security Institute Advisory Council, the chairman of the 18th Annual CSI Conference, founder and past president of the Southeast Michigan Computer Security Special Interest Group, and a former member of the board of directors for (ISC)²®, the security professional certification organization. He has conducted numerous seminars and workshops on various security topics and has led seminars for CSI, Crisis Management, American Institute of Banking, the American Institute of Certified Public Accountants, Institute of Internal Auditors (ISACA®), and Sungard Planning Solutions. He was also an instructor at the graduate level for Eastern Michigan University. He is currently an adjunct professor in the information assurance master's degree program at Norwich University.

Justin Peltier is a senior security consultant with Peltier Associates with over eleven years of experience in information security technologies. As a consultant, Justin has been involved in implementing, supporting, and developing security solutions, and has taught courses on many facets including vulnerability assessment and CISSP preparation. Formerly with Suntel Services, Justin directed its security practice development. Prior to that he was with Netigy where he was involved with the corporate training effort. Justin has led classes for MIS, Netigy, Suntel Services, and Sherwood Associates. Justin currently holds ten certifications in an array of technical products.

Justin has led classes across the United States as well as in Europe and Asia, for Peltier Associates, Sherwood Associates, Computer Security Institute, (ISC)², Mark I. Sobell Training Institute, Netigy Corporation, and Suntel Services. Justin has developed or led the following courses:

- Introduction to Windows NT Security
- Intermediate Windows NT Security
- Advanced Windows NT Security
- Installation and Configuration of Red Hat Linux
- Business Benefits of Virtual Private Networks
- Developing Policies and Procedures
- Risk Assessment Processes
- Conducting a Penetration Test
- Introduction to CheckPoint Firewall-1™ Administration
- Advanced CheckPoint Firewall-1™ Administration
- Conducting a Vulnerability Assessment
- WinX versus Linux: Which Is More Secure?

- Hands-On Wireless
- Hands-On Hacking

Justin has written books on many different subjects related to computer security. His works include two books that are privately owned on Intermediate Windows NT Security and Advanced Windows NT Security. He is co-author of the book *How to Manage a Network Vulnerability Assessment*. He is also a contributing author of the first edition of *The Total CISSP Exam Prep Book: Practice Questions, Answers, and Test Taking Tips and Techniques* and editor of the second edition of the same book. In 2003, Justin co-authored *Information Security Fundamentals*, a set of new sample questions for CISSP and CISM exam preparation. In 2007, Justin is slated to write *Security Testing: Practices, Guidelines, and Examinations* and to edit *Secure Coding and Practices*.

Chapter 1

Information Security Governance

Functional Area Overview

The objective of this job practice area is to focus on the need for a stable security governance program to be in place so all security strategies and processes can be planned, designed, implemented, and maintained. Only with a stable information security governance in place can an organization begin to address the threats to their survivability and profitability. This functional area comprises 21 percent of the CISM® examination and consists of approximately 42 questions.

Security governance is supported by such documents as

- Organization for Economic Co-operation and Development (OECD)
- Institute of Chartered Accountants in England
- ISO/IEC 17799 (ISO 27002)
- British Standard 77 99 (ISO 27001)
- Information Systems Audit and Control (ISACA®), Control Objectives for Information Technology (CobiT®)
- National Institute of Standards and Technology (NIST) Special Publication (SP) 800–55, 800-26, and 800-12

Governance is the process by which governments are selected, held accountable, monitored, and replaced. Corporate governance involves a set of relationships among the organization's management, board, shareholders, and other stakeholders. Corporate governance also provides the structure through which the objectives of the organization are set and the means of attaining those objectives are met, and the ability to monitor performance levels is determined.

In this chapter you will learn about the information security governance tasks:

1. Develop the information security strategy in support of the business strategy and direction.
2. How to obtain senior management commitment and support for information security throughout the organization.
3. Definitions of roles and responsibilities throughout the organization including information security governance.
4. Establish reporting and communication channels that support information security governance activities.
5. Identify current and potential legal and regulatory issues affecting information security and assess their impact on the organization.
6. Establish and maintain information security policies that support business goals and objectives.
7. Ensure the development of procedures and guidelines that support information security policies.
8. Develop a business case which provides an organization value analyses that support information security investments.

CISM® Mapping

When the information security program management functional area is mapped over to ISO 17799 and the domains from the CISSP® common body of knowledge, it shows just how many different areas of knowledge from which we are going to be drawing information. Information security program management is so large that it basically encompasses everything in telecommunication and network security, everything in security architecture, everything in cryptography, and everything in access control systems and methodologies. It is a very, very large functional area (see Table 1.1).

Introduction

The governance section addresses the foundation upon which an organization will build its information security program. Whereas the other four topic areas go into more detail on supportive activities, in this section we get an overview of requirements.

Table 1.1 Mapping CISM Governance to ISO 17799 and CISSP ® Domains

Information Security Program Management *ISO 17799 Section*	*CISSP® Domain*
4. Information Security Policy	3. Security Management
5. Information Security Organization	9. Law, Investigation and Ethics
9. Communications and Operations Management	

The foundation of a successful information security program begins with strong upper-level management support. This support establishes a focus on security within the highest levels of the organization. Without a solid foundation (i.e., proactive support of those persons in positions that control IT resources), the effectiveness of the security program can fail when pressured by politics and budget limitations.

Any information security program must get its direction from executive management (see Figure 1.1). The requirements of today's laws and regulations have identified either the organization's board of directors or an executive management steering committee as responsible for instituting an effective program.

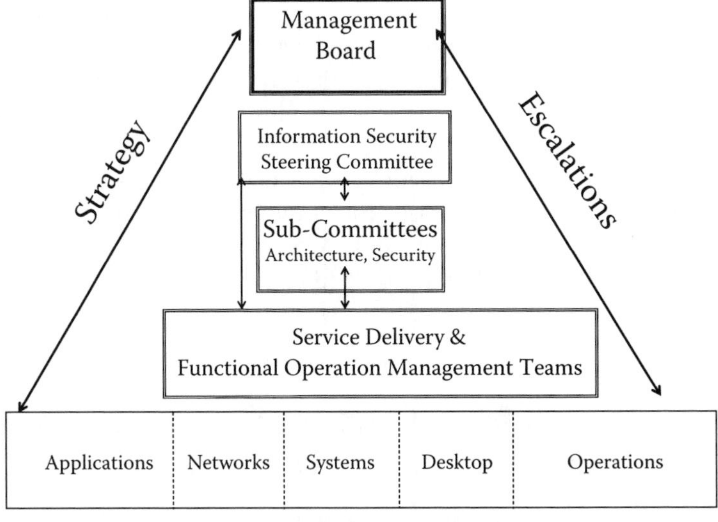

Figure 1.1 Security management hierarchy.

The responsibilities for each group of management and employees must be established (see Table 1.2). Typically the roles and responsibilities are established in a mission statement, which we examine later. The requirements might resemble something like that shown in Table 1.3

The second component of an effective security program is practical security policies and procedures backed by the authority necessary to enforce compliance. Practical security policies and procedures are defined as those that are attainable and provide meaningful security through appropriate controls. The ability to determine the effectiveness of the security program is not easily obtainable if there are no procedures in place.

The third component of developing and establishing an effective security program is the ability to capture and provide meaningful information on program effectiveness. To provide meaningful data, quantifiable security metrics must be based on IT security performance goals and objectives, and be easily obtainable and feasible to measure. They must also be repeatable, provide relevant performance trends over time, and be useful for tracking performance and directing resources.

Finally, the security program itself must emphasize consistent periodic analysis of the program. The results of this analysis are used to apply lessons learned, improve the effectiveness of existing security controls, and plan future controls to meet new security requirements as they occur. Accurate data collection must be a priority with stakeholders and users if the collected data is to be meaningful to the management and improvement of the overall security program.

The success of an information security program implementation should be judged by the degree to which meaningful results are produced. A comprehensive security analysis program (see Table 1.4) should provide substantive justification for decisions that directly affect the security posture of an organization. These decisions include budget and personnel requests, and allocation of available resources. A security program should provide a precise basis for preparation of required security performance-related reports.

Developing an Information Security Strategy in Support of Business Strategy and Direction

When developing an effective information security strategy the information security professional must create the program in full view while working with the other components of the organization. In other words, the program must meet the needs of the organization and not just be an implementation of commonly developed controls.

Table 1.2 Senior Management Requirements

ISO 17799 Section	*Control Requirement*	*HIPAA*	*GLBA*	*Sarbanes-Oxley*
Organizational Security (4.1)	Management Information Security Forum	Risk Management (Required) Sanction Policy (Required) Privacy Officer (Required)	Involve the Board of Directors Assign Specific Responsibilities	Corporation management is responsible for assuring internal controls are adequate

Table 1.3 Governance Roles and Responsibilities

Information Security Roles and Responsibilities		
Governance Body	*Membership*	*Responsibilities*
Information Security Steering Committee	CEO, CFO, COO, CTO VP Business Units Chaired by CISO	Establishes and supports security program
Senior Management	C-level, Senior VPs and Unit VPs	Provides management, operational, and technical controls to satisfy security requirements
Chief Information Security Officer (CISO)	CISO & staff	Directs and coordinates implementation of information security program
Business Unit Managers	Department heads and Supervision	Classifies and establishes requirements for safeguarding information assets

Table 1.4 Security Program Infrastructure

Maturity Level	*Description*
Level 1	Control objectives have been documented in a policy
Level 2	Security control processes have been documented in procedures
Level 3	Supporting procedures have been implemented (stakeholders have been made aware and trained)
Level 4	Policies, procedures and controls are tested and reviewed to ensure continued adequacy
Level 5	Procedures and controls are fully integrated into the culture of the organization

All security decisions must be linked to the organization's business objectives or mission statement. As with other organizationwide policies, the information security program must be established by the implementation of a Global or Tier 1 policy. This type of policy is organizationwide and requires that all areas of the organization comply with the policy. We discuss policies in more detail later in this chapter.

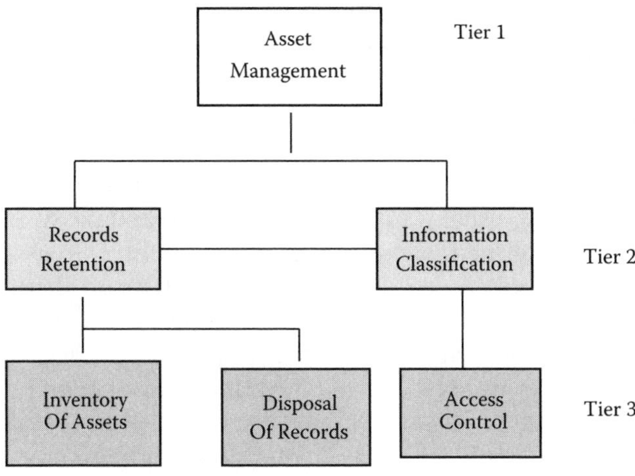

Figure 1.2 Policy and procedure architecture.

To be successful, the security and privacy policies and procedures must have three key elements. They must be:

- Documented
- Communicated
- Current

To supplement an information security policy, the organization must offer awareness programs, user training, and support education. In the hierarchy of documentation we might see a structure such as that shown in Figure 1.2

We go into more detail later in this chapter on policies and supporting documents.

When establishing an information security strategy, the goal of what must be accomplished must be present in all that we create and implement. Information security's goal is not to stop all access to all information but to provide a safe and secure process for all authorized personnel to gain access. The information strategy must, therefore, address three key concepts:

- Identification
- Authentication
- Authorization

To gain access to information and the processing systems everyone needing access must be assigned a unique, individual access code.

Typically this access code is called a userID or an account. There must be procedures in place to provide the information necessary and the approvals required to grant an individual a unique userID.

Once a userID has been established, it will be necessary to authenticate the individual to the system or application they need to access the information. This process is termed authentication and is the process of identifying an individual, usually based on a username and password. A userID and password is termed one-factor authentication. The userID can be teamed up with a token card (such as a SecureID card that changes the password every 60 seconds) or with a biometric (a fingerprint or voiceprint). Many secure systems require two-factor authentication. This means teaming the userID up with a password and one or more of the other methods.

So we have identification, authentication, and the last element is authorization. So once I have identified who I am and authenticated who I am, then I am authorized. I will be authorized to access those things I need to in order to perform my job. There are two key elements regarding authorization and those are *need to know* and *least privilege.* In authentication it is necessary to establish the parameters that verify individuals are who they present themselves to be. Once authenticated, the individual must be authorized to access the resources of the organization. To accomplish that, the individual must present a business need for access. Once business need has been established, the individual is granted only that level of access necessary to perform that specific job function. This process is termed least privilege.

Access can be granted either to an individual or based on the function the individual is performing for the business. You can have individual authorization or you can have group authorization. When somebody comes into a group it signals group authorizations and when they leave they're relieved from the group and those authorizations are taken away. This is a concept known as least privilege. With need to know, you have to have a business need to have access to whatever you're looking at.

An effective security strategy requires at a minimum five key elements: policies, procedures, authentication, authorization, and recovery plan because people have a tendency to wipe things out inadvertently. Sixty-five percent of information loss still comes from errors and omissions. The last thing that you want to hear is, "Oops," or your technician coming in and saying, "Hey, watch this." So you have to have a recovery plan to be able to recover the information as you go through the process. An effective security function requires a well-administered security and privacy policy meaning that not only do we have the written word but that you check it from time to time to make sure it continues to meet the goals and objectives of an organization and that it can be marked through this post-development life cycle. Security strategy must become part of the business and System Development Life Cycle (SDLC). I prefer business process life cycle because the things that we implement in this controlled environment are such that it's not just for information technology; it is for the entire organization. It's a business process because all of those things that we have to do in developing systems and applications are to be done whenever we have a project or business process that is to be developed. So it maps across the entire thing, information by the way is not the IT purview. Information is a corporate activity and corporate function and (here is where we get to the theory part) should not be part of IT.

An effective information security strategy requires four types of controls: preventive, detective, containment, and recovery. Dr. Peter Stephenson has altered these elements to currently address assurance, avoidance, detection, and recovery. Our strategy is to prevent as much as possible; then we want to able to detect when we have problems, to contain the problem, and we want to have the ability to recover from it. Business continuity planning is part of our overall organization process as an example so you understand what business continuity planning is.

Business Continuity Planning, BCP, is a corporate requirement. As you can see later on it is one of the 12 corporate policies. It's not an IT function and it's not run by IT; typically it's run by facilities management, risk management, or physical security. The business unit's BCP must be integrated with the IT Disaster Recovery Plan (DRP) and the organizationwide BCP. Typically we should see each business unit have a line item budget for their BCP and a line item in their budget for their portion of the data center disaster recovery plan.

So the difference between business continuity planning and disaster recovery planning is that all departments within organizations have to do business continuity planning. The IT recovery processing portion is called disaster recovery planning. So in key terms (see Table 1.5) that you should know is to go through and to prepare for the exam on business continuity planning.*

We used to call it business resumption or recovery planning but it's fallen out of favor because that means that you've had an interruption and you couldn't back up when we were selling things. Continuity of operations plans provides procedures and capabilities to sustain the organization's central strategic functions at an alternate site. In order for us to do this we must perform this business in-dropped analysis. This tells us what our most critical systems applications and business processes are and when we get into that we'll talk more about it as we go online but that's talking about

* National Institute of Standards and Technology, Special Publication 800-34Contingency Planning Guide for Information Technology, June 2002.

Table 1.5 Contingency Plan Definitions

Plan	*Purpose*	*Scope*
Business Continuity Plan (BCP)	Provide procedures for sustaining essential business operations while recovering from a significant disruption	Addresses business processes; IT addressed based only on its support for business process
Business Recovery (Resumption) Plan (BRP)	Provide procedures for recovering business operations immediately following a disaster	Addresses business processes; not IT-focused; IT addressed based only on its support for business process
Continuity of Operations Plan (COOP)	Provide procedures and capabilities to sustain an organization's essential, strategic functions at an alternate site for up to 30 days	Addresses the subset of an organization's missions that are deemed most critical; usually written at headquarters level; not IT-focused
Crisis Communications Plan (CCP)	Provide procedures for disseminating status reports to personnel and the public	Addresses communications with personnel and the public; not IT-focused
Cyber Incident Response Plan (CIRP)	Provide strategies to detect, respond to, and limit consequences of malicious cyber incident	Focuses on information security responses to incidents affecting systems and/or networks
Disaster Recovery Plan (DRP)	Provide detailed procedures to facilitate recovery of capabilities at an alternate site	Often IT-focused; limited to major disruptions with long-term effects
Emergency Response Plan (ERP)	Provide coordinated procedures for minimizing loss of life or injury and protecting property damage in response to a physical threat	Focuses on personnel and property particular to the specific facility; not business process or IT system functionality based

bringing up your most critical business processes, systems, and applications at a recovery site. Continuity of operations plans provide procedural capabilities to assist updates.

The crisis communications plan includes senior management, legal, human resources, public relations, and the recovery planning coordinator. Talking about a group that's aptly named, crisis management, this group is responsible for activating and overseeing the recovery processes.

The cyber incident response plans include the normal day-to-day activities and when they have a need for recovery you need to have procedures in place to do them in a structured and formatted manner and not ad hoc.

The data center disaster recovery plan is for the information processing environment and the emergency response plan is one of the elements of an overall plan but is also a key component of the information security strategy. The emergency response plan stabilizes the environment and ensures the safety of the employees. We discuss these topics in depth later in the book.

As part of the information security strategy and the BCP process, it will be necessary to ensure that Service Level Agreements (SLA) are in place between the organization and the service provider. This includes internal as well as external third parties. So whenever there is a new application system or a business process is moved into production, a service level agreement should be implemented to identify service levels. The SLA should include things such as time that it's going to be run, from what period to what period; you'll talk about recovery requirements, backup requirements, and when it has to be up. All of these things are established in service level agreements and you do this internally; you do it externally with third parties.

Testing for the BCP should be done whenever there is a change in the plan or anything in environment business resumption, business continuity planning, or disaster recovery planning which has to be done on a regular basis not to exceed annually. The Office of the Comptroller of the Currency (OCC) requires that you attest that banks and financial institutions have their plans tested at least on an annual basis and that management attests that this has to be done.

When establishing an information security strategy, the information security manager must consider the skills necessary to perform the various security-related activities and the ability to implement the tasks and projects that make up information security. It is management's responsibility to define the skills required to perform these tasks. What often happens is that the security professional confuses the oversight task with the day-to-day administration functions.

A key element in an information security strategy is the concept of conflict of interest. The group or individual responsible for monitoring the activities cannot be the same group or individual doing the task. No one person can be responsible for all of the tasks in a process. However, information security will be involved in establishing the security posture and strategy for such activities as firewall administration, user account administration, anti-virus program, encryption, or privacy compliance. Once these processes are in place, information security is responsible for ensuring that the processes are implemented as required.

Who is in security? It is the information security staff. The group will establish the security program, set the standards, and you work to assess the level of compliance. They do not actually do day-to-day activities. They do awareness and training. They establish the policies, procedures, and standards. They have enough on their plates to do those kinds of activities and don't actually do the day-to-day operations activities.

Obtain Senior Management Commitment and Support

To be successful, the information security program must get the organization's business management involved in the program. Why is it important to achieve a high standard of corporate governance? Why is it important to treat information security as a critical business issue and create a security-positive environment? Why is it important to demonstrate to third parties that the organization addresses information security requirements in a professional manner? Why is it important to apply fundamental principles such as assuming ultimate responsibility for information security, implementing controls that are proactive, and achieving individual accountability?

Let's examine why business continuity and disaster recovery planning fail. The key reason is that these processes have not been presented to management as a business need. Typically there is some external force that is requiring management to do them. It could be because there is an OCC (The Office of the Comptroller of the Currency) requirement, it could be an audit comment, or it could be some external requirement. The reason that BCP and DRP fail is that there has never been an internal risk assessment with the organization's stakeholders to determine what would happen or what the business reasons are why we should be moving forward with business continuity planning or disaster recovery planning.

The same thing is true with information security. There are requirements—HIPAA, GLBA, Sarbanes–Oxley, 7799—to have a security program. Okay, so what? Why do I as a business person need to be learning information security programs? That's IT's responsibility, don't bother me with this. We go back to our key tenants' fiduciary duty and due diligence. The information security program is put together to ensure that management meets its fiduciary duty in protecting the assets of the organization, and this includes our information assets.

Fiduciary duty assigns a trust to management to protect the assets of the organization. The duty or responsibility is made up of two key components: duty of loyalty and duty of care. Duty of loyalty requires that any decision made by management must be made in the best interest of the enterprise. Duty of care requires that management will implement reasonable and prudent controls.

The other key concept is that of due diligence. Due diligence is the process of systematically evaluating information to identify risks and issues relating to a proposed transaction (i.e., verify that information is what it is proposed to be). This ensures that management will make informed business decisions. We address this issue further when we discuss risk management in Chapter 2.

There are three ways that senior management demonstrates their commitment to information security. The first is to become more directly involved in high-level security elements such as policy approval and implementation. This is currently being done by an Information Security Steering Committee (ISSC) made up of representatives of the various business units. The ISSC is the champion and the approver of the policies, the business continuity plan, and business impact analysis results. They are on a hook for that. It's required by law and by international standards.

The second way to demonstrate support is to demonstrate openly their support for the program. This could be as simple as wearing their employee identification badges. Finally, allocating sufficient resources to information security is the third way to demonstrate support. We would all like to have the budget to things.

Information security programs are doomed to failure without the overt support of senior management. To be most effective, information security should not be part of information technology and must be supported by the ISSC.

Information security responsibilities should be defined in each employee's job description. It is a responsibility of management to incorporate information security into the employee standards of conduct document. We discussed unacceptable activities and what will happen if employees are found to be in a noncompliant situation. Compliance with information security should be tied to an employee's performance-based objectives and part of the employee's review progress.

An annual report on the state of information security for the organization has to be presented by the ISSC. Senior management should have a high level of commitment and will then achieve high standards of corporate governance. Information security is a business process that helps maintain confidence in an organization. Corporations need to demonstrate a commitment to information security. This includes keeping all types of private information confidential. Examples of private information would include users, partners and employees' sensitive information, such as wages, social security numbers, and health care information. It is the ultimate responsibility of senior management to assume the fiduciary duty to protect the assets of the organization. From the context of a security program, senior management needs to witness and have demonstrated how these goals and objectives will be met.

Definitions of Roles and Responsibilities

The importance of security governance must be reinforced in every employee's job description. When reviewing the employee's performance annually, their compliance to security regulations, policies, and attitudes should be a factor in the appraisal process. Security-related competencies for various job positions should be defined and documented for inclusion in job descriptions. It is important that information security work with human resources to ensure that this task is completed.

Information security is an enterprisewide management responsibility. Each group has a different role and these roles support the activities of the other roles and responsibilities. Let us examine typical roles found in an organization and what they are responsible for with regard to risk assessment and risk management.

- *Senior Management:* Under the standard of due care, senior management is charged with the ultimate responsibility for meeting business objectives or mission requirements. Senior management must ensure that necessary resources are effectively applied to develop the capabilities to meet the mission requirements. They must incorporate the results of the risk assessment process into the decision-making process.
- *Chief Information Security Officer (CISO):* The CISO is responsible for the organization's planning, budgeting, and performance including its information security components. Decisions made in this area should be based on an effective risk management program.
- *Information Owner:* These are the department managers assigned as functional owners of organization assets and who are responsible for ensuring that proper controls are in place to address integrity, confidentiality, and availability of the information resources of which they are assigned ownership. The term "owner" must be established in the asset classification policy.

- *Business Managers:* The managers (AKA, owners) are the individuals with the authority and responsibility for making cost-benefit decisions essential to ensure accomplishment of organization mission objectives. Their involvement in the risk management process enables the selection of business-oriented controls. The charge of being an owner supports the objective of fulfilling the fiduciary responsibility of management to protect the assets of the enterprise.
- *Information Security Officer:* The security program manager is responsible for the organization's security programs, including risk management.

Obtaining Senior Management Commitment

There are many process and enabling technologies that will ensure the success of an organization's security strategy. These might include:

- Achieving a high level of standards and corporate governance
- Treating information security as a critical business issue and creating a security-positive working culture
- Demonstrating to third parties that the organization manages information security in a professional manner
- Applying fundamental principles such as assuming ultimate responsibility for information security, implementing controls that are proportionate to risk, and achieving individual accountability

As we discussed earlier, management is charged with two key responsibilities and those are fiduciary duty and due diligence. An important deliverable from an effective information security program is the ability for management to demonstrate their compliance with these key requirements.

When we mapped out current legislation requirements and business directives, we saw that senior management must become directly involved in the high-level information security arrangements. Their task is to approve and support policies and allocate sufficient funding to ensure a quality information security program.

Where information security should report is one of the perennial questions that has concerned the information security practitioner for nearly three decades. The computer security group achieved its goals and objectives by working within the IS structure. This security function supported mainframe systems and established its realm based on protecting data and access to the system. The primary responsibilities of this group were access control and disaster recovery planning.

Until the introduction of desktop-based computing, the needs of the organization and the role of the computer security group changed dramatically. The arrival of the personal computer and the ongoing transition to the client/server open systems operating environment, shifted information processing and storage from the mainframe data center to the business unit workplace. This change has forced internal auditing, the "Big 4" accounting firms, and security professionals to reassess the efficient location of the information protection activity.

The National Cyber Security Summit Task Force in 2004 published *Information Security Governance: A Call to Action*. This call to action was a result of the Corporate Governance Task Force which was founded in 2003. This task force was chaired by the CEO of Entrust and CEO of RSA Security and the task force was made up of a Who's-Who of industry, government, and academia.*

Change in Focus

The notion that information security is a function of information technology no longer fits the dynamically changing telecommunication efforts of today's business and industry. With the requirements of the laws and regulations that we have discussed before, and the need to report to executive management on a regular basis, the best and most efficient place for information security to report is to these senior management boards or committees.

The Cyber Security Industrial Alliance published their *National Agenda for Information Security in 2006* in December, 2005. In this document the Alliance noted that "Information assurance in the private sector is critical to creating a more secure infrastructure." The report recommended that the federal government "encourage" CEOs to review cyber security measures at board meetings. This effort will help senior executives understand the security-related implications of Sarbanes–Oxley, GLBA, and HIPAA.**

---

* Corporate Governance Task Force Report, *Information Security Governance A Call to Action*, April 2004.

** Cyber Security Industry Alliance, *National Agenda for Information Security in 2006*, December 2005.

Table 1.6 Roles and Responsibilities

Responsibility	*Task*
Chief Executive Officer (CEO)	– Oversee overall "Organization Security–Posture" (Accountable to Board) Brief Board, customers, public
Chief Information Security Officer (CISO) Chief Risk Officer (CRO) Department/Agency Head (DH)	– Set security policy, procedures, standards, program, training and awareness for Organization – Respond to security breaches (investigate, mitigate, litigate) – Responsible for independent annual audit coordination
Mid-Level Manager (MGR)	– Implement /audit/enforce/assess compliance* – Communicate policies, program, awareness and training
Staff and Employees	– Implement Policy – Report security vulnerabilities and breaches

Responsibilities and Functional Roles

The information security governance responsibilities and role assignments might look like the example shown in Table 1.6.

Figure 1.3 gives a graphic example of how the reporting responsibilities might manifest themselves in a larger and a smaller organization.

A smaller organization may have a number of variations on this theme. Figure 1.4 gives an example of an organization chart for a smaller enterprise.

Where Not to Report

Auditing: Reporting here would put the information security activity into a conflict of interest. It would be the same as having those that make the laws and those that judge compliance with them reporting in the same organization. It is best to establish a partnership between the groups.

Operations: The key problem here is that operations must concentrate on completing the production schedule and keep the system available for the users. Some necessary control measures may be ignored or circumvented if the information security function reported to the head of operations.

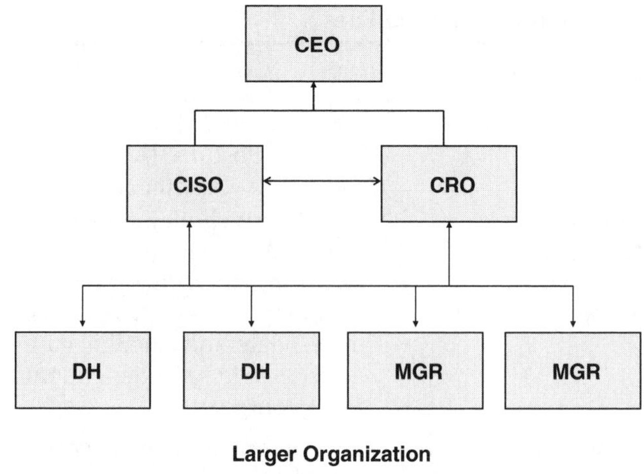

Figure 1. 3 Larger organization reporting matrix.

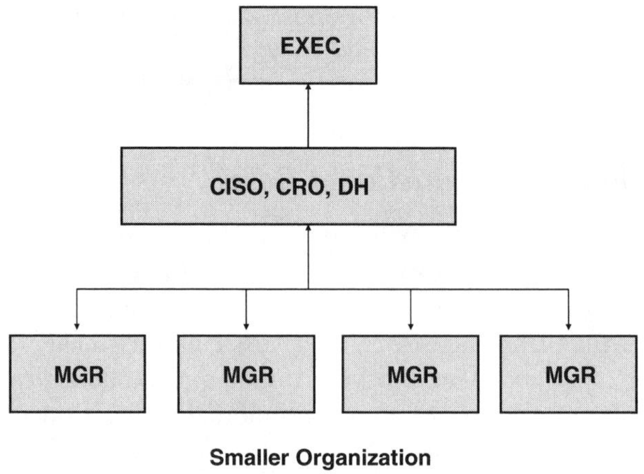

Figure 1.4 Smaller organization reporting matrix.

Physical Security: Many employees associate "security" with guards, dogs, guns, and badges, hardly the image of today's security professional (either physical or information). The problem with having information security report into this structure is that it is a perception problem. For many organizations, security is viewed as being responsible for loss control. Instead of an IP function being viewed as an enabling tool, it may be seen as the "cop."

Recommendation

The information security function must grapple with the new challenges posed by the decentralized client/server workplace and an increased level of legal and regulatory issues. Senior management increasingly recognizes that information is an asset of the organization, and that they are responsible for exercising their fiduciary duty to ensure that organizational information resources are properly protected. A successful information security program requires senior management support, internal and external auditors' recommendations, assigned responsibility, and effective reporting structures.

The user community's perception of information security is equally essential to a program's success. To implement a world-class program, ensure that the business units understand their role in information security. To facilitate the proper image and foster active partnerships, information security needs a semblance of autonomy to be successful. To achieve this, information security should report directly to the CISO.

Establish Reporting Communications That Support Information Security Governance Activities

An annual report of the state of information security should be presented to the Information Security Steering Committee. This reporting requirement has been established in current legislation and information security international standards. This report should not be confused with a standard feature audit performed by the audit staff, nor is it part of some third-party certification process.

Typically the CISO would prepare a report on the levels of compliance currently seen throughout the business units. The report development process normally has two key components: compliance with core information security requirements; and the level of implementation for the current information security initiative. An example questionnaire is shown in Table 1.7.

To ensure that the information security program is relevant, the information security team should be active members of the local chapter of the Information Systems Audit and Control Association (ISACA). ISACA got its start in 1967, when a small group of individuals with similar jobs—auditing controls in the computer systems that were becoming increasingly critical to the operations of their organizations—sat down to discuss the need for a centralized source of information and guidance in the field. In 1969, the group formalized, incorporating as the EDP Auditors Association. In 1976 the association formed an education foundation to

Table 1.7 Information Security Questionnaire

Information Protection Question	*Compliance Yes/No*	*Comments*	*Date*	*Initials*
A Corporate Information Officer (CIO) has been named and the CIO is responsible for implementing and maintaining an effective IP program.				
The Information Protection (IP) program supports the business objective and/or mission statement of the organization.				
An enterprise-wide IP policy has been implemented.				
An individual has been assigned as the corporate information protection coordinator and overall responsibility for the IP program implementation has been assigned.				
The IP program is an integral element of sound management practices.				
Information Protection is identified as a separate and distinct budget item (approximately 1-3% of the overall ISO budget).				
Senior management is aware of the business needs for an effective IP program, and is committed to support its success.				
An effective risk analysis process has been implemented to assist management in identifying potential threats, probability of threat occurrence, and possible counter measures.				
IP controls are based on cost/benefit analysis utilizing risk analysis input.				
IP responsibilities and accountability for all employees with regard to IP are explicit.				

Table 1.7 Information Security Questionnaire (Continued)

Information Protection Question	*Compliance Yes/No*	*Comments*	*Date*	*Initials*
Each business unit, department, agency, etc. has designated an individual responsible for implementing the IP program for that organization.				
The IP program is integrated into a variety of areas both within and outside the computer security field.				
Comprehensive information protection policies, procedures, standards and guidelines have been created and disseminated to all employees and appropriate third parties.				
An ongoing IP awareness program has been implemented for all organization employees.				
A positive, proactive relationship with the audit staff has been established.				
Employees have been made aware that their activities may be monitored.				
An effective program to monitor IP program-related activities has been implemented.				
Employee compliance to IP-related issues is an annual appraisal element.				
The system development life cycle addresses IP requirements during the Initiation or Analysis (first) phase.				
The IP program is reviewed annually and modified where necessary.				

undertake large-scale research efforts to expand the knowledge and value of the IT governance and control field.

Today, membership to ISACA—more than 50,000 strong worldwide—is characterized by its diversity. Members live and work in more than 140 countries and cover a variety of professional IT-related positions: to name just a few, IS auditor, consultant, educator, IS security professional, regulator, chief information officer, and internal auditor. Some are new to the field, others are at middle-management levels, and still others are in the most senior ranks. They work in nearly all industry categories, including financial and banking, public accounting, government and the public sector, utilities, and manufacturing. This diversity enables members to learn from each other, and exchange widely divergent viewpoints on a variety of professional topics. It has long been considered one of ISACA's strengths.

Another organization that supports the information security professional is the Information Systems Security Association (ISSA). ISSA is a not-for-profit, international organization of information security professionals and practitioners. It provides educational forums, publications, and peer interaction opportunities that enhance the knowledge, skill, and professional growth of its members.

With active participation from individuals and chapters all over the world, the ISSA is the largest international, not-for-profit association specifically for security professionals. Members include practitioners at all levels of the security field in a broad range of industries, such as communications, education, healthcare, manufacturing, finance, and government.

The primary goal of the ISSA is to promote management practices that will ensure the confidentiality, integrity, and availability of information resources. The ISSA facilitates interaction and education to create a more successful environment for global information systems security and for the professionals involved.

A third such organization is the Computer Security Institute (CSI). CSI is the world's leading membership organization specifically dedicated to serving and training the information, computer, and network security professional. Since 1974, CSI has been providing education and aggressively advocating the critical importance of protecting information assets.

CSI sponsors two conference and exhibitions each year: CSI NetSec in June, and the CSI Annual Computer Security Conference and Exhibition in November. CSI also offers a full schedule of training classes on encryption, intrusion management, Internet, firewalls, awareness, Windows, and more. CSI membership benefits include the ALERT newsletter, quarterly journal, discounts on CSI conferences and training, and SecurCompass, an automated, standards-based security program assessment tool. They also publish the annual *CSI/FBI Computer*

Crime and Security Survey, *Frontline* end-user awareness newsletter, and *Topline* security brief for executives.

Mission Statement

Throughout the enterprisewide policy document references to information security and the information security program should be incorporated. These concepts should begin with a review of the enterprise's shared beliefs that usually discuss such important concepts as teamwork, accountability, communication, continuous improvement, and benchmarking. Because of the increased emphasis on proper conduct, a formal discussion of the enterprise's support of due diligence concepts should be established.

The use of the term "accountability" when establishing organization goals and beliefs allows the enterprise to commit to the concept that it is willing to accept accountability for the results of decisions made to support the business process or mission of the enterprise. To ensure that appropriate, informed business decisions are made in an open climate of discussion and research, a formal risk analysis process should be implemented to document all management decisions.

By establishing this level of accountability, the enterprise is creating a climate of due diligence throughout the organization. A formal business-related risk management process will ensure that all decisions are made quickly and efficiently and that the process is recorded. This will allow third parties to examine the process and verify that due diligence was performed.

As a security professional, it is very important that due diligence is established as an enterprise objective and guiding principle. Risk management will ensure that all decisions are based on the best needs of the enterprise and those prudent and reasonable controls and safeguards are implemented. With the implementation of more stringent reporting mechanisms and laws (Sarbanes–Oxley) or international standards such as British Standards 7799 (BS 7799) or ISO 17799, the formal adoption of a risk management process will assist in proving the enterprise is being managed in a proper manner.

Another important element found in most enterprisewide policy documents is a section on organizational responsibilities. This section is where the various mission statements of the enterprise organizations are resident along with any associated responsibilities. For example:

> *Auditing:* Auditing assesses the adequacy of and compliance with management, operating, and financial controls, as well as the administrative and operational effectiveness of organizational units.

Information Security: Information Security (IS) is to direct and support the company and affiliated organizations in the protection of their information assets from intentional or unintentional disclosure, modification, destruction, or denial through the implementation of appropriate information security and business resumption planning policies, procedures, and guidelines.

Legal and Regulatory Issues

Security governance is supported by laws, regulations, standards, and other controlling mechanisms that create structure and establish requirements from which the security program can function.

Corporate governance involves a relationship among the company's management, board of directors, shareholders, stakeholders, and anyone with a vested interest in how the organization is run. There are a couple of key terms that will permeate most of the practice areas. The first of these is fiduciary duty: that's what management is charged with; they are charged with protecting the assets of the organization. Laws such as the Foreign Corrupt Practices Act (FCPA) and Sarbanes–Oxley (SOX) require management to attest that they have internal controls and that the internal controls are tested and are found to be adequate. What the FCPA and SOX provide for the information security program is the requirement that management be responsible for two key concepts: fiduciary duty and due diligence.

For many organizations there will be a number of laws, regulations, standards, and internal requirements to which they must adhere. The best way to make sense of all of them is to identify which ones affect your organization. Then using an appropriate standard (we'll use ISO 17799:2000 as the baseline), map the requirements to the standard.

In Table 1.8 I have identified a number of current laws, regulations, and standards that will affect your organization. I found a brief discussion of each to be helpful and you will find it effective when discussing reasons why things must be done,

Once I have identified the external requirements, I then map them to an existing standard that the organization has been using to measure information security compliance levels. An example is illustrated in Table 1.9. These standards could be CobiT or Federal Financial Institutions Examination Council's (FFIEC) directives. Once you have established this mapping process, then it will be easy to perform a gap analysis any time a new requirement is presented.

Once the external laws, regulations, and standards have been identified and mapped it will be necessary to determine how these requirements

Table 1.8 Information Security Legislation

Law	*Definition*
Federal Guidelines for Sentencing for Criminal Convictions	The Federal Sentencing Guidelines define executive responsibility for fraud, theft, and anti-trust violations, and establish a mandatory point system for federal judges to determine appropriate punishment. Since much fraud and falsifying corporate data involves access to computer-held data, liability established under the Guidelines extend to computer-related crime as well. What has caused many executives concern, is that the mandatory punishment could apply even when intruders enter a computer system and perpetrate a crime. While the Guidelines have a mandatory scoring system for punishment, they also have an incentive for proactive crime prevention. The requirement here is for management to show *"due diligence"* in establishing an effective compliance program. There are seven elements that capture the basic functions inherent in most compliance programs: 1. Establish policies, standards, and procedures to guide the workforce; 2. Appoint a high-level manager to oversee compliance with the policy, standards and procedures; 3. Exercise due care when granting discretionary authority to employees; 4. Assure compliance policies are being carried out; 5. Communicate the standards and procedures to all employees and others; 6. Enforce the policies, standards and procedures consistently through appropriate disciplinary measures; 7. Procedures for corrections and modifications in case of violations. These guidelines reward those organizations which make a good faith effort to prevent unethical activity. This is done by lowering potential fines if, despite the organization's best efforts, unethical or illegal activities are still committed by the organization and/or its employees. To be judged effective a compliance program need not prevent all misconduct, however, it must show due diligence in seeking to prevent and detect inappropriate behavior.

Table 1.8 Information Security Legislation (Continued)

Law	*Definition*
The Economic Espionage Act of 1996	The Economic Espionage Act (EEA) of 1996 for the first time makes trade secret theft a federal crime, subject to penalties including fines, forfeiture, and imprisonment. The act reenforces the rules governing trade secrets in that businesses must show that they have taken reasonable measures to protect their proprietary trade secrets in order to seek relief under the EEA. In "Counterintelligence and Law Enforcement: The Economic Espionage Act of 1996 versus Competitive Intelligence"* author Peter F. Kalitka believes that given the penalties companies face under the EEA, that business hiring outside consultants to gather competitive intelligence should establish a policy on this activity. Included in the contract language with the outside consultant should be definitions on: • What is hard-to-get information?; • How will the information be obtained?; • Do they adhere to the Society of Competitive Intelligence Professionals Code of Ethics?; and • Do they have accounts with clients that may be questioned?
The Foreign Corrupt Practices Act (FCPA)	For 20 years, the FCPA was largely ignored by regulators. This was due in part to an initial amnesty program under which nearly 500 companies admitted violations. Now the federal government has dramatically increased its attention on business activities and is looking to enforce the act with vigor. To avoid liability under the FCPA, companies must implement a due diligence program that includes a set of internal controls and enforcement. A set of policies and procedures that are implemented and audited for compliance are required to meet the test of due diligence.
Sarbanes–Oxley (SOX)	Sarbanes–Oxley (SOX) was signed into law on July 30, 2002 and the provisions of the act have a meaningful impact on both public companies and auditors. Two important sections of the act are: • Section 302 (Disclosure Controls and Procedures or "DC&P") that requires quarterly certification of financial statements by CEO and CFO. The CEO and CFO must certify completeness and accuracy of the filings and attest to the effectiveness of internal control.

Table 1.8 Information Security Legislation (Continued)

Law	*Definition*
	• Section 404 (Internal Control Attest), requires annual affirmation of management's responsibility for internal controls over financial reporting. Management must attest to effectiveness based on an evaluation and the Auditor must attest and report on management's evaluation.
Health Insurance Portability and Accountability Act (HIPAA)	The Health Insurance Portability and Accountability Act (HIPAA), is also known as Kassebaum-Kennedy, after the two senators who spearheaded the bill. Passed in 1996 to help people buy and keep health insurance (portability), even when they have serious health conditions, the law sets basic requirements that health plans must meet. Since states can and have modified and expanded upon these provisions, consumers' protections vary from state to state. The law expanded to include strict rules for privacy and security of health information, giving individuals more control over how their health information is used. The privacy and security rules within HIPAA govern the use, disclosure and handling of any identifiable patient information by "covered" healthcare providers. The law covers the information in whatever form it is seen or heard and applies to the information in whatever manner it is to be used. For organizations covered by HIPAA there is a requirement to establish a minimum (regulatory) standard for the security of electronic health information. The act identifies 18 standards which are all required and 36 Implementation Specifications. The Specifications contain 36 required and addressable (risk justified) activities.
Gramm–Leach–Bliley Act (GLBA)	GLBA is the Gramm–Leach–Bliley Act, which was signed into law in 1999. Its primary purpose is to provide privacy of customer information by financial service organizations, and comprehensive data protection measures are required. Depending upon the financial institutions' supervisory authority, GLBA compliance audits are conducted by the Office of the Comptroller of the Currency (OCC), the Federal Reserve Systems (Fed), the Federal Deposit Insurance Corporation (FDIC), or the Office of Thrift Supervision (OTS). All financial service organizations must comply with GLBA data protection requirements. These requirements do not pertain only to providers receiving federal funds.

Table 1.8 Information Security Legislation (Continued)

Law	*Definition*
	GLBA requires financial institutions to: • Ensure the security and confidentiality of customer records and information, • Protect against any anticipated threats or hazards to the security or integrity of such records • Protect against unauthorized access The information security program addressed in GLBA has the following five keys: 1. Involve the Board of Directors; 2. Access risk (manage and control risk) 3. Oversee service provider arrangements 4. Adjust program to meet changing environment 5. Report program effectiveness to the board
Information technology – Code of practice for information security management (ISO/IEC 17799:2000)	A comprehensive set of controls comprising best practices in information security. ISO 17799 is an internationally recognized generic set of information security standards. It is intended to serve as a single reference point for identifying a range of controls needed for most situations where information systems are used in industry and commerce. It identifies ten (10) control objectives essential for a basis for an Information Security Management System and 127 specific controls to choose from.

* Competitive Intelligence Review Volume 8, Issue 3, *Counterintelligence and Law Enforcement: The Economic Espionage Act of 1996 versus Competitive Intelligence,* January 2001.

affect the business or mission of the organization. Once that has been determined, then the information security professional can begin to establish the elements of the information security program. The cornerstone of any program within the organization is a policy that establishes management's beliefs and the general means for implementation.

Not only are there requirements, but the laws and acts define who is responsible and what they must do to meet their obligations (see Table 1.10). The directors and officers of a corporation are required under the "Model Business Corporation Act," which has been adopted in whole or in part by a majority of states, to perform specific duties: a duty of loyalty and a duty of care.

Table 1.9 Mapping Controls Example

ISO 17799 Section	*Control*	*GLBA*	*Sarbanes–Oxley*
	Risk Assessment (2)	Assess Risk	Assess current internal controls
Security Policy	Policy (3.1)	Board approves written policy and program	Policies and procedures must support effective internal control of assets
Organizational Security	Management Information Security Forum (4.1)	Involve the Board of Directors Assign Specific Responsibilities	Corporation management is responsible for assuring internal controls are adequate
Organizational Security	Security Requirements in Outsourcing Contracts (4.3)	Report program effectiveness to Board	Management must report on internal controls effectiveness
Asset Classification & Control	Accounting of Assets (5.1)	Implement policies evaluate sensitivity of customer information	Identify all assets of the corporation
Asset Classification & Control	Information Classification (5.2)	Implement standards and procedures to protect customer information	Information is an asset and the property of the enterprise
Systems Development & Maintenance	Security Requirements of Systems (10.1)	Risk assessment	Assess effectiveness of internal control
Systems Development & Maintenance	Cryptography (10.3)	Assess encryption requirements	
Compliance	Reviews of Security Policy and Technical Compliances (12.2)	Report findings annually to Board	Management must report on internal controls effectiveness

Table 1.10 Legal Concepts

Legal Concept	*Definition*	
Duty of Loyalty	Senior management commits allegiance to the enterprise and acknowledges that interest of the enterprise must prevail over any personal or individual interest. The basic principle here is that senior management should not use their position to make a personal profit or gain other personal advantage	
	Duty of loyalty is evident in certain legal concepts	
	Conflict of Interest	Individuals must divulge any interest in outside relationships that may conflict with the enterprise's interests.
	Duty of Fairness	When presented with a conflict of interest, the individual has an obligation to act in the best interest of all parties.
	Corporate Opportunity	When presented with "material inside information" (advanced notice on mergers, acquisitions, patents, etc.) the individual will not use this information for personal gain.
	Confidentiality	All matters involving the corporation share be kept in confidence until they are made public.
Duty of Care	A director shall discharge his/her duties: • in good faith; • with the care an ordinarily prudent person in a like position would exercise under similar circumstances; and • in a manner he/she reasonably believes is in the best interest of the enterprise.	

The federal sentencing guidelines define executive responsibility for fraud, theft, and anti-trust violations, and establish a mandatory point system for federal judges to determine appropriate punishment. Because much fraud and falsifying of corporate data involve access to computer-held data, liability established under the guidelines extends to computer-related crime as well. What has caused many executives concern is that the mandatory punishment could apply even when intruders enter a computer system and perpetrate a crime.

Although the guidelines have a mandatory scoring system for punishment, they also have an incentive for proactive crime prevention. The requirement here is for management to show "*due diligence*" in establishing an effective compliance program. There are seven elements that capture the basic functions inherent in most compliance programs:

1. Establish policies, standards, and procedures to guide the workforce.
2. Appoint a high-level manager to oversee compliance with the policy, standards, and procedures.
3. Exercise due care when granting discretionary authority to employees.
4. Ensure compliance policies are being carried out.
5. Communicate the standards and procedures to all employees and others.
6. Enforce the policies, standards, and procedures consistently through appropriate disciplinary measures.
7. Have procedures for corrections and modifications in case of violations.

These guidelines reward those organizations that make a good faith effort to prevent unethical activity; this is done by lowering potential fines if, despite the organization's best efforts, unethical or illegal activities are still committed by the organization or its employees. To be judged effective a compliance program need not prevent all misconduct, however, it must show due diligence in seeking to prevent and detect inappropriate behavior.

Recent hacker exploits include accessing 40 million credit card numbers belonging to U.S. consumers, an incident disclosed in June of 2005 by MasterCard International Inc., and records on 310,000 people from the files of LexisNexis in March, 2005. These actions and others prompted a bipartisan group of senators in July to introduce legislation to create a national data privacy law.

The new law will require organizations to develop, implement, and maintain an effective information security program that contains administrative, technical, and physical safeguards for sensitive personal information that the organization sells, maintains, collects, or transfers.

A national law may be necessary to bring order to a state-by-state regulatory structure that has emerged since 2003, when California passed one of the first laws (SB 1386) requiring notification of data theft or loss. Some 17 states have since enacted similar laws, including California, Colorado, Connecticut, Louisiana, Maine, New Jersey, and Nevada.

California legislation SB 1386, signed into law in September 2002, requires all institutions and organizations that collect certain personal information to protect it against possible "identity theft." In addition, if an incident occurs that involves the compromise of personal information, the individuals whose personal information may have been compromised must be notified, and the designated institution or organization authority must notify the Office of the President. IS-3 subsection IV.D describes the requirements that must be met in order to be compliant with law and University of California policy.

Under the proposed federal law (S.1408), the states' laws would be preempted in favor of the national framework. Companies that experience loss or theft of data on more than 1000 people would be required to notify the affected persons or face fines of up to $11 million per incident.

The Senate bill also would bar businesses, schools, and companies from using Social Security numbers on identification cards and other forms of identification, although it contains a potential regulatory loophole allowing those entities to rely on a Social Security number if "no other type of identifier can be used in its place." The measure would allow a consumer to place a "credit freeze" on his or her credit report to prevent identity thieves from taking out a line of credit under the victim's name.

Establish and Maintain Information Security Policies

The cornerstone of an effective information security architecture is a well-written policy statement. This is the source from which all other directives, standards, procedures, guidelines, and other supporting documents will spring. As with any foundation, it is important to establish a strong footing. As discussed in the following, a policy performs two roles, one internal and one external.

The internal portion tells employees what is expected of them and how their actions will be judged. The external portion tells the world how the enterprise is run. Every organization must have policies in place that support sound business practices and they will demonstrate to the world that this organization understands that protection of assets is vital to the successful execution of its mission.

In any discussion regarding written requirements, the term "policy" has more than one meaning. To some, a policy is senior management's directives on how a certain program is to be run, what its goals and objectives are, and to whom responsibilities are to be assigned. Policy may refer to the specific security rules for a particular system such as ACF2 rule sets, RACF permits, or intrusion detection system policies. Additionally, policy may refer to entirely different matters, such as specific management decisions setting an organization's e-mail privacy policy or Internet usage policy.

Security and privacy policies and procedures must have three elements to be effective. They must be documented, communicated, and current.

The actual physical format (layout) of the policy will depend on what policies look like in your own organization. To be successful, it is very important that any policy developed look like published policies from the organization. Some members of the review panel will be unable to read and critique the new policy if it does not look like a policy.

Policies are generally brief in comparison to procedures and normally consist of one page of text using both sides of the paper. In my classes I stress the concept of brevity. However, it is important to balance brevity with clarity. Take all the words you need to complete the thought, but fight the urge to add more information.

There are three types of policies, and you will use each type at different times in your information security program and throughout the organization to support the business process or mission. The three types of policies are:

1. Global (Tier 1): These are used to create the organization's overall vision and direction.
2. Topic-specific (Tier 2): These address particular subjects of concern.
3. Application-specific policies: These focus on decisions taken by management to control particular applications (financial reporting, payroll, etc.) or systems (budgeting system).

Global Policy (Tier 1)

Under the standard of due care, and charged with the ultimate responsibility for meeting business objectives or mission requirements, senior management must ensure that necessary resources are effectively applied to develop the capabilities to meet the mission requirements. They must incorporate the results of the risk analysis process into the decision-making process. Senior management is also responsible for issuing global policies to establish the organization's direction in protecting information assets.

An information security policy will define the intent of management and its sponsoring body with regard to protecting the information assets of the organization. It will include the scope of the program, that is, where it will reach and what information is included in this policy. Finally, the policy will establish who is responsible for what.

The components of a global (Tier 1) policy typically include the following four characteristics.

Topic

The topic portion of the policy defines what specifically the policy is going to address. Because the attention span of readers is limited, the topic must appear quickly, say in the opening or topic sentence. I normally suggest (note it is a guideline not a standard) that the topic sentence also include a "hook." That is, why as a reader I should continue to read this policy. So in the opening sentence we will want to convey two important elements: (1) the topic (it should have something to do with the title of the policy) and (2) the hook, why the reader should continue to read the policy.

An opening topic sentence might read as follows, "Information created while employed by the company is the property of the company and must be properly protected."

Scope

The scope can be used to broaden or narrow either the topic or the audience. In an information security policy statement we could say, "Information is an asset and the property of the company and all employees are responsible for protecting that asset." In this sentence we have broadened the audience to include all employees. We can also say something like, "Business information is an essential asset of the company. This is true of all business information within the company regardless of how it is created, distributed, or stored and whether it is typed, handwritten, printed, filmed, computer-generated, or spoken." Here the writer broadened the topic to include all types of information assets.

Another example of broadening the scope might be as follows, "Information of the company, its subsidiaries, and affiliates in electronic form, whether being transmitted, or stored, is a key asset of the company and must be protected according to its sensitivity, criticality, and value." Here the topic subject is narrowed to "electronic form." However, the audience is broadened to include "subsidiaries and affiliates."

We can also use the scope concept to narrow the topic or audience. In an employment agreement policy, the audience is restricted to a specific group such as the following.

> The parties to this Agreement dated (specify) are (Name of Company), a (specify State and type of company) (the "Company") and (Name of Employee) (the "Executive").
>
> The Company wishes to employ the Executive, and the Executive wishes to accept employment with the Company, on

> the terms and subject to the conditions set forth in this Agreement. It is therefore agreed as follows:

Here the policy is restricted to executives and will then go on to discuss what can and cannot be done by the executives. A sample employment agreement policy is contained in the section titled Tier 2 Policy Examples.

Responsibilities

Typically, this section of the policy will identify who is responsible for what. When writing, it is better to identify the "who" by job title and not by name. Here again the Office Administrator's Reference Guide can be of great assistance. The policy will want to identify what is expected from each of the stakeholders.

Compliance or Consequences

When business units or employees are found to be in a noncompliant situation, the policy must spell out the consequences of these actions. For business units or departments, if they are found in noncompliance, they are generally subject to an audit item and will have to prepare a formal compliance response.

For an employee, being found in noncompliance with a company policy will mean they are in violation of the organization's employee standards of conduct and will be subject to consequences described in the employee discipline policy.

Topic-Specific Policy (Tier 2)

Whereas the global policy (Tier 1) is intended to address the broad organizationwide issues, the topic-specific policy is developed to focus on areas of current relevance and concern to the organization. Management may find it appropriate to issue a policy on how an organization will approach Internet usage or the use of the company-provided e-mail system. Topic-specific policies may also be appropriate when new issues arise, such as when implementing a recently enacted law requiring protection of particular information (GLBA, HIPAA, etc.). The global policy (Tier 1) is usually broad enough that it does not require modification over time, whereas the topic-specific (Tier 2) policies are likely to require more frequent revisions as changes in technology and other factors dictate.

Topic-specific policies will be created most often by an organization. We examine the key elements in the topic-specific policy. When creating an *Information Security Policies and Standards* document, each section in the document will normally begin with a topic-specific policy. The topic-specific policy will narrow the focus to one issue at a time. This will allow the writer to focus on one area and then develop a set of standards to support this particular subject.

Whereas the Tier 1 policies are approved by the Information Security Steering Committee, the topic-specific (Tier 2) may be issued by a single senior manager or director.

As with the Tier 1 policies, Tier 2 policies will address management's position on relevant issues. It is necessary to interview management to determine what their concerns are and what is it that they want to have occur. The writer will take this information and incorporate it into the following structure.

Thesis Statement

This is similar to the topic section discussed in the Tier 1 policies, but it also adds more information to support the goals and objectives of the policy and management's directives. This section is used to discuss the issue in relevant terms and what conditions are included. If appropriate, it may be useful to specify the goal or justification for the policy. This can be useful in gaining compliance with the policy.

When developing a workstation standards document, a topic-specific policy on appropriate software, with supporting standards, would include a discussion on "company-approved" software. This policy would define what is meant by "company-approved" software, which might be "any software not approved, purchased, screened, managed, and owned by the organization." The policy would also discuss the conditions required to have software approved.

Once the terms and conditions have been discussed, the remainder of this section would be used to state management's position on the issue.

Relevance

The Tier 2 policy also needs to establish to whom the policy applies. In addition to whom, the policy will want to clarify where, how, and when the policy is applicable. Is the policy only enforced when employees are in the work-site campus or will it extend to off-site activities? It is necessary to identify as many of the conditions and terms as possible.

Responsibilities

The assignment of roles and responsibilities is also included in Tier 2 policies. For example, the policy on company-approved software will have to identify the process to get software approved. This would include the authority (by job title) authorized to grant approval and a reference to where this process is documented.

This is a good time to discuss deviations from policy requirements. I have established a personal standard in that I never discuss how an entity can gain a dispensation from the policy. I don't like to state that "This is the policy and all employees must comply, except those of you who can find a way around the policy." Most organizations have a process to gain an approved deviation from a policy or standard. This normally requires the petitioner to submit a business case for the deviation along with alternative controls that would satisfy the spirit of the policy. If some organization or person wants a deviation from the policy, let them discover what the process is.

Compliance

For a Tier 2 policy, it may be appropriate to describe, in some detail, the infractions that are unacceptable, and the consequences of such behavior. Penalties may be explicitly stated and should be consistent with the Tier 1 employee discipline policy. Remember, when an employee is found in a noncompliant situation, it is management and human resources that are responsible for disciplining the individual.

Supplementary Information

For any Tier 2 policy, the appropriate individuals in the organization to contact for additional information, guidance, and compliance should be indicated. Typically the contact information would be specified by job title, not by individual name. It may also be prudent to identify who is the owner of this policy. This information will provide the reader with the appropriate information if they have suggestions on how to improve the policy.

To be effective, a policy requires visibility. Visibility aids implementation of the policy by helping to ensure that it is fully communicated throughout the organization. Management presentations, videos, panel discussions, guest speakers, question and answer forums, and newsletters will increase visibility. The organization's information security awareness program can effectively notify users of new policies. The new

Table 1.11 Topic-Specific Policy Categories

ISO 17799 Section
Security Policy
Organizational Security
Organizational Security
Asset Classification & Control
Asset Classification & Control
Systems Development & Maintenance
Systems Development & Maintenance
Compliance

employee orientation program can also be used to familiarize new employees with the organization's policies.

When introducing policies it is important to ensure that management's support is clear, especially in areas where employees feel inundated with directives, regulations, or other requirements. Organization policies are the vehicles used to emphasize management's commitment to effective internal controls and their expectations for employee support and compliance.

At a minimum the Tier 2 or topic-specific policies should address the subject areas identified in the categories from which we mapped our security requirements. See Table 1.11.

Application-Specific Policy (Tier 3)

Global-level (Tier 1) and topic-specific (Tier 2) policies address policy on a broad level; they usually encompass the entire enterprise. The application-specific (Tier 3) policy focuses on one specific system or application. As the construction of the organization information security architecture takes shape, the final element will be the translation of Tier 1 and Tier 2 policies down to the application and system level.

Many security issue decisions apply only at the application or system level. Some examples of these issues include:

- Who has the authority to read or modify data?
- Under what circumstances can data be read or modified?
- How is remote access to be controlled?

Table 1.12 Policy Components

	Tier 1 (Global)	*Tier 2 (Topic-Specific)*	*Tier 3 (Application-Specific)*
Requirements	Topic	Thesis Statement	Subject
	Subject	Relevance	Objective
	Responsibilities	Responsibilities	Roles and Responsibilities
	Compliance	Compliance	Controls
		Supplementary Information	

To develop a comprehensive set of Tier 3 policies, use a process that determines security requirements from a business or mission objective. Try to avoid implementing requirements based on security issues and concerns. Remember, the security staff has been empowered to support the business process of the organization. Typically the Tier 3 policy is more free-form than Tier 1 and Tier 2 policies. As you prepare to create Tier 3 policies, keep in mind the following concepts (see Table 1.12).

- Understand the overall business objectives or mission of the enterprise.
- Understand the mission of the application or system.
- Establish requirements that support both sets of objectives.

Key Security Concepts

When establishing an information security program we often talk about the information security triad of confidentiality, availability, and integrity.

Ensure the Development of Procedures and Guidelines That Support the Information Security Policy

Procedure writing is different from policy writing in that it is not useful to have teams develop the procedures. Procedures will not have to be approved by a management team. So the process is quicker, but will require some work. See Figure 1.5

Unlike the policy development process, the use of a team to develop procedures will actually slow the process down. Many security professionals reach this stage of the information security program and believe

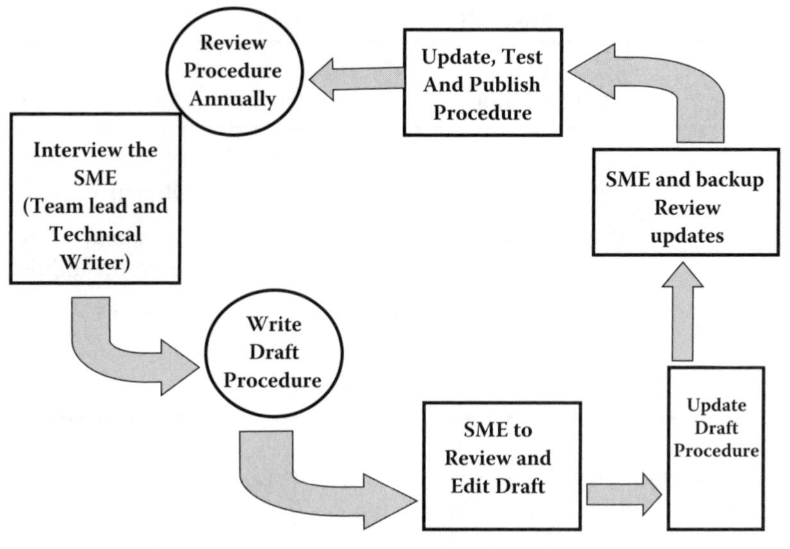

Figure 1.5 Procedure writing process.

that the bulk of their work is complete and now it will be up to the Subject Matter Experts (SME) to write the procedures. This is probably not going to work. The SMEs are usually the same groups of people required now to provide documentation for the work they perform. They are busy with their day-to-day functions and are already hard pressed to find the time to worry about existing paperwork, let alone adding the requirement that they write procedures.

When developing procedures use a technical writer to gather the relevant information from the SME and put that information into one of the procedure formats. It is recommended that you schedule an interview with the SME and let them know in advance what the topic will be. Ask them to bring any written procedures that they may have created on the subject and any other visual aid (perhaps a flow chart or an information flow model).

Schedule the meeting for 45 minutes. This should be long enough to get the information necessary, but not so long as to affect the SME's busy schedule. Remember to treat the SMEs with respect and to listen to what they have to say, but keep them on track. After you have gathered all of the information you can about the subject, inform the SME as to what the next steps will be.

1. The material just discussed will be put into procedure format.
2. A draft procedure will be sent to the SME for review and content editing.

3. The technical writer will update the procedure based on the SME's remarks.
4. The updated procedure will be sent to the SME and the SME backup for a final review.
5. Any additional updates will be incorporated into the procedure.
6. The procedure will be tested (either with the backup or some other person).
7. If the procedure provides the proper results, it will be published in the appropriate procedure document.

Not every procedure will require all of the elements found in the procedure development checklist (see Table 1.13). Some may even require additional steps. As with any checklist, this is only a series of thought starters. The list that will be used by you may have additional items, or fewer.

Develop Business Case and Enterprise Value Analysis Support

Developing business case and enterprise value analysis that supports information security program investments is a vital task of the information security manager. Organizations often justify spending based on a project's value. Two common methods used are Return On Investment (ROI) or Total Cost of Operations (TCO). The information security program also needs a strong business case to justify funding and must be developed by the information security manager.

Because the value of the asset is an unreliable indicator of actual worth, the outcome of the formula of the ROI must be unreliable to determine success or corporate value. However, the ROI formula keeps showing up in annual reports (see Table 1.14).

The degree to which the ROI overstates the economic value depends on at least five factors:

1. Length of project life (the longer, the bigger the overstatement)
2. The capitalization policy (the smaller the fraction of total investment capitalized in the books, the greater the overstatement)
3. The rate at which depreciation is taken (depreciation rates faster than a straight-line basis will result in a higher ROI)
4. The lag between investment outlays and the recouping of these outlays from cash inflows (the greater the time lag, the greater the degree of overstatement)
5. The growth rate of new investment (faster growing companies will have lower ROI)

Table 1.13 Procedure Concepts

Procedure Concept	*Definition*
Title	Establish what the topic of the procedure is going to be. Try to avoid being cute with your choice of words. Remember you are writing for a business environment
Intent	Discuss what the procedure is attempting to accomplish in general terms
Scope	Briefly describe the process that the procedure is going to cover. (i.e., Implementing a UNIX UserID request).
Responsibilities	Identify who is to perform what steps in the procedure. Use job functions rather than individual names
Sequence of Events	It is very important for the user to understand the timing and conditions for performing the tasks identified in the procedure. Some tasks are not executed at a specific time but must be performed when a specific condition is met.
Approvals	Identify any necessary approvals and when these approvals must be met. Approvals will be obtained prior to the execution of the procedure process.
Prerequisites	List any preconditions that must be met before starting the procedure process.
Definitions	Remember the audience. It will be beneficial to include a discussion of any terms and acronyms that are included in the body of the procedure.
Equipment Required	Identify all equipment, tools, documents and anything else the individual executing the procedure will need to perform the tasks.
Warnings	Some tasks, if operated in an improper sequence could cause severe damage to the enterprise. Identify those key tasks and review the importance of understanding exactly when the task is to be executed and under what set of circumstances
Precautions	Identify all steps to be taken to avoid problems or dangers (i.e., "Unplug before performing maintenance").
Procedure Body	These are the actual steps to be performed in the execution of the procedure

Table 1.14 Cost Terms

Term	*Definition*
Return on Investment (ROI)	A figure of merit used to help make capital investment decisions. ROI is calculated by considering the annual benefit divided by the investment amount.
Total Cost of Ownership (TCO)	The total cost of owning a something, including the cost of the building hosting it, operation and maintenance costs, and so on. Total cost of ownership can be significantly higher than the purchase cost, and systems with a lower purchase cost can have higher total cost of ownership.
Return on Security Investment (ROSI)	For a given use of money, ROI calculates how much profit or saving you get from an investment. Security, on the other hand, starts to factor in details such as Risk Management, reduction in perceived vulnerabilities, and loss of downtime.

Business cases and ROI calculations for security have been slow in developing; however, research groups at three universities have developed robust and supportable numbers on the Return On Security Investment (ROSI) data and formulas. Teams at the University of Idaho, Massachusetts Institute of Technology, and Carnegie Mellon University have developed and researched ROSI calculations that the information security manager can integrate into his business case models (see Table 1.15).

Table 1.15 Return on Security Investment (ROSI)

Formula	*Terms*
(R-E) + T = ALE	**T** is the cost of the intrusion detection tool.
	E is the dollar savings gained by stopping any number of intrusions through the introduction of an intrusion detection tool.
	R is the cost per year to recover from any number of intrusions.
R – (ALE) = ROSI	

Table 1.16 Total Cost of Ownership

Formula	*Terms*
DC+IC = TCO	**DC** These costs generally cover the visible IT- and support-related investments and expenses **IC** These costs are less visible and usually are dispersed across the business operations organizations

Recently, the advances in single sign-on and user access provisioning technologies and procedures have resulted in savings in time and cost over traditional manual administration techniques. There are a number of examples that compare the costs of traditional processes against the newer procedures, and these can be used in the business case that most information security managers need to develop.

Idaho researchers developed this formula for calculating the ROI of using intrusion detection as a security defense.

Total Cost of Ownership (TCO; see Table 1.16) is a financial estimate designed to help consumers and enterprise managers assess direct and indirect costs related to the purchase of any capital investment, such as (but not limited to) computer software or hardware. A TCO assessment ideally offers a final statement reflecting not only the cost of purchase but all aspects in the further use and maintenance of the equipment, device, or system considered. This includes the costs of training support personnel and the users of the system, costs associated with failure or outage (planned and unplanned), diminished performance incidents (i.e., if users are kept waiting), costs of security breaches (in loss of reputation and recovery costs), costs of disaster preparedness and recovery, floor space, electricity, development expenses, testing infrastructure and expenses, quality assurance, incremental growth, decommissioning, and more. Therefore TCO is sometimes referred to as Total Cost of *Operation*. When incorporated in any financial benefit analysis (e.g., ROI) TCO provides a cost basis for determining the economic value of that investment.

TCO consists of the costs, direct and indirect, incurred throughout the life cycle of an asset, including acquisition, deployment, operation, support, and retirement.

All of the direct and indirect costs are compiled, computed on an annual basis, and then totaled to provide the total cost of ownership. This exercise can produce some stunning results as studies regularly show that, even in today's world of PCs costing less than $1000, the TCO of a PC continues to average over $5000 per year. A $200 printer could easily have an annual cost of over $1000 when all the supplies and maintenance costs are included. For organizations that want to determine their TCO for a specific area of IT, there are numerous consultants and vendors who will assist in the task.

Summary

Information security governance is the foundation upon which an information security program is built. Governance establishes the relationships among a company's management, its board, its employees, and other stakeholders. Information security governance provides the structure through which the business objectives or mission of the organization are set and the means of attaining those objectives and monitoring performance are determined.

What Was Covered in This Chapter

- Information security concepts
- Relationship between information security and business operations
- Techniques to gain senior management support
- Methods to integrate information security governance into overall enterprise governance
- Policy directives that support senior management objectives
- The Information Security Steering Committee functions
- Security management roles and responsibilities
- The areas of governance
- Legal and regulatory issues
- The process for linking policies to enterprise objectives
- What policies, procedures, standards, and guidelines are and where they work
- A model to measure security program maturity
- Generally accepted international security standards
- Where security should report
- Methodologies for business case value of the security program

Questions

1. The primary responsibility of the information security steering committee is:
   A. Direction setting and performance monitoring
   B. Information security policy development
   C. Information security control implementation

D. Provision of information security training for employees

Answer A

2. Which of the following would be included in an information security strategic plan?
   A. Specifications for planned hardware purchases
   B. Analysis of future business objectives
   C. Target dates for information security projects
   D. Annual budgetary targets for the security department

Answer B

3. The most important responsibility of an information security manager in an organization is:
   A. Recommending and monitoring security policies
   B. Promoting security awareness within the organization
   C. Establishing procedures for security policies
   D. Administering physical and logical access controls

Answer A

4. On which of the following would an information security strategy place the most emphasis?
   A. Business goals and objectives
   B. Technology plans and deliverables
   C. Industry best practices
   D. Security metrics

Answer A

5. Which of the following best describes an information security department's strategic planning process?
   A. The department will have either short-range or long-range plans depending on the organization's broader plans and objectives.
   B. The department's strategic plan must be time and project oriented, but not so detailed as to address and help determine priorities to meet business needs.
   C. Long-range planning for the department should recognize organizational goals, technological advances, and regulatory requirements.
   D. Short-range planning for the department does not need to be integrated into the long-range plans of the organization because technological advances will drive the department plans much quicker than organizational plans.

Answer C

6. To ensure that an organization's password policy is effective, it must provide two key elements: difficult to guess; and
   A. Be encrypted at all times
   B. Contain a number of characters
   C. Must be changed periodically
   D. Controlled by security administration

Answer C

7. "Least privilege" is defined as:
   A. The level of authorization granted to a user that is under investigation
   B. Access to, knowledge of, or possession of information based on need to perform assigned job duties
   C. Only most restrictive privileges granted based on need for job performance
   D. Level of trust that is granted to system users

Answer C

8. An organization's log-on screen must contain three statements: the system is for authorized users, activities will be monitored, and
   A. Wrongful activities will be turned over to HR.
   B. By completing the log-on process you agree to the monitoring.
   C. Password must not be shared.
   D. Violators will be prosecuted.

Answer B

9. Authentication is the process to verify the identity of a user, device, or other entity. The most common forms of authentication used today are passwords. Three types of authentication are: something you know, something you have, and
   A. A combination of any of these two items
   B. Something that you are
   C. A magnetic stripe card
   D. A pass phrase

Answer B

10. The purpose of change control is to:
    A. Track changes to system hardware, software, firmware, and documentation.
    B. Maintain visibility of changes to the system.
    C. Ensure that changes to the system are approved.
    D. To track and approve changes to system hardware, software, firmware, and documentation.

Answer D

11. What data should be subject to a data classification scheme?
    A. Sensitive data
    B. Critical data
    C. Classified data
    D. All data

Answer D

12. The principle of separation of duties is useful in:
    A. Reducing the opportunity for fraud
    B. Identifying critical positions
    C. Developing job descriptions
    D. Conducting background investigations

Answer A

13. What are the three objectives of information security?
    A. Prevent, detect, respond
    B. Integrity, authenticity, and completeness
    C. Confidentiality, integrity, and availability
    D. Identification, authentication, nonrepudiation

Answer C

14. Four deliverables from a risk assessment process are threats identified, controls selected, action plan complete, and
    A. Risk level established
    B. Technical issues quantified
    C. Vulnerability assessment completed
    D. Risk mitigation established

Answer A

15. Need-to-know is defined as
    A. Access to, knowledge of, or possession of information based on need to perform security duties
    B. Possession of information based on need to perform assigned duties
    C. Access to, knowledge of, or possession of information based on need to perform assigned job duties
    D. Knowledge of information or activities based on need to perform job functions

Answer C

16. A financial estimate designed to help consumers and enterprise managers assess direct and indirect costs related to the purchase

of any capital investment, such as (but not limited to) computer software or hardware is termed:

A. Return on investment
B. Return on security investment
C. Total value of asset compensation
D. Total cost of ownership

Answer D

17. The process where senior management commits allegiance to the enterprise and acknowledges that the interest of the enterprise must prevail over any personal or individual interest is termed:

A. Duty of fairness
B. Conflict of interest
C. Duty of loyalty
D. Duty of care

Answer C

18. This recent piece of legislation requires annual affirmation of management's responsibility for internal controls over financial reporting. Management must attest to effectiveness based on an evaluation and the auditor must attest and report on management's evaluation.

A. Foreign Corrupt Practices Act
B. Sarbanes–Oxley
C. Model Business Corporation Act
D. Gramm–Leach–Bliley Act

Answer B

19. An annual report of the state of information security should be presented to the information security steering committee. This reporting requirement has been established in the current legislation and information security international standards. This report should not be confused with a standard feature audit performed by the audit staff nor is it part of some third-party certification process. Who is responsible for presenting this annual report?

A. CISO
B. CTO
C. CEO
D. CFO

Answer A

20. This individual is responsible for the organization's planning, budgeting, and performance, including its information security

components. Decisions made in this area should be based on an effective risk management program.

A. Information owner
B. Information security administrator
C. General auditor
D. Chief information security officer

Answer D

21. This form of emergency plan provides procedures for disseminating status reports to personnel and the public. It addresses communications with personnel and the public and is not IT-focused. This plan is called:
    A. Emergency response plan
    B. Crisis communication plan
    C. Continuity of operation plan
    D. Cyber incident response plan

Answer B

22. Any information security program must get its direction from executive management. The requirements of today's laws and regulations have identified either the organization's board of directors or what other body as responsible for instituting an effective program?
    A. Information security steering committee
    B. Business operations approval team
    C. Crisis management team
    D. Cyber incident response board

Answer A

23. Developing business case and enterprise value analysis that supports information security program investments is a vital task for the information security manager. Organizations often justify spending based on a project's value. Two common methods used are Total Cost of Operations (TCO) and what other widely accepted method?
    A. Cost-benefit analysis
    B. Risk-based assessment
    C. Network vulnerability investment
    D. Return on investment

Answer D

24. Unlike the policy development process, the use of a team to develop procedures will actually slow the process down. Many

security professionals reach this stage of the information security program and believe that the bulk of their work is complete and now it will be up to whom to write the procedures?

A. Technical writer
B. Help desk administrator
C. Subject matter expert
D. Socially awkward male

Answer C

25. There are three types of policies and you will use each type at different times in your information security program and throughout the organization to support the business process or mission. The policy that is used to establish the organization's overall vision and direction is termed:

A. Global (Tier 1)
B. Topic-specific (Tier 2)
C. Application-specific (Tier 3)
D. System-specific (Tier 4)

Answer A

26. A director shall discharge his or her duties: in good faith; with the care an ordinarily prudent person in a like position would exercise under similar circumstances; and in a manner he or she reasonably believes is in the best interest of the enterprise. This responsibility is termed:

A. Duty of loyalty
B. Duty of fairness
C. Fiduciary duty
D. Duty of care

Answer D

27. The group who is charged with the responsibility to "assess the adequacy of and compliance with management, operating, and financial controls, as well as the administrative and operational effectiveness of organizational units" is who?

A. Information security
B. Auditing staff
C. Corporate council
D. Government and regulatory affairs

Answer B

28. This organization got its start in 1967, when a small group of individuals with similar jobs—auditing controls in the computer

systems that were becoming increasingly critical to the operations of their organizations—sat down to discuss the need for a centralized source of information and guidance in the field. This organization is called:

A. Data Processing Management Association (DPMA)
B. Information Systems Security Association (ISSA)
C. Information Systems Audit and Control Association (ISACA)
D. American Society for Industrial Security (ASIS)

Answer C

29. An annual report of the state of information security should be presented to the information security steering committee. This reporting requirement has been established in the current legislation and information security international standards. This report should not be confused with a standard feature audit performed by the audit staff nor is it part of some third-party certification process. Typically the CISO would prepare a report on the levels of compliance currently seen throughout the business units. The report development process normally has two key components: compliance with core information security requirements; and what?
    A. The level of implementation for the current information security initiative
    B. The percentage of overall compliance to agency regulations
    C. Number of liability cases pending
    D. What departments are least compliant with the program

Answer A

30. The Cyber Security Industrial Alliance published their *National Agenda for Information Security in 2006* in December, 2005. In this document the Alliance noted that "Information assurance in the private sector is critical to creating a more secure infrastructure." The report recommended that the federal government "encourage" CEOs to review cyber security measures at board meetings. This effort will help senior executives understand what?
    A. Their personal liability for noncompliance
    B. Their responsibilities when accessing material inside information
    C. The security-related implications of Sarbanes–Oxley, GLBA, and HIPAA
    D. The impact of ROSI on profit margins

Answer C

Chapter 2

Information Security Risk Management

Functional Area Overview

The objective of this job practice area is to identify and manage information security risks to achieve business objectives through a number of tasks utilizing the information security manager's knowledge of key risk management techniques. This functional area comprises 21 percent of the CISM® examination and comprises approximately 42 questions.

Security governance is supported by such documents as:

- Organization for Economic Co-Operation and Development (OECD)
- Institute of Chartered Accountants in England
- ISO/IEC 17799 (ISO 27002)
- British Standard 77 99 (ISO 27001)
- Information Systems Audit and Control (ISACA®), Control Objectives for Information Technology (CobiT®)
- National Institute of Standards and Technology (NIST) Special Publication (SP) 800–55, 800-26, and 800-12

Risk management is the process that allows business managers to balance operational and economic costs of protective measures and achieve gains in mission capability by protecting business processes that support the business objectives or mission of the enterprise.

Table 2.1 Mapping CISM Governance to ISO 17799 and CISSP ® Domains

Information Security Program Management *ISO 17799 Section*	*CISSP Domain*
Introduction Risk Assessment	3. Security Management
5. Information Security Organization	9. Law, Investigation and Ethics
9. Communications and Operations Management	
10. Access Control	

Senior management must ensure that the enterprise has the capabilities needed to accomplish its mission.

Most organizations have tight budgets for security. To get the best bang for the security buck, management needs a process to determine spending.

In this chapter you will learn about the information security risk management tasks:

1. Develop a systematic and continuous risk management process.
2. Ensure risk identification, analysis, and mitigation activities are integrated into the life cycle process.
3. Apply risk identification and analysis methods.
4. Define strategies and prioritize options to mitigate risks to levels acceptable to the enterprise.
5. Report significant changes in risk to appropriate levels of management on both a periodic and event-driven basis.

CISM Mapping

When the information security risk management functional areas are mapped to ISO 17799 and the domains from the CISSP common body of knowledge, as in Table 2.1, it shows just how many different areas of knowledge from which we are going to be drawing information. The information security risk management section is restricted to the risk analysis, assessment, mitigation, and vulnerability assessment.

Introduction

In order to help set the tone for this chapter, let's take a look at questions that normally arise when we discuss or teach risk management techniques.

Is there a difference between risk analysis and risk assessment?

After years of wrestling with this question, it came to me one bright sunny summer day as I read a NIST document on risk management. The answer is: yes, there is a difference. Risk analysis is that first step in the development life cycle when management is required to make an informed business decision to move forward with a new project or capital investment.

Management is charged with showing that "due diligence" is performed during decision-making processes for any enterprise. A formal risk analysis provides the documentation to prove that management considered all of the available options and chose this course of action.

Risk assessment factors into the other key responsibility of management and that is their "fiduciary duty" to protect the assets of the organization. Fiduciary duty has two key elements: a duty of loyalty and duty of care. We discuss this in detail later. Once the decision to proceed with a project is reached (risk analysis), then management must ensure that threats to the project are identified, that the threats are examined to determine the organization's risk of the threat, and what controls or safeguards are available to lessen the risk level to an acceptable range.

Why should a risk assessment be conducted?

It should be conducted because many of our organizations do not know what the threats and risks are to operate in the changing business environment. Risk assessment provides a process to systematically identify threats and then assign risk levels based on the specific organization conducting the assessment. By establishing a risk level or a prioritization of the threats, an organization can best use its limited resources to meet its greatest need.

The output from the risk analysis and risk assessment processes will generally be used twice. The first time will be when decisions are made; for the risk analysis that means deciding whether to proceed on a new project and for the risk assessment, what types of controls or safeguards need to be implemented. For risk assessment, the output will identify what countermeasures should be implemented or that management has determined that the best decision is to accept the risk.

The other time the results will be used is when the "Spam hits the fan." That is, when a problem arises and the organization must show the process it used to reach the decisions that it did. The documentation created in the risk management process will allow the organization to show who was involved, what was discussed, what considered, and what decisions were made.

A risk management process also lets an enterprise take control of its own destiny. With an effective risk analysis process in place, only those controls and safeguards that are actually needed will be implemented. An enterprise will never again face having to implement a mandated control to "be in compliance with audit requirements."

When should a risk analysis be conducted?

A risk analysis should be conducted whenever money or resources are to be spent. Before starting a task, project, or development cycle, an enterprise should conduct an analysis of the need for the project. Understanding the concepts of risk analysis and applying them to the business needs of the enterprise will ensure that only necessary spending is done.

In addition, there will never be the need to implement controls or safeguards unless they are actually needed. As risk management professionals, it is important to understand that there are no such items as "security requirements" or "audit requirements." There are only business objectives or mission requirements. A proper risk management process will ensure that compensating controls are needed to ensure that the business or mission of the enterprise is met.

Who should conduct the risk analysis or risk assessment?

Most risk management projects fail because the internal experts and subject matter experts are not included in the process. A process such as the Facilitated Risk Analysis and Assessment Process (FRAAP) takes advantage of the internal experts. No one knows your systems and applications or your business better than the people who develop and run them. Establishing a team of internal experts will ensure the risk management process has those individuals with in-depth knowledge of the true workings of the business processes. No outsider can understand the nuances of your operations better than those people who must work with it and around it on a daily basis.

Who within the organization should conduct the risk analysis or risk assessment?

If your organization is fortunate enough to have a project management office, then the facilitators from this group would be perfect for conducting the risk management processes. Because this book is directed at the information security profession I would expect to see these professionals conduct the processes.

There are some groups that because of their charters and responsibilities would find a conflict of interest to lead or facilitate these processes. Applications development is a group that could have an impact on both risk analysis and risk assessment. Their job is to create applications and systems as quickly and efficiently as possible. So there could be an appearance of conflict of interest.

The audit staff and systems operations are two other groups that have charters of responsibility which would give an appearance of conflict of interest.

How long should a risk analysis or assessment take?

It should be completed in days, not weeks or months. To meet the needs of an enterprise, the risk management process must be able to complete it quickly with a minimum of impact on the employees' already busy schedule. The key process that we discuss in this book, the FRAAP, was created in response to the needs of the day-to-day workings of business and government agencies.

Time is a very precious commodity and processes such as risk management must be structured to be fast and efficient. As we show, if there is more time available, then there is no end to the different things that can be done. Most organizations, however, have little enough time to spare.

What can a risk analysis or risk assessment analyze?

These processes can be used to review any task, project, or idea. By learning the basic concepts of risk management, the organization can then use them to determine if a project should be undertaken, if a specific product should be purchased, if a new control should be implemented, or if the enterprise is at risk from some threat.

What can the results of a risk management tell an organization?

The process can identify to the enterprise what the threats are and then establish a prioritization of these risks to allow management to concentrate on the biggest concerns.

The greatest benefit of a risk analysis is whether it is prudent to proceed. It allows management to examine all currently identified concerns, prioritize the level of vulnerability, and then to select an appropriate level of control or to accept the risk.

The goal of risk management is not to eliminate all risk. It is a tool to be used by management to reduce risk to an acceptable level.

Who should review the results of a risk analysis?

A risk analysis is rarely conducted without a senior management sponsor. The results are geared to provide management with the information they need to make informed business decisions. The results of a risk assessment are normally classified as confidential and are provided to only the sponsor and to those deemed appropriate by the sponsor.

When working the risk analysis and risk assessment processes it will be necessary to remind all employees that the information discussed in the process is classified as confidential and may not be shared outside the risk management forum. For any third party taking part in the process, it will be necessary to execute a nondisclosure or confidentiality agreement to ensure the protection of information discussed.

How is the success of the risk analysis measured?

The tangible way to measure success is to see a lower bottom line for cost. Risk assessment can assist in this process by identifying only those controls that need to be implemented.

Another way that the success of a risk analysis is measured is if there is a time when management decisions are called into review. By having a formal process in place that demonstrates the due diligence of management in the decision-making process, this kind of inquiring will be dealt with quickly and successfully.

The risk management process is a business process that supports management in its decision-making. It provides the management owners of the assets to perform their fiduciary responsibility of protecting the assets of the enterprise in a reasonable and prudent manner. The process does not have to be a long drawn-out affair. To be effective, risk analysis and risk assessment must be done quickly and efficiently.

Develop a Systematic and Continuous Risk Management Process

Risk management is the process that allows business managers to balance operational and economic costs of protective measures and achieve gains

Table 2.2 Risk Management Definitions

Term	*Definition*
Risk Management	The goal is to identify, control and minimize impact of uncertain events. The objective of risk management is to reduce risk to an acceptable level. Support of this process by senior management is a demonstration of their due diligence.
Risk Analysis	Is a technique to identify and assess factors that may jeopardize the success of a project or achieving a goal? This technique also helps define preventive measures to reduce the probability of these factors from occurring and identify countermeasures to successfully deal with these constraints when they develop.
Risk Assessment	Is the computation of risk. Risk is a threat that exploits some vulnerability that could cause harm to an asset. The risk algorithm computes the risk as a function of the assets, threats, and vulnerabilities. One instance of a risk within a system is represented by the formula (Asset * Threat * Vulnerability). Total risk for a network equates to the sum of all the risk instances.
Risk Mitigation	Is the process in which an organization implements controls and safeguards to prevent identified risks from ever occurring, while at the same time implementing a means of recovery should the risk become a reality in spite of all efforts.
Vulnerability Assessment and Controls Evaluation	Systematic examination of a critical infrastructure, the interconnected systems on which it relies, its information, or product to determine the adequacy of security measures, identify security deficiencies, evaluate security alternatives, and verify the adequacy of such measures after implementation.

in mission capability by protecting business processes that support the business objectives or mission of the enterprise (see Table 2.2). For most of this book we concentrate on the impacts of risk in the information security and information technology areas of an organization. Risk management, however, is not restricted to the information technology and security realm. This is a business process that assists management in meeting its fiduciary duty to protect the assets of the organization.

Risk management is the total process used to identify, control, and minimize the impact of uncertain events. The objective of the risk management program is to reduce the risk of performing some activity or function to an acceptable level and obtain senior management approval.

Risk management is made up of several distinct processes: risk analysis, risk assessment, risk mitigation, and vulnerability assessment and controls evaluation.

Senior management must ensure that the enterprise has the capabilities needed to accomplish its mission or business objectives. As we show, senior management of a department, business unit, group, or other such entity is considered to be the *functional owner* of the enterprise's assets and in their fiduciary duty, act in the best interest of the enterprise to implement reasonable and prudent safeguards and controls. Risk management is the tool that will assist them in the task.

Ensure Risk Identification, Analysis, and Mitigation Activities Are Integrated Into the Life Cycle Process

I do not care for the term "System Development Life Cycle" (SDLC; Figure 2.1) with respect to risk management. The SDLC seems to have been structured to meet the needs of the information technology organization and therefore anything associated with the SDLC must be an IT process. Risk management is a business process and all business decisions should have a Business Process Life Cycle (BPLC). I think the BPLC allows for those elements that make up information technology development, but also takes into account normal business decisions. However, I yield to the logic of the situation and continue with the concept of SDLC throughout this book.

Effective risk management must be totally integrated into the organization's system development life cycle. The typical SDLC has five phases and they can be termed almost anything. Regardless of what the phases are labeled, they all have the same key concepts:

1. Analysis
2. Design
3. Construction
4. Test
5. Maintenance

The National Institute of Standards and Technology (NIST) uses the following terms: Initiation, Development or Acquisition, Implementation, Operation or Maintenance, and Disposal. As Table 2.3 points out, risk analysis is mapped throughout the SDLC. The first time risk analysis needs

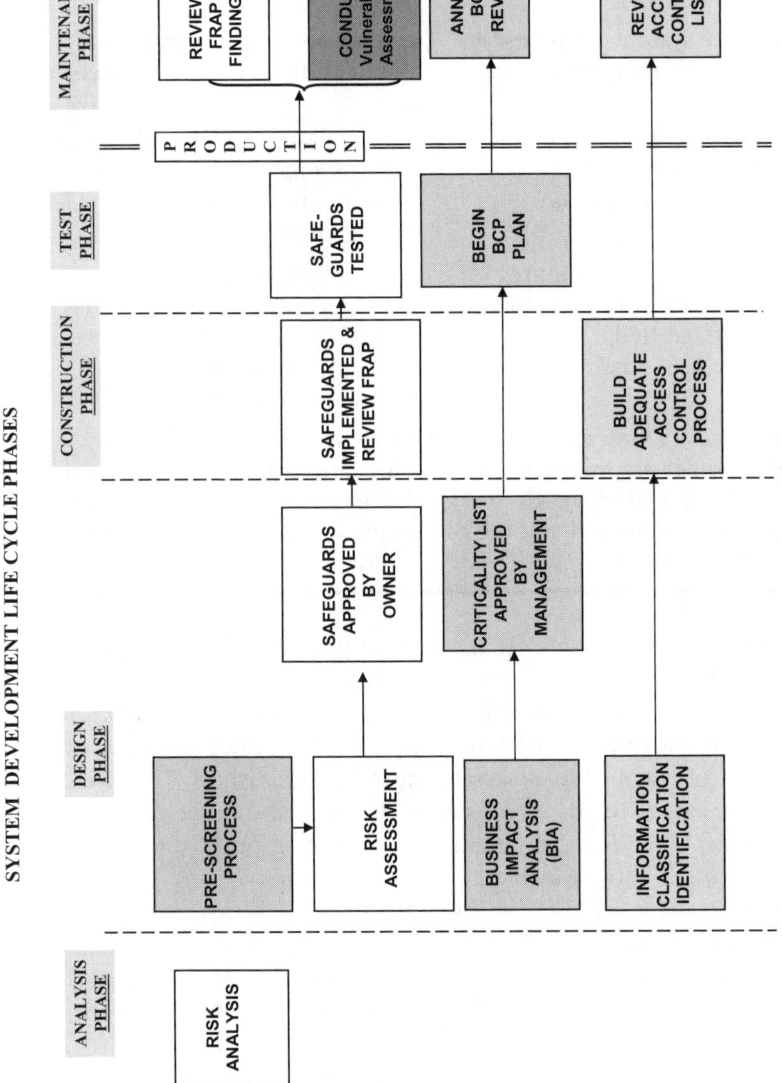

Figure 2.1 System Development Life Cycle (SDLC).

Table 2.3 SDLC vs. Risk Management Table

SDLC Phases	*Risk Management Activities*
Analysis – The need for a new system, application or process and its scope are documented.	Analysis – identified risks are used to support the development of system requirements, including security needs.
Design – The system or process is designed and requirements are gathered.	Design – Security needs lead to architecture and design tradeoffs.
Development – The system or process is purchased, developed, or otherwise constructed.	Development – The security controls and safeguards are created or implemented as part of the development process.
Test – System security features should be configured, enabled, tested, and verified.	Test – Safeguards and controls are tested to ensure that decisions regarding risks identified are reduced to acceptable levels prior to movement to production.
Maintenance – When changes and/or updates are made to the system, the changes to hardware and software are noted and the risk analysis process is revisited.	Maintenance – Controls and safeguards are re-examined when changes or updates occur or on regularly scheduled intervals.

to be done is when there is a discussion of whether a new system, application, or business process is required.

Risk management is a management responsibility. To be successful, the risk management process must be supported by senior management and the concept of ownership of assets must be established. This concept is typically presented to the organization through the asset or information classification policy. Sample language for this portion of the policy might be similar to that shown in Figure 2.2

Employees have different roles and these roles support the activities of the other roles and responsibilities. To establish a level of understanding throughout this book, let us examine typical roles found in an organization and what they are responsible for with regard to risk analysis and risk management.

Table 2.4 shows only examples of the types of roles and responsibilities that are found in a typical organization. It will be necessary to ensure that all employees have as part of their job description the concept of support of information security. The organization's information classification policy will also establish the key concepts of owner, custodian, and user.

```
Employees are responsible for protecting corporate information from
unauthorized access, modification, destruction, or disclosure,
whether accidental or intentional.  To facilitate the protection of
corporate information, employee responsibilities have been
established at three levels: Owner, Custodian and User.

Owner:  Is a The Company manager of a business unit or office where
the information is created, or who is the primary user of the
information.  Owners are responsible to:
     Identify the classification level of all corporate information
       within their organizational unit,
     Define and implement appropriate safeguards to ensure the
       confidentiality, integrity, and availability of the
       information resource,
     Monitor safeguards to ensure their compliance and report
       situations of non-compliance,
     Authorize access to those who have a business need for the
       information, and
     Remove access from those who no longer have a business need for
       the information.
Custodian:  Employees designated by the Owner to be responsible for
protecting information by maintaining safeguards established by the
Owner.
User:  Employees authorized by the Owner to access information and
use the safeguards established by the Owner.
```

Figure 2.2 Policy on employee responsibilities: example.

When implementing risk management, it will be necessary to view this process as part of the ongoing information security life cycle. As with any business process, the information security life cycle (see Figure 2.3) starts with a risk analysis. Management is charged with showing that "due diligence" is performed during the decision-making process to proceed with any new task or project. A formal risk analysis provides the documentation that due diligence is performed.

Once the risk analysis is complete, the next step in the security life cycle is to conduct a risk assessment. As we have stated before, the results of a risk analysis or assessment will be used on two occasions: when a decision needs to be made and when there arises a need to examine the decision-making process.

A risk assessment also allows an enterprise take control of its own destiny. With an effective risk assessment process in place, only those controls and safeguards that are actually needed will be implemented. An enterprise will never again face having to implement a mandated control to "be in compliance with audit requirements."

A risk analysis should be conducted whenever money or resources are to be spent. Before starting a task, project, or development cycle, an enterprise should conduct an analysis of the need for the project.

Table 2.4 Typical Employee Responsibilities – Example

Typical Role	*Risk Management Responsibility*
Senior Management	Under the Standard of Due Care, senior management is charged with the ultimate responsibility for meeting business objectives or mission requirements. Senior management must ensure that necessary resources are effectively applied to develop the capabilities to meet the mission requirements. They must incorporate the results of the risk analysis process into the decision-making process.
Chief Information Security Officer (CISO)	This position was at one time called the Chief Information Officer (CIO) but many organizations simple named their head of IT to this position and, therefore the CIO has become the position known as the CISO. The CISO is responsible for the organization's planning, budgeting, and performance including its information security components. Decisions made in this area should be based on an effective risk management program.
Resource Owners	These are the business unit managers assigned as functional owners of organization assets and are responsible for ensuring that proper controls are in place to address integrity, confidentiality and availability of the information resources that they are assigned ownership. The term "owner" must be established in the asset classification policy. The managers (aka, Owners) are the individuals with the authority and responsibility for making cost-benefit decisions essential to ensure accomplishment of organization mission objectives. Their involvement in the risk management process enables the selection of business-orientated controls. The charge of being an owner supports the objective of fulfilling the fiduciary responsibility of management to protect the assets of the enterprise.
Information Security Professional	The security program manager responsible for the organization's security programs, including risk management. The ISA has changed its designation because designation "officer" is normally restricted to senior executives. The officers can be held personally liable if internal controls are not adequate.

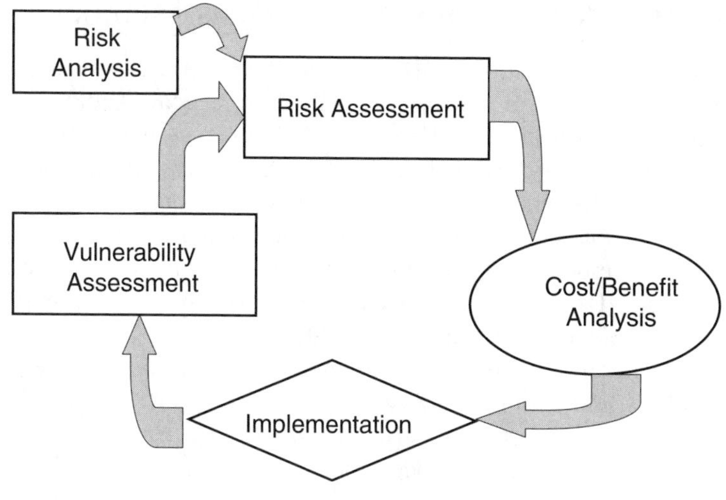

Figure 2.3 Information security life cycle.

Understanding the concepts of risk analysis and applying them to the business needs of the enterprise will ensure that only necessary spending is done.

Once a risk analysis has been conducted it will be necessary to conduct a risk assessment to determine what threats exist to the project and business mission. These threats must be prioritized and possible safeguards and controls must be selected. To be effective, a cost-benefit analysis to determine which controls will help mitigate the risk to an acceptable level at a cost the enterprise can afford must be part of this process. It is unwise to implement controls or safeguards just because they seem to be the right thing to do or because other enterprises are doing so. Each organization is unique, and the levels of revenue and exposure are different. By conducting a proper risk analysis, the controls or safeguards will meet the enterprise's specific needs.

Once the controls or safeguards have been implemented, it is appropriate to conduct an assessment to determine if the controls are working. In the information security profession, the term *vulnerability* has been defined as a condition of a missing or ineffectively administered safeguard or control that allows a threat to occur with a greater impact or frequency or both. When conducting a Network Vulnerability Assessment (NVA), the team will be assessing existing controls, safeguards, and processes that are part of the network. This process, the assessment, will ensure that controls are effective and that they will remain so.

Apply Risk Identification and Analysis Methods

Risk analysis is a technique used to identify and assess factors that may jeopardize the success of a project or achieving a goal. Another term for this process is a project impact analysis. This process will require a cost-benefit analysis be conducted. The cost-benefit process should incorporate the features and benefits of the asset or process under review.

Part of the review will examine the costs of the project. These costs include procurement or development, operation, and maintenance costs, which include: documentation development, user and infrastructure support training, and possible upgrades. Other costs that must be factored into the analysis are conversion or migration costs. All costs are examined both in dollars and staffing implications.

Although it is important to consider all of the elements of cost in deciding to move forward, procurement is just one variable. The cost of not moving forward with the new project must be factored into the analysis process. What would be the impact on the enterprise if it were decided to delay or not approve the project? How would not moving forward affect the competitive advantage of the organization? How would this decision affect the ability to meet the mission of the enterprise? How would strategic business partners, suppliers, vendors, and other stakeholders be affected?

Another important factor to consider in this process is the impact of regulatory compliance issues. The new project should, whenever possible, enhance regulatory requirements. Sometimes a new idea or concept is drafted by a department, such as marketing, and it gains support and management acceptance before the infrastructure, budget, and security personnel get the opportunity to perform a project impact analysis.

Whenever money or resources are to be spent, a risk analysis should be conducted. This will provide the business reasons that should be used to justify the decision to move forward. This is a way that management can demonstrate that due diligence has been performed. The output from the risk analysis process will be used twice. The first time is when decisions need to be made. Typically the only other time the results would be examined is when the enterprise is being examined by a third party and management is asked to show its decision-making process.

For risk analysis and risk assessment the need to demonstrate due diligence is an important factor. However, the overriding reason to conduct these processes is that it makes good business sense. The enterprise proceeds on certain paths based on need and the ability of the organization to meet those specific business or mission needs.

Risk assessment is the second process in the risk management life cycle. Organizations use risk assessment to determine what threats exist to a specific asset and the associated risk level of that threat. The threat prioritization (establishing the risk level) provides the organization with the information needed to select appropriate control measures, safeguards, or countermeasures to lower the risk to an acceptable level.

As we discussed earlier, the need to reduce a threat risk level to zero is counterproductive. Organizations must establish their threshold or concern and implement sufficient countermeasures to reduce the risk to a management-determined level.

As we examine the risk assessment portion of the risk management process, we discuss six steps that will provide us with the three deliverables we need. Risk is a function of the probability that an identified threat will occur, and then the impact that the threat will have on the business process or mission of the asset under review. Each of the six steps will require that the risk assessment team explore their contents and be as thorough as possible.

Step 1: Asset Definition

To be successful this first step in the risk assessment process must be as thorough as possible. It will be difficult to conduct an accurate risk assessment if not all of the team members have the same vision of what is to be reviewed.

During step one the risk assessment team lead (lead) and the owner are to define the process, application, system, or asset that is under review. The key here is to establish the boundaries of what is to be reviewed. Most failed projects come to grief because the scope of the project was poorly defined to begin with or because the scope was not managed well and was allowed to "creep" until it was out of control. If you are going to manage risk assessment as a project, then the asset definition must be looked upon as a scope statement. All of the elements that go into writing a successful scope statement should be used to define the asset and what will be expected from the risk analysis process.

As with any project, the deliverable from the asset definition step is to reach agreement with the owner on what the assessment is to review and all relevant parameters. The objective here is to put in writing a risk assessment statement of opportunity that consists of two elements: project statement, and specifications.

For the project statement, identify the desired outcome. For example, "The team will identify potential threats to the asset under review and will prioritize those threats by assessing the probability of the threat occurring and the impact to the asset if the threat happened. Using the prioritized list of risks, the team will identify possible controls, countermeasures, or safeguards that can reduce the risk exposure to an acceptable level." This will become the risk assessment scope statement and provide the focus for the specifications.

Take enough time during the scope statement development to discuss and clarify the parameters of the project. Although these parameters will vary from project to project, the following items should be considered each time.

- *Purpose:* Fully understand the purpose of the project. What is the need driving the project? If the purpose is to correct a problem, identify the cause of the problem. A risk analysis has been performed that has decided that the project is to move forward. Review the results of this process to better understand the project's purpose.
- *Customer:* Your customer is the person or unit that has the need this project is meant to fill. Determine who the real customer is and note other stakeholders.
- *Deliverables:* These are specific things that are to be delivered to the customer.
- In a risk assessment the deliverables typically are:
  - Threats identified
  - Risk levels established
  - Possible controls identified
- *Resources:* What resources will be required to accomplish the project? Resources include:
  - Money
  - Personnel
  - Equipment
  - Supplies
  - Services
- *Constraints:* Identify those activities that could affect the deliverables of the project. Consider such things as:
  - Laws
  - Policies
  - Procedures
  - Resource limitations
- *Assumptions:* Identify those things that the project team believes to be true or complete.
  - Infrastructure risk assessment has been completed.
  - Baseline set of controls has been implemented.
- *Criteria:* Agree on specifically how the customer will evaluate the success of the project. What are the customer's criteria for the project?
  - Timeliness

- Cost
- Quality
- Criteria should be relevant and valid measures of how well the project accomplishes its stated purpose. You may need to help the customer clarify their true needs in order to ensure that the criteria to be used are valid indicators of project success.

Step 2: Threat Identification

We define a threat as an undesirable event that could affect the business objectives or mission of the business unit or enterprise. Some threats occur when existing controls, that were either implemented incorrectly or have passed their usefulness, now provide a weakness or threat to the infrastructure that can be exploited to circumvent the intended behavior of the control. This process is known as exploiting vulnerability.

A threat-source is defined as any circumstance or event with the potential to cause harm to the asset under review. You will want to create as complete a list of threat-sources as possible. Typically there are three major categories of threat-sources. These include:

1. Natural threats: floods, earthquakes, tornadoes, landslides, avalanches, electrical storms, and other such events.
2. Human threats: events that are either enabled by or caused by human beings, such as unintentional acts (errors and omissions) or deliberate acts (fraud, malicious software, unauthorized access). Statistically the threat that causes the largest loss to information resources remains human errors and omissions.
3. Environmental threats: long-term power outages, pollution, chemical spills, liquid leakage.

To create a complete list of threats there are a number of different methods that can be used. These include developing checklists. Although I think checklists are important and need to be used, I must caution you that if used improperly a checklist will affect the free flow of ideas and information. So use them to ensure that everything gets covered or identified, but don't rely on them to complete the risk assessment process.

Another method of gathering threats is to examine historical data. Research what types of events have occurred and how often they have done so. Once you have the threat, it may be necessary to determine the Annual Rate of Occurrence (ARO). This data can be obtained from a number of sources. For natural threats, the National Weather Center is a good place to get these rates of occurrence. For accidental human threats an insurance underwriter will have these figures. For deliberate threats, then local law enforcement or the organization's security force will have them. For environmental threats, facilities management and the local power companies will have this information.

The method that I like best is brainstorming. I like to get a number of people (stakeholders) together and give them a structure to focus thought and then let them identify all of the threats they can. When we brainstorm there are no wrong answers. We want to ensure that all threats get identified. Once we have completed the information gathering, then we will clean up duplicates and combine like threats. See Figure 2.4.

Threat	Applicable Yes / No	Probability 1 = Low 2 = Medium 3 = High	Impact 1 = Low 2 = Medium 3 = High	Risk Level	Control Selected	New Risk Level
Natural Threat						
Electrical storm						
Ice storm						
Snowstorm/Blizzard						
Major landslide						
Mudslide						
Tsunami						
Tornado						
Hurricane/Typhoon						
High Winds (70+ mph)						
Tropical storm						
Tidal flooding						
Seasonal flooding						
Local flooding						
Upstream dam /reservoir failure						
Sandstorm						
Volcanic activity						
Earthquake (2 – 4 on Richter scale)						
Earthquake (5 or more)						
Epidemic						
Human - Accidental						
Threat	**Applicable Yes / No**	**Probability** 1 = Low 2 = Medium 3 = High	**Impact** 1 = Low 2 = Medium 3 = High	**Risk Level**	**Control Selected**	**New Risk Level**
Fire: Internal-minor						
Fire: Internal-major						
Fire: Internal-Catastrophic						
Fire: External						
Accidental explosion – on site						
Accidental explosion – off site						

Figure 2.4 Threat table by threat source.

Threat	Applicable Yes / No	Probability 1 = Low 2 = Medium 3 = High	Impact 1 = Low 2 = Medium 3 = High	Risk Level	Control Selected	New Risk Level
Aircraft crash						
Train crash						
Derailment						
Auto/Truck crash at site						
Fire: Internal-minor						
Human error – maintenance						
Human error – operational						
Human error – Programming						
Human error – users						
Toxic contamination						
Medical emergency						
Loss of key staff						

Human - Deliberate

Threat	Applicable Yes / No	Probability 1 = Low 2 = Medium 3 = High	Impact 1 = Low 2 = Medium 3 = High	Risk Level	Control Selected	New Risk Level
Sabotage/Terrorism: External - Physical						
Sabotage/Terrorism: Internal - Physical						
Terrorism: Biological						
Terrorism: Chemical						
Bombing						
Bomb Threat						
Arson						
Hostage taking						
Vandalism						
Labor dispute/Strike						
Riot/Civil disorder						
Toxic contamination						

Environmental

Threat	Applicable Yes / No	Probability 1 = Low 2 = Medium 3 = High	Impact 1 = Low 2 = Medium 3 = High	Risk Level	Control Selected	New Risk Level
Power flux						
Power outage – internal						
Power outage – external						
Water leak/plumbing failure						
HVAC failure						
Temperature inadequacy						
Telecommunications failure						

Figure 2.4 (Continued)

Step 3: Determine Probability of Occurrence

Once a list of threats has been finalized and the team has agreed on the definitions of each threat, then it will be necessary to determine how likely that threat is to occur. The risk management team will want to derive an overall likelihood that indicates the probability that a potential threat may be exercised against the risk assessment asset under review. It will be necessary to establish definitions of probability and a number of other key terms.

The following is a sample definition of the probability or likelihood that a threat may occur.

- *Probability:* The likelihood that a threat event will occur
  - *High Probability:* Very likely that the threat will occur within the next year
  - *Medium Probability:* Possible that the threat may occur during the next year
  - *Low Probability:* Highly unlikely that the threat will occur during the next year

When the team is preparing the definitions, they will want to ensure that the probability timeframe meets the needs of the organization. When establishing the project scope statement, a review of the definitions is one of the tasks to be completed.

Step 4: Determine the Impact of the Threat

Once we have determined the probability that a threat might occur, it will then be necessary to determine the impact that the threat will have on the organization. Before determining the impact value, it is necessary to ensure that the scope of the risk analysis has been properly defined. It will be necessary to ensure that the risk management team understands the objectives or mission of the asset under review and how it affects the organization's overall mission or objectives.

When determining the risk level (probability and impact) it will be necessary to establish the framework in which the evaluation is to occur. That is, how will existing controls affect the results? Typically, during the initial review or an assessment of infrastructure, the threats are examined as if there were no controls in place. This will enable the risk management team to establish a baseline risk level from which controls and safeguards can be identified and their effectiveness measured.

Although we make the assertion that no controls are in place, in the scope statement we will identify assumptions and constraints. These assumptions might include the concepts that a risk assessment has been performed on the supporting infrastructure elements and that appropriate controls have been implemented. This will mean that such an activity will have to have taken place or is scheduled to be done as soon as possible. By establishing these assumptions, the risk management team can focus on the threats and impacts related directly to the asset under review.

The results of the review of the probability and impact are the identification of a risk level that can be assigned to each threat (see Figure 2.5). Once the risk level has been established, then the team can identify appropriate actions. Steps three and four determine the likelihood that a given threat may occur and the magnitude of the impact should the threat occur. The risk-level assessment process can be done again after a control has been selected. This will allow the team to determine if the selected control provides the desired reduction in the risk level.

The risk-level process will require the use of a definition for impact as well as a matrix table that will allow the team to establish a risk level. The following are sample definitions for impact that can be used with the probability definition described above.

- *Impact:* The measure of the magnitude of loss or harm to the value of an asset
  - *High Impact:* Shutdown of critical business unit that leads to a significant loss of business, corporate image, or profit
  - *Medium Impact:* Short interruption of critical process or system that results in a limited financial loss to a single business unit
  - *Low Impact:* Interruption with no financial loss

PROBABILITY	IMPACT		
	HIGH	MEDIUM	LOW
HIGH	HIGH	HIGH	MEDIUM
MEDIUM	HIGH	MEDIUM	LOW
LOW	MEDIUM	LOW	LOW
	RISK LEVEL		

Figure 2.5 Probability impact matrix.

Step 5: Controls Recommended

After the risk level has been assigned the team will identify controls or safeguards that could possibly eliminate the risk or at least reduce the risk to an acceptable level. Remember that one of the goals of risk assessment is to document the organization's due diligence when making business decisions. Therefore, it will be important to identify all of the controls and safeguards that the team believes could reduce the risk to an acceptable level. By doing this the team will be able to document all of the options that were considered.

There are a number of factors that need to be considered when recommending controls and alternative solutions. For instance, how effective is the recommended control? One way to determine the relative effectiveness is to perform the risk-level process (probability and impact) to the threat with the control in place. If the risk level is not reduced to an acceptable point, then the team may want to examine another option.

There may also be legal and regulatory requirements to implement specific controls. With so many new and expanding requirements mandated by government agencies, controlling boards, and laws, it will be necessary for the risk management team to be current on these requirements.

When selecting any type of control, it will be necessary to measure the operational impact on the organization. Every control will have an impact in some manner. It could be the expenditure for the control itself. It could be the impact of productivity and turnaround time. Even if the control is a new procedure, the effect on the employees must be reviewed and used in the determination on whether or not to implement.

A final consideration is the safety and reliability of the control or safeguard. Does the control have a track record that demonstrates that it will allow the organization to operate in a safe and secure mode? The overall safety of the organization's intellectual property is at stake. The last thing that the risk management team wants to do is to implement a control that puts the enterprise at a greater risk.

The expenditure on controls must be balanced against the actual business harm. A good rule of thumb is that if the control costs more than the asset it is designed to protect, then the return on investment is probably going to be low. One way to identify a good "bang for the buck" is to identify each control and cross-reference it to all of the threats that could be mitigated by the implementation of that specific control. This process will provide the team with an initial idea of which control is most cost effective.

In order to be effective, the risk analysis process should be applied across the entire organization. That is, all of the elements and methodology that make up the risk analysis process should be standard and all business units trained in its use (see Table 2.5). The output from the risk analysis will lead the organization to identify controls that should reduce the level of threat occurrence.

Another way to map controls is by using some standard such as ISO 17799 (see Table 2.6). The numbers in parentheses in the figure are the matching section numbers found in ISO 17799. ISO 17799 is actually "a comprehensive set of controls comprising best practices in information security." It is essentially, in part (extended), an internationally recognized generic information security standard.

Its predecessor, titled BS7799-1, has existed in various forms for a number of years, although the standard only really gained widespread recognition following publication by ISO (the International Standards Organization) in December of 2000. Formal certification and accreditation were also introduced around the same time.

The object of the controls list is to identify categories of controls that will lead the team to determine the specific control required. When developing your list, be sure to be thorough, but don't be so lengthy that the list of controls is similar to reading *War and Peace*.

Step 6: Documentation

Once the risk analysis is complete, the results need to be documented in a standard format and a report issued to the asset owner. This report will help senior management, the business owner, make decisions on policy, procedures, budget, and systems and management change. The risk analysis report should be presented in a systematic and analytical manner that assesses risk so that senior management will understand the risks and allocate resources to reduce the risk to an acceptable level.

Cost-Benefit Analysis

To allocate resources and implement cost-effective controls, organizations, after identifying all possible controls and evaluating their feasibility and effectiveness, should conduct a cost-benefit analysis. This process should be conducted for each new or enhanced control to determine if the control recommended is appropriate for the organization. A cost-benefit analysis should determine the impact of implementing the new or enhanced control and then determine the impact of not implementing the control.

Remember that one of the long-term costs of any control is the requirement to maintain its effectiveness. It is, therefore, necessary to factor this cost into the benefit requirement of any control. When performing a

Table 2.5 Controls by IT Organization

Control Number	*IT Group*	*Descriptor*	*Definition*
1	Operations Controls	Backup	Backup requirements will be determined & communicated to Operations including a request that an electronic notification that backups were completed be sent to the application System Administrator. Operations will be requested to test the backup procedures.
2	Operations Controls	Recovery Plan	Develop, document, and test, recovery procedures designed to ensure that the application and information can be recovered, using the backups created, in the event of loss.
3	Operations Controls	Risk Analysis	Conduct a risk analysis to determine the level of exposure to identified threats and identify possible safeguards or controls.
4	Operations Controls	Anti-Virus	1) Ensure LAN Administrator installs the corporate standard anti-viral software on all computers. 2) Training and awareness of virus prevention techniques will be incorporated in the organization IP program.
5	Operations Controls	Interface Dependencies	Systems that feed information will be identified and communicated to Operations to stress the impact to the functionality if these feeder applications are unavailable.
6	Operations Controls	Maintenance	Time requirements for technical maintenance will be tracked and a request for adjustment will be communicated to management if experience warrants.
7	Operations Controls	Service Level Agreement	Acquire service level agreements to establish level of customer expectations and assurances from supporting operations.

Table 2.5 Controls by IT Organization (Continued)

Control Number	*IT Group*	*Descriptor*	*Definition*
8	Operations Controls	Maintenance	Acquire maintenance and/or supplier agreements to facilitate the continued operational status of the application.
9	Operations Controls	Change Management	Production Migration controls such as search and remove processes to ensure data stores are clean.
10	Operations Controls	Business Impact Analysis	A formal business impact analysis will be conducted to determine the asset's relative criticality with other enterprise assets.
11	Operations Controls	Backup	Training for a backup to the System Administrator will be provided and duties rotated between them to ensure the adequacy of the training program.
12	Operations Controls	Backup	A formal employee security awareness program has been implemented and is updated and presented to the employees at least on an annual basis.
13	Operations Controls	Recovery Plan	Access Sourced: Implement a mechanism to limit access to confidential information to specific network paths or physical locations.
14	Operations Controls	Risk Analysis	Implement user authentication mechanisms (such as firewalls, dial-in controls, Secure ID) to limit access to authorized personnel.
15	Application Controls	Application Control	Design and implement application controls (data entry edit checking, fields requiring validation, alarm indicators, password expiration capabilities, check-sums) to ensure the integrity, confidentiality, and availability of application information.

Table 2.5 Controls by IT Organization (Continued)

Control Number	IT Group	Descriptor	Definition
16	Application Controls	Acceptance Testing	Develop testing procedures to be followed during applications development or during modifications to the existing application that include user participation and acceptance.
17	Application Controls	Training	Implement user programs (user performance evaluations) designed to encourage compliance with policies and procedures in place to ensure the appropriate utilization of the application.
18	Application Controls	Training	Application developers will provide documentation, guidance, and support to the operations staff (Operations) in implementing mechanisms to ensure that the transfer of information between applications is secure.
19	Application Controls	Corrective Strategies	The Development Team will develop corrective strategies such as: reworked processes, revised application logic, etc.
20	Security Controls	Policy	Develop policies and procedures to limit access and operating privileges to those with business need.
21	Security Controls	Training	User training will include instruction & documentation on the proper use of the application. The importance of maintaining the confidentiality of user accounts, passwords, and the confidential and competitive nature of information will be stressed.
22	Security Controls	Review	Implement mechanisms to monitor, report, and audit activities identified as requiring independent reviews, including periodic reviews of user-IDs to ascertain and verify business need.

Table 2.5 Controls by IT Organization (Continued)

Control Number	*IT Group*	*Descriptor*	*Definition*
23	Security Controls	Asset Classification	The asset under review will be classified using enterprise policies, standards, and procedures on asset classification.
24	Security Controls	Access Control	Mechanisms to protect the database against unauthorized access, and modifications made from outside the application, will be determined and implemented.
25	Security Controls	Management Support	Request management support to ensure the cooperation and coordination of various business units.
26	Security Controls	Proprietary	Processes are in place to ensure that company proprietary assets are protected and that the company is in compliance with all third-party license agreements.
27	Security Controls	Security Awareness	Implement an access control mechanism to prevent unauthorized access to information. This mechanism will include the capability of detecting, logging, and reporting attempts to breach the security of this information.
28	Security Controls	Access Control	Implement encryption mechanisms (data, end-to-end) to prevent unauthorized access to protect the integrity and confidentiality of information.
29	Security Controls	Access Control	Adhere to a change management process designed to facilitate a structured approach to modifications of the application, to ensure appropriate steps and precautions are followed. "Emergency" modifications should be included in this process.

Table 2.5 Controls by IT Organization (Continued)

Control Number	*IT Group*	*Descriptor*	*Definition*
30	Security Controls	Access Control	Control procedures are in place to ensure that appropriate system logs are reviewed by independent third parties to review system update activities.
31	Security Controls	Access Control	In consultation with Facilities Management, facilitate the implementation of physical security controls designed to protect the information, software, and hardware required of the system.
32	Systems Controls	Change Management	Backup requirements will be determined & communicated to Operations including a request that an electronic notification that backups were completed be sent to the application System Administrator. Operations will be requested to test the backup procedures.
33	Systems Controls	Monitor System Logs	Develop, document, and test, recovery procedures designed to ensure that the application and information can be recovered, using the backups created, in the event of loss.
34	Physical Security	Physical Security	Conduct a risk analysis to determine the level of exposure to identified threats and identify possible safeguards or controls.

cost-benefit analysis it will be necessary to consider the cost of implementation based on some of the following:

- Costs of implementation including initial outlay for hardware and software
- Reduction in operational effectiveness
- Implementation of additional policies and procedures to support the new controls

Table 2.6 Controls Using ISO 17799:2000

Control Number	*ISO 17799 Section*	*Class*	*Control Description*
1		Risk Assessment (2)	Conduct an accurate and thorough assessment of the potential risks and vulnerabilities to the confidentiality, integrity and availability of information resources.
2	Security Policy	Policy (3.1)	Develop and implement an Information Security Policy.
3	Organizational Security	Management Information Security Forum (4.1)	Establish a corporate committee to oversee information security. Develop and implement an Information Security Organization mission statement.
4	Organizational Security	Security of Third Party Access (4.2)	Implement a process to analyze third party connection risks and implement specific security standards to combat third party connection risks.
5	Organizational Security	Security Requirements in Outsourcing Contracts (4.3)	Ensure the security requirements of the information owners have been addressed in a contract between the owners and the outsource organization.
6	Asset Classification & Control	Accounting of Assets (5.1)	Establish an inventory of major assets associated with each information system.
7	Asset Classification & Control	Information Classification (5.2)	Implement standards for security classification and the level of protection required for information assets.
8	Asset Classification & Control	Information Labeling and Handling (5.2)	Implement standards to ensure the proper handling of information assets.

Table 2.6 Controls Using ISO 17799:2000 (Continued)

Control Number	*ISO 17799 Section*	*Class*	*Control Description*
9	Personnel Security	Security in Job Descriptions (6.1)	Ensure that security responsibilities are included in employee job descriptions.
10	Personnel Security	User Training ((6.2)	Implement training standards to ensure that users are trained in information security policies and procedures, security requirements, business controls and correct use of IT facilities.
11	Personnel Security	Responding to Security Incidents and Malfunctions (6.3)	Implement procedures and standards for formal reporting and incident response action to be taken on receipt of an incident report.
12	Physical & Environmental Security	Secure Areas (7.1)	Implement standards to ensure that physical security protections exist, based on defined perimeters through strategically located barriers throughout the organization.
13	Physical & Environmental Security	Equipment Security (7.2)	Implement standards to ensure that equipment is located properly to reduce risks of environmental hazards and unauthorized access.
14	Physical & Environmental Security	General Controls (7.3)	Implement a clear desk, clear screen policy for sensitive material to reduce risks of unauthorized access, loss, or damage outside normal working hours.

Table 2.6 Controls Using ISO 17799:2000 (Continued)

Control Number	*ISO 17799 Section*	*Class*	*Control Description*
15	Communications and Operations Management	Documented Operating Procedures (8.1)	Implement operating procedures to clearly document that all operational computer systems are being operated in a correct, secure manner.
16	Communications and Operations Management	System Planning and Acceptance (8.2)	Implement standards to ensure that capacity requirements are monitored, and future requirements projected, to reduce the risk of system overload.
17	Communications and Operations Management	Protection from Malicious Software (8.3)	Implement standards and user training to ensure that virus detection and prevention measures are adequate.
18	Communications and Operations Management	Housekeeping (8.4)	Establish procedures for making regular back-up copies of essential business data and software to ensure that it can be recovered following a computer disaster or media failure.
19	Communications and Operations Management	Network Management (8.5)	Implement appropriate standards to ensure the security of data in networks and the protection of connected services from unauthorized access.
20	Communications and Operations Management	Media Handling and Security (8.6)	Implement procedures for the management of removable computer media such as tapes, disks, cassettes, and printed reports.

Table 2.6 Controls Using ISO 17799:2000 (Continued)

Control Number	*ISO 17799 Section*	*Class*	*Control Description*
21	Communications and Operations Management	Exchanges of Information and Software (8.7)	Implement procedures to establish formal agreements, including software escrow agreements when appropriate, for exchanging data and software (whether electronically or manually) between organizations.
22	Access Control	Business requirement for System Access (9.1)	Implement a risk analysis process to gather business requirements to document access control levels.
23	Access Control	User Access Management (9.2)	Implement procedures for user registration and deregistration access to all multiuse IT services.
24	Access Control	User Responsibility (9.3)	Implement user training to ensure users have been taught good security practices in the selection and use of passwords.
25	Access Control	Network Access Control (9.4)	Implement procedures to ensure that network and computer services that can be accessed by an individual user or from a particular terminal are consistent with business access control policy.
26	Access Control	Operating System Access Control (9.5)	Implement standards for automatic terminal identification to authenticate connections to specific locations.
27	Access Control	Application Access Control (9.6)	Implement procedures to restrict access to applications system data and functions in accordance with defined access policy, and based on individual requirements.

Table 2.6 Controls Using ISO 17799:2000 (Continued)

Control Number	*ISO 17799 Section*	*Class*	*Control Description*
28	Access Control	Monitoring System Access and Use (9.7)	Implement audit trails that record exceptions and other security-relevant events, produced and maintained to assist in future investigations and in access control.
29	Access Control	Remote Access and Telecommuting (9.8)	Implement a formal policy and supporting standards that address the risks of working with mobile computing facilities, including requirements for physical protection, access controls, cryptographic techniques, back up, and virus protection.
30	Systems Development & Maintenance	Security Requirements of Systems (10.1)	Implement standards to ensure that analysis of security requirements is part of the requirement analysis stage of each development project.
31	Systems Development & Maintenance	Security in Application Systems (10.2)	Implement standards to ensure that data that is input into applications systems is validated, to ensure that it is correct and appropriate.
32	Systems Development & Maintenance	Cryptography (10.3)	Implement policies and standards on the use of cryptographic controls, including management of encryption keys, and effective implementation.
33	Systems Development & Maintenance	Security of System Files (10.4)	Implement standards to exercise strict control over the implementation of software on operational systems.

Table 2.6 Controls Using ISO 17799:2000 (Continued)

Control Number	*ISO 17799 Section*	*Class*	*Control Description*
34	Systems Development & Maintenance	Security in Development and Support Environments (10.5)	Implement standards and procedures for formal change management process.
35	Business Continuity Management	Aspects of Business Continuity Planning (11.1)	Implement procedures for the development and maintenance of business continuity plans across the organization.
36	Compliance	Compliance with Legal Requirements (12.1)	Implement standards to ensure that all relevant statutory, regulatory, and contractual requirements are specifically defined and documented for each information system.

- Cost of possibly hiring additional staff or at a minimum, training existing staff in the new controls
- The cost of education support personnel to maintain the effectiveness of the control

Risk mitigation is a systematic methodology used by senior management to reduce organizational risk. Once the risk assessment has been conducted (threats identified, risk levels established, controls chosen) then management can use various risk mitigation techniques to complete the process. Risk mitigation can be achieved through a number of different methods. We take, identify, and discuss the six most common methods of risk mitigation.

1. *Risk Assumption:* After examining the threats and determining the risk level, the team's findings lead management to determine that it is the best business decision to accept the potential risk and continue operating. This is an acceptable outcome of the risk assessment process. If, after completing the risk assessment process, management decides to accept the risk, then they have performed their due diligence.

2. *Risk Alleviation:* Senior management approves the implementation of the controls recommended by the risk management team that will lower the risk to an acceptable level.
3. *Risk Avoidance:* This is where after performing the risk assessment management chooses to avoid the risks by eliminating the process that could cause the risks. For example, foregoing certain functions or enhancements to systems or applications because the risk assessment results lead management to conclude that to proceed would place the organization at too great an exposure.
4. *Risk Limitation:* This is the process used to limit the risk by implementing controls that minimize the adverse impact of a threat that would exercise a threat. This is the standard process that is worked when a risk assessment is completed. By identifying threats, establishing the risk level, and selecting reasonable and prudent controls, management is limiting risk exposure.
5. *Risk Planning:* This is a process where it is decided to manage risk by developing an architecture that prioritizes, implements, and maintains controls.
6. *Risk Transference:* Here management transfers the risk by using other options to compensate for a loss, such as purchasing an insurance policy.

Whichever risk mitigation technique is used, the business objectives or mission of an organization must be considered when selecting any of these techniques. It may not be practical.

Define Strategies and Prioritize Options to Mitigate Risks to Levels Acceptable to the Enterprise

To be effective, the risk assessment process must be accepted as part of the business process of the enterprise. The risk management professional looks to ensure that the analysis and assessment processes support the business objectives or mission of the organization. For years I have been trying to tell security and audit professionals that security or audit requirements are not what the business needs. There are only business or mission recommendations or solutions. Remember, part of the success of a process is its acceptance by the user community. Trying to mandate requirements to managers can be counterproductive. An effective risk assessment process will search for the business needs of the enterprise and will work with the business owners to identify safeguards to meet those needs.

To be successful, the needs of the customer must be identified and met. Every time the risk assessment is to be conducted, the risk management professional must meet with the client to determine what is to be reviewed, what kinds of risk elements are to be examined, and what the client needs as a deliverable or as results from the process.

For an information security professional most of the focus of the risk assessment process revolves around the information security triad of integrity, confidentiality, and availability of information resources. As we discussed before, the only inhibiting factor in risk assessment is what you can conceive of to conduct a risk assessment against. These are only initial examples of what can be examined by an effective risk analysis process. Throughout the book we review a number of risk assessment methods and critique them. By looking at different methods, you will be able to build a risk assessment process that will meet your organization's specific needs.

According to *Systems Management* magazine, top IS project managers were asked what functional capability they most needed to be successful; the number one answer was risk management. Projects often have involuntary controls or requirements imposed on them. The owner and project-lead do not recognize or understand the need for the seemingly arbitrary set of controls, and therefore don't understand the need. As a result, the project manager is often surprised by negative consequences and the project sponsor suffers unmet expectations.

The risk assessment process must be geared to support the business or mission of the enterprise. Many times owners are told that certain controls are being implemented because the controls are "audit requirements" or "security requirements." As we discussed, there are only business or mission requirements. Our job is to help the owner find business-friendly controls or countermeasures.

The role of security (whether physical or information) is to assist management in meeting its fiduciary responsibility to adequately protect the assets of the enterprise. With capital assets, it is easy to see that stealing property affects the enterprise's ability to conduct business. So, now we must help management to identify intellectual property and implement effective, cost-efficient safeguards.

Every enterprise has to establish its own set of requirements for the protection of information assets. These are typically documented through an information classification policy and handling standards. The individual safeguards will differ depending on sensitivity and criticality of the information resource. Therefore the goal of an enterprisewide information security program and risk assessment process is to determine the threat impact on information assets based on:

- Integrity: The information is as intended without inappropriate modification or corruption.

- Confidentiality: The information is protected from unauthorized or accidental disclosure.
- Availability: Authorized users can access applications and systems when required to perform their jobs.

It may be necessary to create a more specific definition or example of each of these elements to provide the team with a better frame of reference from which to work.

The process for classifying information needs to be well defined and a methodology to assist the users in determining the level of classification must also be implemented as part of the risk management process. Later we use qualitative risk assessment methods to demonstrate how you can create a user-friendly classification process. To assist the information risk management process, it will be necessary to have the users visualize the elements that make up the value of the information asset (see Table 2.7). These might include some, all, or more than the following:

- The cost of producing the information
- The value of the information on the open market
- The cost of reproducing the information if destroyed
- The benefit the information brings to the enterprise in meeting its business objectives or mission
- The repercussions to the enterprise if the information were not readily available
- The advantage it would give to a competitor if they could use, change, or destroy the information
- The cost to the enterprise if the information were released, altered, or destroyed
- The loss of client or customer confidence if the information were not held and processed securely
- The loss of public credibility and embarrassment if the information were not secure

The value of a particular information resource must be determined by the business manager owner where the information resource is created or is the primary user of that resource. This is a process that cannot be discharged to the information security staff or to audit or to any other third party, it must remain with the business unit.

The risk assessment process consists of four elements: asset scoped, threats identified, risk level established, and possible controls selected. In the previous chapter we discussed creating a project scope statement to define the asset that is to be the subject of the review.

Table 2.7 Review Element Definition Table

Review Element	*Definition*
Loss of Integrity	System and data integrity refers to the requirement that information be protected from improper modification. Integrity is lost if unauthorized changes are made to the data or the system either intentionally or accidentally changes the data. If the loss of system or data integrity is not corrected, continued use of the contaminated system or corrupted data could result in inaccuracy, fraud, or erroneous decisions. Also, violation of integrity may be the first step in a successful attack against system availability or confidentiality.
Loss of Availability	If a mission-critical system is unavailable to its end users, the organization's mission may be affected. Loss of system functionality and operational effectiveness may result in loss of productive time and therefore impede the end users' performance of their tasks in supporting the organization's mission.
Loss of Confidentiality	System and data confidentiality refers to the protection of information from unauthorized disclosure. The impact of unauthorized disclosure of confidential information can range from the jeopardizing of non-public, personal private information to loss of competitive advantage or trade secret information. Unauthorized, unanticipated, or unintentional disclosure could result in loss of public confidence, competitive advantage, organization embarrassment, legal or regulatory action.

Just as a review, what then is an asset? An accountant might say that an asset is anything of value. However, many times the "asset" in question is a tangible piece of property that can be seen. However, the physical assets are not the only assets that must be protected. Another way of dividing assets is into at least these major headings:

- Physical: those items that can be seen
- Logical: the intellectual property of the enterprise

Other classification levels might include people, physical and environmental, telecommunications, hardware, software, and data or information. Another list might include topics such as hardware, software, data, information, and people and procedures. All too often, management tends to focus on the enterprise's physical assets. Although important, the intellectual assets of an organization are often more valuable and harder to protect than the physical assets.

As we have seen, the proper definition of the asset to be reviewed in the risk assessment process is vital to the success of the risk assessment process. The ability to precisely identify what a specific asset is cannot be overemphasized.

We now review the remaining three elements of the risk assessment process.

Step 1: Threat Identification

After you have identified the asset that needs to be protected, you must begin to look for and identify threats to those assets. What then is a threat? Based on the context in which it is used, threat can mean a number of things, none of them typically good. It is normally looked upon as an "intent to do harm to someone or something." According to *Webster's*, a threat is "An indication of impending undesirable event," or, my favorite, "An expression of intention to inflict evil, injury, or damage."

There can be an unlimited number of threats that can be of concern to your enterprise. Any number of typical or common threats can be identified, such as fire, flood, or fraud. It is very important to consider all threats, no matter how unlikely they may seem. Later in the risk-level process we can weed out those threats that have little or no possibility of occurring. As a starting point, you want to consider those threats that might actually affect your organization.

When attempting to identify potential threats, it might prove beneficial to create scenarios that will help the team expand its search pattern. You will want to examine circumstances or events that could cause harm to the asset under review or to the mission or business objectives of the organization.

As we discussed in the previous chapter, there are three common sources for threats and they can be classified as natural, human, or environmental. Remember that human threat is divided into two subcategories: accidental and deliberate.

When searching for threats it is important to consider all potential sources or scenarios that could lead to an impact on the organization. Try not to overlook the obvious. For example, you may have a data center located in Mesa, Arizona. The idea of a "natural flood" may be dismissed by the team as being too remote a likelihood to consider. However, an environmental threat such as a broken water main could quickly flood the data center and cause severe damage to the assets. So be sure to examine the source of each threat, natural, human, or environmental, before dismissing it.

As we have mentioned before, the human threat must be viewed through intentional acts, such as deliberate attacks by malicious persons or disgruntled employees, or unintentional acts, such as negligence and errors. A deliberate attack can be either an attempt to gain unauthorized access to a system or application by password guessing or cracking, or by using a Post-it® note attached to the workstation to remember the access codes.

You will want to include discussions on what would motivate a threat source to act. Remember, motivation is pretty much limited to the human source. Although I have many times thought that Mother Nature had it in for me when I had to work outside, I am fairly certain that these acts were not deliberately aimed at me. It may help to put together a discussion table for the team members to facilitate discussion (see Table 2.8).

Table 2.8 Threat Source Table

Source	*Motivation*	*Threat*
External hacker	Challenge Ego Game-playing	• System hacking • Social engineering • Dumpster diving
Internal hacker	Deadline Financial problems Disenchantment	• Trap-door • Fraud • Poor documentation
Cracker	Destruction of information Monetary gain Unauthorized data alteration	• Spoofing • System intrusion • Impersonation • Denial of service attack
Terrorist (environmental)	Revenge	• System attack
	Greenmail Strident cause	• Social engineering • Letter bombs • Viruses • Denial of service
Poorly trained employees	Unintentional errors	• Corruption of data
	Programming errors Data entry errors	• Malicious code introduced • System bugs • Unauthorized access

When examining threats, experts identify these elements that are associated with threats:

- The *agent* is the catalyst that performs the threat. The agent can be human, machine, or nature.
- The *motive* is something that causes an agent to act. These actions can be either accidental or intentional. Based on the elements that make up an agent, the only motivating factor that can be both accidental and intentional is human.
- The *results* are the outcome of the applied threat. For the information security profession, the results normally lead to a loss of access, unauthorized access, modification, disclosure, or destruction of the information asset.

During the risk assessment process it will be necessary to identify as many threats as possible. There are a number of ways that this can be accomplished. The first way may be to review current risk management textbooks and develop a list of possible threats.

Step 2: Threat Vulnerability

Identifying a threat is just the first part of the analysis phase. It will be necessary to determine just how vulnerable your enterprise is to that threat. There are a number of factors that will affect a threat. There are nearly as many factors affecting the threat and its impact on your enterprise as there are threats.

Your geographical location can have an impact on the threat model. If you are located in the Midwest, then some natural threats will not be part of your areas of concern. There are very few dust storms in Lincoln, Nebraska. Although Detroit and the northern states and cities are used to handling ice and snow, just the threat of an inch of snow can send southern cities into a panic. Beyond the natural threats, geography can also affect the infrastructure supporting your enterprise. The northeast United States has too many people and businesses for the existing support infrastructure. Telecommunications, power, electricity, and roads are stretched to their capacity, and any additional impact can and often does cause problems.

The facility that your enterprise is housed in can affect threats. Depending on the age of the building, it can either be an asset or a threat. Don't get confused by thinking that only newer construction is safer. In many instances the older structures are able to withstand some pretty impressive happenstance. Look to see the construction of the complex and determine if there is an active fire suppression system installed and tested.

Who you share the facility with and who your neighbors are can affect the level of vulnerability the threat presents to your enterprise. During a recent physical security review, the seven-story office complex was typical when it came to security officers in the lobby, additional level of access for restricted areas, and a fire suppression system that is tested. The biggest threat we found to the enterprise was the fact that they shared their building with noncompany law enforcement agencies.

Other factors that might affect the level of vulnerability include those shown in Table 2.9.

Table 2.9 Threat Impact Table

Impacts to Threats	*Concern*
Information sensitivity	What kinds and type of information does your enterprise generate?
Employee emergency training	Have employees been trained to respond to emergency incidents? Are there procedures in place that will assist employees during an emergency?
Protection and detection features	Are there additional asset protection features in place? Can the enterprise detect when a threat is happening?
Employee morale	Are employees unusually dissatisfied? Is there unrest within the ranks?
Local economic conditions	Is the surrounding area economically deprived?
Visibility	Is your organization a high profile company or agency?
Redundancies	Are there backup systems in place?
Proficiency level of employees	Are employees properly trained?
Written procedures	Are there written desk procedures in place? Are these procedures used to train backup personnel?
Employee security awareness	Do employees attend annual security awareness sessions?
Past prosecutions	Has the enterprise ever sought relief in the courts for attacks on their assets? Has information been turned over to law enforcement for criminal prosecution?

Once assets and threats have been identified, it will be necessary to establish some link between the two. One of the most basic forms of risk analysis is a process known as an Annual Loss Exposure or (ALE). The ALE takes the value of an asset and then uses the likelihood of a threat occurrence in a formula to calculate the ALE. The asset value (V) multiplied by the likelihood (L) of the threat ($V \times L$ = ALE).

Getting and understanding the likelihood of an occurrence is going to take some work. For natural threats, the local and national weather center can and does track the number of times a specific weather threat happens during a calendar year. The risk management team will need to research these findings and then develop a table. This table can be an average based on the number of occurrences and then divided by the number of years. Or you can track the number of occurrences over a five-year period and develop a rate of occurrence with the lowest number at one end of the range and the highest number at the other.

For all other types of threats, it will be necessary to do additional research. For criminal activities, the risk management team can look to local law enforcement, the FBI, and state agencies. Each entity keeps a log on the number of times a specific activity has occurred within their jurisdiction. This information, along with the information gathered by your internal audit and security staffs will provide the rates of occurrence found through the weather bureaus.

For some threats it may be necessary to contact your enterprise's insurance company to see if they have information that they can share with you. Don't forget to review the system incident logs to determine errors, omissions, hardware failure, software bugs, and other types of system-related threats.

Once you've done your leg work, you may use something like the table in Table 2.10 to show annual rates of occurrence.

The ALE would work like this. You have a $3 million data center located in a flood area. A major flood that would destroy the data center occurs once every 100 years.

Value = $3 million
Likelihood = once every 100 years (using the table above L = .01)
$3 million × .01 = $30,000.

Insurance companies use the ALE to assist them in determining what kind of premium they should charge. For the risk management professional, this form of risk analysis is often misleading. The loss if a flood occurred is not $30,000 but actually $3,000,000. Among the problems with using the ALE method is the inability to predict how soon a threat will occur.

Table 2.10 Threat Occurrence Rate

Rate of Occurrence		*Multiplier Factor*
Never	0	0.0
Once in 300 Years	1/300	0.00333
Once in 200 Years	1/200	0.005
Once in 100 Years	1/100	0.01
Once in 50 Years	1/50	0.02
Once in 25 Years	1/25	0.04
Once in 5 Years	1/5	0.20
Once in 2 Years	1/2	0.50
Yearly	1/1	1.0
Twice a Year	1/.5	2.0
Once a Month	12/1	12.0
Once a Week	52/1	52.0
Once a Day	365/1	365.0

Once the threat list has been reviewed, consolidated, and edited it will be necessary to establish a risk level for each threat. We examine that process next.

Once a list of threats has been finalized, it will be necessary to determine how likely that each threat is to occur. The risk assessment team will want to derive an overall likelihood that indicates the probability that a potential threat may be exercised against the risk assessment asset under review. When establishing probability levels it will be necessary to include governing factors such as motivation from the source of the threat and the existence of current controls.

When examining the threat there are two key ways to assess the probability and impact. The first method is to establish probability without consideration for existing controls. This method is typically used when conducting an initial risk assessment for an enterprise infrastructure resource such as a network segment, platform, or information security program. This method will give the team a baseline of exposure levels from which to build the control program.

The other method is to examine the risk level by taking into account existing controls. This will allow the team to examine existing controls and establish a risk level based on how effective the existing controls are. This method is typically used when examining a specific LAN, application, or subnet.

Table 2.11 Sample Definitions for Probability

Probability Level	*Definition*
High	The threat-source is highly motivated and has sufficient capability, and controls are inadequate to keep the threat from being exercised.
Medium	The threat-source is motivated and capable, but controls are in place that may impede the successful exercise of the threat.
Low	The threat-source lacks motivation or capability, or controls are in place to prevent, or at least significantly impede, the threat from being exercised.

The likelihood the organization is susceptible to a specific threat is typically described as high, medium or low (see Table 2.11).

Once the probability that a threat might occur has been determined, then the impact that the threat will have on the organization must be addressed. Before determining the impact value, it is necessary to ensure that the scope of the risk assessment has been properly defined. It will be necessary to ensure that the risk assessment team understands the objectives or mission of the asset under review and how it affects the organization's overall mission or objectives. Before beginning the impact analysis, it is necessary to obtain the following:

- *Asset mission:* This was accomplished as part of the project scope statement. The scope statement must be discussed with the team at the start of the risk assessment process.
- *Information sensitivity:* To conduct a successful risk assessment, everyone must know the sensitivity of the information that will be handled by the asset under review. We will discuss this process later.
- *Asset criticality:* How important is this asset to the mission of the organization? It will be necessary to conduct a Business Impact Analysis (BIA) on the asset to determine its relative criticality. We discuss these processes later in the book.

Again, when determining the impact, the team has to know how existing controls are to be considered. The scope statement will include the establishment of assumptions and constraints. These assumptions might include the concepts that a risk assessment has been performed on the supporting infrastructure elements and that appropriate controls have been implemented. This will mean that such an activity will have to have taken place or be scheduled to be done as soon as possible. By establishing these assumptions, the risk management team can focus on the threats and impacts related directly to the asset under review.

Some tangible impacts can be measured quantitatively in lost revenue, cost of repairing the system, or the level of effort required to correct problems caused by a successful threat occurrence. Other impacts, the intangible ones such as loss of public confidence, loss of credibility, and damage to the organization's reputation cannot be measured in specific units but must be qualified in terms of high, medium, and low impacts. See Table 2.12 for some sample definitions.

Once the team has established the probability level and the impact level, it will be able to assign a risk level to the threat. This can be done by creating the type of risk level matrix we discussed in the previous chapter (also see Figure 2.6). Try to keep the levels as clear and concise as possible.

Step 3: Controls and Safeguards

After the risk level has been assigned the team will identify controls or safeguards that are in place or could be put in place to possibly eliminate the risk or at least reduce the risk to an acceptable level. One of the goals of risk assessment is to document the organization's due diligence when making business decisions. Therefore, it will be important to identify as many controls and safeguards as possible that could reduce the risk exposure level. By doing this the team will be able to document all of the options that were considered.

There are a number of factors that need to be considered when recommending controls and alternative solutions. For instance, how effective is the recommended control? One way to determine the relative effectiveness is to perform the risk-level process (probability and impact) on the threat with the identified control in place. If the risk level is not reduced to an acceptable point then the team may want to examine another option.

There may also be legal and regulatory requirements to implement specific controls. With so many new and expanding requirements mandated by government agencies, controlling boards, and laws, it will be necessary for the risk management team to be current on these requirements.

When selecting any type of control, it will be necessary to measure the operational impact on the organization. Every control will have an impact in some manner. It could be the expenditure for the control itself. It could be the impact on productivity and turnaround time. Even if the control is a new procedure the effect on the employees must be reviewed and used in the determination of whether to implement.

Table 2.12 Sample Definitions for Impact

Impact Level	*Definition*
High	The loss of confidentiality, integrity or availability could be expected to have severe or catastrophic adverse effect on organizational operations, assets or individuals. • Severe degradation or loss of mission capability to an extent and duration that the organization is not able to perform its primary functions • Results in major damage to the organization's assets • Results in major financial loss • Results in severe or catastrophic harm to individuals involving loss of life or serious life threatening injuries
Medium	The loss of confidentiality, integrity or availability could be expected to have serious adverse effect on organizational operations, assets, or individuals. • Significant degradation in mission capability to an extent and duration that the organization is able to perform its primary functions, but the effectiveness is reduced • Results in significant damage to the organization's assets • Results in significant financial loss • Results in significant harm to individuals but not loss of life or serious injuries
Low	The loss of confidentiality, integrity or availability could be expected to have limited adverse effect on organizational operations, assets, or individuals. • Degradation in mission capability to an extent and duration that the organization is able to perform its primary functions, but the effectiveness is reduced • Results in minor damage to the organization's assets • Results in minor financial loss • Results to minor exposure to harm

A final consideration is the safety and reliability of the control or safeguard. Does the control have a track record that demonstrates that it will allow the organization to operate in a safe and sound mode? The overall safety of the organization's intellectual property is at stake. The last thing that the risk assessment team will want to do is to implement a control that puts the enterprise at a greater risk.

The expenditure on controls must be balanced against the actual business harm. A good rule of thumb is that if the control costs more than the asset it is designed to protect, then the return on investment is probably going to be low. One way to identify a good return on investment is to

PROBABILITY	IMPACT			
		HIGH	MEDIUM	LOW
	HIGH	HIGH	HIGH	MEDIUM
	MEDIUM	HIGH	MEDIUM	LOW
	LOW	MEDIUM	LOW	LOW
		RISK LEVEL		

Figure 2.6 Probability–impact matrix example.

identify each control and cross-reference it to all of the threats that could be mitigated by the implementation of that specific control. This process will provide the team with an initial idea of which control is most cost effective.

Therefore, the goal of this step in the risk assessment process is to analyze the controls that have been implemented, or are planned for implementation. Security controls encompass the use of technical and nontechnical methods. The technical controls are safeguards that are incorporated into computer hardware, software, or firmware. These would include access control mechanisms, identification and authentication processes, encryption tools, and intrusion detection software. Nontechnical controls are management and operational controls such as policies, procedures, standards, personnel security, and environmental control mechanisms.

The control categories for both technical and nontechnical control methods can be further classified as avoidance, assurance, detection, and recovery. The team should concentrate on controls that will allow the mission of the enterprise to function while providing an adequate level of protection. It may be prudent to establish a list of possible controls in each of the layers that will help the enterprise meet its business objectives.

- *Avoidance* controls are proactive safeguards that attempt to minimize the risk of accidental or intentional intrusions.
- *Assurance* controls are tools and strategies employed to ensure the ongoing effectiveness of the existing controls and safeguards.
- *Detection* controls are techniques and programs used to ensure early detection, interception, and response for security breaches.
- *Recovery* controls are planning and response services to rapidly restore a secure environment and investigate the source of the breaches.

During this step, the risk assessment team will determine the security controls generally based on existing security architecture, some regulatory requirement, a business standard, or a combination of all three. As we discussed in the previous chapter, the *Information Technology—Code of Practice for Information Security Management* (ISO/IEC 17799) is a good basis for establishing a set of controls.

There are other sources for standards, and each year the risk assessment teams seem to receive new regulations discussing the need to protect information and information-processing assets. Other sources might include some of the following.

- Security Technologies for Manufacturing and Control Systems (ISA-TR99.00.01-2004)
- Integrating Electronic Security into Manufacturing and Control Systems Environment (ISA-TR99.00.02-2004)
- Federal Information Processing Standards Publications (FIPS Pubs)
- National Institute of Standards and Technology
- CobiT Security Baseline
- Health Insurance Portability and Accountability Act (HIPAA)
- The Basel Accords
- Privacy Act of 1974
- Gramm–Leach–Bliley Act (GLBA)
- Sarbanes–Oxley Act (SOX)
- Information Security for Banking and Finance (ISO/TR 13569)
- FFEIC Examination Guidelines

When I find that a new set of standards or controls has been introduced, I try to map them to an established industry standard such as ISO 17799. This allows me to be certain that any new item is assimilated into the controls list and that items are not duplicated. By doing this, management is given the opportunity to see that the new standards or industry requirements have already been addressed in the existing practices of the organization.

First I map out the new requirements such as HIPAA (see Table 2.13). After mapping out the new standards, I map those to the organization's existing control standards or to ISO 17799. That might look like the mapping shown in Table 2.14.

Step 4: Cost-Benefit Analysis

To allocate resources and implement cost-effective controls, organizations, after identifying all possible controls and evaluating their feasibility and effectiveness, should conduct a cost-benefit analysis. This process should

Table 2.13 HIPAA Requirements

Category	Control	Classification	HIPAA Control Description
Security Management Process			Implement policies and procedures to prevent, detect.
1	Risk Analysis	Required	Conduct an accurate and thorough assessment of the potential risks and vulnerabilities to the confidentiality, integrity and availability of Electronically Protected Health Information (EPHI).
2	Risk Management	Required	Implement security measures sufficient to reduce risks and vulnerabilities to a reasonable and appropriate level.
3	Sanction Policy	Required	Apply appropriate sanctions against workforce members who fail to comply with the security policies and procedures of the covered entity.
4	Information System Activity Review	Required	Implement procedures to regularly review records of information systems activity.
Assigned Security Responsibility			Identify the security official who is responsible for the development and implementation of the policies and procedures.
5	Privacy Officer	Required	Identify a single person responsible for the development and implementation of the policies and procedures supporting HIPAA compliance.

Table 2.13 HIPAA Requirements (Continued)

Category	Control	Classification	HIPAA Control Description
Administrative Safeguards			Implement policies and procedures to ensure that all members of its workforce have appropriate access to EPHI, and to prevent those workforce members who are not authorized to have access under the Information Access Management standard from obtaining access to electronic health information.
6	Authorization/ Supervision	Addressable	Implement procedures for the authorization and/or supervision of workforce members who work with EPHI or in locations where it might be accessed.
7	Workforce Clearance Procedure	Addressable	Implement procedures to determine that the access of a workforce member to EPHI is appropriate.
8	Termination Procedure	Addressable	Implement procedures for terminating access to EPHI when the employment of a workforce member ends or as required by access authorization policies.
Information Access Management			Implement policies and procedures for authorizing access to EPHI.
9	Isolate Healthcare Clearinghouse Functions	Required	If a Covered Entity (CE) operates a healthcare clearinghouse, it must implement policies and procedures to protect the EPHI maintained by the clearinghouse from unauthorized access by the larger organization.

Table 2.13 HIPAA Requirements (Continued)

Category	*Control*	*Classification*	*HIPAA Control Description*
10	Access Authorization	Addressable	Implement policies and procedures for granting access to EPHI, for example through access to a workstation, transaction, program, process, or other mechanism.
11	Access Establishment and Modification	Addressable	Implement policies and procedures that, based on the entity's access authorization policies, establish, document, review and modify a user's right of access to a workstation, transaction, program or process.
Security Awareness and Training			Implement a security awareness and training program for all members of the workforce including management.
12	Security Reminders	Addressable	Periodic security reminders.
13	Protection from Malicious Software	Addressable	Procedures guarding against, detecting and reporting malicious software.
14	Log-in Monitoring	Addressable	Procedures to monitor log-in attempts and report discrepancies.
15	Password Management	Addressable	Procedures to create, change and safeguard passwords.
Security Incident Procedures			Implement policies and procedures to address security incidents.

Table 2.13 HIPAA Requirements (Continued)

Category	*Control*	*Classification*	*HIPAA Control Description*
16	Response and Reporting	Required	Identify and respond to suspected or know security incidents; mitigate to the extent practicable harmful effects of the security incidents that are known to the CE; and document security incidents and their outcomes.
Contingency Plan			Establish (and implement as needed) policies and procedures for responding to an emergency or other occurrence that damages systems that contain EPHI.
17	Data Backup	Required	Establish and implement procedures to create and maintain retrievable exact copies of EPHI.
18	Disaster Recovery Plan	Required	Establish (and implement as needed) procedures to restore any loss of data.
19	Emergency Mode Operations Plan	Required	Establish (and implement as needed) procedures to enable continuation of critical business processes to assure access to EPHI and to provide for adequate protection of EPHI while operating in emergency mode.
20	Testing and Revision Procedures	Addressable	Implement procedures for periodic testing and revision of contingency plans.
21	Applications and Data Criticality	Addressable	Assess the relative criticality of specific applications and data in support of other contingency plan components.

Table 2.13 HIPAA Requirements (Continued)

Category	Control	Classification	HIPAA Control Description
Evaluation			
22			Perform a periodic technical and non-technical evaluation, based initially upon the security rule standards, and subsequently in response to environmental or operational changes affecting the security of EPHI that establish the extent to which a CE security policies and procedures meet the requirements.
Business Contracts			
23			A CE may permit a business associate to create, receive, maintain, or transmit EPHI on its behalf only if the CE obtains satisfactory assurances that the BA will appropriately safeguard the information.
Physical Safeguards			
Facility Access Control			Implement policies and procedures to limit physical access to EPHI systems and the facilities in which they are housed, while ensuring that properly authorized access is allowed.
24	Contingency Operations	Addressable	Establish (and implement as needed) procedures that allow facility access in support of restoration of lost data under the disaster recovery plan and emergency mode operations plan in the event of an emergency.

Table 2.13 HIPAA Requirements (Continued)

Category	*Control*	*Classification*	*HIPAA Control Description*
25	Facility Security Plan	Addressable	Implement policies and procedures to safeguard the facility and the equipment therein from unauthorized physical access, tampering, and theft.
26	Access Control and Validation Procedures	Addressable	Implement procedures to control and validate a person's access to facilities based on their role or function, including visitor control, and control of access to software programs for testing and revision.
27	Maintenance Records	Addressable	Implement policies and procedures to document repairs and modifications to the physical components of a facility which are related to security.
Workstation Use			Implement policies and procedures that specify the proper functions to be performed, the manner in which those functions are to be performed, and the physical attributes of the surroundings of a specific workstation or class of workstation than can access EPHI.
28	Workstation Security	Standard	Implement physical safeguards for all workstations that access EPHI to restrict access to authorized users.

Table 2.13 HIPAA Requirements (Continued)

Category	Control	Classification	HIPAA Control Description
29	Device and Media Control	Standard	Implement policies and procedures that govern the receipt and removal of hardware and electronic media that contain EPHI into and out of a facility, and the movement of these items within a facility.
30	Disposal	Required	Implement policies and procedures to address the final disposition of EPHI and/or the hardware or electronic media on which it is stored.
31	Media Reuse	Required	Implement procedures for removal of EPHI from electronic media prior to re-use.
32	Accountability	Addressable	Maintain a record of the movement of hardware and software and any person responsible for movement.
33	Data Backup and Storage	Addressable	Create a retrievable, exact copy of EPHI, when needed, prior to moving equipment.
Technical Safeguards			
Access Control			Implement technical policies and procedures for electronic information systems that maintain EPHI to allow access only to those person or software programs that have been granted access rights as specified.
34	Unique User Identification	Required	Assign a unique name or number for identifying and tracking user identity.
35	Emergency Access Procedure	Required	Establish (and implement as needed) procedures for obtaining necessary EPHI during an emergency.

Table 2.13 HIPAA Requirements (Continued)

Category	*Control*	*Classification*	*HIPAA Control Description*
36	Automatic Logoff	Addressable	Implement electronic procedures that terminate an electronic session after a predetermined time of inactivity.
37	Encryption and Decryption	Addressable	Implement a mechanism to encrypt and decrypt EPHI.
38	Audit Controls	Standard	Implement hardware, software, or procedural mechanisms that record and examine activity in information systems that contain or use EPHI.
39	Integrity	Standard	Implement policies and procedures to protect EPHI from improper alteration or destruction.
40	Authentication	Standard	Implement procedures to verify that a person or entity seeking access to EPHI is the one claimed.
41	Transmission Security	Standard	Implement technical security measures to guard against unauthorized access to EPHI that is being transmitted over an electronic communications network.
42	Business Associate Contracts	Standard	The contract between the CE and its BA must meet the (following) requirements, as applicable: A CE is not in compliance if it knew of a pattern of activity or practice of the BA that constituted a material breach or violation of the BA's obligation under the contract, unless the CE took reasonable steps to cure the breach or end the violation, and if such steps were unsuccessful to

Table 2.13 HIPAA Requirements (Continued)

Category	Control	Classification	HIPAA Control Description
			(A) terminate the contract, if feasible; or (B) report the problem to the Secretary of HHS, if not.
Policies and Procedures			Implement reasonable and appropriate policies and procedures to comply with the standards, implementation specifications, and other requirements.
43	Documentation	Standard	Maintain the policies and procedures required by the security rule in writing which may be electronic; and If an action, activity, or assessment is required to be documented, maintain a written record which may be electronic.
44	Time Limit	Required	Retain the documentation required by the Security Rule for six years from the date of its creation or the date when it was last in effect, whichever is later.
45	Availability	Required	Make documentation available to those person responsible for implementing the procedures to which the documentation pertains.
46	Updates	Required	Review documentation periodically, and update as needed, in response to environmental and operational changes affecting the security of the EPHI.

Table 2.14 HIPAA - ISO 17799 Mapping

ISO 17799 Section	*Control*	*HIPAA*
	Risk Assessment (2)	Risk Analysis (Required)
Security Policy	Policy (3.1)	Isolate Healthcare Clearinghouse Functions (Required) Integrity (Standard)
Organizational Security	Management Information Security Forum (4.1)	Risk Management (Required) Sanction Policy (Required) Privacy Officer (Required)
Organizational Security	Security of Third Party Access (4.2)	Business Associate Contracts (Standard)
Organizational Security	Security Requirements in Outsourcing Contracts (4.3)	Audit Controls (Required)
Asset Classification & Control	Accounting of Assets (5.1)	Inventory all assets
Asset Classification & Control	Information Classification (5.2)	Information is an asset and the property of the enterprise
Asset Classification & Control	Information Labeling and Handling (5.2)	
Personnel Security	Security in Job Descriptions (6.1)	
Personnel Security	User Training (6.2)	
Personnel Security	Responding to Security Incidents and Malfunctions (6.3)	
Physical & Environmental Security	Secure Areas (7.1)	Workstation Security (Standard)

Table 2.14 HIPAA - ISO 17799 Mapping (Continued)

ISO 17799 Section	*Control*	*HIPAA*
Physical & Environmental Security	Equipment Security (7.2)	
Physical & Environmental Security	General Controls (7.3)	
Communications and Operations Management	Documented Operating Procedures (8.1)	Response and Reporting (Required) Emergency Mode Operations Plan (Required) Transmission Security (Standard)
Communications and Operations Management	System Planning and Acceptance (8.2)	
Communications and Operations Management	Protection from Malicious Software (8.3)	
Communications and Operations Management	Housekeeping (8.4)	Data Backup (Required)
Communications and Operations Management	Network Management (8.5)	
Communications and Operations Management	Media Handling and Security (8.6)	Device and Media Control (Standard) Media Reuse (Required)
Communications and Operations Management	Exchanges of Information and Software (8.7)	
Access Control	Business requirement for System Access (9.1)	Risk Analysis (Required)
Access Control	User Access Management (9.2)	Authentication (Standard)
Access Control	User Responsibility (9.3)	

Table 2.14 HIPAA - ISO 17799 Mapping (Continued)

ISO 17799 Section	*Control*	*HIPAA*
Access Control	Network Access Control (9.4)	
Access Control	Operating System Access Control (9.5)	Emergency Access Procedure (Required)
Access Control	Application Access Control (9.6)	Unique User Identification (Required)
Access Control	Monitoring System Access and Use (9.7)	
Access Control	Remote Access and Telecommuting (9.8)	
Systems Development & Maintenance	Security Requirements of Systems (10.1)	Risk Analysis
Systems Development & Maintenance	Security in Application Systems (10.2)	
Systems Development & Maintenance	Cryptography (10.3)	
Systems Development & Maintenance	Security of System Files (10.4)	
Systems Development & Maintenance	Security in Development and Support Environments (10.5)	
Business Continuity Management	Aspects of Business Continuity Planning (11.1)	Data Backup (Required) Disaster Recovery Plan (Required) Emergency Mode Operations Plan (Required)
Compliance	Compliance with Legal Requirements (12.1)	
Compliance	Reviews of Security Policy and Technical Compliances (12.2)	Information System Activity Review (Required) Audit Controls (Required)

be conducted for each new or enhanced control to determine if the control recommended is appropriate for the organization. A cost-benefit analysis should determine the impact of implementing the new or enhanced control and then determine the impact of not implementing the control.

One of the long-term costs of any control is the requirement to maintain its effectiveness. It is, therefore, necessary to factor these costs into the benefit received from any control. When performing a cost-benefit analysis it is necessary to consider the cost of implementation based on some of the following.

- Costs of implementation including initial outlay for hardware and software
- Reduction in operational effectiveness
- Implementation of additional policies and procedures to support the new controls
- Cost of possibly hiring additional staff or at a minimum, training existing staff in the new controls
- The cost of education support personnel to maintain the effectiveness of the control

Step 5: Documentation

Once the risk assessment is complete, the results need to be documented in a standard format and a report issued to the asset owner. This report will help senior management make decisions on policy, procedures, budget, and systems and management change. The risk assessment report should be presented in a systematic and analytical manner that assesses risk so that senior management will understand the risks and allocate resources to reduce the risk to an acceptable level.

The following is an example of what might be included in a management summary report for the risk assessment process. At a minimum the report should contain the following.

Assessment Team:
Gilbert Godfried
Katherine Turner
Bill Aikman
Leonard Elmore
Myra Osmond
Mike Illich

Facilitator:	Thomas R. Peltier	Peltier and Associates
Scribes:	Lisa Bryson	Peltier and Associates
	Julie Peltier	Peltier and Associates

Risk Assessment Scope Summary:

On October 23, 2004 the GLBA Bank (GLBA) risk assessment team and Peltier and Associates met to review the scope of a risk assessment to be conducted on Nonpublic Personal Customer Information held or processed at GLBA. The team discussed the most recent Office of the Comptroller of the Currency (OCC) examination of GLBA. The team also reviewed the December 21, 2003 Visioneering, Inc. (VI) information system audit; the Gross Technology Partners (GTP) November 18, 2003 Penetration Test and Network Vulnerability Assessment report; and the GLBA Internal Audit report of November 30, 2003. The findings of these reviews, assessments, and audits were used to develop a risk assessment scope statement.

On October 24, 2004, GLBA Bank (GLBA) staff at the 45 North Main Avenue, Buzzover, Utah, conducted the risk assessment. The intent of this process was to identify threats that could signify risk to the integrity, confidentiality, and availability of Nonpublic Personal Customer Information being held or processed by GLBA.

Fifteen (15) GLBA employees participated in the process. These employees represented a variety of users with a broad range of expertise and knowledge of GLBA operations and business processes. The various Bank areas represented helped support a multidisciplinary and knowledge-based approach to the risk assessment process. These employees were asked to participate within a candid reflective atmosphere so that a thorough and clear representation of GLBA's potential business risks to customer information could be developed.

Assessment Methodology Used:

The Facilitated Risk Analysis and Assessment Process (FRAAP) was created by Peltier and Associates in 1993. The FRAAP was received within the information security industry through its inclusion as a course in the 1995 Computer Security Institute's calendar of classes. The FRAAP was further promoted in the industry upon publication of the book *Information Security Risk Analysis* by Auerbach Publications/CRC Press. The General Accounting Office (GAO) reviewed the FRAAP in 1998 and issued Government Accounting Office May 1998 Executive Guide for Information Security Management (GAO/AIMD 98-68). This executive guide supplemented the Office of Management and Budget revision of Circular A-130, Appendix III recommending qualitative risk analysis for government agencies. The FRAAP process is consistent with the National Institute of Standards and Technology October 2001 Special Publication *Risk Management Guide of Information Technology Systems* and the FFIEC December 2002 *Information Security Risk Assessment.*

A senior facilitator led the process, assisted by GLBA information security personnel. Participants were asked to identify risks to the availability, confidentiality, and integrity of customer information held or processed by GLBA Bank.

All risks were reviewed and consolidated to eliminate redundancy. All risks were then examined to determine if an existing control or safeguard was in place at GLBA. Typically, the examination of existing controls is conducted after the risk level has been established. Due to time constraints, these steps were transposed to effect a more streamlined, accelerated risk assessment process.

Participants were asked to rate each risk in terms of probability of occurrence (high, medium, and low) and then business impact (high, medium, and low). The GLBA risk assessment team, with assistance from Peltier and Associates, examined the controls identified to determine whether existing controls were adequate. Low criticality items are not included in final counts summarized in the assessment findings below, as they are normally deferred to a "Monitor" status in final recommendations.

Assessment Findings and Action Plan:

The risk assessment process identified one hundred and thirteen (113) potential risks in the areas of confidentiality, integrity, and availability. Approximately sixty (60) percent of the risks identified were classified by the team as moderate to low level of risk. Of the remaining risks, six (6) were categorized as Priority A (requiring immediate correction), and fifty-four (54) Priority B (corrective action should be taken). The open number of priority risks has been significantly reduced through diligent efforts undertaken by the GLBA team.

The threat scenario categories with the highest rated risk levels are shown in Table 2.15.

The risk assessment identified five key areas of concern:

Table 2.15 Threat Scenario Evaluation

Risk Level	*Number of Similar Threats*	*Description of Threat Scenario*
A	4	Physical intrusion
A	2	Power failure
B	10	Information handling and classification
B	4	Password weakness or sharing
B	4	People masquerading as customers
B	3	Firewall concerns
B	2	Computer viruses
B	2	Workstations left unattended
B	2	Employee training

1. Restricted physical access areas should be considered throughout GLBA.
   Action Plan: A physical security risk assessment will be conducted to determine if there is a need to create restricted access areas or increase physical access controls.
2. Power failure could cause corruption of information or prevent access to the system.
   Action Plan: Network UPS may not be adequate for a power outage out of regular business hours. Install a backup domain controller at Ualena Street and connect it to the Ualena Street UPS.
3. Information classification scheme is incomplete.
   Action Plan: GLBA has created a draft Information Classification Policy that addresses five categories: Public, Internal Use, Restricted, Confidential, and Classified. The new policy requirements are to be disseminated to the GLBA staff and will become part of the new employee orientation and the annual employee awareness program.
4. The weakness of passwords for some information system user accounts could allow compromise of the password and permit unauthorized access to GLBA systems and information.
   Action Plan: The GLBA Passwords Policy is to be modified to require strong passwords. GLBA Information Security Department (ISD) will investigate software solutions to enforce a strong password requirement.
5. Someone could impersonate a customer to corrupt or access bank records or accounts.
   Action Plan: Concern to be addressed in GLBA employee awareness program and new employee orientation.

Full Findings Documentation:

The completed risk assessment worksheets have been turned over to the GLBA Information Security Officer and are available through that office.

Conclusion:

The results of this risk assessment exercise proved to be fairly comprehensive in the breadth of the threat scenarios considered. The breadth of consideration can be directly attributed to the collaborative approach to the risk assessment process embraced by the GLBA participants. The results of this assessment should provide a solid foundation upon which to build and enhance future risk assessment efforts as GLBA moves forward to ensure that assessments are completed whenever changes to any relevant factors, such as new products, business processes, or new technologies, occur.

Practically no system or activity is risk free, and not all implemented controls can eliminate the risk that they are intended to address. The purpose of risk management is to analyze the business risks of a process, application, system, or other asset to determine the most prudent method for safe operation. The risk assessment team reviews these assets with the business objectives as their primary consideration. A security program that has as its goal one hundred percent security will cause the organization to have zero percent productivity.

The risk assessment process has two key objectives: to implement only those controls necessary and to document management's due diligence. As company representatives we must be aware that the goal is to provide support for the mission of the company. By implementing an effective risk management and risk assessment process, this objective will be met and embraced by our constituents.

Quantitative Versus Qualitative Risk Assessment

There are as many different styles and types of risk analysis as there are enterprises trying to run them. In the 2003 Computer Security Institute's *Buyers Guide* there were 26 different ads for risk analysis products, software, and consulting services. The organizations that are most satisfied with their risk analysis process are those that have defined a relatively simple process that can be adapted to various business units and involved a mix of individuals with knowledge of business operations and technical aspects of the systems or resources being analyzed.

Table 2.16 Qualitative Risk Assessment Attributes

Qualitative Risk Assessment	*Attributes*
	Minimally quantified estimates Exposure scale ranking estimates Easier to conduct than quantitative risk assessment

In conducting the risk assessment, consideration should be given to the advantages and disadvantages of quantitative and qualitative assessments. The main advantage of the qualitative style of risk assessment (see Table 2.16) is that it prioritizes the risks and identifies areas for immediate action and improvement. The disadvantage of qualitative risk assessment is that it does not provide specific quantifiable measurements of the magnitude of the impacts, therefore making a cost-benefit analysis of recommended controls more difficult.

The major advantage of quantitative risk assessment is that it provides a measurement of the impact's magnitude, which can be used in the cost-benefit analysis of recommended controls. The disadvantage is that, depending on the numerical ranges used to express the measurement, the meaning of the quantitative risk assessment may be unclear, requiring the results to be interpreted in a qualitative manner. Additional factors often must be considered to determine the magnitude of the impact (see Table 2.17). These may include, but are not limited to:

- An estimate of the frequency of the threat occurrence rate over a specified period, usually in one-year increments
- An approximate cost for each occurrence of the threat
- A weighted factor based on a subjective analysis of the relative impact of a specific threat

Table 2.17 Quantitative Risk Assessment Attributes

Quantitative Risk Assessment	*Attributes*
	Quantified estimates of impact, threat frequency, safeguard effectiveness and cost, and probability Powerful aid to decision making Difficult to conduct

In 1998 the Government Accounting Office (GAO) visited the organizations that were previous winners of the Computer Security Institute's Information Security Program of the Year Award. Their task was to identify best practices. The found that "Organizations that are most satisfied with their risk analysis procedures are those that have defined a relatively simple process that can be adapted to various organizational units and involved a mix of individuals with knowledge of business operations and technical aspects of the enterprise's systems and security controls."

Government Accounting Office May 1998 Executive Guide for Information Security Management (GAO/AIMD 98-68) states:

> *OMB's 1996 revision of Circular A-130, Appendix III, recognizes that federal agencies have had difficulty in performing effective risk assessments. . . . For this reason, the revised circular eliminates a long-standing federal requirement for formal risk assessments. Instead, it promotes a risk-based approach and suggests that, rather than trying to precisely measure risk, agencies should focus on generally assessing and managing risks.*

Each process has its advantages and also its disadvantages. The best way for you to determine which assessment style is best for your organization is to map out the benefits and pitfalls of each. Typically you would want to do something such as that shown in Table 2.18.

Qualitative risk analysis provides for a systematic examination of threats and risks and provides for a review of proposed countermeasures and safeguards to determine the best cost-benefit for implementation. By establishing a quality risk management team, this subjective analysis can rely on the expertise of the enterprise's internal experts. The entire process is subjective in nature and therefore the team must be properly screened, and populated with knowledgeable personnel.

Qualitative risk analysis is a technique that can be used to determine the level of protection required for applications, systems, facilities, or other enterprise assets. During the systematic review of threats the team will be able to establish the probabilities of threats occurring, the impact of loss if the threats do occur, and how well the safeguards or countermeasures designed to reduce the risks will work to reduce risk to an acceptable level. The qualitative methodology attempts only to prioritize the various risk elements in subjective terms.

Table 2.18 Quantitative – Qualitative Pros and Cons

Quantitative Risk Assessment Advantages	*Qualitative Risk Assessment Advantages*
The results are based substantially on independently objective processes and metrics	Calculations are simple
Great effort is put into asset value definition and risk mitigation	Not necessary to determine $ value of asset
Cost/benefit assessment effort is essential	Not necessary to quantify threat frequency
Results can be expressed in management-specific language	Easier to involve non-security and non-technical staff
	Provides flexibility in process and reporting
Disadvantages	*Disadvantages*
Calculations are complex	Very subjective in nature
Historically only works well with a recognized automated tool and associated knowledge base	Limited effort to develop monetary value for targeted assets
Large amount of preliminary work	No basis for the cost-benefit analysis of risk mitigation
Not presented on a personnel level	
Participants cannot be coached easily through the process	
Difficult to change directions	
Difficult to address "out-of-scope" issues	

Report Significant Changes in Risk

Reporting significant changes in risk to appropriate levels of management on both a periodic and event-driven basis is a primary role of the information security manager. The risk assessment that the information security manager uses to develop and implement security processes and procedures should be considered. As changes occur within the organization, the risk assessment should be updated to ensure it remains an accurate representation. The information security manager should have periodic update meetings with upper management to present the status of the organization's overall security program. That update should include any significant changes to the organization's risk profile.

In addition, the security program should include a process whereby a significant security breach or security event will trigger a special report to upper management. The information security manager should have defined processes whereby the security event can be evaluated based on its impact on the organization. Based on this evaluation, it may warrant a special report to upper management to inform them of the event, the impact, and the steps being taken to mitigate the risk. Care should be taken to ensure that when such a special report is communicated, a secure channel is utilized so that potentially sensitive information does not fall into the wrong hands.

Knowledge Statements

Gap Analysis

Gap analysis (Figure 2.7) is used to assess generally accepted practices against current security conditions. Gap analysis measures the maturity level of the security program and it uses standards of good practice or accepted standards to set targets for future attainment. Once future targets are established, an assessment should be conducted to determine the current state of effectiveness of information security management. Once the gaps have been identified, an action plan is established. Typically one might use ISO 17799:2000 for Gap analysis.

4 SECURITY POLICY **Note: ISO17799 Sections 1 and 2 are non-action items, and are not included in this checklist.**			
4.1 Information Security Policy	Management direction and support for information security must be clearly established.		
4.1.1 Information Security Policy Document Development	Has an information security policy document been developed?	Y____ N ___	
4.1.2 Information Security Policy Document Publication	Has an information security policy document been published?	Y ___ N ___	

Figure 2.7 Gap Analysis Example.

Standards of good practice include:

- ISO 17799 (ISO 27002)
- CobiT
- NIST CSRC
- The Security Risk Analysis Directory
- OCC
- FFIEC

Recovery Time Objectives

To determine Recovery Time Objectives (RTO) the security manager should have knowledge of recovery time objectives for their organization. The organization's business drives the RTO. To determine the RTO the organization must conduct a Business Impact Analysis (BIA) to address all potential disasters including sudden outages and rolling disasters. The information will allow the organization to achieve established RTO and Recovery Point Objectives (RPO).

The RTO and RPO are covered in more detail in Chapter 5 on Response Management.

Data (Information) Classification

Information is an asset and the property of the organization. All employees are to protect information from unauthorized access, modification, disclosure, or destruction. Before employees can be expected to protect information, they must first understand what they have. An information classification policy and methodology will provide them with the help they need.

There are four essential aspects of information classification: (1) information classification from a legal standpoint, (2) responsibility for care and control of information, (3) integrity of the information, and (4) the criticality of the information and systems processing the information. Examples of how the classification process fits into the application and system development life cycle are presented to assist you in the development of your own information classification process.

Organizations classify information in order to establish the appropriate levels of protection for those resources. Because resources are limited, it will be necessary to prioritize and identify what really needs protection. One of the reasons to classify information is to ensure that scarce resources are allocated where they will do the most good. All information is created equally, but not all information is of equal value.

The old concept in computer security was that everything is closed until it is opened. However, after nearly 20 years of working with companies in establishing information classification systems, I have found that nearly 90 percent of all enterprise information needs to be accessed by employees or is available through public forums. Because resources are limited, the concept that all information is open until it requires closing is perhaps a better way of protecting information.

Most organizations do not have information that is all of the same value. Therefore, it is necessary to at least develop an initial high-level attempt at classification. This should be done, if for no other reason than to ensure that budgeted resources are not misused in protecting or not protecting information assets. Before employees can protect information assets, they must first have a mechanism in place that allows them to establish the value of the information. An information classification system and a scoring methodology that rely on common sense and a knowledge of the corporate culture and market sensitivity can be a significant advantage over most organizations.

Keep the number of information classification categories to as few as possible. If two possible categories don't require substantially different treatment, then combine them. The more categories that are available, the greater the chance for confusion among managers and employees. Normally, three or four categories should be sufficient to meet your organization's needs.

Additionally, avoid the impulse to classify everything the same. In order to simplify the classification process, some organizations have flirted with having everything classified as confidential. The problem with this concept is that confidential information requires special handling. This would violate the concept of placing controls only where they are actually needed. This method would require the organization to waste limited resources protecting assets that do not really require that level of control.

Another pitfall to avoid is taking the information classification categories developed by another enterprise and adopting them verbatim as your own. Use the information created by other organizations to assist in the creation of your organization's unique set of categories and definitions.

Classified information normally declines in sensitivity with the passage of time. Downgrading should be as automatic as possible. If the information owner knows the date that the information should be reclassified, then it might be labeled as: *Confidential until (Date)*. There should be an established review process for all information classified as confidential, and reclassified when it no longer meets the criteria established for such information.

Part of an effective information classification program is to destroy documents when they are no longer required. Placing restrictions on copying classified documents will ensure that the documents and data sets are controlled and logged as to the number of copies created and to whom those copies were assigned. To assist in this process, it may be convenient to create an information-handling matrix.

Information classification drives the protection control requirements and this allows information to be protected to a level commensurate with its value to the organization. The costs of overprotection are eliminated and exceptions are minimized. When a policy and methodology specifications are clear an accountability is established.

There are costs associated with implementing a classification system. The most identifiable costs include labeling classified information, implementing and monitoring controls and safeguards, and proper handling of confidential information.

Information, wherever it is handled or stored, needs to be protected from unauthorized access, modification, disclosure, and destruction. Not all information is created equal. Consequently, segmentation or classification of information into categories is necessary to help identify a framework for evaluating the information's relative value. By establishing this relative value, it will be possible to establish cost-effective controls that will preserve the information asset for the organization.

Summary

Information security risk management is one of the key building blocks for an effective information security program. In this section we covered risk management, risk analysis, risk assessment, and risk mitigation of cost-benefit analysis. We also discussed the pros and cons of qualitative and quantitative risk assessment. All of the concepts in this chapter are evolving concepts that are changing. These areas are some of the oldest in information security and as such most of the concepts will continue to evolve and mature.

What Was Covered in This Chapter

- Business Impact Analysis (BIA)
- Countermeasures
- Criticality analysis (see BIA)
- Data classification
- Exposure
- ISO 17799:2000
- Recovery Point Objectives (RPO)

- Recovery Time Objectives (RTO)
- Residual risk
- Risk analysis
- Risk assessment
- Risk avoidance
- Risk mitigation
- Risk transfer
- Threat analysis

Questions

1. Which of the following is a key drawback in the use of quantitative risk analysis? It:
   A. Applies numeric measurements to qualitative elements
   B. Attempts to assign numeric values to exposures of assets
   C. Is based on a criticality analysis of information assets
   D. Produces the results in numeric (percentage, probability) form

Answer A

2. Acceptable risk is usually:
   A. Subjectively determined
   B. Objectively determined
   C. Less than residual risk
   D. Based on loss expectancy

Answer A

3. The cost of mitigating a risk should not exceed the:
   A. Annual loss expectancy
   B. Value of the physical asset
   C. Expected benefit to be derived
   D. Cost to the perpetrator to exploit the weakness

Answer C

4. Which of the following is the best source for developing Recovery Time Objectives (RTO)?
   A. Industry averages
   B. Tape restore statistics
   C. Business impact analysis
   D. Previous recovery test results

Answer C

5. In providing risk reporting to management, the most appropriate vehicle for the initial reporting of a major security incident would be to include it in a:
   A. Quarterly report
   B. Special report
   C. Monthly report
   D. Weekly report

Answer B

6. Risk mitigation includes all of the following except:
   A. Risk assumption
   B. Risk planning
   C. Risk limitation
   D. Risk identification

Answer D

7. To determine if a threat poses a risk, the risk management team must determine the impact and
   A. Vulnerability
   B. Probability
   C. Identification
   D. Reason

Answer B

8. To accept the potential risk and continue operating or to implement controls to lower the risk to an acceptable level is termed:
   A. Risk assumption
   B. Risk avoidance
   C. Risk sharing
   D. Risk management

Answer A

9. Two forms of risk assessment are:
   A. Analytical and assessment
   B. Technical and procedural
   C. Qualitative and quantitative
   D. Subjective and objective

Answer C

10. The process used to demonstrate that the costs of implementing controls can be justified by the reduction of a risk level is:
    A. Probability and impact
    B. Vulnerability assessment

C. Compliance checking
D. Cost benefit

Answer D

11. The process for determining the acceptable level of impact on organization applications, systems, and business processes is called:
A. Risk analysis
B. Risk assessment
C. Business impact analysis
D. Project impact analysis

Answer C

12. Three basic threat categories include human, natural, and what additional category?
A. Possible
B. Probable
C. Engineering
D. Environmental

Answer D

13. The potential for a particular event to successfully exercise a particular vulnerability is called:
A. Threat
B. Risk
C. Impact
D. Probability

Answer A

14. Another term for project impact analysis is:
A. Risk assessment
B. Cost benefit
C. Security management
D. Risk analysis

Answer D

15. Four deliverables from a risk assessment process are threats identified, controls selected, action plan complete, and
A. Risk level established
B. Technical issued quantified
C. Vulnerability assessment completed
D. Risk mitigation established

Answer A

16. Risk management encompasses three processes: risk assessment, risk mitigation, and what other element?
    A. System development life cycle
    B. Risk analysis
    C. Evaluation and assessment
    D. Threat analysis

Answer C

17. Risk management is the process that allows IT managers to balance the operational and what other element of protective measures?
    A. Cost
    B. Technology
    C. Mission
    D. Politics

Answer A

18. Effective risk management must be totally integrated into what process?
    A. IPL
    B. SDLC
    C. Security perimeter
    D. Disposal

Answer B

19. Senior management depends on an effective risk analysis process to make informed business decisions. This management responsibility is called:
    A. Due diligence
    B. Due proxy
    C. Due date
    D. DEW line

Answer A

20. What is the first process in the risk management methodology?
    A. Records retention
    B. Likelihood
    C. Fault tolerance
    D. Risk analysis

Answer D

21. The results of the likelihood that a given threat-source were to be used is termed:
    A. Vulnerability

B. Risk
C. Control
D. Probability

Answer A

22. There are three basic forms of threat-sources. These are human threats, environmental threats, and what other kind of threat?
    A. Tangible
    B. Intangible
    C. Terror
    D. Natural

Answer D

23. A flaw or weakness in system security procedures, design, implementation, or internal controls that could be exercised and result in a security breach or violation of the system's security policy is called:
    A. Vulnerability
    B. Typical
    C. Virus
    D. Logic bomb

Answer A

24. Two major types of risk analysis are:
    A. Threat and controls
    B. Errors and omissions
    C. Quantitative and qualitative
    D. Vulnerability and management

Answer C

25. A systematic methodology used by senior management to reduce mission risk is termed:
    A. Risk transfer
    B. Risk limitation
    C. Accepting the risk
    D. Risk mitigation

Answer D

26. To convey a risk by using other options to compensate for loss, such as purchasing insurance, is referred to as:
    A. Risk transfer
    B. Risk assumption
    C. Risk planning

D. Risk limitation

Answer A

27. To check a risk by implementing controls that minimize the adverse impact of the threat's exercising a vulnerability (such as use of supporting, preventive, detective controls) is referred to as:
    A. Risk transfer
    B. Risk assumption
    C. Risk planning
    D. Risk limitation

Answer D

28. The types of controls focused on stopping a security breach from occurring in the first place are termed:
    A. Containment
    B. Preventive
    C. Detection
    D. Recovery

Answer B

29. An audit log is an example of what type of control?
    A. Containment
    B. Preventive
    C. Detection
    D. Recovery

Answer C

30. To allocate resources and implement cost-effective controls, organizations, after identifying all possible controls and evaluating their feasibility and effectiveness, should perform what form of additional analysis?
    A. Vulnerability analysis
    B. Cost-benefit analysis
    C. Qualitative
    D. Quantitative

Answer B

Chapter 3

Information Security Program Management

Functional Area Overview

The information security program management functional area deals with processes and technical solutions that implement the information security governance framework. This functional area comprises 21 percent of the CISM® examination and comprises approximately 42 questions.

In this chapter you will learn about the following terms.

- The OSI and other models
- Common uses and applications of Internet Protocol (IP)
- Roles and responsibilities of information security
- The System Development Life Cycle (SDLC)
- The role and use of cryptography

CISM Mapping

When the information security program management functional area is mapped over to ISO 17799 and the domains from the CISSP® common body of knowledge, it shows just how many different areas of knowledge from which we are going to be drawing information (see Table 3.1). Information security program management is so large that it basically encompasses everything in telecommunication and network security,

Table 3.1 Information Security Program Management

ISO 17799 Section	*CISSP Domain*
3. Information security policy	2. Telecommunications and network security
4. Information security organization	3. Security management
5. Asset classification and control	5. Cryptography
9. System access control	7. Applications and systems development
	9. Access control systems and methodologies

everything in security architecture, everything in cryptography, and everything in access control systems and methodologies. It is a very, very large functional area.

Introduction

This functional area deals with many different concepts in the realm of information security management. There are many topics covered in this section, and most of the technical security controls will be included in this functional area. As such the information security program management functional area is the longest of the five functional areas in terms of terms and ideas that are covered.

The OSI Model

The Open Systems Interconnection reference model or the OSI layer model is one of the most commonly used models in all of telecommunications and information security. Most reference guides on networking or TCP/IP will begin with the OSI model and build from there. Because this is such a tried and true approach there really is no reason to try to reinvent the wheel. This means that we start with the OSI Model just as every other reference does.

The model defines a seven-layer model of data communication, as shown in Figure 3.1. Each layer of the OSI model provides a set of functions to the layer above and, in turn, relies on the functions provided by the layer below. Although messages can only pass vertically through the stack from layer to layer, from a logical point of view, each layer communicates directly with its peer layer on other nodes.

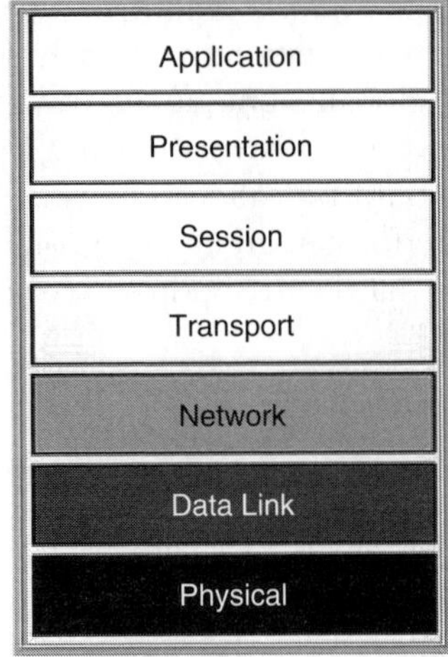

Figure 3.1 OSI model's seven layers.

Layer 1: Physical

The physical layer is the least complex layer of the OSI model. As such, the physical layer is responsible for physically transmitting the data over the communication link. It provides the mechanical, electrical, functional, and procedural standards to access the physical medium. This means that the physical layer deals with the electrical impulses traveling over the network cable. This layer only sees information as binary ones and zeros and does not see the larger patterns of data. The best examples of physical layer devices are repeaters, hubs, and network cards. The function of a repeater is to boost a weak network signal so that a receiving station that is a great distance away from the sending station still has a strong enough signal to differentiate between the electrical ones and zeros that the sending station sent. Information sent on the network at the physical layer would be called bits.

Layer 2: Data Link

The data link layer is the next least complex layer of the OSI model. The data link layer provides the functions and protocols to transfer data between network entities and to detect (and possibly correct) errors that may occur in the physical layer. This layer acts upon the hardware or Media Access Controller (MAC) address. These addresses are statically assigned by the manufacturer and are held in the firmware of the device.

Every network device should have a unique hardware address, each switch, each network card in a workstation, and each server network interface card should all have a globally unique hardware address. Examples of data link layer devices would be switches and bridges. Information sent on the data link layer would be called frames.

In Figure 3.2 I have performed an *ipconfig* command from my Windows XP machine to see the hardware address associated with an external network card.

Layer 3: Network

As opposed to the statically coded addresses previously mentioned in the data link layer, the network layer provides administratively assigned addresses. This functionality allows the network layer to provide the means to establish connections between networks. The standard also includes procedures for the operational control of internetwork communications and for the routing of information through multiple networks. Thus protocols such as IP (Internet Protocol) are an example of network layer protocols. There are other network layer protocols such as IPX (Internet Packet Exchange), but IP is by far the most common network layer protocol. Due to the administratively assigned addresses, the network layer is where we see administratively assigned addresses and many other processes such as Dynamic Host Configuration Protocol (DHCP) and routing. DHCP is a mechanism that automates the process of assigning administrative (IP) addresses to a system, in most cases based on the hardware (MAC) address. Network layer devices include the packet filter firewall, the stateful inspection firewall, routers, and smart or layer-three switches. The concept of routing exists at the network layer of the OSI model. Information sent at the network layer would be called packets.

In Figure 3.3 I show the configuration options for setting an IP address on my Windows XP machine. This can be seen on most Windows systems by clicking on the start button, Control Panel, Network Connections, Local Area Connection, Internet Protocol, Properties. The example below has a statically coded IP address. The other common option used is the aforementioned DHCP. On a network that uses static IP addresses an administrator needs to configure each machine to tell that machine which address to use. DHCP certainly makes the administration of IP addresses easier. However, there is a security risk involved with using DHCP. The risk is that any system can plug a network connection into the network and immediately get a network address assigned. An attacker would certainly like to receive an address through DHCP inasmuch as it is far easier than determining the IP address to use through other slower processes.

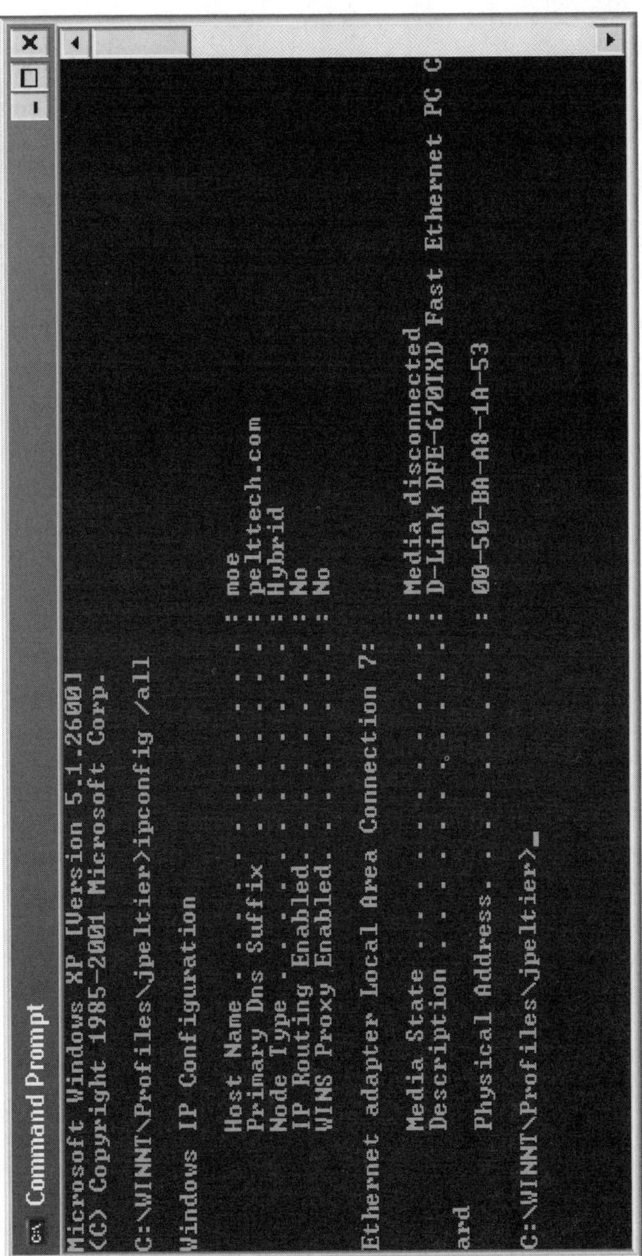

Figure 3.2 Data link layer.

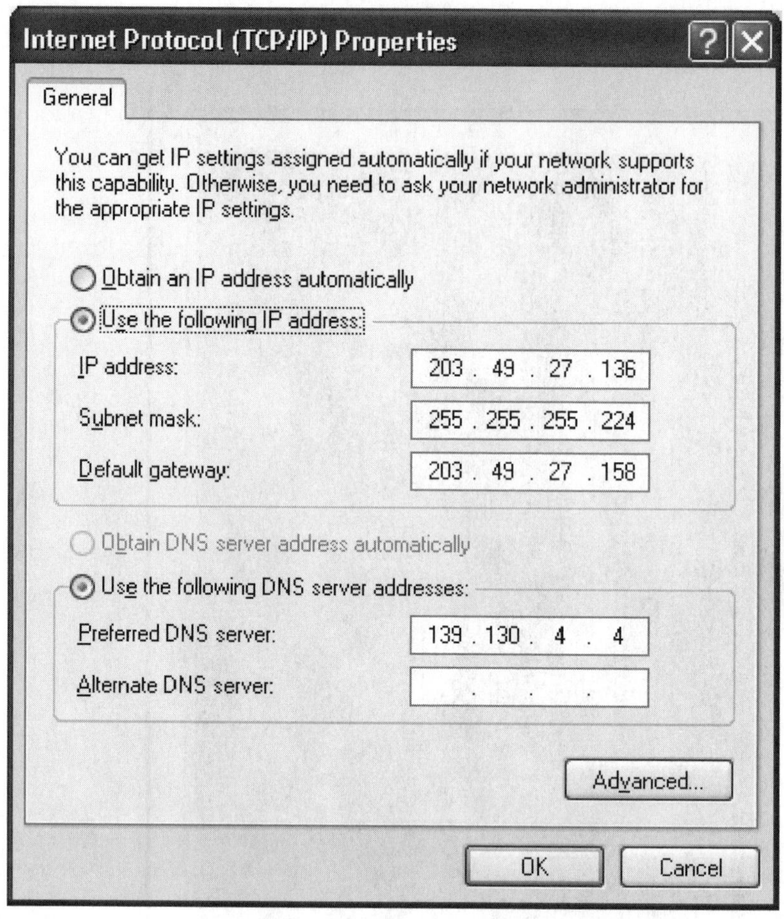

Figure 3.3 Windows IP configuration.

We examine IP address assignment and construction later in this chapter.

Layer 4: Transport

The transport layer provides transparent and reliable end-to-end data transfer, relying on lower-layer functions for handling the peculiarities of the actual transfer medium. The transport layer is responsible for the following tasks.

- Flow control: A mechanism for adjusting the flow of data from one device to another to ensure that the receiving device can handle all of the incoming data
- Windowing: A process that dynamically adjusts the amount of outstanding (unacknowledged by the recipient) data a sender can send on a particular connection before it gets an acknowledgment back from the receiver that it has gotten some of it
- Data sequencing: A process for reassembling data packets if they arrive out of order to ensure the conversation is understood by the receiver as the sender meant it to be
- Recovery: A process for resending information that was damaged or not received by the sender

Transmission Controls Protocol (TCP) and User Datagram Protocol (UDP) are examples of a transport layer protocol (see Figure 3.4). The best examples of transport layer communication components are ports. We go into ports in great detail later in the chapter, but for now just know that ports exist at the transport layer. Information sent at the transport layer would be called segments.

Layer 5: Session

The session layer provides mechanisms for organizing and structuring interaction between applications or devices and is also responsible for keeping multiple data streams separate. Information sent at the session, presentation, and application layer would all be called data.

Layer 6: Presentation

The presentation layer is concerned with the representation of user or system data. This is done to ensure that information sent by the application layer of one system is formatted in a manner in which the destination system's application layer can read it. This includes necessary conversations (e.g., a printer control character) and code translation (e.g., ASCII to EBCDIC).

Layer 7: Application

The most complex layer in the OSI model is the application layer. The application layer is the layer closest to the user and it gives the user access to all the lower OSI functions; its purpose is to support semantic exchanges

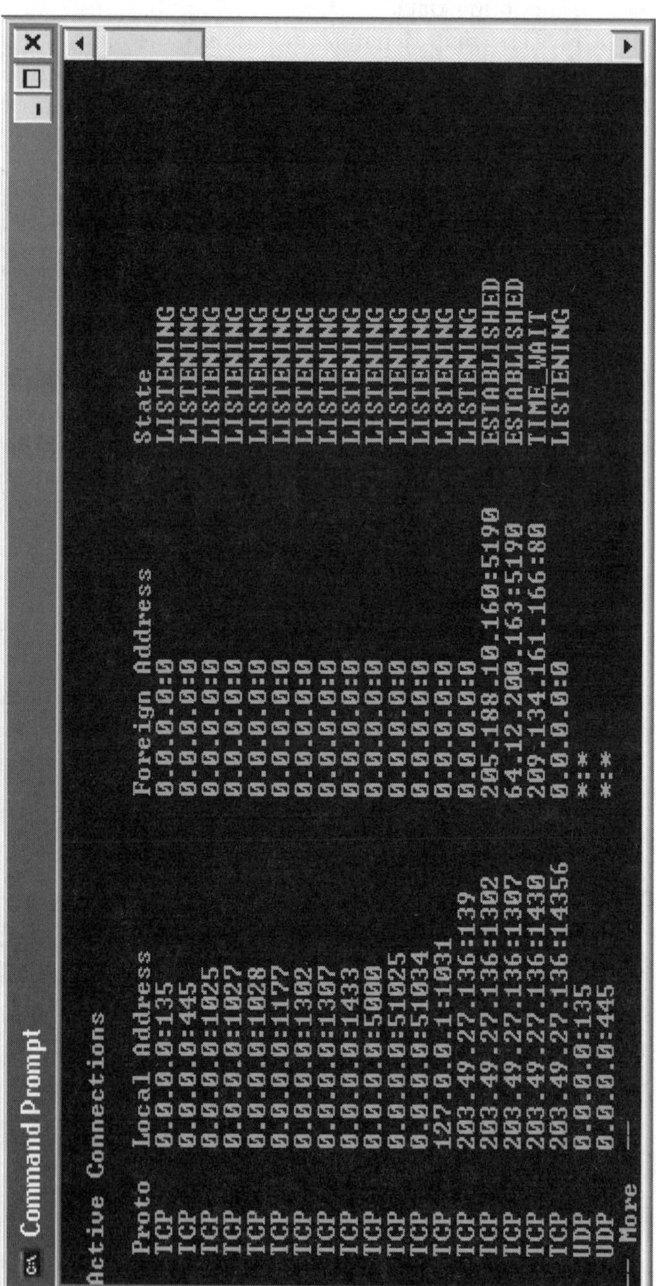

Command Prompt
Active Connections
Proto Local Address Foreign Address State
TCP 0.0.0.0:135 0.0.0.0:0 LISTENING
TCP 0.0.0.0:445 0.0.0.0:0 LISTENING
TCP 0.0.0.0:1025 0.0.0.0:0 LISTENING
TCP 0.0.0.0:1027 0.0.0.0:0 LISTENING
TCP 0.0.0.0:1028 0.0.0.0:0 LISTENING
TCP 0.0.0.0:1177 0.0.0.0:0 LISTENING
TCP 0.0.0.0:1302 0.0.0.0:0 LISTENING
TCP 0.0.0.0:1307 0.0.0.0:0 LISTENING
TCP 0.0.0.0:1433 0.0.0.0:0 LISTENING
TCP 0.0.0.0:5000 0.0.0.0:0 LISTENING
TCP 0.0.0.0:51025 0.0.0.0:0 LISTENING
TCP 0.0.0.0:51034 0.0.0.0:0 LISTENING
TCP 127.0.0.1:1031 0.0.0.0:0 LISTENING
TCP 203.49.27.136:139 0.0.0.0:0 LISTENING
TCP 203.49.27.136:1302 205.188.10.160:5190 ESTABLISHED
TCP 203.49.27.136:1307 64.12.200.163:5190 ESTABLISHED
TCP 203.49.27.136:1430 209.134.161.166:80 TIME_WAIT
TCP 203.49.27.136:14356 0.0.0.0:0 LISTENING
UDP 0.0.0.0:135 *:*
UDP 0.0.0.0:445 *:*
-- More --

Figure 3.4 TCP and UDP ports.

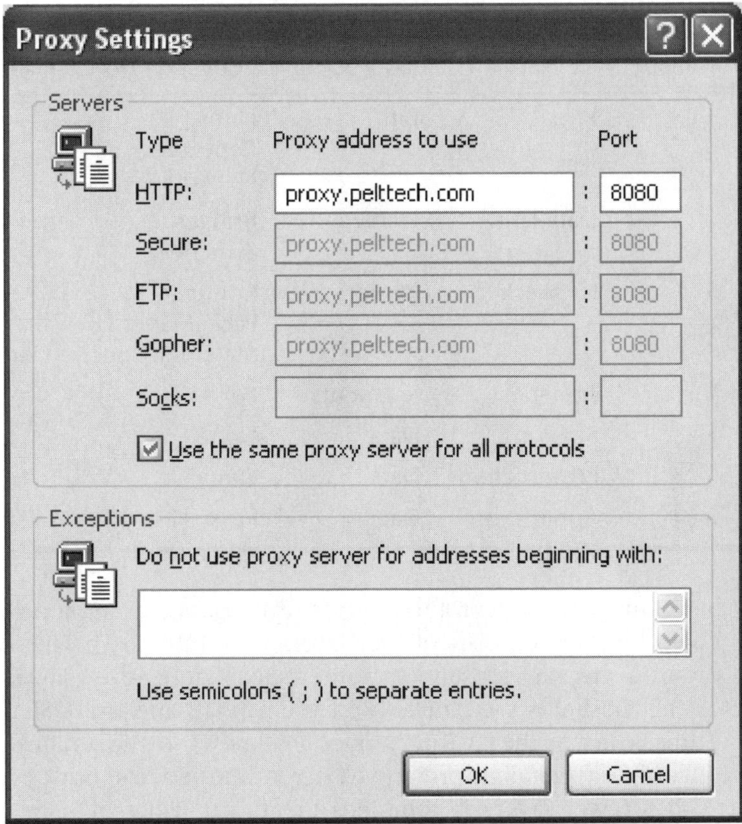

Figure 3.5 Proxy configuration screen in Internet Explorer.

between applications existing in open systems. It is often said the mistakes made at lower layers of the OSI model can be corrected with programming at the application layer. A common example of an application layer device is a proxy-based firewall (see Figure 3.5).

The TCP/IP Model

The OSI model (Table 3.2) is not the only model and in fact the OSI model was created after TCP/IP was already a standard. This is part of the reason that IP does not map as cleanly to the OSI model as other protocols do.

The Transmission Control Protocol/Internet Protocol (TCP/IP) model provides the foundation and framework for many computer networks, including the world's largest, the Internet. As in the OSI model and most

Table 3.2 OSI Layers Summary

Layer Number	*Layer*	*Data Name*	*Common Device Examples*
1	Physical	Bits	Hubs Repeaters Network Cards
2	Data Link	Frames	Bridges Switches
3	Network	Packets	Routers Packet Filter Firewall Stateful Inspection Firewall
4	Transport	Segments	Ports
5	Session	Data	None
6	Presentation	Data	None
7	Application	Data	Proxy Firewall

other data communication protocols, TCP/IP consists of a protocol stack; in this case, the stack consists of four layers (see Table 3.3). The TCP/IP model's four layers may loosely tie to the OSI model's seven layers.

Figure 3.6 illustrates the similarity of the TCP/IP and the OSI model. Many of the layers in the TCP/IP model are known by two names. You can see that the layers align pretty well across the models, but obviously with TCP/IP's fewer layers it combines the functionality of several OSI layers into a single layer.

IP Addressing

As an information security manager it can be necessary to read Requests For Comment (RFC) documents to understand the latest technology. RFCs are a series of notes about the Internet, started in 1969 (when the Internet was the ARPANet). An Internet Document can be submitted to the IETF (International Engineering Task Force) by anyone, but the IETF decides if the document becomes an RFC. Eventually, if it gains enough interest, it may evolve into an Internet standard.

Each RFC is designated by an RFC number (see Figure 3.7). Once published, an RFC never changes. Modifications to an original RFC are assigned a new RFC number.

My favorite site to get not just RFCs, but also opinion documents of those RFCs, is freesoft. Freesoft is available at http://www.freesoft.org.

Table 3.3 TCP/IP Model Layers

Layer	Name	Description
4	Application Layer	The Application layer consists of application programs and serves as the windows, or network interface. It is through this window that all exchange of meaningful information occurs between communication users. Examples include Telnet and SMTP.
3	Transport (Host to Host) Layer	Provides end-to-end data delivery services. The protocols at this layer are TCP and UDP.
2	Internetwork (Internet) Layer	Defines the datagram or frame format and handles routing data through an internetwork. Examples include IP and ICMP.
1	Link (Network Interface) Layer	Defines how to access a specific network topology such as Ethernet or Token-Ring.

This organization is home to a great resource called "Connected: An Internet Encyclopedia."

There are many RFCs that are just silly to look at. Some of my personal favorites are:

- RFC 1149: A Standard for the Transmission of IP Datagrams on Avian Carriers

  This memo describes an experimental method for the encapsulation of IP datagrams on avian carriers. This specification is primarily useful in Metropolitan Area Networks. This is an experimental, not recommended standard. Distribution of this memo is unlimited.

- RFC 1925: The Twelve Networking Truths

  This memo documents the fundamental truths of networking for the Internet community. This memo does not specify a standard, except in the sense that all standards must implicitly follow the fundamental truths.

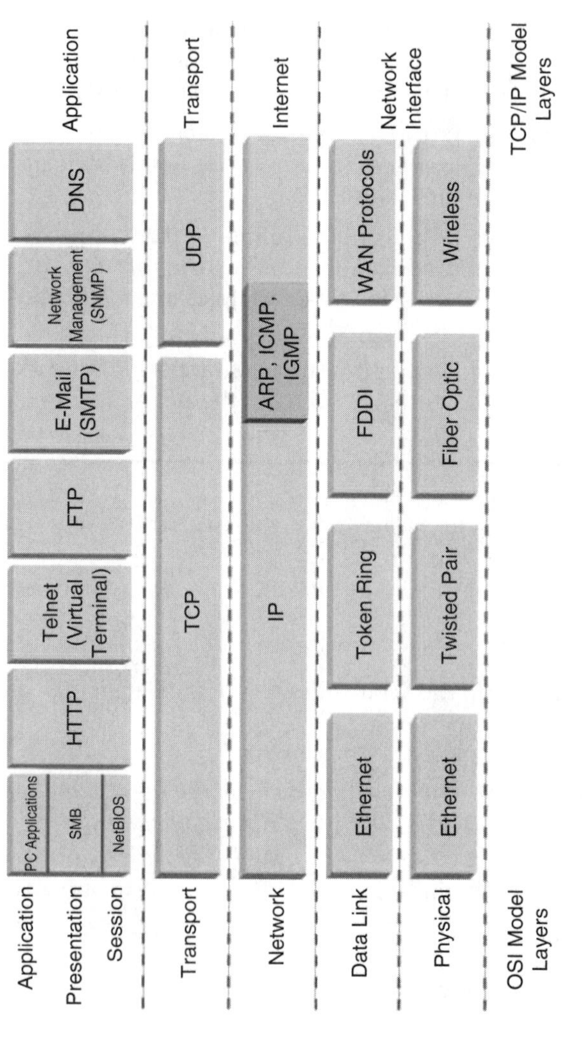

Figure 3.6 Mapping OSI to TCP/IP model.

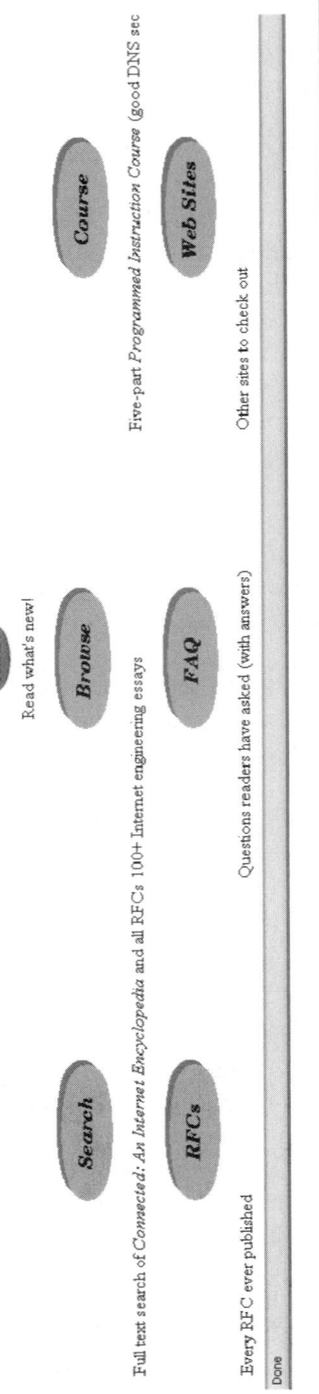

Figure 3.7 Connected.

- RFC 2324: Hypertext Coffee Pot Control Protocol (HTCPCP/1.0)

  This document describes HTCPCP, a protocol for controlling, monitoring, and diagnosing coffee pots.

- RFC 2549: IP over Avian Carriers with Quality of Service

  This memo amends RFC 1149, "A Standard for the Transmission of IP Datagrams on Avian Carriers," with Quality of Service information. This is an experimental, not recommended standard.

- RFC 2795: The Infinite Monkey Protocol Suite (IMPS)

  A protocol suite which supports an infinite number of monkeys that sit at an infinite number of typewriters in order to determine when they have either produced the entire works of William Shakespeare or a good television show. The suite includes communications and control protocols for monkeys and the organizations that interact with them.

There are some standards that have more to do with information security than the IP over carrier pigeon documents listed above and these should be understood by most security professionals. These are:

- RFC 793: Transmission Control Protocol (TCP)
- RFC 768: User Datagram Protocol (UDP)
- RFC 792: Internet Control Message Protocol (ICMP)
- RFC 1918: Address Allocation for Private Intranets (IP)

Protocols

We are going to start with the last standard from the list and discuss IP. To fully understand IP we need to start with a definition of a protocol. A protocol is an agreed-upon format for transmitting data between two devices. Take a conversation between two people. When the two people begin talking they will typically begin speaking in a language; in the case of where I am from (Detroit), it is English. There is also a mechanism for error checking: if the other person does not understand what you have said she will have to ask for clarification. There are also rules regarding contention; it is usually considered poor form to talk while someone else is talking. So before you talk, you make sure the network (air) is clear so you will not interfere with someone else's speaking. Even the medium is specified in the conversation protocol: the conversation will typically take place through the air. So it can be said that the protocol determines the following.

- The type of error checking to be used
- Data compression method, if any
- How the sending device will indicate that it has finished sending a message
- How the receiving device will indicate that it has received a message

At its most basic, a protocol is a set of rules to ensure that information transmitted from one station can be understood by the other. There are many different protocols from which programmers and manufacturers can choose. Each has particular advantages and disadvantages; for example, some are simpler than others, some are more secure, some are more interoperable, some are more reliable, and some are faster than others.

Internet Protocol (IP) Details

When it comes to modern networks almost all use the IP protocol. The way that IP works on an IP network is that each computer is allocated a unique IP address. In the current version of IP protocol, IP version 4, an IP address is 4 bytes. The addresses are usually written as x1.x2.x3.x4, with x1, x2, x3, and x4 each describing one byte of the address. For example, address 16843009 (hex 1010101) is written as 1.1.1.1, because each byte of this address has a value of 1.

Because an address is 4 bytes, the total number of available addresses is 2 to the power of 32 = 4,294,967,296. This represents the total theoretical number of computers that can be directly connected to the Internet. In practice, the real limit is much smaller for several reasons.

Internet Protocol (IP) Network and Host

Each physical network has to have a unique network number, comprising some of the bits of the IP address. The rest of the bits are used as a host number to uniquely identify each computer or resource on that network. The number of unique network numbers that can be assigned in the Internet is therefore much smaller than the four billion number mentioned above, and it is very unlikely that all of the possible host numbers in each network number are fully assigned.

An address is divided into two parts: a network number and a host number. The idea is that all computers on one physical network will have the same network number, a bit like the street name; the rest of the address defines an individual computer, a bit like house numbers within a street.

Subnet Masks and Internet Protocol (IP) Classes

The size of the network and host parts depends on the class of the address, and is determined by the address network mask. The network mask is a binary mask with ones in the network part of the address, and zero in the host part.

To allow for a range from big networks, with a lot of computers, to small networks, with a few hosts, the IP address space is divided into four classes, called class A, B, C, and D. The first byte of the address determines to which class an address belongs.

Class A Networks

Network addresses with the first byte between 1 and 126 are class A, and can have about 17 million hosts each. A class A network address has the leading bit set to 0, a 7-bit network number, and a 24-bit local host address. The first octet ranges from 0 to 127, although 0 and 127 are reserved and cannot be assigned to networks and hosts. When we break our IP addresses down into their binary form we get results as shown in Figure 3.8. Notice in the figure that in all cases the first bit is set to zero. This is the distinction between a class A and class B IP address range. There is more information on class B IP address ranges below.

Class B Networks

Network addresses with the first byte between 128 and 191 are class B, and can have about 65,000 hosts each. A class B network address has the two highest-order bits set to 1-0, a 14-bit network number, and a 16-bit local host address. The first octet ranges from 128 to 191, as illustrated by Figure 3.9.

Class C Networks

Network addresses with the first byte between 192 and 223 are class C, and can have 256 hosts. A class C network address has the three leading

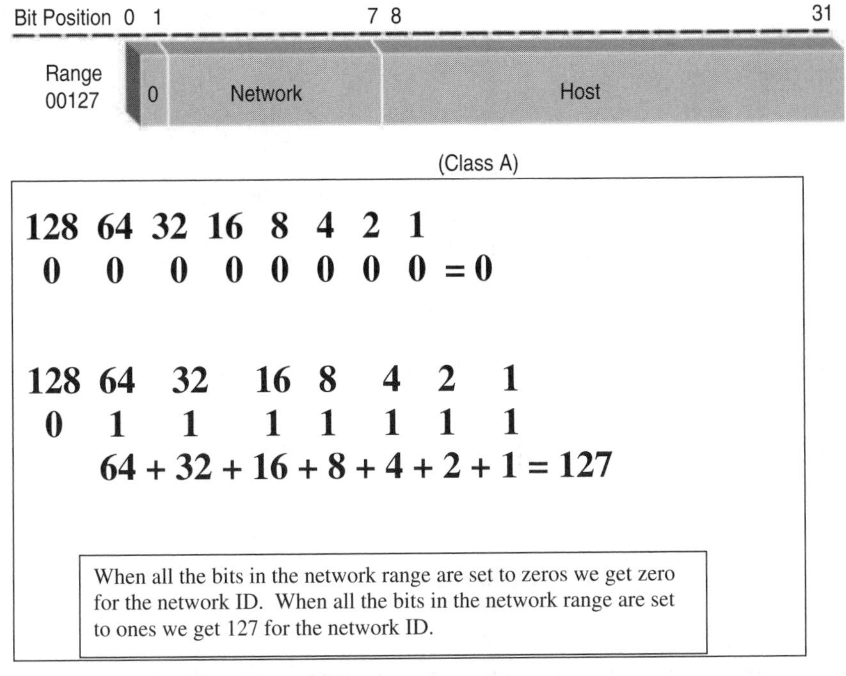

Figure 3.8 Class A network.

bits set to 1-1-0, a 21-bit network number, and an 8-bit local host address. The first octet ranges from 192 to 223, as is shown in Figure 3.10.

Beyond Class C Networks

All other networks are class D, which is used for special functions (such as multicast network traffic) or class E, which is reserved. Figure 3.11 shows a summary of class A, B, and C networks.

IP Address Availability and Internet Protocol (IP) Version 6

Most class A and B addresses have already been allocated, leaving only class C available. This means that the total number of available addresses on the Internet is 2,147,483,774. Each major world region has an authority that is given a share of the addresses and is responsible for allocating them to Internet Service Providers (ISPs) and other large customers. Because of routing requirements, a whole class C network (256 addresses) has to be assigned to one client at a time; the clients (e.g., ISPs) are then responsible for distributing these addresses to their customers.

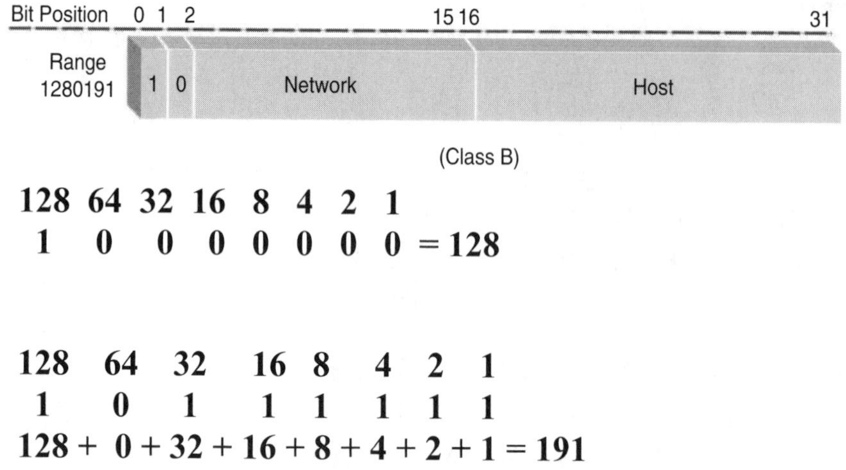

Figure 3.9 Class B network.

Although the number of available addresses seems large, the Internet is growing at such a pace that it will soon be exhausted. The next generation IP protocol, IP version 6, allows for larger addresses; however, it will take years before the existing network infrastructure migrates to the new protocol.

IP Hosts

In the world of IP, there are basically three categories of addresses according to RFC 1918. These types are:

- *Category 1:* Hosts that do not require access to hosts in other enterprises or the Internet at large; hosts within this category may use IP addresses that are unambiguous within an enterprise, but may be ambiguous between enterprises.
- *Category 2:* Hosts that need access to a limited set of outside services (e.g., e-mail, FTP, netnews, remote log-in) which can be handled by mediating gateways (e.g., application layer gateways or proxies). For many hosts in this category an unrestricted external access (provided via IP connectivity) may be unneces-

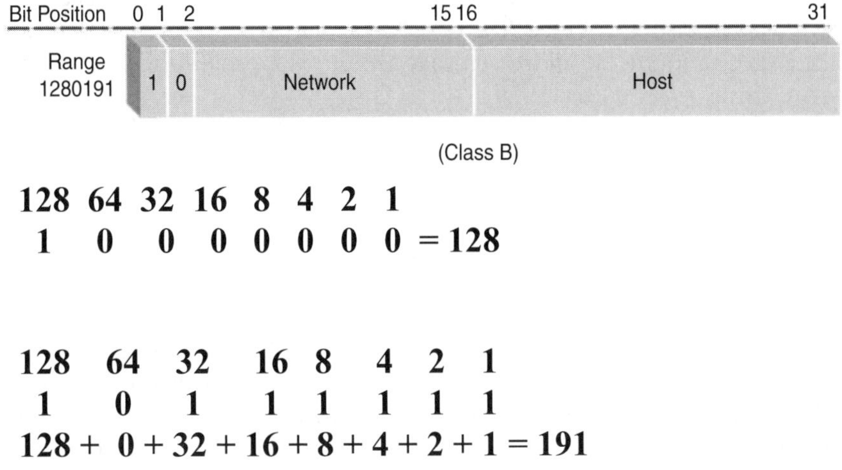

When all the bits but the first one are set to zeros we get 128 for the network ID. When all the bits but the second bit in the network range are set to ones we get 223.

Figure 3.10 Class C network.

	1 byte (8 bits)	1 byte (8 bits)	1 byte (8 bits)	1 byte (8 bits)
Class A	Network	Host	Host	Host
Class B	Network	Network	Host	Host
Class C	Network	Network	Network	Host

Class	Network Range	Binary Representation
Class A	001-127	00000001 - 01111111
Class B	128-191	10000000 - 10111111
Class C	192-223	11000000 - 11011111

Figure 3.11 Summary of Class A, B, C networks.

sary and even undesirable for privacy or security reasons. Just as with hosts within the first category, such hosts may use IP addresses that are unambiguous within an enterprise, but may be ambiguous between enterprises.

- *Category 3:* Hosts that need network layer access outside the enterprise (provided via IP connectivity); hosts in the last category require IP addresses that are globally unambiguous.

We refer to the hosts in the first and second categories as "private." We refer to the hosts in the third category as "public."

Private Internet Protocol (IP) Networks

There are three special IP address ranges that are specified by the Internet Assigned Numbers Authority (IANA) now called the Internet Corporation for Assigned Names and Numbers (ICANN). The following three blocks of the IP addresses provide addresses for private intranets and will never be in use on the public Internet. This allows an organization to utilize the following ranges without fear that there will ever be an address conflict with an existing device on the Internet. These three private ranges are:

10.0.0.0–10.255.255.255 (10/8 prefix)
172.16.0.0–172.31.255.255 (172.16/12 prefix)
192.168.0.0–192.168.255.255 (192.168/16 prefix)

We refer to the first block as the "24-bit block," the second as the "20-bit block," and to the third as the "16-bit" block. Note that the first block is nothing but a single class A network number, whereas the second block is a set of 16 contiguous class B network numbers, and the third block is a set of 256 contiguous class C network numbers.

Network Address Translation (NAT)

Although this might not seem as if it has much to do with information security management, I assure you that it does. Many organizations take advantage of the private IP addresses. First, it allows for the organization to need fewer Internet valid IP addresses. Secondly, any machine with a private IP address cannot communicate with the Internet directly. If an organization is using private IP addressing and wishes to allow Internet access some of Network Address Translation (NAT) needs to be done. This can be accomplished by many different types of network devices, but some of the most common devices to perform NAT are:

- Layer three switches
- Routers
- Proxies

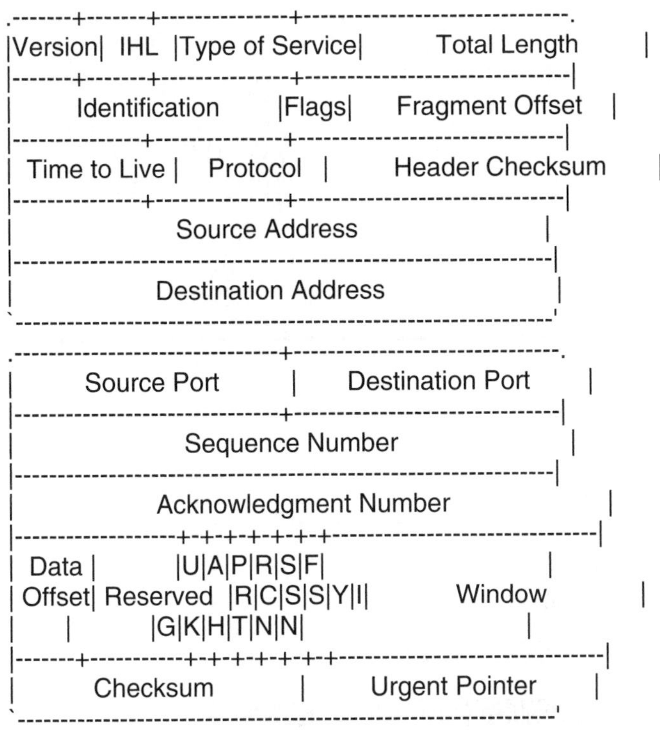

Figure 3.12 NAT packet structure.

- Firewalls
- Wireless access points
- Cable/DSL modems

All of these devices will substitute an invalid IP address in an IP packet for a valid IP address.

Figure 3.12 shows the header structure as listed in RFC 791. The first diagram is that of the IP header and the second is the transport header. In this case the second header is a TCP header. We break down the TCP header in an upcoming section of this chapter.

The Internet Protocol (IP) Header

From our diagram in the previous section, it is the first header that gets modified when network address translation occurs. In most cases on an outgoing packet (one that is leaving the organization's network to initiate

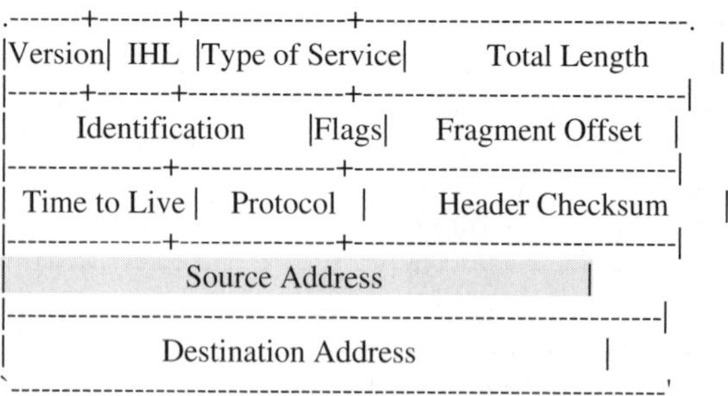

Figure 3.13 Generic IP header.

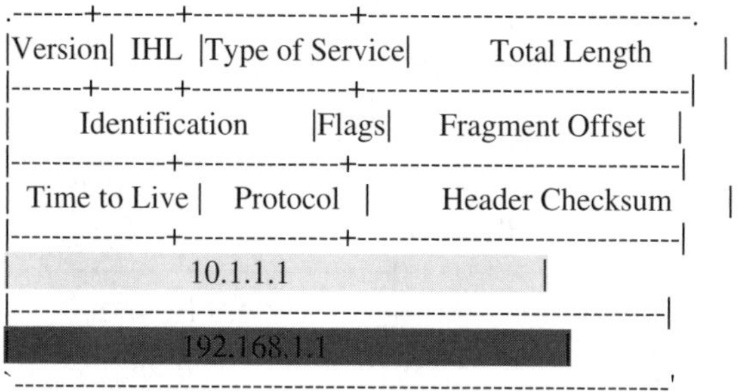

Figure 3.14 Original IP header.

a connection) the source address is what is going to be modified. See Figure 3.13 for a generic IP header.

Network address translation will change this source field, in most cases, from a private IP address to a public address to allow communication with the Internet. Take, for example, the packet header in Figure 3.14 in which an organization's user, whose IP address is 10.1.1.1, is initiating a communication with my Web server whose IP address is 192.168.1.1 (not my real Web server address as this is a private IP as well). The outgoing packet header will look like the diagram in the figure.

Once this packet has been passed through the device that is going to do the address translation, the source IP address will be changed to an Internet valid or public IP address. In this example we use a public IP address of 203.49.27.136. This would result in the packet header shown in Figure 3.15.

Notice how the source IP field, highlighted in yellow, has changed. Once this packet has made the journey over the Internet to the Web server at 192.168.1.1 the Web server will then create a response packet.

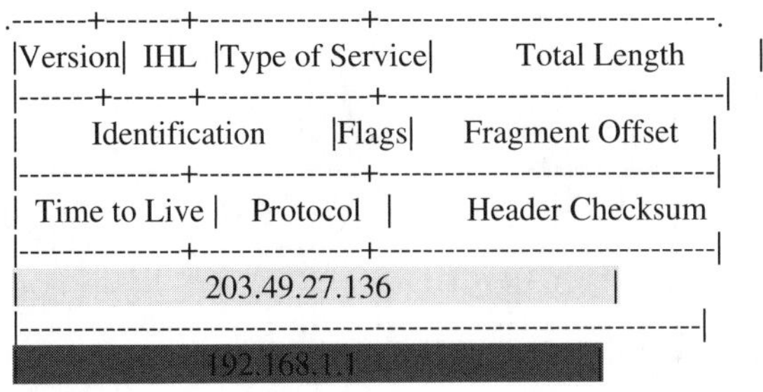

Figure 3.15 Network address translated IP header.

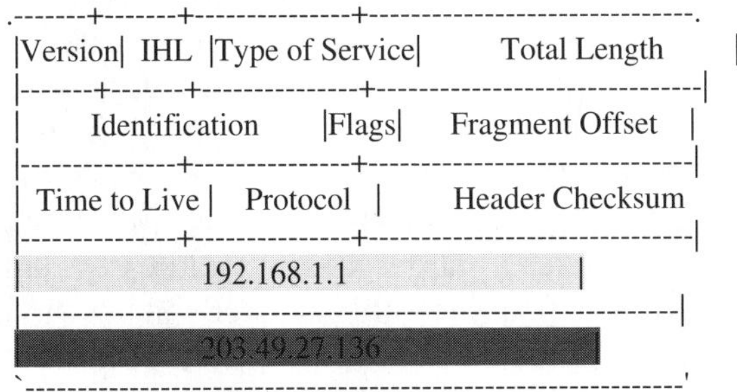

Figure 3.16 Original response packet.

The packet header for this packet will reverse the source and destination IP fields because the packet is now going in the other direction. The response packet will have the IP packet header shown in Figure 3.15.

Notice in the diagram in Figure 3.16 that the response packet uses the address translated IP address as the destination address and not the private IP address. This packet will now travel over the Internet and back to our organization's network address translation device. At this point the address translation device will reverse the process that was done previously and substitute the public IP address for the private IP address of the requesting client. The IP packet header will look like the example in Figure 3.17.

This packet will then be forwarded to the client organization's network where it can be delivered to the client who made the original request. This entire process is done for two previously mentioned reasons:

1. To conserve dwindling Internet available (public) IP addresses
2. To provide security because the Internet at large never knows your organization's true IP addresses on client machines

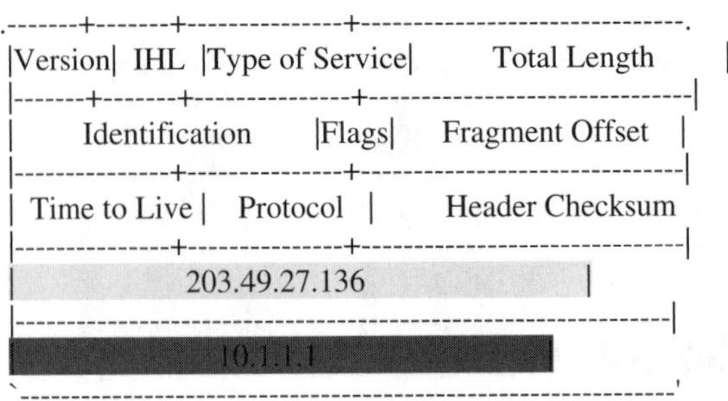

Figure 3.17 Network address translated response packet.

With those reasons listed above, it is still true that machines behind a firewall can use these internal IP addresses to communicate among themselves. This is not a foolproof way of constantly disguising your internal (private) IP addresses. Attackers will be looking for these IP address ranges and they can be revealed in a number of common ways such as in e-mail headers. The e-mail header will give the attacker the internal IP addresses and this allows the attacker to target these IP addresses directly. To try to attack using these private IP address the attacker will have to use a common attack and attempt to "spoof" the IP address in hope of fooling a misconfigured network address translation device, firewall, or router.

Datagram Structure

The IP header we discussed above has many more fields than those that were mentioned. This is a good time to go through the other fields in the IP header and discuss exactly for what these fields are used (see Figure 3.18).

(Note: This is the structure of an IPv4 datagram.)

- *Version:* Describes the IP version; typically 4. As of this writing according to IPv6.org the IP version 6 is currently in proposed standard status. IPv6 is the next generation of IP communication, and depending on the final standard and implementation can change things considerably from current IPv4 structure.
- *Internet header length:* The IHL specifies the length of the IP datagram header, measured in 32-bit double words. When all fields, including options are filled, the header is 24 bytes in length. Hence the IHL would be 6 (i.e., 6 ∞ 4 bytes). Without any options, the IHL is 5.

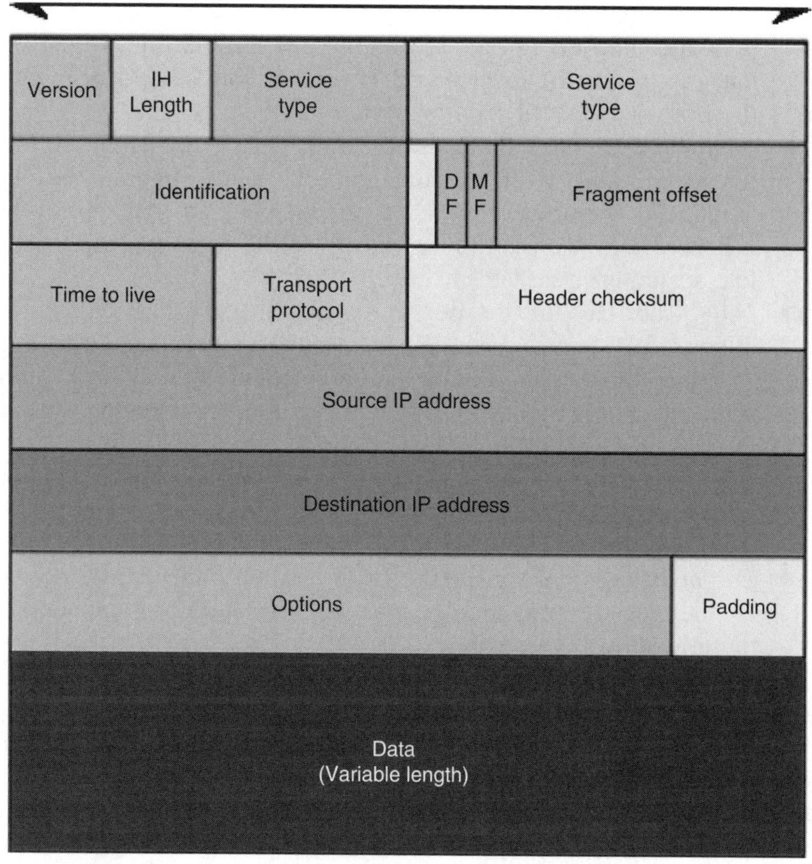

Figure 3.18 Detailed IP packet header.

- *Service type:* This 8-bit field specifies the datagram's precedence (importance), delay, throughput, and reliability. The original intention was for a sending host to specify a preference for how the datagram would be handled as it made its way through an internetwork (the Internet, for example). For instance, one host could set its IPv4 datagram's ToS field value to prefer low delay, whereas another might prefer high reliability. In practice, the ToS field has not been widely implemented. However, a great deal of experimental, research, and deployment work has focused on how to make use of these eight bits.
- *Total length:* This field defines the entire datagram size, including header and data, in 8-bit bytes. The minimum-length datagram is 20 bytes and the maximum is 65,535. The maximum size datagram that any host is **required** to be able to handle is 576 bytes, but

most modern hosts handle much larger packets. Sometimes subnetworks impose further restrictions on the size, in which case datagrams must be *fragmented.* Fragmentation is handled in either the host or packet switch in IPv4.

- *Identification:* Each datagram assembled receives a unique identification number. If the datagram becomes fragmented, this identification number is used to reassemble the datagram when it is received. We play more with the IPID field while discussing idle scanning in a later chapter.
- *Flags:* The flags are the next three bits in the datagram. The first is unused. The next is the DF (Don't Fragment) flag. If this is set to 1, then the datagram cannot be fragmented. If the IP layer cannot send datagrams across the network without fragmenting, and the DF flag is set, then no datagrams can be sent. The next flag is MF (More Fragments), and specifies that the current datagram is part of a fragmented message and that more fragments are to follow. If MF is set to 0, then this is the last fragment in the message.
- *Fragment offset:* When MF is set, this field indicates the position of the current fragment relative to the starting fragment, and thereby allows reassembly.
- *Time to live:* The TTL specifies how long a datagram can remain on the network. It is usually set to 15 or 30. Whenever a datagram passes through a host or router, the TTL is decreased by 1. If a datagram reaches 0, the current node discards it and sends a message back to the originator so that it can resend. This process ensures that gateways do not become bottlenecked, and ensures that datagrams do not travel forever if a network path contains a loop.
- *Transport protocol:* This field contains a code representing the transport protocol of the segment passed to the IP layer. In turn, at the receiving end, this field indicates which upper layer protocol is to receive the data portion of the IP datagram. Common values are 1 for ICMP, 6 for TCP, and 17 for UDP.
- *Header checksum:* A form of CRC, the checksum is calculated using a quick algorithm, using data in the IP header only. Because the TTL value is decreased at every node the datagram passes through, the checksum must also be recalculated at each stage. This checksum gives some protection against corruption.
- *IP addresses:* The 32-bit source and destination IP addresses.
- *Options:* These fields are often not used. There are a few options, but those most commonly used are the routing and time-stamping options which can be used to trace the passage of a datagram through a network.

Transmission Control Protocol (TCP)

Inasmuch as we have discussed IP for quite a while, it is time to move into a more in-depth discussion of some of the protocols that run on top of IP. The next three sections deal with transport layer protocols (TCP, UDP, and ICMP). Because TCP is more complex than the other two transport layer protocols, we start there.

TCP is a connection-oriented stateful protocol (meaning that an application establishes a connection with a destination and then all transmission between source and target use this connection) and can therefore implement reliability and error recovery. The best analogy for TCP is to think of a phone call. In a phone call you typically start out with a hello exchanged on both sides. This becomes the cue that it is time to start talking (exchanging data). Every so often you will check to verify that the other party is still listening and at these intervals you will expect and hope to hear a response. Once you are done talking (sending data) it is typical to terminate the conversation by saying goodbye on both ends. This is a very reliable method for exchanging information, but as you have probably seen, the overhead can be a bit taxing. In the computer world, resending lost datagrams is handled by TCP, rather than by the applications themselves. TCP also provides flow control, which ensures that the rate of data transmission does not overload the system and cause data loss. In our phone conversation example this flow control would be a way of ensuring that you are not speaking faster than the person on the other end of the phone can understand. I can tell you from personal experience that most phone conversations really lack a mechanism for flow control and that some people that I speak to frequently just speak way too fast.

TCP Ports

In order to explain more about TCP we need to have a basic discussion of ports. The best place to start is probably by starting with what a port actually is. A port is a memory address space running on a system. Ports allow us to have multiple services running on a single host. An analogy to ports is to think of ports as phone extensions within a company. The primary number of the company would be equivalent to the IP address and the extension to reach an individual person would be the port. Because of ports, this means that a Web server can also be an FTP server and a DNS server all by having a different extension (port). There are a pretty large number of ports to choose from; ports are numbered from 0 all the way up to 65,535. These 65,535 ports are broken into three primary classifications.

Well-Known Ports

The first group of ports is known as the well-known ports. These are ports 0 through 1023. The well-known port numbers are reserved for assignment by the Internet Corporation for Assigned Names and Numbers (ICANN) and are used by the applications that have been assigned to these ports. These are the most prevalent ports in use on the Internet. For example, Web traffic, e-mail, and FTP are all assigned to well-known ports.

Registered Ports

The next group of ports is the registered ports, sometimes called the high ports. The ports are those from 1024 through 49,151. These ports are applications not typically as popular as the well-known ports, but are still registered with the ICANN. Other applications can use these ports, and many often do, so traffic on these ports is not guaranteed to correspond to the registered application.

Dynamic Ports

The last group of ports is the dynamic or private ports and are those from 49,152 through 65,535. These ports are available for any application to use and are not registered through the ICANN. The lists of applications and their corresponding ports are available at http://www.iana.org/assignments/port-numbers.

It is worthy of note that both UDP and TCP have separate memory address spaces from 0 to 65,535. This allows two applications to be running on the same port as long as they are on different protocols. In theory, this means that one application could use UDP port 80 and a completely different application could use TCP port 80. This is something that is not common, but there are still a few applications that are assigned only TCP or UDP ports. For example, take the TCP/UDP port number 2005. A snippet from the IANA assigned port number document shows us that two different applications can share the same port on two different protocols. A chart of common ports is given in Figure 3.19.

```
berknet   2005/tcp
oracle    2005/udp
```

One port is a bit unique when compared to other ports. This is port 0. The chart in Figure 3.20 was taken from snort.org and this chart gives information about port 0 and port 0 attacks.

Service	Port Type	Port Number
DNS Zone Transfers	TCP	53
DNS Lookups	UDP	53
TFTP Daemon	UDP	69
Link	TCP	87
SUN RPC	TCP & UDP	111
BSD UNIX	TCP	512 – 514
LPD	TCP	515
UUCPD	TCP	540
Open Windows	TCP & UDP	2000
NFS	TCP & UDP	2049
X Windows	TCP & UDP	6000 – 6255
Small services	TCP & UDP	20 and below
FTP	TCP	21
SSH	TCP	22
Telnet	TCP	23
SMTP (except external mail relays)	TCP	25
NTP	TCP & UDP	37
Finger	TCP	79
HTTP (except to external web servers)	TCP	80
POP	TCP	109 &110
NNTP	TCP	119
NTP	TCP	123
NetBIOS in Windows NT	TCP &UDP	135
NetBIOS in Windows NT	UDP	137 & 138
NetBIOS	TCP	139
IMAP	TCP	143
SNMP	TCP	161 &162
SNMP	UDP	161 &162
BGP	TCP	179
LDAP	TCP &UDP	389
SSL (except to external web servers)	TCP	443
NetBIOS in Win2k	TCP &UDP	445
Syslog	UDP	514
SOCKS	TCP	1080
Cisco AUX port	TCP	2001
Cisco AUX port (stream)	TCP	4001
Lockd (Linux DoS Vulnerability)	TCP &UDP	4045
Cisco AUX port (binary)	TCP	6001
Common high order HTTP ports	TCP	8000, 8080, 8888

Figure 3.19 Chart of common ports and applications.

Message	BAD-TRAFFIC top port 0 traffic
Rule	alert top $EXTERNAL_NET any <> $HOME_NET 0 (msg:"BAD-TRAFFIC top port 0 traffic"; flow:stateless; classtype:misc-activity; sid:524; rev:8;)
Summary	This event is generated when TCP traffic to port 0 is detected. This should not be seen in normal TCP communications.
Impact	Possible reconnaisance. This may be an attempt to verify the existence of a host or hosts at a particular address or address range.
Detailed Information	TCP traffic to port 0 is not valid under normal circumstances. an indicator of unauthorized network use, reconnaisance activity or system compromise. These rules may also generate an event due to improperly configured network devices
Affected Systems	Any
Attack Scenarios	The attacker could send packets to a host with a destination port of 0. The attacker might also be using hping to verify the existance of a host as a prelude to an attack.
Ease of Attack	Simple
False Positives	None Known If you think this rule has a false positives, please help fill it out.
False Negatives	None Known If you think this rule has a false negatives, please help fill it out.
Corrective Action	Disallow TCP traffic to port 0.
Contributors	Original rule writer unknown Sourcefire Research Team Nigel Houghton <nigel.houghton@sourcefire.com>

Figure 3.20 Snort.org Port 0 listing.

Port Scanning

Most computer attackers will almost always perform a port scan as part of a security test. This will identify open or listening ports running on different hosts throughout the target network. From a security perspective it is best to have as few ports open as possible. The more ports that are open, the more potential points there are for an attacker to break into a system. Think of each port as a door or a window into your house. As long as all the doors and windows are locked there is no major security risk, but as with any home, the more doors and windows that exist the greater the chance that one door or window will have been forgotten and not locked.

As an information security manger it is important to realize that the only ports that should be available are those that are necessary for the business to function. Any time a new port is going to be turned on in an organization a risk assessment should be performed to determine if the business need is worth the risk for allowing traffic on the new port. This is all part of the system development life cycle which we discuss later in the chapter.

Each port will respond to a port scan, and these responses will differ depending on the state of the application and also the security measures protecting the port. The three most common responses by a port to a port scan are:

1. Open—allows communication
2. Closed—responds with port closed response
3. Filtered—no response given typically this means that a firewall is blocking the request

The TCP Header

Because we have spent some time covering a little about TCP and a little time covering what ports are, we are now ready to start dissecting the TCP packet header. The TCP header has fields just like the IP header and the TCP header has just a few more options. The diagram in Figure 3.21 shows the TCP field and the relationships among them.

- Source Port: Length 16 bits: This is the port number from the client sending the packet. This is usually a high port (from 1025–65,535).
- Destination Port: Length 16 bits: This is the port number of the application on the destination machine (often a server). In most cases this port will be a well-known port (1 to 1024). For example, Web traffic (http) will be on port 80.

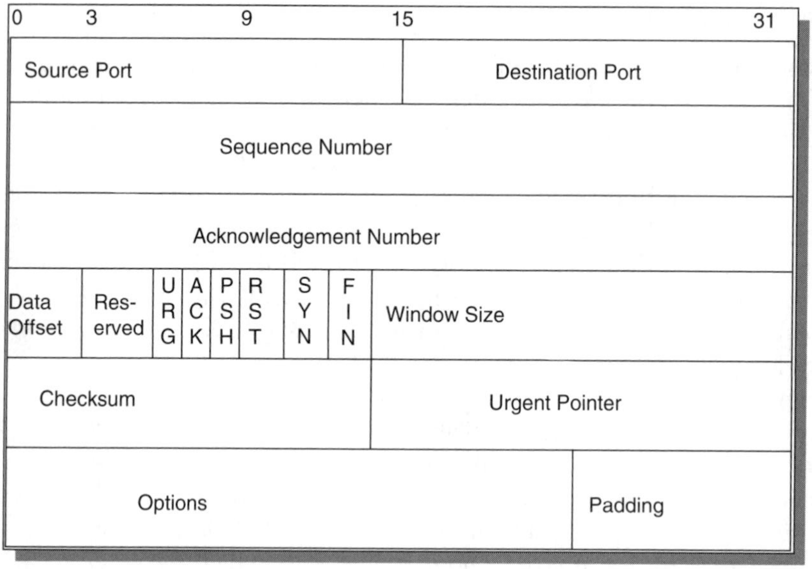

0 3	9	15	31
Source Port		Destination Port	
Sequence Number			
Acknowledgement Number			
Data Offset	Res-erved	U R G, A C K, P S H, R S T, S Y N, F I N	Window Size
Checksum		Urgent Pointer	
Options			Padding

Figure 3.21 TCP header structure.

- Sequence Number: Length 32 bits: This field is used to provide the reliability of TCP. Sequence numbers are used to reassemble a sequence of TCP packets that arrived out of order at the destination. It is tightly tied to the acknowledgment (ACK) number that is listed below. In the next section we explain all about sequence and acknowledgment numbers. For now it is sufficient to understand that sequence numbers are used to keep packets in order.
- Acknowledgment Number: Length 32 bits: The acknowledgment number is tied to the sequence number above. This field is used to verify that all data was received by the receiving station. We break these numbers down in the next section as well.
- Data Offset: Length 4 bits: Data offset is the value that indicates where the data begins, implying the end of the header and start of data. This is necessary because the length of the TCP header can change based on the number of bits that are set in the options field. This number will always be a multiple of 32 bits. If the TCP header is shorter than a 32-bit multiple then bits will be added to the padding field to increase the size to a 32-bit multiple.
- Reserved: Length 6 bits: Nothing going on here. This must be set to zero.
- Control Bits: Length 6 bits (from left to right): These are often called the flags. Each flag is a single bit that can be set to 1 for on and 0 for off. Not all flags are implemented by all manufacturers and

this allows for unique IP stack fingerprints. Here are the flags and the uses of each flag:

- URG: Urgent pointer field significant: This flag is often not implemented, but it is used to specify that this network packet is critical and needs to receive priority processing.
- ACK: Acknowledgment field significant: This bit is implemented in all systems and is used to specify that the packet is a response packet. It is used with the acknowledgment number to verify that all information was received.
- PSH: Push function: This flag is often not implemented, but is used to signal to the operating system to bypass the network buffer and send this traffic directly to the application.
- RST: Reset the connection: This flag is implemented by almost all manufacturers. It is used as either a nongraceful teardown or is sent in response to an error packet. It basically terminates communication.
- SYN: Synchronize sequence numbers: This flag is implemented in all systems and is used to start communication between systems. This flag is used to start the process of getting the sender and receiver to synchronize sequence numbers.
- FIN: No more data from sender: This flag is implemented in all systems and is used to specify a "gentle close" to a connection. A FIN flag is sent when data transfer is complete and the receiving system can release session information from memory.

- Window: Length 16 bits: The window field is used to tell the source how fast to send the packets. When the destination reaches its limit and cannot process any more packets, the window field is set to zero. When the destination finishes previous packets and is ready to handle more, it increases the window size.
- Checksum: Length 16 bits: This is an error-checking mechanism. This checksum is the checksum for the TCP header plus some parts of the IP header. These fields from the IP header are the Source IP, Destination IP, the protocol number, and the TCP length.
- Urgent Pointer: Length 16 bits: This is used if the urgent (URG) flag is set on the packet. The urgent pointer points to the sequence number of the octet following the urgent data.
- Options: Length variable: There are a few different options that can be set here. All must be a multiple of eight bits in length according to the RFC. The most common option is the MSS or Multiple Segment Size. This is sent on SYN flagged packets and is used to set the size of the largest segment the sender of the segment wishes to receive.

- Padding: Length variable: This is used to add bits to the TCP header so that it will be a multiple of 32 bits long. The padding field is filled with zeros.

The TCP Three-Way Handshake

As we mentioned above, TCP has six flags that can be set in every TCP packet. These flags are tied together to do everything from ensuring the reception of packets to closing error connections. Even with six options (or flags) to choose from, there is an orderly progression to how these flags are used during a normal data session. There are three steps that are taken: the first step is where the client requests initiation of a session with the server. In each of the example figures that follow Sally is always the requesting client and Bob is the server that responds.

The First Shake: The SYN Packet

Sally will always begin the process by sending out a flag with the SYN option set. The SYN flag as mentioned above is set to synchronize sequence numbers between the systems. In this case Sally will be sending her Initial Sequence Number (ISN) to Bob. This is illustrated in Figure 3.22.

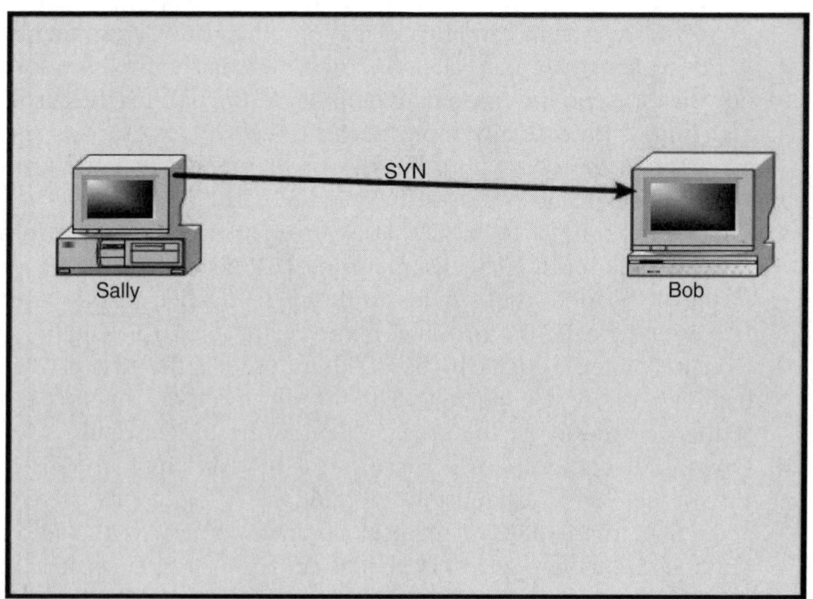

Figure 3.22 The SYN packet.

The initial sequence number

It would seem logical that when a TCP session is started the initial sequence number should be set to 1 for each session. So a valid question is, "Why wouldn't we always just start off each TCP connection by selecting a sequence number of 1?" Because sequence numbers are arbitrary this would, by far, be the easiest way to do it.

In an ideal world, this would probably work, but we don't live in an ideal world. The problem with starting off each connection with a sequence number of 1 is that it introduces the possibility of packets from many different conversations getting confused. Suppose we established a TCP connection and sent a segment containing bytes 1 through 30. However, there was a problem with the inner network that caused this segment to be delayed and, eventually, the TCP connection itself to be terminated. So after the first session was terminated we started another session and set the sequence number to 1, but as soon as this new connection was started the old session's packets showed up at the receiver. Because both packets would have a conversation with the sequence numbers labeled 1 to 30, the receiver would erroneously think those bytes were part of the new connection and not the old connection that was discarded.

This is one of several similar problems that can occur if we select 1 as our ISN for each conversation. To avoid these problems, each TCP device, at the time a connection is initiated, chooses a more unique 32-bit (ISN) for the connection. Each device has its own ISN, and they should not be the same.

Selecting the initial sequence number

Traditionally, each device chose the ISN by making use of a timed counter, like a clock of sorts, which was incremented every four microseconds. This counter was initialized when TCP started up and then its value increased by one every four microseconds until it reached the largest 32-bit value possible (4,294,967,295) at which point it "wrapped around" to 0 and resumed incrementing. Any time a new connection was set up, the ISN was taken from the current value of this timer. Because it takes over four hours to count from 0 to 4,294,967,295 at four microseconds per increment, this virtually assured that each connection would not conflict with any previous ones.

One issue with this method is that it makes ISNs predictable. A malicious person could write a program to analyze ISNs and then predict the ISN of a subsequent TCP connection based on the ISNs used in earlier ones. This represents a security risk, which has been exploited in the past.

Most implementations now use a more complex algorithm to select pseudo-random initial sequence numbers. These numbers are still relatively predictable between operating systems, and utilities such as Nmap can determine the operating system through ISNs.

The Second Shake: The SYN/ACK Packet

Once Bob has received Sally's SYN packet and processed it, Bob will respond with a SYN-ACK or SA packet to Sally. The function of the SA packet is twofold. The first function is for Bob to send his own ISN to Sally and the second is to acknowledge that Bob has received Sally's ISN. This process is illustrated in Figure 3.23.

The Third Shake: The ACK Packet

Once Sally has received the SYN-ACK packet from Bob she will respond with an ACK packet. This ACK packet represents the third and final part of the TCP three-way handshake. This packet will acknowledge that Sally has received Bob's initial sequence number and that data transfer is now all set to occur. This ACK packet is illustrated in Figure 3.24.

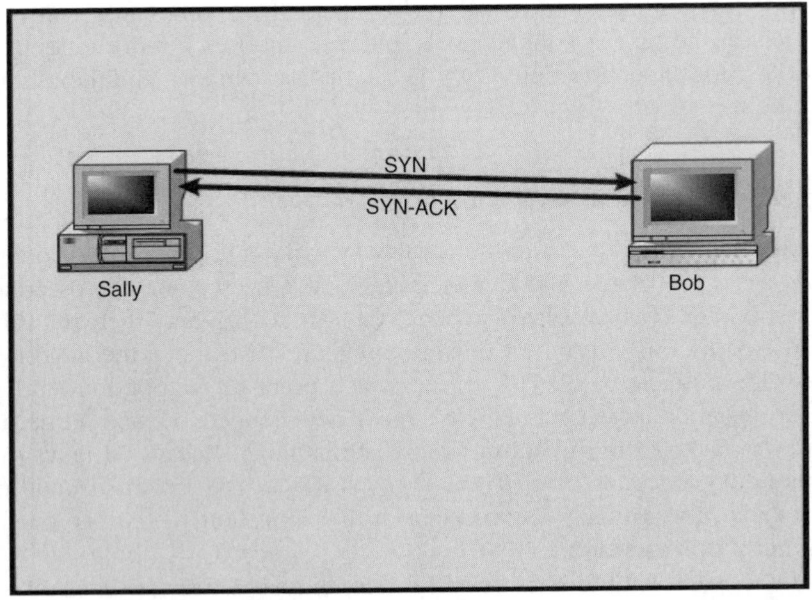

Figure 3.23 SYN-ACK packet.

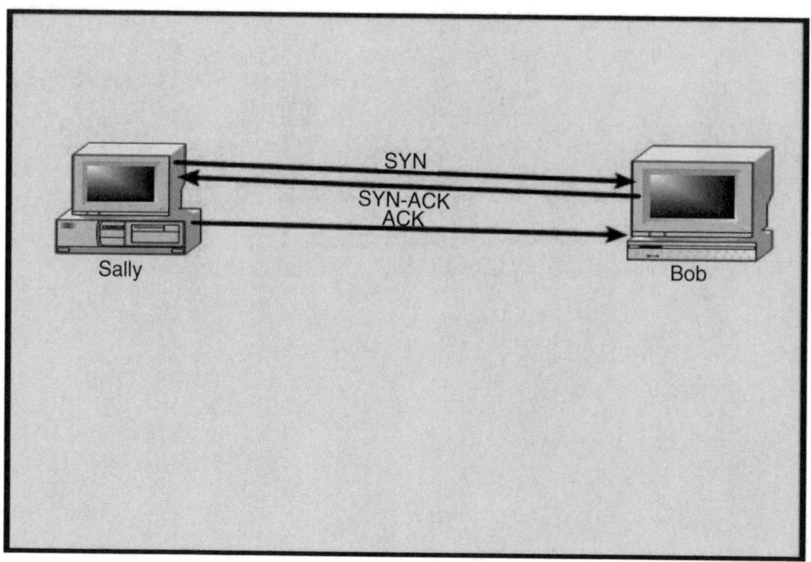

Figure 3.24 ACK packet.

After the Shaking

Once the three-way handshake is complete Bob and Sally can transfer datafiles between the systems. Over 95 percent of Internet traffic runs over TCP, so most communications are set up in this fashion. Once Sally has received all of the data that she wants from Bob she can terminate the connection. Sally will do this by sending a packet with the FIN flag set. This packet is to tell Bob that the communication is done, that the connection can be closed, and the resulting memory can be released. This process is often called the graceful close because it gives the server (Bob) a chance to terminate the connection without an error being sent. This process is illustrated in Figure 3.25.

TCP Summary

Because TCP is used for more than 95 percent of all Internet traffic, an information security manager should have a good knowledge of how TCP functions. Skilled network attackers certainly know how TCP functions and will try many different tricks with TCP packets to bypass security devices and gather information about the system. Malformed (manipulated by attacker) TCP packets may cause the target system to give up information about itself, such as the OS, grant access through a security device that should be blocking access, or fail to provide service (with a DoS such as a SYN flood).

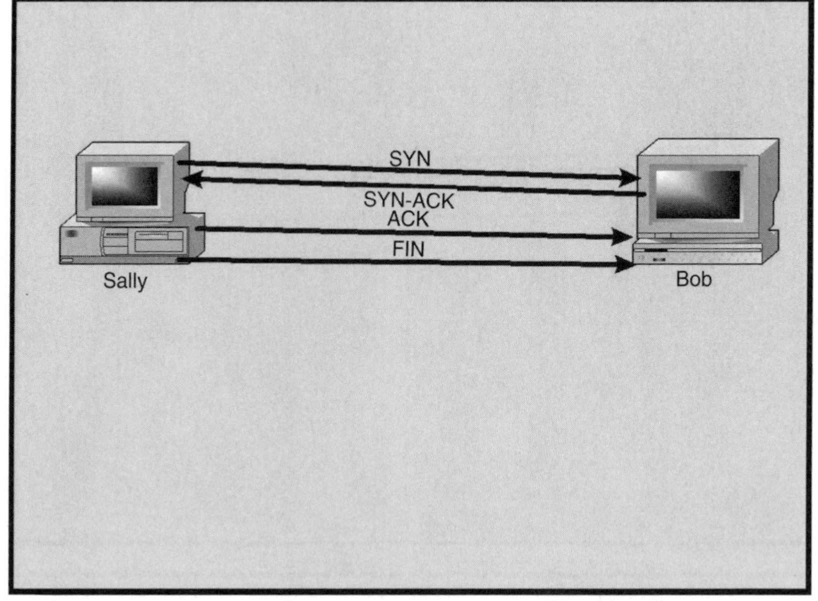

Figure 3.25 FIN packet.

Some of the common manipulations that attackers will do are changing the TCP flags, not respond to SYN-ACK packets, starting a session with a SYN-ACK (response) packet instead of a SYN (start) packet, or sending bad flag combinations (SYN-FIN) (open–close). This is done for a number of different reasons. One of the biggest reasons is that the RFC for TCP only covers what to do in the event of normal network traffic and does not cover much about erroneous or abnormal network packets. This means that error responses are up to the IP stack developer, usually the OS developer, and are often unique to each operating system environment. This gives each OS its own unique "fingerprint" that an attacker can use to determine what is running on the target system.

User Datagram Protocol (UDP)

We have spent quite some time discussing TCP, but TCP is not the only transport layer protocol that is commonly used with IP. Another protocol is the user datagram protocol. UDP is a connectionless transport protocol and as such does not offer reliability or error recovery. This means that there are no flags or sequence numbers with UDP packets and conversations (see Figure 3.26). The best analogy for UDP is a postcard. As opposed to TCP which is like a phone call, UDP is like a postcard. With a postcard, you

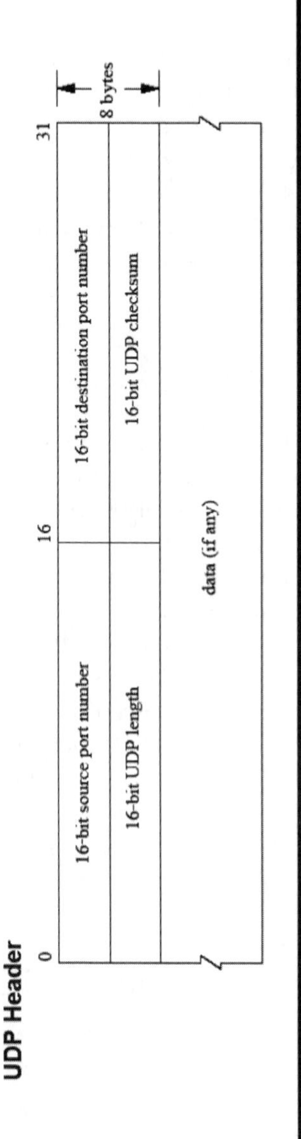

Figure 3.26 UDP header.

fill out the postcard and drop it in the mail. If the postcard gets there, it gets there. If the postcard does not arrive, then there is no harm done. You would not often use UDP for critical data because it may just never show up. Furthermore, UDP does not offer flow-control. This means that UDP is much simpler in its packet structure than TCP. UDP is most often used where speed of data transfer is preferred over reliability. UDP is faster than TCP but not reliable. Due to UDP not having flags, states, sequence numbers, or acknowledgment numbers the overhead can be kept minimal. Applications that are message-based, that is, do not require consecutive messages to be in a particular order (such as DNS), broadcast intensive (such as the routing protocol, RIP), or time-sensitive (e.g., Voice over IP) may benefit from using UDP rather than TCP.

However, because reliability is usually a high priority, TCP is the more dominant transport protocol.

UDP Error Messages

A unique component to UDP is how UDP handles error packets or packets addressed to a UDP port that is not open. UDP cannot send a RST (reset) packet as can TCP, so UDP responds instead with an ICMP error message. This is a rather unique example of a protocol using another protocol for communication. Because of its simplicity, UDP is a favorite target for attackers. Because the protocol maintains no state information and has no session establishment (three-way handshake) it can be difficult for firewalls and other security devices to understand and secure UDP well. This was actually the case for quite some time with many popular firewalls. However, more current versions of firewalls will maintain a virtual UDP state and will treat UDP much like TCP. Because older security devices could have had a bit of a problem securing UDP well, it became a favorite place for attackers to place a backdoor into an already compromised system.

Internet Control Message Protocol (ICMP)

The last transport layer protocol that we discuss is the ICMP protocol. As opposed to TCP and UDP the primary goal of ICMP was not so much to transport data as it was to help troubleshoot networks. ICMP was designed to go hand-in-hand with IP and carry out error reporting. In the event that an IP, especially UDP, packet does not reach its destination, ICMP often allows the sending station to be informed.

ICMP is a transport-layer protocol just as TCP and UDP are, and follows the IP header in normal packet structure. The ICMP header usually does not contain data that is critical. The data portions of ICMP packets are often filled with nonsense characters to make the size of the ICMP packet appropriate. Look at the data view of Ethereal in Figure 3.27. It is hoped you will notice that the ICMP packet contains a pattern of the ASCII characters (abcdefghijklmnopqrstuvwxyz) repeating to fill the size of data necessary.

ICMP Header

The ICMP header is what actually contains a message and it has a very specific structure. It is the IP layer of the receiving station that "interrogates" an ICMP packet and determines that it is in fact an ICMP message. Up until this point, the destination believes the packet to be a normal IP packet.

ICMP defines an extensive set of messages, defined by the value of the *Type* field in the ICMP datagram (see Figure 3.28). These messages may be in response to network errors, or they may be purely informational.

ICMP Packet Structure

The ICMP packet, being an IP packet, contains the usual IP header. This is followed by an ICMP header that varies slightly among the different types of ICMP message. The general format is shown in Figure 3.28.

The following are explanations of what each field does in the ICMP header and also what some common values are.

- Type: Length 8 bits: This field defines the type of ICMP message. This basically lets the receiving station know for what the message is supposed to be used. Some valid values are shown in Table 3.4.
- Code: Length 8 bits: This field provides further information about the message. The exact meaning of the value contained within this field depends on the message type. For example, with an ICMP Type 3 message ("Destination unreachable"), a Code value of 0 means "Network unreachable," which implies a router failure. A Code of 1 means "Host unreachable." The following are common ICMP codes.
  - 0—Network Unreachable
  - 1—Host Unreachable
  - 2—Protocol Unreachable
  - 3—Port Unreachable
  - 4—Fragmentation Needed and Don't Fragment Was Set
  - 5—Source Route Failed

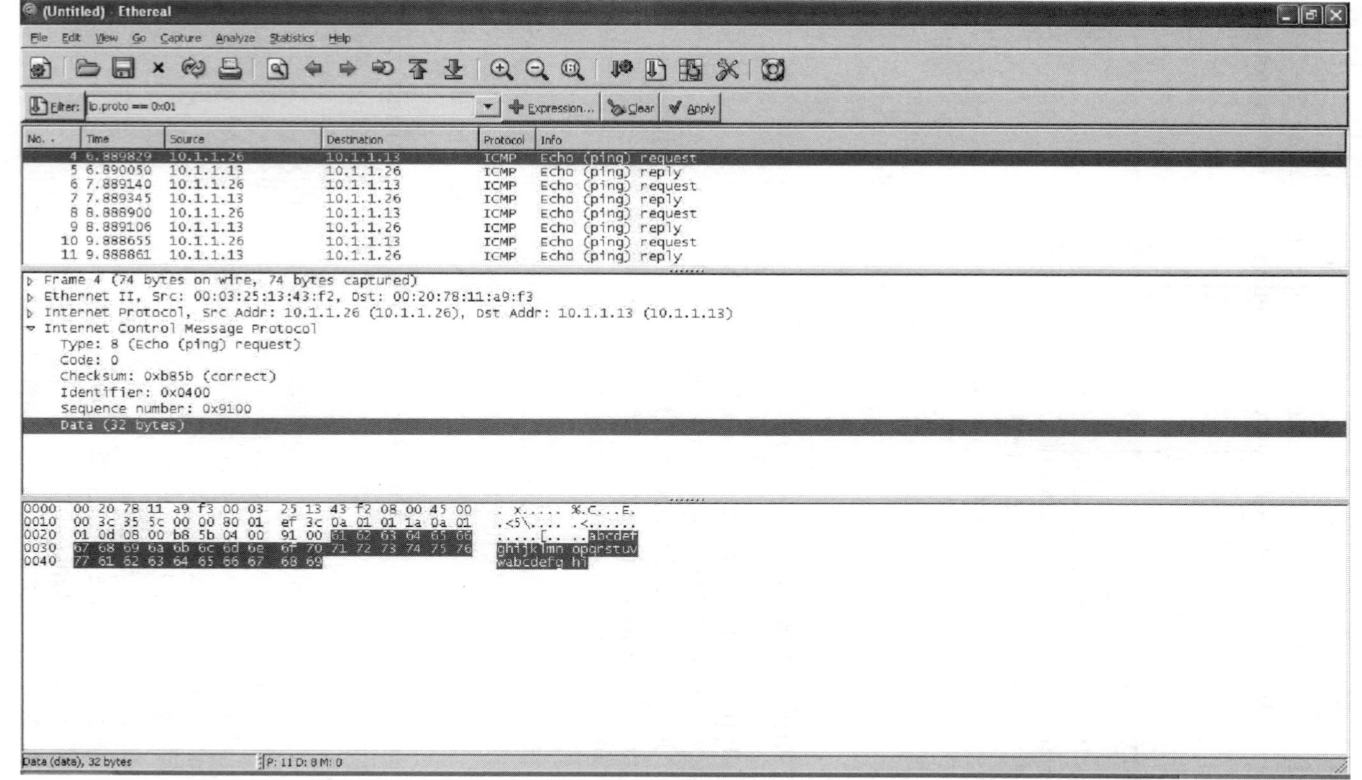

Figure 3.27 Packet capture of ICMP.

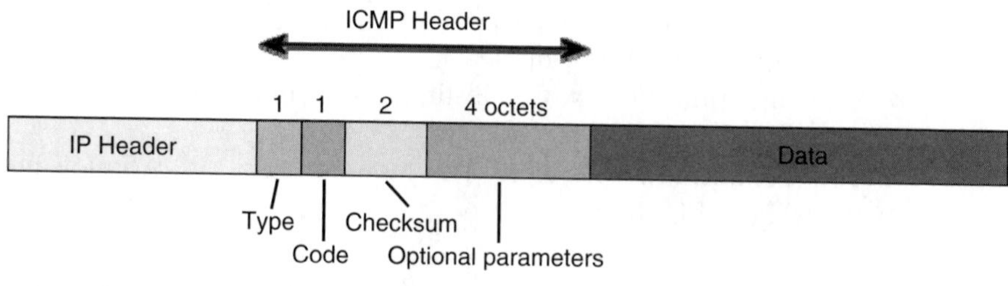

Figure 3.28 ICMP header.

Table 3.4 Valid Values

Type	*Message*
0	Echo reply
3	Destination unreachable
4	Source quench
5	Redirect
8	Echo request
9	Router advertisement
11	Time exceeded
12	Parameter (IP) unintelligible
13	Timestamp request
14	Timestamp reply
15	Information request
16	Information reply
17	Address mask request
18	Address mask reply
30	Traceroute
33	IPv6 Where-Are-You
34	IPv6 I-Am-Here
37	Domain name request
38	Domain name reply

- 6—Destination Network Unknown
- 7—Destination Host Unknown
- 9—Communication with Destination Network is Administratively Prohibited
- 10—Communication with Destination Host is Administratively Prohibited

- Checksum: Length 16 bits: The checksum field is calculated in the same way as the IP header checksum and is used for error checking.
- Parameters: Variable length usually 8 bits if used: Whether this field is used depends on the type of message. For example, Type 3 messages do not use this field, whereas Type 0 and 8 messages use the field to store an identifier and sequence number.
- Data: Variable length: Typically, the data is the IP header and first 64 bits of the original packet; this is usually the one that failed to arrive successfully at the destination and prompted the ICMP message. Including the first 64 bits of the original packet allows the ICMP message to be matched to the packet that caused it.

ICMP Common Examples

The core function of ICMP is troubleshooting. The following are examples of ICMP error messages and the corresponding types.

For example, a *Type 4* ICMP packet corresponds to a *source quench* message. If a router receives more packets than it can handle, it eventually runs out of network buffer space. At this time, it can no longer store incoming packets and simply starts discarding them. Whenever it receives a packet that it is forced to drop, it also sends a *source quench* ICMP message back to the host that sent the diagram, thereby requesting that the host send fewer messages.

A *Type 3* ICMP packet corresponds to a *host unreachable* message. A router will return this type of message if it cannot forward a packet onto the next hop in the path. Typically this happens when the destination is secured by a firewall or other security device.

The ICMP *Type 8* message is the *echo request*. Despite its simplicity, the capability to send an *echo request* is the magic ingredient in what is perhaps the world's most often used network diagnostic tool: *ping*! When the ping command (Figure 3.29) is executed, a *Type 8* packet is sent to the destination IP address. ICMP defines that when a host receives such a packet, it must respond by sending an *echo reply* (*Type 0*) message. Ping is very commonly used by attackers as part of the preamble or reconnaissance attack. These

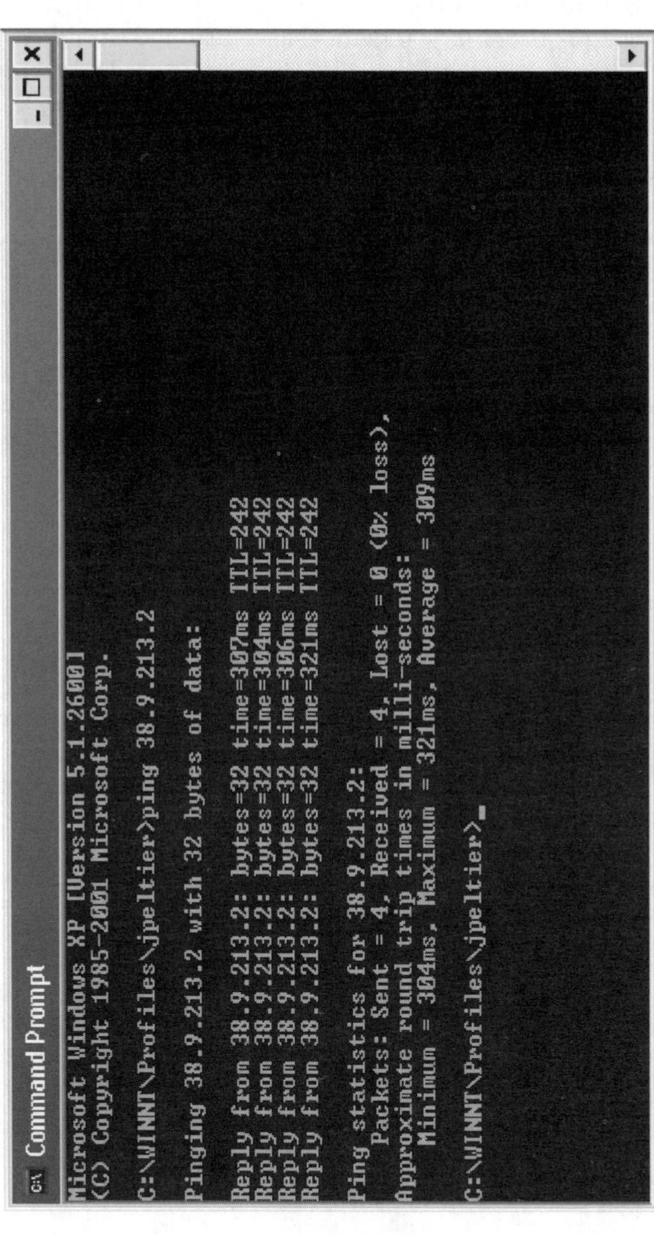

Figure 3.29 Ping.

are used to gather information about a network to find hosts that are alive. To see the prevalence of these types of probes try installing a personal firewall and see how often your device is pinged. The story of ping is actually quite interesting and the author's Web site is available at http://ftp.arl.mil/~mike/ping.html. If you get a chance read the story.

Another diagnostic tool that makes use of ICMP messages is *trace route* (Figure 3.30). Trace route works by sending a series of IP packets to the destination IP address. However, the first IP packet has the *time to live* field set to 1. When the packet reaches the first router along the journey, the router decrements the TTL by 0 and then, accordingly, returns a *Type 11* (*time exceeded*) message. This packet will contain the IP address of the first router and as such, the host machine can determine the IP address of the first router in the journey. Then, the host sends another IP packet with the TTL set to 2. In this case, the first router in the journey reduces the TTL to 1 and the second router reduces the TTL to 0. Therefore, in this case, the second router returns an ICMP *time exceeded* message. Consequently, the sending host can now determine the IP address of the second router on the journey. This process continues until *trace route* has determined the IP addresses of all routers along the way.

Risks and Vulnerabilities Associated with IP Protocols

Computers can be attacked at each of the OSI model's seven layers or the TCP/IP's four layers. As many of these protocols are susceptible to attack, it is clear that a single-layer security mechanism (often targeted only at the application layer) will be defeated by attacks directed at protocols on any other level. In large part this is due to the fact that IP was designed with two major characteristics in mind:

1. Interoperability
2. Redundancy

IP was never designed for security. At the outset IP was created to provide a protocol for military organizations and some academic institutions to exchange information. IP and the Internet in general were never designed to allow access to the millions of machines currently connected to the Internet.

Common Threats

From the hacker sitting up to all hours of the night finding ways to steal the company's secrets, to the dedicated employee who accidentally hits

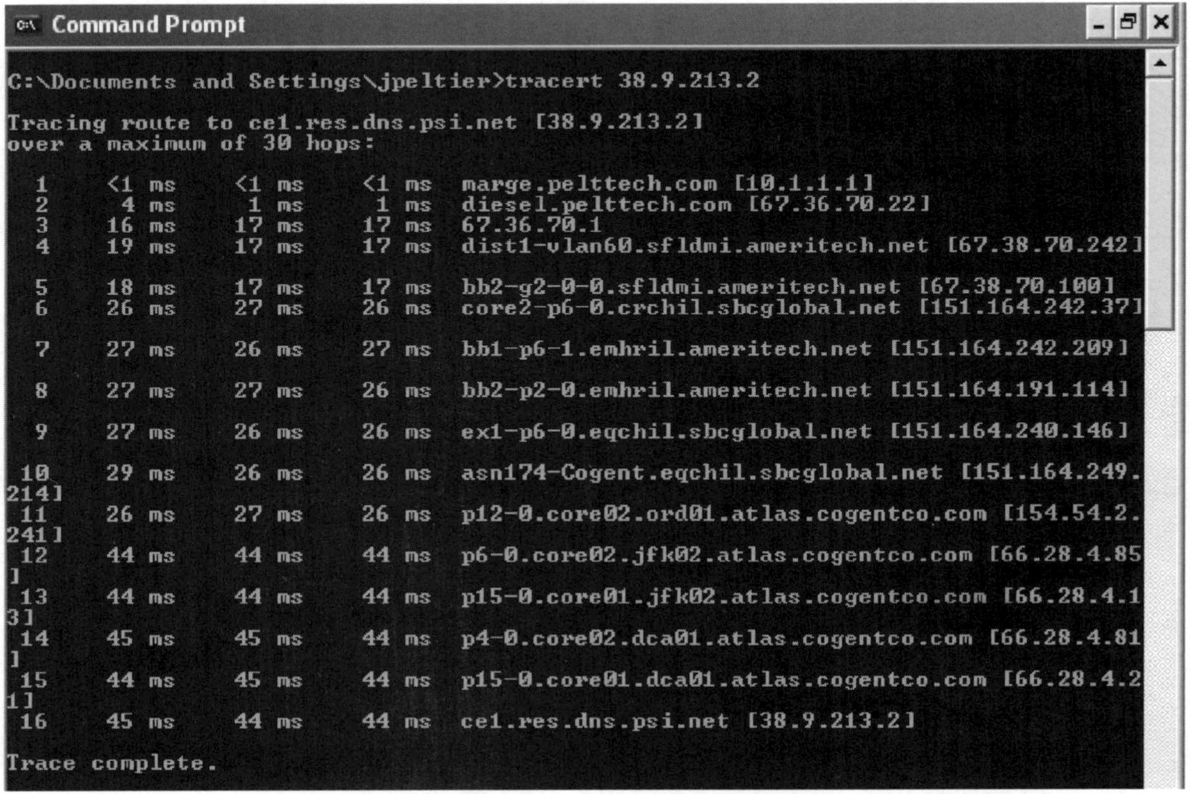

Command Prompt

```
C:\Documents and Settings\jpeltier>tracert 38.9.213.2

Tracing route to ce1.res.dns.psi.net [38.9.213.2]
over a maximum of 30 hops:

  1    <1 ms    <1 ms    <1 ms  marge.pelttech.com [10.1.1.1]
  2     4 ms     1 ms     1 ms  diesel.pelttech.com [67.36.70.22]
  3    16 ms    17 ms    17 ms  67.36.70.1
  4    19 ms    17 ms    17 ms  dist1-vlan60.sfldmi.ameritech.net [67.38.70.242]

  5    18 ms    17 ms    17 ms  bb2-g2-0-0.sfldmi.ameritech.net [67.38.70.100]
  6    26 ms    27 ms    26 ms  core2-p6-0.crchil.sbcglobal.net [151.164.242.37]

  7    27 ms    26 ms    27 ms  bb1-p6-1.emhril.ameritech.net [151.164.242.209]

  8    27 ms    27 ms    26 ms  bb2-p2-0.emhril.ameritech.net [151.164.191.114]

  9    27 ms    26 ms    26 ms  ex1-p6-0.eqchil.sbcglobal.net [151.164.240.146]

 10    29 ms    26 ms    26 ms  asn174-Cogent.eqchil.sbcglobal.net [151.164.249.
214]
 11    26 ms    27 ms    26 ms  p12-0.core02.ord01.atlas.cogentco.com [154.54.2.
241]
 12    44 ms    44 ms    44 ms  p6-0.core02.jfk02.atlas.cogentco.com [66.28.4.85
]
 13    44 ms    44 ms    44 ms  p15-0.core01.jfk02.atlas.cogentco.com [66.28.4.1
3]
 14    45 ms    45 ms    44 ms  p4-0.core02.dca01.atlas.cogentco.com [66.28.4.81
]
 15    44 ms    45 ms    44 ms  p15-0.core01.dca01.atlas.cogentco.com [66.28.4.2
1]
 16    45 ms    44 ms    44 ms  ce1.res.dns.psi.net [38.9.213.2]

Trace complete.
```

Figure 3.30 Traceroute.

the delete key, there are many foes of information security. Due to the many different types of threats, it is very difficult to try to establish and maintain information security. Our attacks come from many different sources, so it is much like trying to fight a war on multiple fronts. Our good policies can help fight the internal threats and our firewall and intrusion detection system can help fight the external threats. However, a failure of one component can lead to an overall failure to keep our information secure. This means that even if we have well secured our information from external threats, our end users can still create information security breaches. Recent statistics show that the majority of successful compromises are still coming from insiders. In fact, the Computer Security Institute (CSI) in San Francisco estimates that between 60 and 80 percent of network misuse comes from inside the enterprises where the misuse has taken place.

CIA Triad

In addition to the multiple sources of information security attacks, there are also many types of information security attacks. A well-known model helps illustrate this point. The information security triad (Figure 3.31) shows the three primary goals of information security. The three components of the triad are integrity, confidentiality, and availability. When these three tenets are put together our information will be well protected.

The first tenet of the information security triad we discuss is integrity. Integrity is defined by ISO 17799 as "the action of safeguarding the accuracy and completeness of information and processing methods." This can be interpreted to mean that when a user requests any type of information from the system the information will be correct. A great example of a lack of information integrity is commonly seen in large

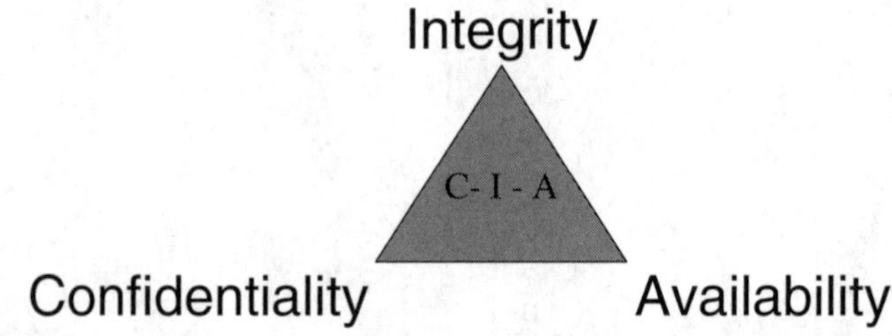

Figure 3.31 CIA triad.

home-improvement warehouses. One day, I ventured to the local home-improvement megamart looking for a hose to fix my sprinkler system. I spent quite some time looking for the hose before I happened upon a salesperson. Once I had the salesperson's attention I asked about the location and availability of the hoses for which I was looking. The salesperson went to his trusty computer terminal and pulled up information about the hose that I needed. The salesperson then let me know that I was in luck and they had 87 of the particular type of hose that I needed in stock. So I inquired as to where these hoses could be found in the store and was told that just because the computer listed 87 in the store it did not mean that there really were any of the hoses available.

Although this example really just ruined my Sunday, the integrity of information can have much more serious implications. Take your credit rating. It is just information that is stored by the credit reporting agencies. If this information in inaccurate, or does not have integrity, it can stop you from getting a new home, car, or job. The integrity of this type of information is incredibly important, but is just as susceptible to integrity errors as any other type of electronic information.

The second tenet of the information security triad we discuss is confidentiality. Confidentiality is defined by ISO 17799 as "ensuring that information is accessible only to those authorized to have access to it." This can be one of the most difficult tasks to ever undertake. To attain confidentiality you have to keep secret information secret. It seems easy enough, but remember the discussion on threat sources above. People from both inside and outside your organization will be threatening to reveal your secret information.

The last tenet of the information security triad is availability. Once again as defined by ISO 17799, availability is ensuring that authorized users have access to information and associated assets when required. This means that when a user needs a file or system, the file or system is there to be accessed. This seems simple enough but there are so many factors working against your system availability. You have hardware failures, natural disasters, malicious users, and outside attackers all fighting to remove the availability from your systems. Some common mechanisms to fight against this downtime are fault-tolerant systems, load balancing, and system failover.

Fault-tolerant systems incorporate technology that allows the system to stay available even when a hardware fault has occurred. One of the most common examples of this is RAID. According to the folks over at linux.org the acronym RAID means Redundant Array of Inexpensive Disks. I have heard much debate as to what those little letters actually stand for, but for our purposes let's just use that definition. RAID allows the system to maintain the data on the system even in the event of a hard-drive crash. Some of the simplest mechanisms to accomplish this are through disk mirroring and disk duplexing. With disk mirroring the system would have two hard drives attached to the same interface or controller. All data would be written to both drives simultaneously. With disk duplexing the two hard drives are attached in the system to two different controllers. Duplexing allows for one of the controllers to fail without the system losing any availability of the data. But RAID configuration can get significantly more complex than disk mirroring or disk duplexing. One of the more common advanced RAID solutions is RAID level 5. With level 5 RAID data is striped across a series of disks, usually three or more, so that when any one drive is lost no information is destroyed. The disadvantage with using any of the systems mentioned above is that you lose some of the storage space from the devices. For example, a RAID 5 system with five 80-gigabyte hard drives would only have 320 gigabytes of actual storage. For more information on RAID look at the chart in Table 3.5.

The technologies we just talked about provide system tolerance, but do not provide improved performance under heavy utilization conditions. To improve system performance with heavy utilization we need load balancing. Load balancing allows the information requests to be spread across a large number of servers or other devices. Usually a front-end component is necessary to direct requests to all of the back-end servers. This also provides tolerance, due to the fact that the front-end processor can just redirect the requests to the remaining servers or devices.

A technology that would be between load balancing and RAID in terms of most availability would be system failover. With a failover environment when the primary processing device has a hardware failure a secondary device begins processing. This is a common technology to use with firewalls. In most organizations, to avoid having the firewall be a single point of failure on the network, the organization implements two firewalls that communicate with each other. In the event that the primary firewall cannot communicate with the secondary firewall, the secondary firewall takes over and begins processing the data.

As we have discussed, the job of the information security manager is difficult. There are many tasks to adequately protect the resources of an organization and one slip along any of them can lead to systems breach. This is why the task of defending information systems is rather difficult. In the next section we look at possible implementations of security devices that will create the CIA triad for the information security manager.

Table 3.5 RAID Chart

Raid Level	*Activity*	*Name*
0	Data striped over several drives. No redundancy or parity is involved. If one volume fails, the entire volume is unusable. It is used for performance only.	Striping
1	Mirroring of drives. Data is written to two drives at once. If one drive fails, the other drive has the exact same data available.	Mirroring
2	Data striping over all drives at the bit level. Parity data is created with a hamming code, which identifies any errors. This level specifies the use of up to 39 disks: 32 for storage and 7 for error recovery data. This is not used in production today.	Hamming code parity
3	Data striping over all drives and parity data held on one drive. If a drive fails, it can be reconstructed from parity drive.	Byte-level parity
4	Same as level 3, except data is striped at the block level instead of the byte level.	Block-level parity
5	Data is written in disk sector units to all drives. Parity is written to all drives also, which ensures that there is not a single point of failure.	Interleave parity
6	Similar to level 5 but with added fault tolerance, which is a second set of parity data written to all drives.	Second parity data (or double parity)
10	Data is simultaneously mirrored and striped across several drives and can support multiple drive failures.	Striping and mirroring

PPPN

The PPPN model is a unique model used by the ISACA® organization and it is part of the CISM. The PPPN model breaks down to

- Process
- Physical
- Platform
- Network

Each component of the PPPN model represents a different set of controls that can be used to increase the integrity, confidentiality, and availability of the data in our organization. Each set of controls can differently affect the CIA triad for the entire organization.

Process

The first phase of this model is the process phase. Processes include the policies, procedures, and guidelines to make sure they address confidentiality, integrity, and availability of all systems in an organization. Process comes first for a reason. There is another RFC standard (RFC2146). It is a document that denotes that policies are what they actually call the "backbone of your Information Security Program." In CISM terms this would be part of the information security framework and this is going to be what drives the information security program (see Figure 3.32).

Physical

When it comes to the physical layer we are going to be implementing controls that modify the physical space or physical access to systems: things such as biometrics to get into a secure location, building ID cards, and visitor badges. Those types of security controls are going to be the physical controls and are going to alter the physical space. Included in this layer will be controls such as locks, sensors, and UPS (Uninterruptible Power Supplies). A UPS is a device that will help maintain availability of a system in the event of power failure, but will also provide integrity of the data because it allows the system to shut down gracefully if power is lost for an extended period of time.

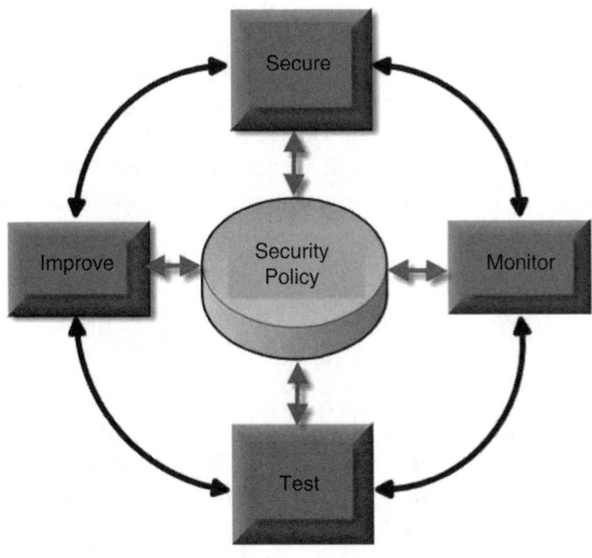

Figure 3.32 Information security wheel.

Platform

Platform is the next layer, and platform controls are those controls that are typically those controls that a technician would think of as either system security or host security depending on the nomenclature that you use. Platform controls are going to be those controls that can be used to verify the confidentiality, integrity, and authenticity of a single device or host. Some examples of platform controls include operating system security controls. Other examples of platform controls would be application security. In an example of a Web-enabled application, a security control could be a SSL (Secure Sockets Layer) connection to protect the information as it is in transit. Protection mechanisms such as virus detection would also be platform controls. Most of the examples of platform controls that we have discussed have increased the confidentiality of the data, but there are also platform controls that increase the integrity of our data. One such example of this type of platform integrity control would be a trip wire. Typically a trip wire program will protect a system from modification of a critical file, system file, or configuration file. If these types of files are modified, the trip wire program is going to create an alert.

Network

Network layer controls are going to be more commonly thought of controls and also more commonly used controls. Network layer controls are going to help secure the network against attacks on the data's confidentiality, availability, and integrity. Examples of network layer controls would be firewalls, intrusion detection/intrusion prevention systems, Virtual Private Network devices (VPNs), and 802.1X architectures. We cover each of these topics in the upcoming sections in this chapter.

Threats

Information security has many different threats. As mentioned above, threats can range from accidental to deliberate and also from natural disaster to component failure. An information security manager needs to have the ability to manage all of the resources that can assist in mitigation of these threats to information security. Some of the resources available to the information security manager include:

- Vendors
- Consultants
- Security research and standards bodies

Each of these resources can provide important and unique insight in the evolving world of information security threats. The following sections provide information about common threats to information security.

Malicious Hackers

There are several groups of Internet users out there that will attack information systems. The three primary groups are hackers, crackers, and phreaks. Although common nomenclature terms all three of the groups "hackers," there are some differences among the groups. A hacker is a user who penetrates a system just to look around and see what is possible. The etiquette of the hackers is that after they have penetrated the system, they will notify the system administrator to let the administrator know that the system has a vulnerability. It is often said that a hacker just wants security to be improved on all Internet systems. The next group, the crackers, are the group to really fear. A cracker has no etiquette on breaking into a system. Crackers will damage or destroy data if they are able to penetrate a system. The goal of the cracker is to cause as much damage as possible to all systems on the Internet. The last group, phreaks,

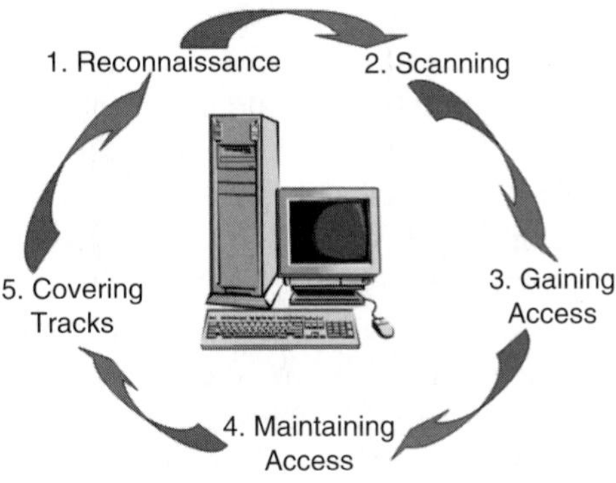

Figure 3.33 Attacking methodology.

tries to break into your organization's phone system. The phreaks can then use the free phone access to disguise the phone number that they are calling from, and also stick your organization with the bill for long distance phone charges.

The way that a hacker will attack a system can vary tremendously. Each attacker has his or her own bag of tricks that can be used to break into a system. There are several books on just the subject of hacking currently available, but we cover the basic hacker methodology briefly here.

The basic hacker methodology (Figure 3.33) has five main components: reconnaissance, scanning, gaining access, maintaining access, and covering tracks. It might seem odd to think of a methodology for hackers, but as with anything else time matters. So to maximize time most hackers follow a similar methodology.

Attacking Methodology

The first phase in the methodology is the reconnaissance phase. In this the phase the attacker tries to gain as much information about the target network as possible. There are two primary ways an attacker can do this: active and passive. Most attackers would generally begin with passive attacks. These passive attacks can often generate a lot of good information about the network or organization the hacker wants to attack. The hacker would often begin by reading through the Web site at the organization to see if any information can be gained. The attacker would look for contact information for key employees (this can be used for social engineering), information on the types of technology used at the organization, and any other nugget of information that could be used in an attack. After the attacker has gone through the Web site he would probably move to

Internet search engines to find more information about the network he wishes to attack. He would be looking for bad newsgroup postings, posts at sites for people who are upset with the company, and any other details that could help in the attack. The attacker would then look for information in the DNS servers for the attack organization. This would provide a list of server and corresponding IP addresses. Once this is done the hacker would move over to active attacking.

To perform an active reconnaissance attack a hacker would perform ping sweeps, SNMP network scans, banner grabbing, and other similar attacks. The attacks would help the attacker weed out the number of dead IP addresses and find the live hosts to move on to the next phase, scanning.

An attacker would begin scanning looking for holes to compromise to gain access to the network. The attacker would scan all servers that are available on the Internet looking for known vulnerabilities. These vulnerabilities could be in a poorly written Web-enabled application or from applications that have known security vulnerabilities in them. The attacker would also look at the organization's firewall and routers to see if vulnerabilities exist there as well. Once an attacker has compiled a list of vulnerabilities, then he would move on to the next stage: gaining access.

There are many ways for an attacker to gain access to the target network. Some of the more common entry points into the network are through the target server's OS, through an application that was developed in-house, through an application with known vulnerabilities, as well as through the network devices that can be seen from the Internet, and if all else fails the attacker performs a denial-of-service attack. Once the attacker has access all he wants to do is make sure that he can keep it.

To maintain access an attacker would commonly upload custom applications onto the compromised server. These applications would then be backdoors into the target organization, and would allow the attacker to come and go at will. In addition to uploading new programs an attacker can alter existing programs on the system. The advantage to doing this is that a well-informed administrator may know the files on her system and she might recognize if new files were installed on her servers. By modifying already existing files the system would appear to be unmodified at first glance. One common way of doing this is with a group of files called a rootkit. A rootkit allows an attacker to replace normal system files with files of the same name that also have Trojan horse functionality. The new system files would allow the attacker in just as if he added additional files to the target server. An attacker may not need long access to the system and he might just wish to download the existing programs or data from the target server.

Once an attacker has put his mechanism for getting back into the server the last step in the hacker methodology is to cover the tracks.

To cover the tracks an attacker would go through the system audit log files and remove any trace of the attacker on the system. This would hide her access from the system administrator and would also leave less evidence behind in case the system administrator wishes to have a forensics examination performed on the compromised host. The level of skill of an attacker is often apparent in this phase. A crude attacker may delete the entire log file, making it easy for the system administrator to determine that someone has been in the system, but a more skillful attacker may just modify the log entries to show that the traffic was originating from a different IP address.

Malicious Code

Although malicious users can attack your system, programs released by the same group of people will often be more successful in reaching the protected parts of your organization. Malicious code is defined as any code that is designed to make a system perform any operation without the knowledge of the system owner. One of the fastest ways to introduce malicious code into a target organization's protected network is by sending the malicious code via e-mail.

There are many different types of malicious code; in this chapter we look at a few of the more common ones including virus, worm, Trojan horse, and logic bomb. The most commonly thought-of type of malicious code is the virus.

Virus

A virus is a code fragment, or a piece of code, that can be injected into target files. A virus then waits, usually until the file is opened or accessed to spread to another file where the malicious code is then injected into that file. With a virus-infected system you can often find in excess of 30,000 infected files. There are many different types of viruses out there. There are viruses that attack the boot sector of the hard drive, there are file system infectors, there are macro viruses that use the Office scripting functionality, and there are viruses for all major operating systems.

Worms

Another type of malicious code is the worm. A worm is typically a complete file that infects one place on a given system and then tries to replicate to other vulnerable systems on the network or Internet. A number of the highly publicized attacks have, lately, been worms. Nimda is one example of a recent highly publicized attack that was a worm.

Trojan Horses

Trojan horses are a different type of malicious code and can be quite deceiving to the end user. A Trojan horse appears to have a legitimate function on the surface, but also has malicious code underneath. There are a number of freeware programs on the Internet that allow an attacker to insert a malicious code the attacker wants to send into most of the common executables. The only way to help stop the Trojan horses is to educate the end users not to open file attachments unless they know exactly what the attachment will do.

Logic Bomb

The last type of malicious code that we look at is the logic bomb. The logic bomb is a generic term for any type of malicious code that is waiting for a trigger event to release the payload. This means that the code could be waiting for a period of time, such as one month, before it executes. A well-known example of a logic bomb was the Michelangelo attack. This logic bomb was waiting for Michelangelo's birthday before it would trigger the malicious code.

Denial-of-Service Attacks

As an attacker if you cannot get access to the target network, often the best thing that you can do is make sure that no one gets access to the network. Enter the denial-of-service attack. The denial-of-service or DoS attack is designed to either overwhelm the target server's hardware resources or to overwhelm the target network's telecommunication lines. For years there were a number of common "one-to-one" DoS attacks. In these attacks the hacker would launch an attack from his system against the target server or network. Syn floods, Fin floods, Smurfs, and Fraggles are all examples of these "one-to-one" attacks. Although all of these attacks are still successful on some target networks today, most organizations have implemented technology to stop these attacks from causing a service disruption in their organization.

Distributed Denial-of-Service Attacks

In February of 2000 DoS attacks hit the next level. In that month a number of high-profile targets were taken offline by the next generation of DoS attacks: the Distributed Denial-of-Service (DDoS). These DDoS attacks were no longer the familiar "one-to-one" attacks of the past. These attacks used zombie hosts to create a many-to-one attack. These zombie hosts were devices that were compromised and had code uploaded onto them that would allow for a master machine to contact them, and have them all release the DoS attack at the same time. There were tens of thousands of zombie hosts available and the attacker could use a number of common tools from which to launch the attack. Some of the common tools were Trinoo, TFN2K, and Stacheldraht. These tools were pretty straightforward to use and allowed for an attacker to release a devastating attack against the target.

The new DDoS attacks are very difficult to defend against. Most of the tools denied service not by overwhelming the processing server, but by flooding the telecommunications lines from the Internet Service Provider (ISP). Most organizations are still vulnerable to this sort of attack. The mechanism that has currently curtailed most of the DDoS attacks tries to minimize the number of zombie-infected hosts available. As soon as a new and better infection mechanism surfaces, another round of DDoS attacks is sure to spring up.

Social Engineering

Social engineering is the name given to a category of security attacks in which someone manipulates others into revealing information that can be used to steal data, access to systems, access to cellular phones, money, or even their own identity. Such attacks can be very simple or very complex. Gaining access to information over the phone or through Web sites that you visit has added a new dimension to the role of the social engineer.

Social engineering is the acquisition of sensitive information or inappropriate access privileges by an outsider, based upon the building of an inappropriate trust relationship with insiders. Please note that the term "outsider" does not refer only to nonemployees. An outsider can be an employee that is attempting to circumvent established policies and standards.

The goal of social engineering is to trick someone into providing valuable information or access to that information or resource. The social engineering exploiter preys on qualities of human nature, such as:

- The desire to be helpful. We have trained our employees well. Make sure the customer is satisfied. The best way to a good appraisal is to have good responses from those needing assistance. Most of our employees want to be helpful and this can lead to giving away too much information.
- A tendency to trust people. Human nature is to actually trust others until they prove that they are not trustworthy. If someone tells us that she is a certain person, we usually accept that statement. We must train our employees to seek independent proof.
- The fear of getting into trouble. Too many of us have seen negative reaction by superiors because verification of identity took too long or some official was offended. Management must support all employees who are doing their assignments and protecting the information resources of the enterprise.
- The willingness to cut corners. Sometimes we get lazy. We post passwords on the screen or leave important material lying out.

What scares most companies about social engineers is that the sign of truly successful social engineers is that they receive what they are looking for without raising any suspicion. It is the bad social engineers that we know about, not the good ones.

According to the *Jargon Dictionary* "wetware" is the human being attached to a computer system. People are usually the weakest link in the security chain. In the 1970s, we were told that if we installed access control packages then we would have security. In the 1980s we were encouraged to install effective anti-virus software to ensure that our systems and networks were secure. In the 1990s we were told that firewalls would lead us to security. Now in the twenty-first century, it is intrusion detection systems or public key infrastructure that will lead us to information security. In each and every iteration, security has eluded us because the silicon-based products have to interface with carbon-based units. It is the human factor that will continue to appear in our discussion on social engineering.

A skilled social engineer will often try to exploit this weakness before spending time and effort on other methods to crack passwords or gain access to systems. Why go to all of the trouble of installing a sniffer on a network, when a simple phone call to an employee may gain the needed userID and password? Social engineering is the hardest form of attack to defend against because it cannot be defended with hardware or software alone. A successful defense will require an effective information security architecture starting with policies and standards and following through with a vulnerability assessment process.

Attacks Against Access Control Systems

Hackers for many years have used two common types of password attacks to gain unauthorized access to a network device. These two techniques are the dictionary attack and the brute force attack. With a dictionary attack the attacker uses a dictionary of varying size to guess many common passwords in short order. This attack is often successful, because many users tend to use the easiest password the network or desktop operating system will allow them to use. In many cases this means that the password will either be a dictionary word or it will be based on a dictionary word. The attacking choice is very popular with attackers because the attacker can run through a complex dictionary in a very short period of time.

The other well-known attack, the brute force attack, tries every possible combination of characters until the password is broken. And given enough time this type of attack will succeed. However, this type of attack can be enormously time consuming and can take months in order to defeat a secure password. Because of the amount of time necessary to perform a brute force attack many attackers will resort to the method only as a last resort or when time will permit.

A more recent development in password attacking is the hybrid attack. A hybrid attack tries to combine the speed of a dictionary attack with the thoroughness of the brute force attack. In most cases a hybrid attack will start with a dictionary of common passwords and it will add in special characters and make simple substitutions to try to defeat the password. This type of attack takes longer than the dictionary attack, but is still considerably faster than a full-on brute force attack.

Man in the Middle (MITM)

The man-in-the-middle attack you can often see written as the MITM. What you are trying to do is, you are inserting yourself into the key exchange and this is something that as long as you have physical access to one side or the other can actually be done.

Well, the man-in-the-middle-attack kind of works. My two favorite people are Bob and Sally, and Bob and Sally happen to share a network with me and I am the security administrator. And Bob and Sally are married, just not to each other. And they are having a torrid affair. So me being a security administrator, I don't have enough to do. So I like to play practical jokes. I know what's going on between Bob and Sally. After all, Bob would probably tell me. So I am sitting on the network one day, and I see a message coming out from Bob that says, "Sally, send me your encryption key so I can send you an encrypted message." So what I do is I say, "Hey Sally, I am Bob, please send me your encryption key." Now

Sally turns around and says, "All right Bob, you can have my encryption key." But I spoofed that I am Bob; I have actually stopped Bob's message here. And so Sally gives who she thinks is Bob her key. But it actually turns out it's me. So I turn around and I say, "Hey Bob, here is the key." But I don't give him Sally's key; I can't decrypt messages with Sally's key. I send Bob my key. And when Bob encrypts the message using my key, I can decrypt the message. So why did I go through the process of getting the key from Sally?

Threats Summary

There are many threats to information security, and those mentioned above are just a sample of the most prevalent threats. The understanding that our information systems are constantly under attack is a key concept to understanding the difficulty in protecting the confidentiality, integrity, and availability of our data. To help protect these systems we use controls.

Controls

There are many controls that can be used to help mitigate the risk from threats such as those listed in the previous section. It is important to note a few key details about controls in general. The first concept to remember is the value of a control should not outweigh the value of an asset. This means that it would be foolhardy to purchase a $100,000 firewall to protect a database that only contains $10 worth of information. In addition to costs concerns for controls, it is also important to remember that the goal of information security is acceptable levels of risk and not zero risk. Zero risk for information systems only occurs when a system is turned off and protected from electronic, magnetic, and physical damage. This system that has zero risk also has zero availability and therefore does not meet the three primary objectives of information security management.

The last concept to remember about controls is that the controls used should have the lowest level of impact on the productivity of the user community. If a control is going to have any impact on the user community, it is recommended to have a metric or calculation to show the business justification for implementation of such a control. In the case of justifying a control that will have a negative impact on the user community, an Annualized Loss Expectancy (ALE) should only be used as a last resort. The primary reason for caution when using an ALE is that the numbers used for an ALE are usually just an estimate and can be wildly inaccurate if the values and risks are not adequately assessed.

Now that we have established some rules for controls in general, it is time to delve into specific controls. It is worthy to note that no control is perfect, no matter what the manufacturer might have on their marketing materials. Due to the imperfection of controls, it is important for an information security manager to understand three elements of each control. These elements are:

1. Benefits of this control when compared against other similar controls
2. Drawbacks of this control when compared against other similar controls
3. Environment in which the control is the most appropriate to implement

Access Control

The primary control in information security is access control. Access control can take many forms, from the software-based access control solution used in conjunction with an operating system, to the ruleset of a hardware firewall, to an intrusion detection system profile. The goal of any access control system is to provide access to authorized users while restricting access to unauthorized users. In addition to allowing and denying access to system resources, most access control packages also attempt to create a level of granularity that will allow for other information security goals such as the principle of least privilege and separation of duties.

If we are going to create a dichotomy of access control by splitting the access control world into two halves, we would divide it between Mandatory Access Control (MAC) and Discretionary Access Control (DAC) first.

Mandatory Access Control

Mandatory access control (MAC) is where access control is being set by a policy. This leads to mandatory access control being implemented only by organizations that have the highest of security standards that need to be followed. Typically MAC is implemented by government agencies and also consultants that support the government agencies. These are just about the only examples of organizations that use mandatory access control. In order to effectively use mandatory access control you have to have a policy established. MAC security permissions are usually set through a background check, need to know, and security classification level. The rules for the amount of access given (based on the three criteria mentioned above) are defined in the policy itself. MAC requires that every person, every document, and every system be classified through an information classification process. MAC requires every person to get his or her security classification and every document has to be classified. Once every user, program, document, and system has been classified a label is applied. A label is formally defined as a marking or an attribute applied to a subject or an object. Informally, a label is the assigned information classification level.

As you might imagine there are certainly some advantages and disadvantages of using MAC. The biggest advantage is MAC generally provides greater security than discretionary access control. Because security is defined by policy, a change to policy is necessary to change the relative security of a user of a resource. The disadvantages of MAC are the cost of MAC is typically higher than that of DAC and also MAC introduces more administrative overhead. This is typically the reason larger organizations tend to use MAC more often than smaller organizations. Another small component of MAC is that data owners cannot assign ownership of the data to other people as is possible in DAC. Although this is stressed in a number of resources on the subject of MAC versus DAC, it is minor part of the overall difference between the two.

Typically there is an essential role inside mandatory access control that allows for the ability to change the security policy and change the limitations on what permissions can be given by other than the data owner. This specific position is often referred to as the trusted subject. The trusted subject is similar to the Key Maker from the *Matrix* movies. He is the one person who can go in and make changes to the system itself. He is the person who can assign additional access permissions. Having a trusted subject stops users from assigning permissions to those things that they have created.

Discretionary Access Control

The other primary access control system is discretionary access control. DAC allows permissions to be assigned by a data custodian or an administrator, at the behest of the data owner, to the user based on job function. The rules of access are defined within the system and examples of these system access control systems would be RACF, Top Secret, Microsoft's Active Directory, and Novel Directory Services. DAC does not necessarily require a written policy for access control for the entire organization.

Because DAC is typically based on your job role, implemented by a data custodian, and defined within the system, it is less expensive with less administrative overhead than MAC. Also DAC tends to be more flexible and this tends to favor organizations that have rapidly changing environments. Because of this flexibility DAC can often be modified and over time this can lead to security breaches and decreased security. DAC is used by just about all organizations that are not government agencies or support organizations for government agencies.

Lattice-Based Access Control

Any organization can use a lattice-based access control system (Figure 3.34). Regardless of which access control system an organization utilizes (mandatory or discretionary access control) a lattice-based model can be used. A lattice-based access control system is a model that lays out users (subjects) and files (objects) for the purpose of defining relationships between the access permissions. Organizations that tend to use mandatory access control tend to also use a lattice-based model more frequently because of the need for extensive labeling. So what would typically be additional overhead, in terms of labeling in DAC, would already be in place with mandatory access control. However, there are organizations that use discretionary access control which will also utilize a lattice-based model. After all, a lattice-based model is just a model that helps define access control relationships between users and files.

Document Sensitivity →	Object 1	Object 2	Object 3
Subject 3	W	W	RW
Subject 2	W	RW	R
Subject 1 (↑ Security Clearance)	RW	R	R

Figure 3.34 Lattice-based access control.

The advantage to using a lattice-based model is that it allows an information security manager to see security violations, lack of security, and also where additional security needs to be implemented.

Rule-Based Access Control

Besides MAC and DAC there are some other types of access control that can be used. Rule-based access control (Figure 3.35) is basically an if-then statement. For example, you could have a device, such as a firewall, that has a rule defined that states if a request originates from a specific IP address you can access the payroll system. Examples of devices that tend to use rule-based access control include firewalls, routers, some layer three switches, and intrusion detection/prevention systems.

Role-Based Access Control

Another mechanism for applying access control is Role-Based Access Control (RBAC). Role-based access control is different from rule-based access control because as opposed to assigning permissions to users, job functions are created and permissions are assigned to the job function. Once the permissions have been assigned to the job function, the user is then assigned to that job function. Role-based access control is most often used for those roles in the organization that have a high employee turnover rate. One example of a high turnover job is the help desk. Typically you would create help desk objects and you would assign people to the help desk. Also roles such as backup operators tend to be a role-based access control due to the rotational responsibility of tape backup operations. The major advantage to RBAC is that RBAC allows for reduced administration overhead.

Access Control Lists

Regardless of the type of access control system in use, the devices that implement access control use access control lists. Every operating system, every firewall, and every router all have access control lists saying who can access those systems or which types of data can bypass these systems. Most systems provide some mechanism to view the access control list. This is done so that the access control list on the system can be audited for completeness and correctness. See Figure 3.36 for an example.

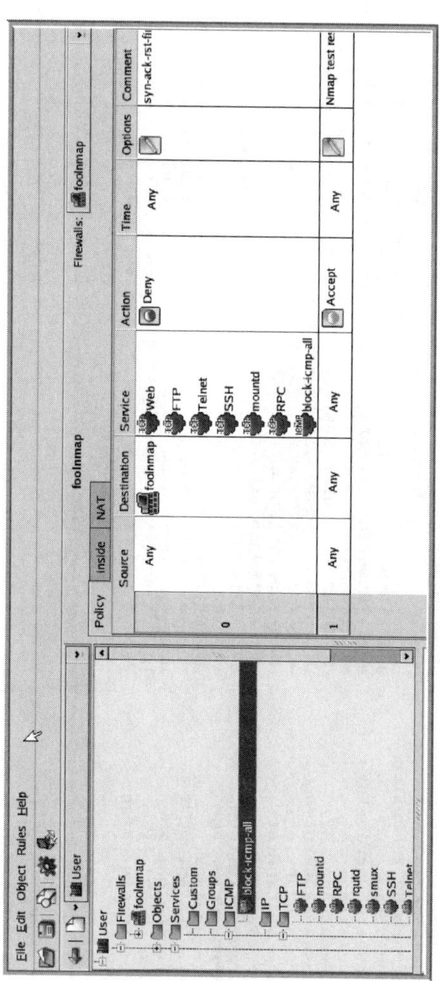

Figure 3.35 Rule-based access control.

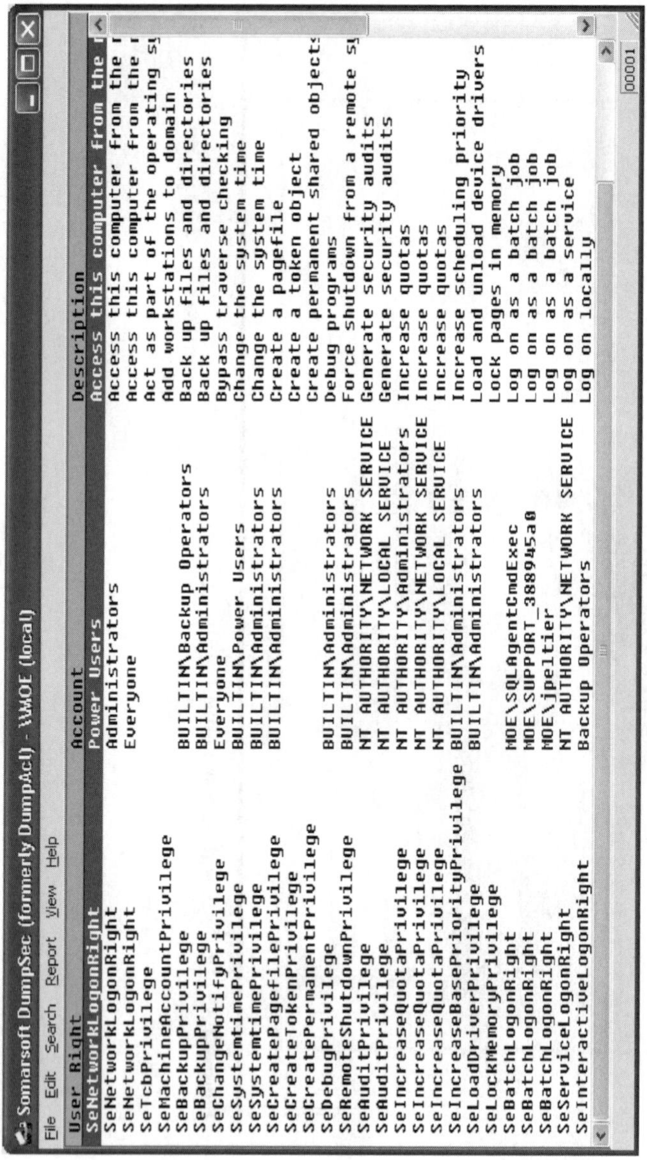

Somarsoft DumpSec (formerly DumpAcl) - \\MOE (local)

File Edit Search Report View Help

User Right	Account	Description
SeNetworkLogonRight	Power Users	Access this computer from the r
SeNetworkLogonRight	Administrators	Access this computer from the r
SeNetworkLogonRight	Everyone	Access this computer from the r
SeTcbPrivilege		Act as part of the operating sy
SeMachineAccountPrivilege		Add workstations to domain
SeBackupPrivilege	BUILTIN\Backup Operators	Back up files and directories
SeBackupPrivilege	BUILTIN\Administrators	Back up files and directories
SeChangeNotifyPrivilege	Everyone	Bypass traverse checking
SeSystemtimePrivilege	BUILTIN\Power Users	Change the system time
SeSystemtimePrivilege	BUILTIN\Administrators	Change the system time
SeCreatePagefilePrivilege	BUILTIN\Administrators	Create a pagefile
SeCreateTokenPrivilege		Create a token object
SeCreatePermanentPrivilege		Create permanent shared objects
SeDebugPrivilege	BUILTIN\Administrators	Debug programs
SeRemoteShutdownPrivilege	BUILTIN\Administrators	Force shutdown from a remote sy
SeAuditPrivilege	NT AUTHORITY\NETWORK SERVICE	Generate security audits
SeAuditPrivilege	NT AUTHORITY\LOCAL SERVICE	Generate security audits
SeIncreaseQuotaPrivilege	NT AUTHORITY\Administrators	Increase quotas
SeIncreaseQuotaPrivilege	NT AUTHORITY\NETWORK SERVICE	Increase quotas
SeIncreaseQuotaPrivilege	NT AUTHORITY\LOCAL SERVICE	Increase quotas
SeIncreaseBasePriorityPrivilege	BUILTIN\Administrators	Increase scheduling priority
SeLoadDriverPrivilege	BUILTIN\Administrators	Load and unload device drivers
SeLockMemoryPrivilege		Lock pages in memory
SeBatchLogonRight	MOE\SQLAgentCmdExec	Log on as a batch job
SeBatchLogonRight	MOE\SUPPORT_388945a0	Log on as a batch job
SeBatchLogonRight	MOE\jpeltier	Log on as a batch job
SeServiceLogonRight	NT AUTHORITY\NETWORK SERVICE	Log on as a service
SeInteractiveLogonRight	Backup Operators	Log on locally

00001

Figure 3.36 Microsoft access control list.

Single Sign-On

Another access control technique is Single Sign-On (SSO). Single sign-on is a bit of a myth. What is more prevalent is RSO or Reduced Sign-On. It becomes difficult for the average end user to remember so many different userIDs and passwords for all of the different systems and Web sites that require authentication. For people who work in IT or IS the number is about three times that of the average end user. Remembering all these passwords leads to a major security issue: weak passwords. It is human nature to pick the password that is easiest to remember that just meets the minimum requirements of the access control system. SSO provides a mechanism by which each user only has to remember one password and one userID. This single userID–password combination is entered only once and the SSO system grants access to all of the systems to which the user needs access. As you can imagine, it is difficult to find a mechanism that will complete all of the necessary authentication steps. Later in this section we discuss RADIUS, which is a current standard that is bringing information technology closer to the SSO goal than ever before.

Script-Based Single Sign-On

There are different ways that SSO can be implemented. An older method that is not very much used today is the script-based method of doing single sign-on. This is where you log into a primary network operating system and the NOS stores your passwords and authentication mechanism for other systems. When you log on, the network operating system passes your authentication credentials to all other systems. The drawback to script-based SSO is typically those passwords are stored in plaintext and they are transmitted over the network in plaintext. If you have ever written or seen a log-in script, you have an idea for how script-based SSO operates. The major drawback to the method is the lack of encryption of sensitive information, userIDs, and passwords. Any attacker running a network sniffer can uncover the authentication credentials and bypass the access control system in place.

Host-Based Single Sign-On

The SSO method that is more commonly used currently is host-based single sign-on. Host-based SSO uses a centralized authentication server that all other applications and systems utilize for authentication purposes. One of the major problems with any type of host-based single sign-on is you create an SPF, a Single Point of Failure. If that authentication server goes down, your network becomes nonfunctional. Because no authentication can take place it is as if all systems were lost on the network. A second security concern is what happens if that userID and password get compromised by an attacker? Does the attacker get access to only one system? No, the attacker gets access to everything. It's the keys to the access control kingdom.

Access Control Methods

There are three ways that a user can authenticate to access control systems: knowledge based, characteristics based, and possession based. Examples of knowledge-based authentication would be based on passwords or Personal Identification Numbers (PINs). Characteristics-based authentication would be biometrics or behavior such as a fingerprint reader or a voiceprint system. Possession-based authentication would include tokens and tickets. A token is typically a hardware device that can be stored in a pocket or on a key chain and carried with the user. These devices can be pricey and are easy to lose for many end users. The advantage to token-based authentication is that the token will introduce a level of complexity to the authentication and this helps mitigate the risk of weak passwords. The concept of a token when applied to a software environment instead of a hardware environment is known as a ticket. Some authentication protocols such as Kerberos use tickets as the way of passing authentication credentials. There are other less-known software packages that also make use of the term ticket for describing their authentication software.

One-Time Passwords

A one-time password is good for one log-in only. So what common type of network attack would a one-time password help stop? One-time passwords mitigate the risk of an attacker using a network sniffer to record a userID and password as they are sent over the network and reusing the credentials to authenticate to the access control system. One-time passwords should be good for one log-in only, but that does not mean that every manufacturer's one-time password implementation actually does that. There are some manufacturers that create a password that is usable for authentication for a short time period of around 50 seconds to a minute. Although this system mitigates the risk of a network sniffer attack slightly, it does not eliminate the threat completely. For an attacker to be successful in defeating the second type of one-time password system, the attacker has to be pretty darn fast at capturing and entering a legitimate user's userID and password before it expires.

Password Selection

Creating a standard for an organization's password selection is a difficult task. Password selection is another information security example where security and ease of use are opposite each other. Each password selection standard has to be created to fit each organization so that passwords are as resistant to attack as possible without creating a situation where the password is either written down or repeated calls to the help desk are necessary to change the password. Some of the most commonly used criteria for password selections include:

- Passwords should not be based on a dictionary word.
- Passwords should be changed regularly.
- Passwords should include at least one unique character.

In addition to selecting the strongest passwords possible the information security manager should have a count revocation process in place so you can revoke user accounts when an employee leaves the company or when an employee no longer needs permissions to access a resource. All of these security mechanisms are used to mitigate the risk of a password-guessing or password-cracking attack.

Access Control Goals

The primary goal of access control is to create nonrepudiation from a userID and password combination. Nonrepudiation can only exist when a userID is tied, without any chance of compromise, to one person. So if a message comes from a user's e-mail account we know that that user really sent the e-mail. Nonrepudiation is difficult based on just userID and password combinations because passwords can be cracked, guessed, borrowed, or stolen. All of these factors would stop true nonrepudiation. To create a system that moves closer to the goal of nonrepudiation, the authentication would require more than just a password. This is one of the biggest concepts for access control, two-factor authentication.

Two-Factor Authentication

Due to the inherent weaknesses in passwords, access control is improved when passwords are bundled with another mechanism for authentication. Two-factor authentication pulls from two of the three categories mentioned in the previous sections. These categories are:

- Something you know
- Something you have
- Something you are

For two-factor authentication to be the most effective the authentication has to be from two of the three categories. An example of a password and a PIN is not two-factor authentication. That scenario is just two examples of something you know. The information security manger should perform cost analysis to verify that two-factor authentication is appropriate for the organization. If this is the case, the information security manager should ensure that controls are in place because it will be one step stronger than passwords. Two-factor authentication will move the access control system closer to the goal of nonrepudiation.

RADIUS

One of the most commonly used host-based single sign-on technologies is RADIUS. RADIUS is the Remote Authentication Dial-In User Service. RADIUS is popular not just because of the single sign-on, but also because of newer wireless network authentication schemes. RADIUS is an authentication protocol that allows for the use of dynamic passwords. There are many examples of commercial products that allow for RADIUS authentication such as Microsoft's Active Directory on Windows Server 2000 and Windows Server 2003. RADIUS support is a component of the Internet Authentication Service (IAS). Other popular RADIUS manufacturers include Funk Software and their product Steel Belted Radius™. In addition to the number of commercially available RADIUS solutions there are also freeware RADIUS systems. Currently RADIUS is used as the authentication component of the 802.1x standard for network authentication.

802.1x

Originally 802.1x was a standard written for education institutions and campus-sized networks. Because of the very nature of a campus network the environment is dynamic and constantly changing. A student may be logging onto the university's network from her dorm room at noon and a campus lecture hall computer lab an hour later. With this sort of unique dynamic environment in mind the 802.1x standard was created. 802.1x provides extensible authentication through the use of its sister protocol Extensible Authentication Protocol (EAP). 802.1x and EAP change the role of authentication to the user for many components that were traditionally associated with the machine, such as IP address assignment via DHCP.

So when a user logs into the network authentication system it is the userID that specifies which IP address the user is going to have assigned to the system.

In addition to the assignment of a specific IP address the extensible component of EAP allows for other dynamic configuration to take place. For example, the network can dynamically configure itself to put the user on the correct Virtual Local Area Network (VLAN) with those resources to which the user needs to have access. Additional checks can also be done as part of the authentication. For example, software packages can ensure that the user is running the appropriate anti-virus or personal firewall. Also 802.1x can be used to dynamically load the correct firewall ruleset or ACL for the user. As long as the user is logging in with the correct userID these security controls will follow the user account to any location. 802.1x creates a network environment that has nothing to do with the hardware a user is using to access the network from, because the unique features of the network are tied to the user account.

The Role of RADIUS in 802.1x

RADIUS is often the back-end authentication mechanism for 802.1x networks. This may not be the case for long. There are newer protocols that are aiming to replace RADIUS as the most commonly used authentication system for SSO, RSO, wireless, and 802.1x. The newer proposed protocol is named Diameter. In typical computer geek humor Diameter is the name of the standard because diameter is twice radius. RADIUS uses UDP as its transport-layer protocol. As we discussed earlier in the chapter UDP is not connection-oriented so authentication packets can potentially be lost on the network without the client being made aware of the lost packet. Diameter is proposed to use TCP as its transport-layer protocol instead of UDP. This will provide greater reliability for Diameter-based authentication. It will be interesting to see how the Diameter/RADIUS standards work out over the next few years. Because RADIUS is so commonly used it may be difficult to replace.

TACACS

TACACS is another authentication protocol like the aforementioned RADIUS. Currently most organizations utilize TACACS+ instead of TACACS because of increased authentication options that TACACS+ can support. TACACS uses TCP for its transport-layer protocol and TACACS can provide much of the same functionality that RADIUS can as listed in the examples above.

Access Control Zone of Control

When it comes to access control, the zone of control is the area of an organization for which an information security manager is responsible for setting the security policy. Typically a zone of control is either a physical or a logical zone of control. One example of a physical zone of control would be the fourth floor of an office building. An example of a logical zone of control would be the research and development department. For a communication to be considered inside the zone of control both the sender and the receiver have to be located within the zone of control. This means the devices such as Internet-available Web sites do not fall into a zone of control because there is no mechanism to enforce a security policy on the entire Internet. This is true no matter how hard we wish it were otherwise.

Firewalls

There are many technical controls besides the access control systems, mentioned above, which can be put in place to help secure systems. One of the most popular information security controls is a firewall. A firewall is basically a device that is going to sit on your network and divide your network up into segments of trusted versus untrusted and different levels of trust on your network. By splitting up, or segmenting, your network a firewall is going to enforce your security policy. The firewall's enforcement will force users attempting to access resources on another segment to pass through the firewall's policy. This concept is illustrated in Figure 3.37.

Types of Firewalls

For an enterprise there are three primary types of firewalls. Please note that this discussion is of enterprise-class firewalls, which differ from personal firewalls which are discussed later in this chapter. An information security manager should be familiar with the three primary types of firewalls and the pros and cons of each type of device. The three types of firewalls are packet filter, stateful inspection, and proxy-based firewalls. Each of these devices has different strengths and weaknesses. If we are looking at the OSI model, the proxy-based firewall is an application-layer device. It works at the most complex layer of the OSI model. This concept is illustrated in Figure 3.38.

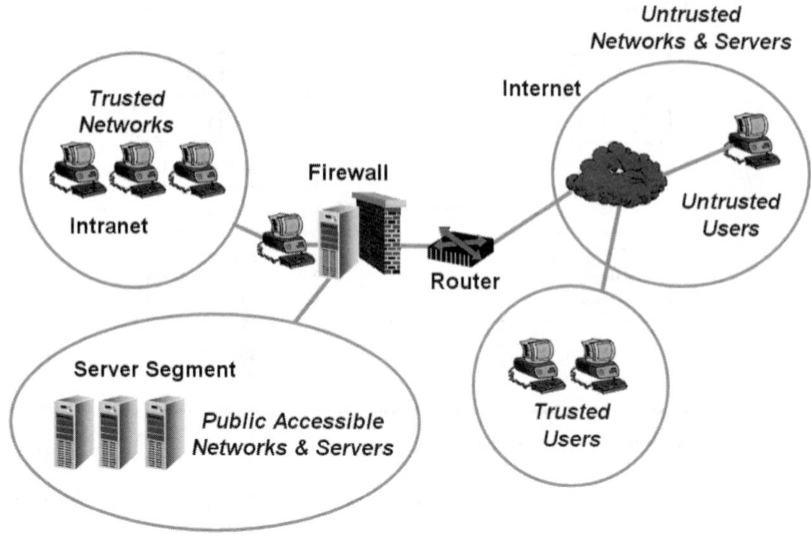

Figure 3.37 Firewall.

OSI Layer	Firewall
Application	Application Layer Gateway (Proxy)
Presentation	
Session	
Transport	
Network	Packet Filtering and Stateful Inspection
Data Link	
Physical	

Figure 3.38 OSI layers and firewalls.

Packet-Filtering Firewalls

The reason for this is packet filter firewalls were the first firewalls that really came about. Packet filter firewalls would basically be transparent to the user community. In this example this would be the user's IP stack talking to the server's IP stack with no interference from the firewall whatsoever. This concept is illustrated in Figure 3.39.

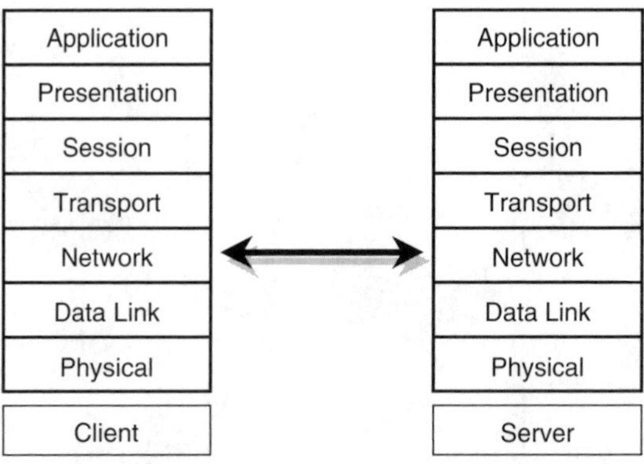

Figure 3.39 Packet filter communication.

Let's take a look at the packet filter firewall in action. In this example, a packet filter firewall is going to be configured to allow a corporate client machine to browse to Acme Corporation's Web site. This example will require a total of four configuration rules in the packet filter firewall. In order to do this we are going to have to configure a total of four rules on our packet filter firewall to allow this to happen. The basic format of the rules that we are going to put into this firewall is source, destination, source port, and destination port.

The first rule in the ruleset of a packet filter firewall would have a source of our corporate client, and a destination of a DNS server (Table 3.6). The DNS server's role is to resolve the name of www.acmecorp.com to an IP address so the information can be routed. The source port for

Table 3.6 Sample Packet Filter Ruleset

Rule Number	*Source*	*Destination*	*Source Port*	*Destination Port*	*Action*
1	Corporate Client	DNS Server	UDP Any	UDP-53	Accept
2	DNS Server	Corporate Client	UDP-53	UDP Any	Accept
3	Corporate Client	DNS Server	TCP 1025-65535	TCP-80	Accept
4	DNS Server	Corporate Client	TCP-80	TCP 1025-65535	Accept

the corporate client system is going to be some UDP port, and this is shown in the chart as UDP Any. UDP Any means there are 65,535 possibilities. The destination port is known and it will be UDP Port 53. That is the first rule in the packet filter firewall's ruleset.

Remember that just because the first rule is allowing outbound traffic that does not mean that the response packet is going to be allowed to come back in through the packet filter firewall. With only the first rule configured the client can query the DNS server but the response will be blocked. In order to get the response packet back to the corporate client a second rule is necessary. This second rule is configured with a source of the DNS server and a destination of the corporate client. The source port from the DNS server will be UDP port 53, but the destination port for our corporate client is unknown so the rule needs to be configured for UDP Any as the destination port. This second rule says that the DNS server can packet to the corporate client at any time as long as the source port is UDP Port 53. This means the DNS server can send network information to the corporate client at any time and this creates a bit of a security concern. These two rules simply allow for the corporate client to resolve www.acmecorp.com to an IP address.

Two more rules will need to be added to the ruleset in order to allow the client to actually browse to Acme Corporation's Web site. The next rule in the ruleset will permit the Web query from the corporate client to www.acmecorp.com. The source of this rule would be set to the corporate client and the destination would be set to www.acmecorp.com. The source port of this rule is unknown, but not quite as unknown as was the case with the UDP rules one and two. With TCP there are high ports that are dynamically used (this was described in detail earlier in this chapter); these ports are numbered from 1025–65,535. Although the source port is somewhat unknown, the destination port is. The destination port is going to be TCP port 80. The same conundrum applies to this rule as it did with the first rule. This rule only allows the outgoing packet and it does not allow the response in automatically. This is why rule four is necessary.

Rule four will allow www.acmecorp.com to respond to the corporate client. The source of this rule will be www.acmecorp.com and the destination will be our corporate client. The source port will be set to TCP Port 80, and the destination port will be set to TCP 1025 to 65,535.

Two rules in this configuration are going to introduce security problems for any organization. These are rules number two and four. These rules allow systems on the Internet to send information to corporate clients at any time as long as traffic originates on the appropriate ports. The even greater security concern is that a packet filter firewall restricts traffic to very, very few ports. If we are looking at the entire port space available, UDP has ports from 1 to 65,535 and TCP has the same range from 1 to

65,535. Of all of these ports (which number 131,000 and change) we are actually only securing 1024 of them which means we still have more than 129,000 ports that Internet systems can use to send unsolicited information to corporate clients. These major security concerns minimize the use of packet filter firewalls by most organizations.

Packet Filter Firewall Recap

Packet filter firewalls are the least secure of the three types of firewalls that are currently available. A packet filter firewall is often called the first generation firewall. Right now packet filter firewalls come free with the purchase of some other network device. Examples of these devices include low-end cable modems, low-end DSL modems, DSL routers, and low-end wireless access points. The major advantage to packet filter firewalls is that they are fast. These devices look at very little of the information inside a network packet. They basically look at source address, destination address, and ports to make the determination whether that information should be blocked or permitted. The major trade-off to the use of packet filter firewalls is relative level of security. A secondary advantage is cost. As mentioned before, the trade-off is the firewall creates holes that you could drive a truck through. Packet filter firewalls have another advantage in that they support custom-written applications as long as the applications use common transport-layer protocols such as TCP, UDP, and ICMP.

Stateful Inspection Firewalls

The next firewall that an information security manager should be aware of is the stateful inspection firewall. A stateful inspection firewall is built upon packet filter firewall technology, but the stateful inspection firewall mitigates some of the exposures that are associated with the packet filter firewall. A stateful inspection firewall builds, through a process usually known as the inspection engine, a small dynamic database with connection information. This process monitors incoming and outgoing packets in terms of the direction. This concept is illustrated in Figure 3.40.

Because of the connection state database used by stateful inspection firewalls the configuration for the same example that is used above for the packet filter firewall would require only two rules (Table 3.7). The first rule would be the same as the packer filter firewall first rule and the second rule in the stateful inspection ruleset would be the same as the fourth rule in the packet filter firewall. The stateful inspection firewall Table 3.7) creates the packet filter firewall's Rules 2 and Rules 4 dynamically. In this example, if the corporate client makes a request outbound, the firewall will open up a response rule for 40 seconds to 2 minutes

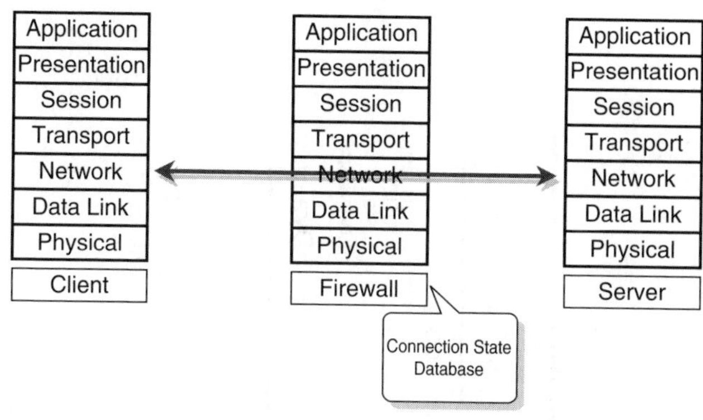

Figure 3.40 Stateful inspection firewalls.

depending on the manufacturer. This allows the network information to come back into the corporate network as long as the response takes less than the 40 seconds to 2 minutes. If the response takes longer than the 40 seconds to 2 minute window, the firewall will have closed the dynamic rule and will drop the packet. Likewise if this corporate client has not created a request the firewall will drop packets that originate from the Internet.

This process of dynamically opening and closing the response rules in the stateful inspection firewall removes the primary exposure points from the packet filter firewall. This process is not without certain trade-offs. Because the stateful inspection firewall can dynamically reconfigure itself, and therefore the security policy of the organization, it is vulnerable to spoofing attacks. These spoofing attacks are when an attacker creates fraudulent packets that fool the stateful inspection firewall into assuming the packet was a request originating from an internal resource. In actuality the spoofed packet was created by an Internet attacker with the intent of creating an incorrect dynamic rule to allow the attacker's packets into the corporate network.

Most modern stateful inspection firewalls include good anti-spoofing features to protect against such attacks. However, not all firewalls contain anti-spoofing technology and some manufacturers have a more secure anti-spoofing feature than other manufacturers do. With some of the earliest stateful inspection firewalls, the firewall could not use both anti-spoofing functionality and network address translation. This left the information security manager with the choice of using either one of the security mechanisms. In this case, most organizations chose network address translation over anti-spoofing and this decision left many organizations open to spoofing attacks. An advantage to stateful inspection firewalls is that stateful inspection tends to be relatively inexpensive technology when

Table 3.7 Stateful Inspection Ruleset

Rule Number	*Source*	*Destination*	*Source Port*	*Destination Port*	*Action*	*Type*
1	Corporate Client	DNS Server	UDP Any	UDP-53	Accept	Static
2	DNS Server	Corporate Client	TCP-80	TCP 1025-65535	Accept	Static
	DNS Server	Corporate Client	UDP-53	UDP Any	Accept	Dynamic
	Corporate Client	DNS Server	TCP 1025-65535	TCP-80	Accept	Dynamic

compared to proxy-based firewalls. The higher-end stateful inspection devices can sell for as much as $15,000 but the lower-end devices can sell for as little as $20.

Stateful Inspection Recap

Another feature of the stateful inspection firewall is that it operates on the network layer of the OSI model. Because of this, the stateful inspection firewall will make its primary determinations based on source address, destination address, and ports. This allows the stateful inspection firewall to be very fast. The drawbacks to stateful inspection technology are the anti-spoofing problem (mentioned above) and the sometimes complex configuration of the anti-spoofing feature. Another advantage to stateful inspection firewalls is they also tend to support custom applications as well as the packet filter firewalls do.

Proxy Firewalls

With two of the three primary types of firewalls already discussed, stateful inspection and packet filter, we just have one left to discuss. The last firewall is the proxy-based firewall (Figure 3.41). The proxy-based firewall actually maintains two separate one-way conversations. In the example above, a proxy-based firewall configuration never allows the corporate user to directly access the Internet. The corporate user sends information to the proxy firewall, and the firewall makes the request to the Internet. Proxy-based firewalls operate at the application layer of the OSI model, and because of this the filtering decisions are based upon the proxy firewall processing more network information. Consequently proxy-based firewalls tend to be slower and they tend to be more expensive. Because a proxy-based firewall is using more information to determine whether

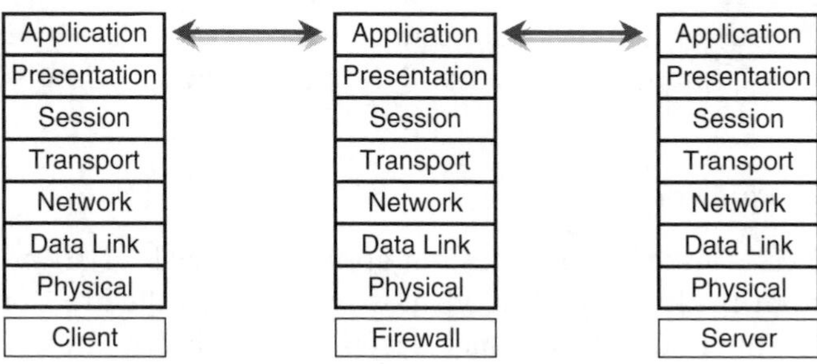

Figure 3.41 Proxy firewalls OSI model.

to pass or block a packet it could, in theory, be more secure than any other type of device. Because of the performance issues most proxy-based firewalls tend to use the same type of decision processes that a stateful inspection firewall is going to use.

Caching

To provide greater speed most proxy-based firewalls are actually proxy cache firewalls. When a corporate user browses www.acmecorp.com using a proxy cache firewall the packets are usually not sent to the Internet and a local, or cached, copy of www.acmecorp.com is sent back to the client. What actually happens is that when one user requests www.acmecorp.com, a copy of the first request is saved to either the hard drive or the memory of the proxy cache firewall. All subsequent users that request www.acmecorp.com are just seeing a copy of www.acmecorp.com's Web page from the hard drive of the proxy cache firewall. Regardless of whether the proxy firewall has a cache feature, there are two primary types of proxy-based firewalls. These are transparent and nontransparent proxy firewalls.

Transparent and Nontransparent Proxy Firewalls

There are transparent and nontransparent proxy-based firewalls. A transparent proxy requires no client configuration and this is used most often in hotel and other high user turnover networks. A nontransparent proxy requires configuration in every Web browser in order to access the Internet through the proxy firewall. A transparent proxy is easier on corporate user communities but less secure because network clients do not need to have a configuration change to know where the proxy server is. A nontransparent proxy introduces administrative overhead because each client has to be configured. The advantage to the nontransparent proxy based firewall is that malicious or inappropriate users on a network will not have access to the Internet from the network until the proxy configuration is changed.

Proxy Firewall Recap

Proxy servers do not support custom applications well. If an organization has a custom banking application most proxy firewalls are not going to support it. This is due to the fact that the proxy-based firewall looks at the data portion of the packet and in order for the proxy-based firewall to determine if the packet is a legitimate packet requires that the proxy firewall understand that application. For every application that the proxy firewall is going to support, it requires custom-written code to support that application on the firewall. Common applications such as Web requests (HTTP), file transfer (FTP), and e-mail, are almost always supported. Proxy-based firewalls support most common applications, but custom applications are usually not supported. Proxy-based firewalls tend to be slower, but have the theoretical ability to be more secure. As a rule of thumb, proxy-based firewalls tend to be the most expensive because of the additional hardware and software necessary to perform the deeper inspection of the packet.

Network Segmentation/Subdomain Isolation

Firewalls and access control are some of the most common security controls, but they are by no means the entire list of security controls. The next group of controls that we discuss is controls that create segmentation or subdomain isolation. These controls are common network devices such as routers, switches, and firewalls. The goal here is to stop one part of the network from directly interacting with another.

Virtual Local Area Networks (VLANs)

One of the most common controls used to create network segmentation/subdomain isolation is a Virtual Local Area Network or VLAN (Figure 3.42). In the previous section on 802.1X we mentioned dynamic reconfiguration of the network based on the userID such that each user was only able to interact with those devices and resources the user needed access to regardless of from where the user logged in. That's what a VLAN is: a virtual local area network. A VLAN will take a physical switch and break it into two or more logical network segments. To the user community, it appears that there are actually two physical switches and two completely separate networks. The drawback to VLANs is that VLANs require configuration and sometimes the configuration can be difficult. The disadvantages of VLANs are VLANs can be expensive and typically a skilled attacker will be able to jump from one virtual local area network to another virtual local area network. VLANs will still stop inadvertent traffic from one network to another network.

Physical Distance

The cheapest option to create segmentation or subdomain isolation is to use physical distance (Figure 3.43). This method can also be called inserting

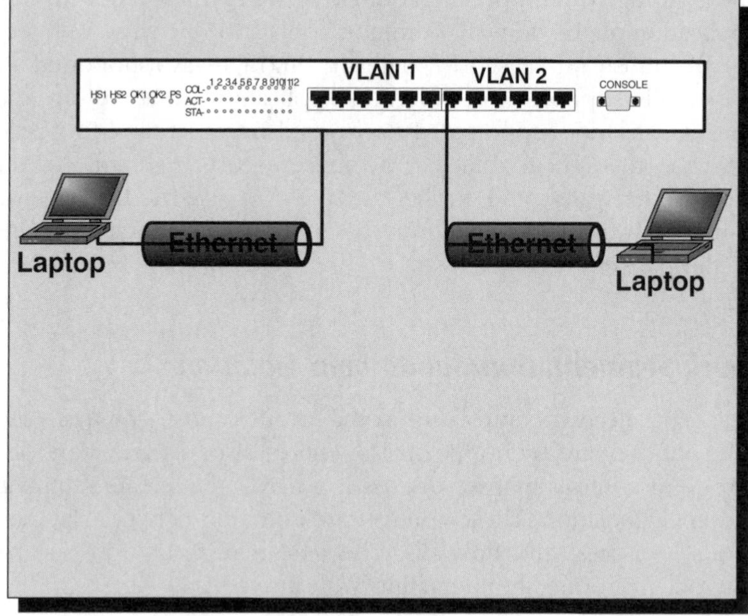

Figure 3.42 Virtual local area network.

an air gap. To create physical distance the networks do not physically touch each other. This of course costs nothing because air is all you are inserting. The drawback here is the security. If somebody inadvertently plugs network A into network B your security is gone away. The advantage to physical distance is that the cost is free; the disadvantage is that the security is minimal.

Subnetting for Isolation

Segmentation or subdomain isolation can also be created above the physical layer at the network layer by assigning two different IP address ranges for the different networks. In the example in Figure 3.44 one network has 10.X.X.X IP addresses and the other has 192.168.X.X IP addresses. Assigning to separate ranges will stop the two networks from communicating with each other. The problem is if a user recognizes that the other network exists she can reconfigure her systems and become part of that other network. So, once again the cost here is none, but the drawback is a user can potentially get around it.

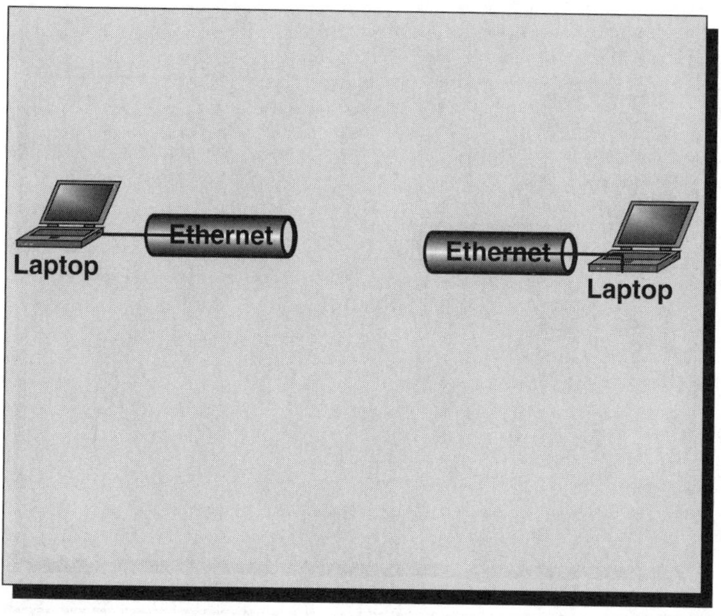

Figure 3.43 Physical distance.

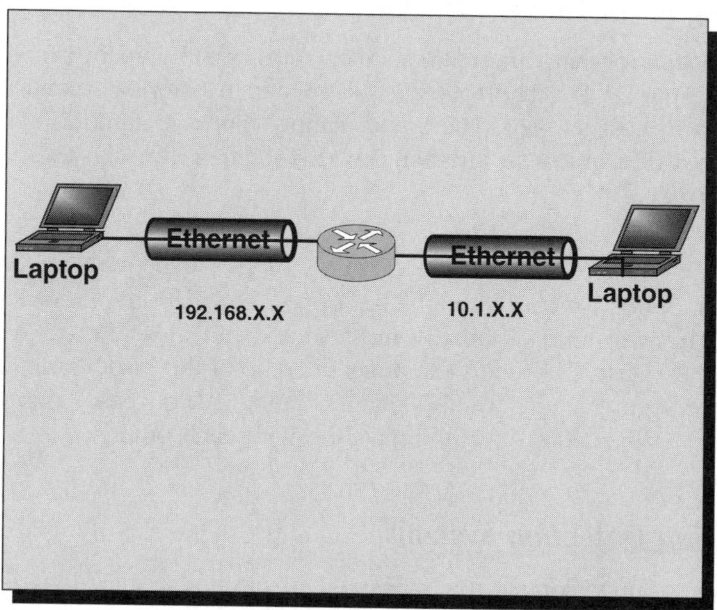

Figure 3.44 Subnetting.

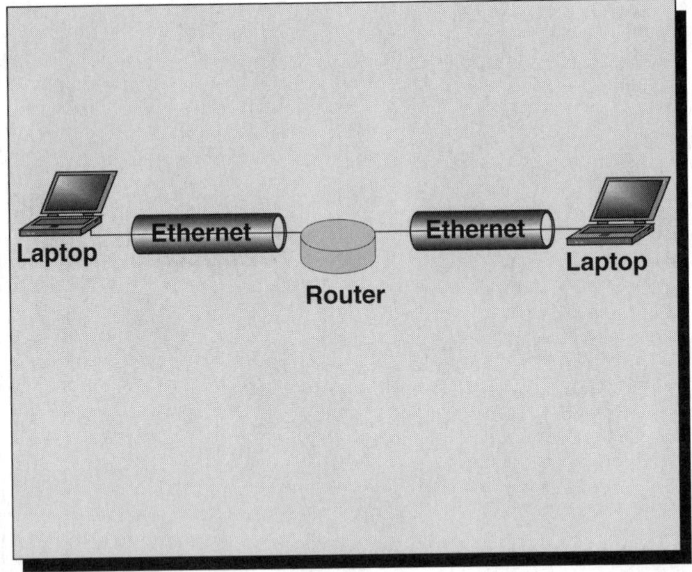

Figure 3.45 Routing.

Routing for Isolation

Another control that can create segmentation or subdomain isolation is a router (Figure 3.45). The router is far greater in complexity and security but also in cost as well. The router simply blocks communication from one network segment to another network segment through an ACL.

Firewall for Isolation

The best option is going to be the last option and that's the firewall (Figure 3.46). This will tend to be the most secure but also tend to have the greatest expense. These are examples of some of the most common ways to create segmentation or subdomain isolation. All of these controls stop different groups from directly interacting with each other.

Intrusion Detection Systems

Another security control that we need to discuss is intrusion detection systems. In order to understand intrusion detection systems we need to start by discussing intrusions.

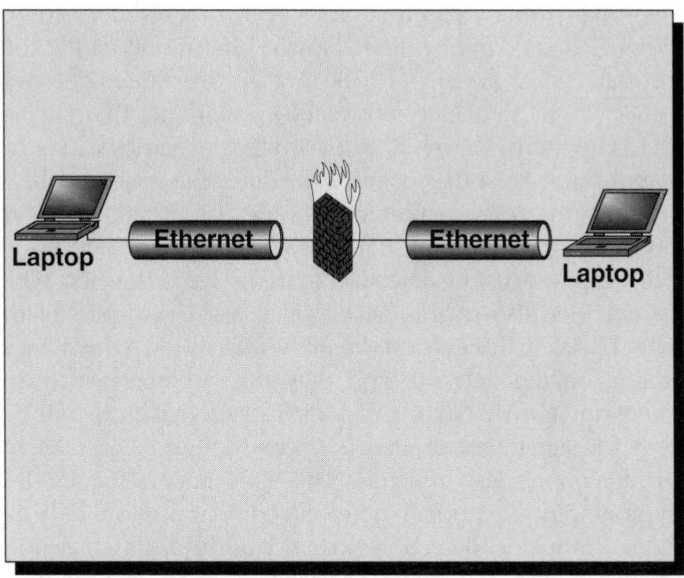

Figure 3.46 Firewall.

Types of Intrusions

Intrusions are typically broken down as internal versus external. Most statistics are showing that about 70 percent of intrusions are going to be done by internal employees. External intrusions are going to be the hackers coming in from outside the network or over the Internet. In addition to internal and external intrusions there are many motivations for intrusions. These are unintentional and malicious intrusions. The vast majority of intrusions are malicious. It used to be that it was possible to accidentally intrude into a system (think of the movie *War Games*) but this has not been common for quite some time. Keep in mind the majority of intrusions usually come from internal sources.

Network- Versus Host-Based Intrusion Detection Systems

Intrusion detection systems have two primary ways to gather information. They can be either Host-based Intrusion Detection Systems (HIDS) or Network-based Intrusion Detection Systems (NIDS). Host-based intrusion detection systems are going to monitor a single critical device, such as a server, a firewall, or a router. And HIDS are going to monitor for attacks coming directly to that critical device.

There are many, many different types of host-based intrusion detection systems. There is a program called Tripwire that monitors file integrity to make sure that critical system files do not get modified. There are other packages that will monitor network traffic coming into that device. Finally there are HIDS systems that will monitor log file entries to see what that system is reporting. Host-based intrusion detection systems are currently in vogue right now. More manufacturers are using host-based and more organizations are implementing host-based intrusion detection.

Network-based intrusion detection systems were the first IDS systems on the market. Because of this NIDS still has a larger part of the install base. NIDSs basically function as a network sniffer, which means they monitor traffic on the network and they then compare it against other types of network traffic. NIDS can look for anomalies or NIDS systems can monitor for signatures of attacks. Network-based intrusion detection systems are becoming less effective. The main reason for this is because of the cryptography to protect network communication and attacks. A network-based intrusion detection system cannot distinguish normal network traffic from attack network traffic if there is encryption in place. NIDS systems are also very prone to false positives. This is where a NIDS device mistakes normal network traffic for a network attack. Many organizations have moved away from using network-based intrusion detection systems because of the thousands of alerts (some false positives and some legitimate) that were generated on a daily basis.

IDS Information Processing

Regardless of how the intrusion detection system gathers the information (host-based or network-based) there is going to be some sort of back-end processing mechanism that is going to be used. IDS systems can either use attack signature identification or anomaly identification. Attack signature identification works like your anti-virus package. Your anti-virus package looks at things and says, "Oh, this matches the signature, or this matches the function, or it looks like a virus." Once this has happened the IDS system will alert you that there is a virus on your system. This type of processing is limited because it only knows what is known. A signature for an attack may not have been written, distributed, or installed. In some cases the update process can take up to a month.

Anomaly Identification

The current trend in IDS processing is a move towards anomaly identification. There are two primary ways to achieve anomaly identification.

One is that an anomaly identifier can set up a baseline for your network. Note: This is different from the baseline that we discussed previously, which concerns a baseline level of controls. Anomaly identification baseline requires the IDS system to monitor your network for a period of time such as 30 days, 60 days, or 90 days. During this period the anomaly identification will determine how your network functions on a day-to-day basis. The IDS system will report any deviations from this standard baseline in terms of network usage and standard network traffic. That is the first type of anomaly identification. The second type of anomaly identification monitors your network for any type of traffic that deviates from the RFCs or other guideline for the specific type of network traffic. If there is any deviation from those RFCs, the IDS system will alert you to the type of inappropriate network traffic.

This method for IDS processing is very popular right now and it tends to be very commonly used by security device manufacturers. The disadvantage to anomaly identification is new applications. New applications are released often and many do not comply with RFCs. This type of anomaly identification may not work well in your organization if your organization is using Voice over IP. This is because Voice over IP does not conform to RFC standards. Back when they were designing TCP and UDP they were not envisioning people using it for voice information. So the RFC writers never thought about it. This results in an anomaly identification system reporting Voice over IP traffic as a kind of fragmentation attack usage.

IDS Response

Regardless of the processing of the IDS system, signature matching or anomaly identification, the security of IDS is up to the response. This is how the IDS system may benefit the security of your organization. There are two primary types of response to an IDS alert. The basic choice of IDS response breaks down to automated versus manual. An automated response occurs when your intrusion detection system can actively block. This is usually achieved when the IDS system can send a message to a firewall or to a router and have it reconfigure its security profile or access control list to block the attacker's address. The drawback to automated responses from an IDS is that if the IDS is using anomaly identification as its processing facility and a new application emerges that does not conform to the RFCs the IDS system may block legitimate traffic. In addition, if an attacker recognizes that your IDS system is performing automated blocking, the attacker can start spoofing packets that include a known attack to create a denial-of-service attack. An attacker can use fraudulent source addresses to get the intrusion detection system to block everybody and can create a denial-of-service attack.

Manual Response — If you choose not to use an automated response your IDS can utilize a manual response. A manual response can use a pager or an e-mail or a screen pop-up to send notification to the response team. The biggest problem with any manual response is operator inattention. Operator inattention is going to be directly related to the number of false positives your intrusion detection system creates. This reduces the likelihood of a new application being blocked or a denial-of-service attack, but many attacks may be allowed to continue if the alert for the IDS system is ignored.

IDS Versus IPS

There have been three generations of IDS systems (Figure 3.47), if IPS is considered the third generation of IDS and not a new technology. The first generation of IDS systems provided no mechanism for automated response or other communication with the organization's firewall. These devices did not communicate, they did not talk to each other, and they did not understand each other; they were basically two independent security controls.

The second generation began when intrusion detection systems could communicate with firewalls and routers and engage in some active defending. The third generation is intrusion prevention. Intrusion prevention packages are supposed to encompass intrusion detection technology with vulnerability assessment technology with anti-virus technology and firewall technology all built into one security device or software package. In the event of an attack, your intrusion prevention system is supposed to make the first check to see if your network's even vulnerable to that attack. This should take place before any alert (manual or automated) is made. Next, if your organization is vulnerable to the attack and that attack is directed at a vulnerable system, the IPS system should proceed to automated blocking mode. Currently most IPS packages do not have all of the mentioned functionality, but each version of the IPS system moves closer to that end.

Cryptography

Cryptography is different from the controls that we have previously discussed because cryptography, or crypto, protects information while it is in transit from one system to another. In addition, crypto is different

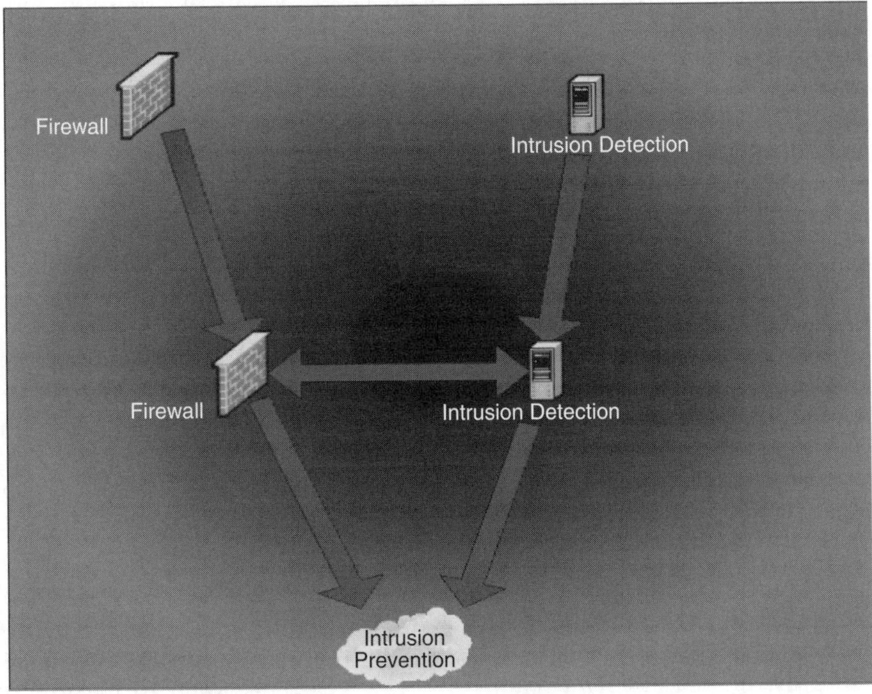

Figure 3.47 Intrusion detection generations.

from other controls because crypto has its own CIA triad. Other controls utilize a CIA triad of confidentiality, integrity, and availability. In cryptography the A of the CIA triad is authenticity. This is because cryptography and availability are diametrically opposed forces that work against each other. For example, if a file is encrypted it is less available and if a file is highly available it is less encrypted. The CIA triad for cryptography is illustrated in Figure 3.48.

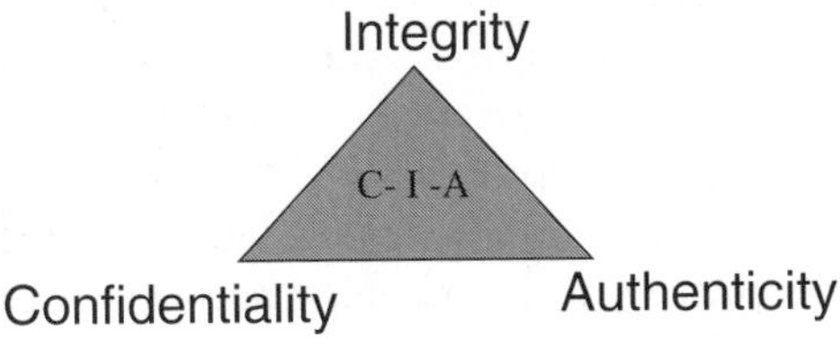

Figure 3.48 Cryptography CIA triad.

In this chapter we cover cryptography in greater depth than other topics because many exam candidates are more uncomfortable with cryptography than any other concept.

Goals of Cryptography

The primary goal of cryptography is secrecy. Cryptography has its basis in military operations. Crypto was designed as a way to exchange information so the enemy cannot intercept and read the communication. The history of cryptography can be traced back to either the Egyptians with hieroglyphics or the Greeks with the Scytale cipher. We do not spend any more time on the history of cryptography because it is not really part of the CISM exam.

It is still important to know the primary goal of cryptography is secrecy. There are also some secondary goals with cryptography. The easiest way to explain the secondary goals of crypto is to look at an example. For this example let's pretend that we going to send a message from military headquarters to the military troops in the field. The content of this message is to tell the troops to move 3 kilometers south of the city. There are several goals that we need to achieve with this message. We want to make sure the enemy (1) can't read that message; (2) we want to make sure that when the message reaches the troops in the field they know it actually came from headquarters and didn't come from the enemy; and (3) we want to ensure that the message contents are accurate. A very simple miscalculation in encrypting and decrypting the message, such as adding an extra 0, could switch the contents of the message from 3 kilometers to 30 kilometers and our troops could lose their lives.

Nonrepudiation

A term that is commonly used with cryptography is nonrepudiation of origin. We have discussed nonrepudiation in the earlier section on access control. Nonrepudiation of origin guarantees the message's authenticity and integrity. With nonrepudiation of origin you know the person who sent it and you know the message has not been modified in the encryption process. Nonrepudiation of origin does not include confidentiality, but that is still the primary goal of cryptography.

Whether cryptography is an art or a science is something that can be well debated. I tend to view cryptography as a science because of the amount of math that is included in crypto. However, as I tend to spend more time working cryptography I see more of the artistry to it.

Cryptographic Definitions

What is cryptography to the information security manager? Cryptography is the implementation of the science of secret writing. This is often called by academic sorts as applied cryptography. In information security the cryptosystem is the overlying concept that provides the secrecy of the message. The cryptosystem includes the mechanism for exchange of cryptographic keys, the message integrity system, the algorithm that provides the transformation of the data, and the ability to authenticate the sender.

The secrecy our cryptosystem gives us is not absolute secrecy; it does not keep a message secret forever. Rather, the cryptosystem's goal is to keep the message secret for such a period of time that if the cryptosystem were defeated it would take longer than the time the message has to be kept secret. The goal of the cryptosystem is twofold: first is the time component we just discussed and the second is the cost to defeat the cryptosystem. If it costs our competitor more money to defeat our cryptosystem than the costs of the message if it is read by our competitor then the cryptosystem has accomplished its goal. For example, if we are trying to protect our corporate earnings information, and we are going to make the earnings announcement 30 days from today, we would only need cryptography strong enough to stop the attacker or cryptanalyst from breaking the crypt on the message for 30 days.

A term that is related to the breaking of cryptography is work factor. Work factor is the amount of time, effort, and resources that it takes to defeat the cryptosystem. Work factor does not just refer to the amount of CPU time necessary to defeat the cryptosystem, but also the time that is necessary to develop the system that will go about defeating the cryptosystem as well.

If our competitor is trying to break our encrypted corporate earnings statement by defeating our cryptosystem then our competitor is using cryptanalysis. Cryptanalysis is the term for trying to defeat the cryptosystem without the appropriate key. A term that is similar to cryptanalysis is cryptology. The academic study of cryptosystems that includes the study of the relative strength of the cryptosystem but performing cryptanalysis is cryptology.

Our cryptosystem transforms data from one form to another. The form that is able to be read by anyone is called plaintext or cleartext. Once the data has been processed through the cryptosystem, it becomes readable by only the intended recipient and this type of scrambled data is called ciphertext.

Enciphering and deciphering are cryptographic mechanisms. Encipher is to go from plaintext/cleartext to ciphertext. Decipher is a process with which I am sure you are all familiar. I get this regularly when I am out

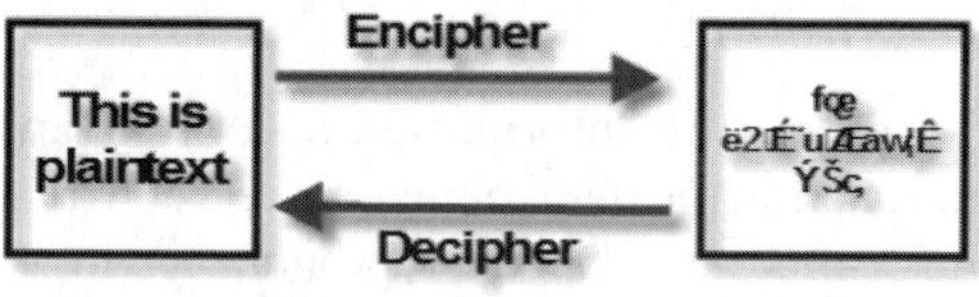

Figure 3.49 Encipher–decipher.

of town, like yesterday. My wife will take down phone messages for me and when I get home I always have to decipher the phone messages because it always appears that the cat wrote them, because I can't determine exactly what those messages say. What I am trying to do is figure out what the message said. The process of deciphering is to attempt to uncover the plaintext from the ciphertext. These concepts are illustrated in Figure 3.49.

Kerckhoff's Principle

In 1883, a mathematician named Auguste Kerckhoff published a paper. In this paper he stated that the only secret component of a cryptosystem should be the key. The component of the cryptosystem that actually transforms the data is the algorithm. The algorithm is pretty easy to distinguish from the rest of the cryptosystem; it is the part with all the math involved in it. Kerckhoff stated that all encryption algorithms should be publicly known because this is the only way that an algorithm can be reviewed for security holes. Kerckhoff also stated that any algorithm that was not publicly known would have more security holes than a publicly known algorithm. This axiom is still true today; most cryptosystems use algorithms that are publicly known. This means that anyone can look at most algorithms to see how the transformation of data occurs. So if it's not how we transform the data that's secret, what keeps the message secret?

It's the key. The key is like the password for cryptography. One of the greatest tasks of the information security manager in the field of cryptography is keeping the key secure.

Key Clustering and Key Escrow

Because the encryption key always needs to be kept secret, it can present a problem distributing keys to our user community. Many users can lose their encryption keys, and the data often still needs to be recovered. One of the many components that allows for this data to be recovered is key clustering. With key clustering another key can be used to encrypt and decrypt the data. Another term that works along with key clustering is key escrow. Key escrow is when a key, often used in emergency purposes, is distributed to different individuals. This allows for the data to be recovered only when two people are working together. This stops an administrator from using his key for malicious purposes.

The Algorithm

The algorithm is going to be the part of cryptography that actually transforms the data. The way I think of the algorithm is that it is the math part that actually switches the bits from one format to another. It's a component of the cryptosystem as we mentioned before.

Private or Secret Key Cryptography

Private key cryptography is also called symmetric key cryptography. The best way to explain private key cryptography is through an analogy. The best analogy of private key cryptography is if we picture a safe as our cryptosystem. So imagine I want to encrypt a message for Larry and the cryptosystem is going to be a safe. I begin by writing a message that states, "Meet me at the bridge at midnight." This is now our message that we wish to encrypt. In order to encrypt the message I walk up to the safe and I open the door. In order to open the safe I need to put the combination into the safe. Once I have placed the message in the safe and closed the door I have encrypted the message.

Now anyone can walk by and see that there is a safe, just as an attacker can see that a message is encrypted on the network. Unless the attacker has some kind of superpowers, she is not going to be able to actually look in the safe and determine what the message says. Later, when it is time for Larry to decrypt and read the message, he must walk up to the safe, put in the combination, open the door, and finally, read the message. The combination in this analogy is the key. The combination to the safe is the same when I encrypted the message and when Larry opened the safe to decrypt the message. As the combination illustrates, there is only one key with private key cryptography. This message must be given to both parties before the message can be encrypted and decrypted.

This type of cryptography is known as symmetric cryptography, because the process that is done to decrypt the message is the exact opposite of the process used to encrypt the message. With private key cryptography the greatest challenge is to keep the private key secure. There is an old adage: two people can keep a secret when one is dead. When applied to private key cryptography, it is of critical importance to keep the private key secure. In our above analogy of the safe, we need to ensure that the secret key (the combination) is never written down, and especially that it is never written down on a sticky note and attached to the safe. Private key cryptography can have some problems with key distribution and key management (the exchange of the combination of the safe). Typically private key cryptography is going to be simpler to set up for a small user community. However, private key cryptography does not scale to large numbers of users because the number of key pairs (combinations) that need to be managed grows quite large quickly. In most cases private key cryptography is considered to be faster than public key cryptography, but less secure. The next item that we discuss is public key cryptography which is generally considered more secure but slower than private key cryptography.

As we mentioned before, private key cryptography utilizes a single key, which is used to both encrypt and decrypt the data. This key needs to be distributed to all parties. The hard part is how do you distribute to this key to people; how do you give them this information? Usually this is going to take place in some out-of-band mechanism. Unfortunately the most common way for this key to be exchanged is through e-mail which is not a secure mechanism. The second most common method is the fax machine, which is once again not a secure mechanism. The third most common method is through a phone conversation.

Another issue of private key crypto is key recovery. In this example I am setting up a Virtual Private Network (VPN) connection to the Commuter Hospital and Data Corporation (Chad). Chad and I decide to set up a VPN between our offices and I call the administrator for Chad's firewall, I give him the key, he plugs it into his VPN device, and we communicate just fine. Sometime later Chad and I get in a big fight because his favorite wrestler is the Wacko Taco, whereas mine is the Salsa Slammer. We decide that we can't work together anymore so I need to revoke your access from the Chad corporation. How do I go about making sure there are no copies of that key that exist anywhere at the Chad offices? The problem is, I told it to the administrator and he wrote it down. It is impossible to make sure I get a copy of that key back from him. In addition I would have put the brain-sucking device on him and make sure I get that piece of information out of his brain. This just goes to show that key recovery of private key cryptographic systems can result in some tricky situations. More common than the brain sucker is just having to replace the keys and reissue keys to everyone else.

Another problem with private key cryptography is the storage and destruction of those keys. An information security manager needs to make sure that the keys are going to be handled securely, that the keys are not going to be written down, and if there are any written copies they are going to be destroyed at the appropriate time.You also run into problems with key strength. Because these keys can be generated by humans they often are weak keys because they tend to be:

- Short
- Based on a dictionary word
- Contain only letters and numbers

Just as we mentioned with passwords, the keys for private key cryptosystems need to be securely chosen.

Examples of Private Key Cryptography

When it comes to examples of private key cryptography, the two most commonly used examples are the Data Encryption Standard (DES) and the Advanced Encryption Standard (AES). DES was originally developed by IBM in the 1960s, under the codename of Lucifer. In 1977–1978 the American National Standards Institute (ANSI) approved DES as a standard. Eventually it became a NIST standard and in 1987 the U.S. government threatened to decertify DES. DES is a 56-bit algorithm and in 1987 security concerns started to arise because computers were getting faster and everyone knew that eventually most computers would be able to brute force a DES key at 56-bits. The U.S. government proposed a switch to a classified 80-bit algorithm called the Skipjack algorithm. The major issue with Skipjack was the government backdoor that was the clipper chip. Skipjack was intended to be implemented in secure hardware and the encrypting Skipjack chip was to be put into only secure machines. Once the clipper chip story was leaked to the media, public outcry forced the government to stop supporting the clipper chip. Skipjack is a large part of the reason for software-based encryption being so popular today.

When the Skipjack effort failed, the government through NIST recertified DES for five-year terms in both 1988 and 1993. In 1999 NIST no longer certified DES and the certification moved to Triple-DES (3DES). Triple-DES is basically performing DES encryption on a message three times. We discuss 3DES later in this section. DES is a nonlinear block cipher that uses a 64-bit block of text. DES is considered a 56-bit algorithm, but DES is actually a 64-bit algorithm. The difference is due to the fact that 8 bits are not used for transposing or changing the data; these bits are used for error checking. These bits are referred to as the parity bits. A 56-bit key creates 70 quadrillion possible keys. DES uses 16 rounds of simple operations, substitution, and transposition. Substitution is switching one bit for another, and transposition is switching the order of the bits. The DES algorithm is known, so DES security is derived from the secrecy of the key.

DES has four modes of operation. The first mode is the default mode for most DES implementations and it is the Electronic Code Book. The problem with ECB mode is that you are going to see the nonrandomness of the ciphertext. The next mode of DES is Cipher Block Chaining (CBC): this is the process illustrated in the block cipher section of this chapter. CBC works by combining a little bit of the ciphertext from the previous message and combining it with the key for the next block so that the key becomes randomized. It defeats that resulting nonrandomness of the ciphertext. The third mode of DES is cipher feedback mode, Cipher feedback mode operates by combining the ciphertext from the previous message with the plaintext from the following message to help disguise the nonrandomness of the language being used. The last mode of DES is output feedback mode (OFB). This is the one instance where DES functions as a stream cipher. OFB uses a key stream generator and it exclusively ORings (OR) the plaintext before encrypting the message with the normal DES process.

Double-DES and Triple-DES — Double-DES was popular for about two weeks. You may remember briefly seeing Double-DES VPN implementations that had to be upgraded to Triple-DES when the cryptanalysts realized that Double-DES was not really any more secure than Single-DES. Triple-DES is still widely used and as mentioned before 3DES simply performs DES encryption three times on a single message. Because the message is encrypted three times the 3DES process is quite slow. 3DES is still popular, but it is becoming a legacy cryptosystem as it has been supplanted by AES.

The Advanced Encryption Standard

Because it was possible to crack DES and performing DES three times with Triple-DES was slow, in 1997 the government proposed the hunt for a new encryption algorithm, AES. The AES project was announced, and as opposed to how things were handled with Skipjack, NIST along with the NSA allowed algorithms to be published and all testing to be made public. In 1998 15 candidate algorithms were submitted and in 1999 five finalists were selected.

Eventually the AES project selected the Rijndael algorithm which was created by two Belgians. Rijndael eventually won because of the algorithm's complexity and speed. In 2001, NIST and the NSA allowed for a one-year comment period where cryptologists could review the algorithm and test it for cryptographic strength. Later in 2001 AES was certified for the next five years. This means that the first certification of AES expires this year (2006) and what happens with AES will be interesting to see. AES is similar to DES in that it is a block cipher. AES has different modes, and it usually uses 128-bit blocks. AES also allows for a variable key length, anywhere from a 128-bit to 256-bit key, which is significantly longer than the keys used for plain DES. The mathematical problem is based on polynomials. AES has, for most cryptanalysts, been easy to analyze but most of the attacks have failed against it. There have been some successful attacks against AES because of the way AES picks the data encrypting keys. The method is not random enough and so there are actually some mathematical prediction attacks. As of this writing the attacks only slightly reduce the strength of AES and messages encrypted with AES are still considered incredibly secure.

Public Key Cryptography

The other type of cryptography opposite that of private key cryptography is public key cryptography. I'll try to explain public key crypto by modifying the analogy that we used above. In this example we have the same safe from our previous analogy, but this time picture the safe having a mail slot on the top of it. The process starts the same as before when I write, "Meet me at the bridge at midnight," on a piece of paper. We now have our message. To encrypt this message we simply drop the message into the mail slot on top of the safe. Anybody can walk by and drop something in the mail slot. In this analogy the mail slot represents our public key. This is the key that is available for everyone and in this example the public key is used to encrypt the message.

Now how do we go about decrypting the message? Are we going to reach our hand down the mail slot, grab the message, and pull it out? Not this time. Public key cryptography is an asymmetric process. This means that we are going to use a different process from the encryption to decrypt the message. To get the message we are going to decrypt the safe by putting in the combination and opening the door. This combination represents the private key. Please don't confuse the two keys. There is private key cryptography (the example above) and the private key in public key cryptography, which is the example here. This private key needs to be known by only one person: the person decrypting the message. No one else needs to know the combination to the safe. Public key cryptography has two keys: one to encrypt the message and another key to decrypt the message. The public key can be read by all, but the key still needs to be protected from modification and damage. The private key needs to be kept private and if this key is exposed our public key cryptosystem will provide no confidentiality. This concept can also be explained as asymmetric cryptography or as public key cryptography that has two keys.

The major advantage to public key cryptography is that public key cryptography allows for better scalability. If we have a job function at our organization where every day it requires a message to be decrypted and one day I am out of the office and I can't decrypt the message, what do we do? Someone else cannot decrypt that particular message so we have to reassign somebody else and have him decrypt a new message that is encrypted with his public key. With public key cryptography you do not share keys. This private key is kept only by the owner and is used for decrypting the messages.

In public key cryptography the private and public keys are related to each other such that anything that is encrypted with the public key can be decrypted with the private key and anything that's encrypted with the private key can be decrypted with the public key. So these two keys are related to each other. However, you can't have one half of the equation, the private key, and be able to determine what the public key is or have the public key and determine what the private key is. The mathematical problem is related to the difficulty of factoring very large prime numbers. One of the most interesting examples of factoring prime numbers is the number 3701; it happens to be a number where the only two factors are 37 and 73. It's a product of those two prime numbers being multiplied together. So when you are encrypting a message with the public key all you have is 37; when you are encrypting a message with the private key all you have is 73.

As mentioned above, public key cryptography uses two keys, a public key and a private key. Public key cryptography is a one-way function. We discuss one-way functions at greater length later in the chapter, but for now understand that a one-way function is simple to do in one direction, but very difficult to do in the other direction. Dropping a glass off a table is a good example of this concept. Breaking the glass is very easy to do, but it is very difficult to do the reverse process: to recreate the glass from the glass shards. Public key cryptography is a one-way function.

Public key cryptography creates a mathematical trapdoor that allows the encrypted message to be revealed. After all, public key cryptography is breakable given a long enough time. Remember the mathematical problem is factoring very large prime numbers that have been multiplied together. A computer will eventually be successful in figuring out the two prime numbers, but at current speeds it will take trillions of years. A cryptographic concept similar to public key cryptography is elliptical curve cryptography. Elliptical curve cryptography is like public key cryptography in construct and uses, but it uses a different mathematical problem. Elliptical curve cryptography is not based on factoring two prime numbers that have been multiplied together as is public key cryptography. ECC uses the mathematical problem of finding two points on a parabola. Elliptical curve cryptography is supposedly faster than traditional public key cryptography. The RSA algorithm that is part of the Secure Sockets Layer (SSL) protocol is the best example of a public key algorithm.

When it comes to public key cryptography key distribution and management it's more difficult to set up public key cryptography initially, but once it is up and running, especially in large implementations public key cryptography is going to be the way to go. In large part this is because public key cryptography allows for easier ongoing administration. Typically there is going to be an automated process where you are going to have key generation and key distribution. People are going to be able to request their own keys and the keys are going to be generated by a server or other system and sent out to the user. The key recovery process for public key cryptography is something that's a bit interesting. With public key cryptography typically the key recovery process is simply to list that key as bad in the server that issued that key. This process is actually done through something called the certificate revocation list. We discuss this more in the upcoming section on PKI components. When it comes to key strength you usually do not have the same problems with public key cryptography that you do with private key cryptography. The complexity of keys is greater because the entire process is computer generated.

Public key cryptography requires network components in order to function. These components are referred to as public key infrastructure, and are covered later in this chapter.

Stream Ciphers

In this section we look at the methods that a cryptosystem can use for transforming data. The two most common options are block ciphers and stream ciphers. A stream cipher (Figure 3.50) encrypts the message a bit

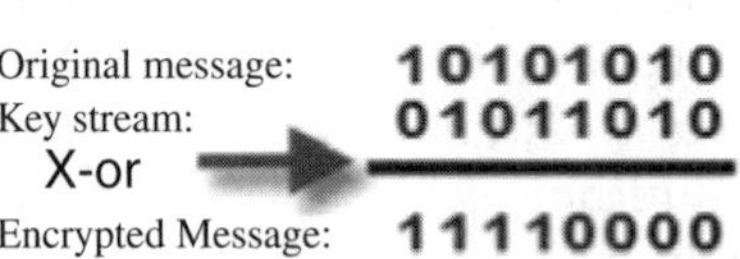
Take the following example:
Original message: 10101010
Key stream: 01011010
X-or
Encrypted Message: 11110000

Figure 3.50 Stream ciphers.

of text at a time. This means that a stream cipher breaks a message down into 1s and 0s before the message is encrypted. To encrypt the stream of ones and zeros from the message the stream cipher uses a component known as a key stream generator. The key is then input into the key stream generator to generate a stream of random ones and zeros. The original message is then put through a mathematical process known as exclusive ORing (X-OR) where the two bits are compared. If the bit from the original message is a one and the bit from the key stream generator is a one then the encrypted message would send out a zero or the first bit. If the two bits are the same the X-OR process yields zero; if the two bits are different the process yields a one.

Because a stream cipher is generally less complex in terms of lines of code necessary to implement it, a stream cipher is often used in hardware. The encryption protocol Wired Equivalent Privacy (WEP) used by wireless networks uses a stream cipher called RC4.

Because the randomness of the ones and zeros coming from the key stream generator is critical to the security of a stream cipher, there are rules that must apply to a key stream generator.

1. A key stream generator must have long periods where the key stream does not repeat.
2. The key stream must be functionally complex, which means that the key stream cannot be the key and then the key in reverse and then the key.
3. The key stream must be statistically unpredictable which means there are no patterns to the key stream.
4. The key stream has to be unbiased which means there are as many ones as zeros.
5. The key stream cannot be easily related to the key.

All of the rules increase the security and secrecy of a stream cipher (see Figure 3.51).

The only unique concept of the one-time pad is that this key could only be used for one message and when that message is done the key is discarded and never used again. And so the key that you would be using, you would have a whole bunch of onion skins with you and they would be sent the next message you are using; you are just using the next key online and headquarters would have to keep track of them. So the keys were exchanged ahead of time. This is what it looks like if I am drawing it out in video; this shows you the key goes into the key stream generator. It generates the key stream of random ones and zeros. The plaintext gets exclusively ORd with the key stream and gives you the resulting ciphertext. What's the most common stream cipher that we are seeing today?

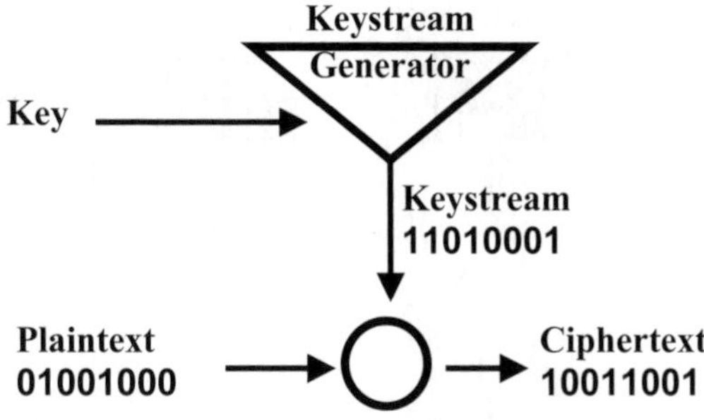

Figure 3.51 Stream cipher.

Block Ciphers

As opposed to encrypting a bit of text at a time a block cipher encrypts a block of text at a time. Block ciphers work on fixed-size blocks of text; as an example a block could be 8 characters. The Data Encryption Standard happens to be a 64-bit block cipher, and it just so happens that 64 bits equate to roughly 8 characters. The problem with encrypting this way is a relationship can form between the input and the output. If we are encrypting the same block of text with the same key we are going to get the same resulting ciphertext. When this permutation is created patterns can be discovered in the ciphertext. This is due to the fact that words or phrases in the English language are used more frequently than other words and combinations. These patterns start to be noticeable in the ciphertext. That form of cryptanalysis is called the ciphertext-only attack.

Block ciphers (Figure 3.52) are more complex than stream ciphers in terms of the mathematical operations. Typically you are not going to see block ciphers implemented in hardware but typically you are going to see block ciphers implemented in software.

Devices like DES accelerator cards and Triple-DES accelerator cards are the exception to the hardware/software rule of cryptosystems. In most cases block ciphers are implemented in software.

The Initialization Vector

The Initialization Vector (IV) is an attempt to try to make encrypted messages appear different so that permutations are not defined between the plaintext and the ciphertext. The advantage to using an initialization vector is that the nonrandom pattern of language will not be apparent in the resulting ciphertext. An initialization vector is a way to make the key appear more random. The initialization vector is a string that will be

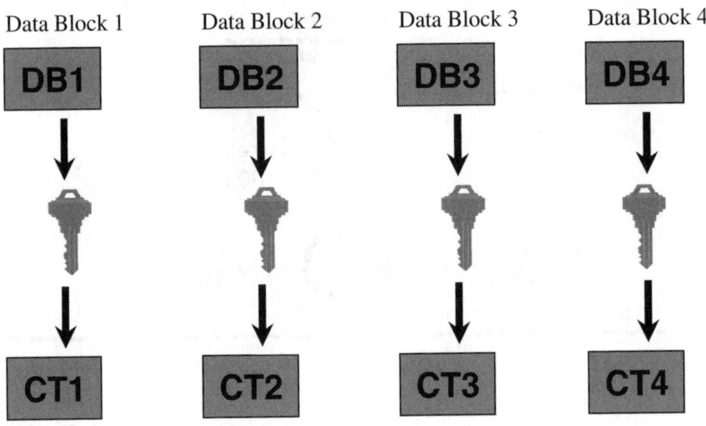

Figure 3.52 Block cipher.

combined with the key for each message in such a way that the resulting ciphertext will look unique even if the corresponding plaintext is exactly the same. This concept can be expanded on to form another cryptographic concept: the Cipher Block Chain (CBC). A CBC begins with a pseudo-random initialization vector being chosen from the permissible IV values. Once this is done each future message uses part of the previous message's ciphertext to combine with the key to create a more random-appearing key. This concept is easier to see through illustration and it is shown in the diagram in Figure 3.53.

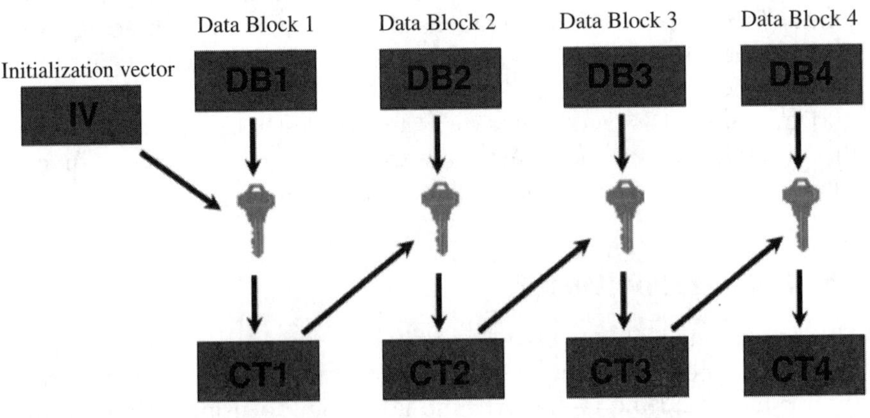

Figure 3.53 Cipher block chaining.

Methods of Attack

Bad guys do cryptanalysis. Well, not just guys and not all of them are bad, but cryptanalysis is the process of trying to defeat cryptography without the secret key. The most common type of cryptanalysis is the ciphertext-only attack. This is where an attacker looks at the encrypted messages with a utility such as a network sniffer and looks at the stream of ciphertext to see if patterns emerge. A twist on the ciphertext-only attack is known as the birthday attack. With a birthday attack an attacker looks at the stream of messages to find two or more messages that are the same being transmitted. This is much more efficient than the attacker encrypting his own message and then watching the stream of encrypted messages for one that matches his encrypted message. The birthday attack takes advantage of the nonrandomness of the English language. Because some words are used more frequently than others, those words will be encrypted more often than others, and will show up more often in the stream of encrypted words. There are many other types of attack a cryptanalyst can do. Here are some of the types of attack and a brief summary of what the attack is:

- *Known plaintext attack:* Sample of ciphertext and the corresponding plaintext is available as well.
- *Chosen plaintext attack:* Cryptosystem is loaded with hidden key provided and input of any plaintext. The attacker can then see the output to determine how the algorithm functions.
- *Adaptive chosen plaintext attack:* Same as above except you are able to choose plaintext samples dynamically, and alter your choice based on results of previous encryptions.
- *Chosen ciphertext attack:* The cryptanalyst may choose a piece of ciphertext and attempt to obtain the corresponding decrypted plaintext.
- *Man-in-the-middle attack:* The attacker inserts himself during the key exchange between parties and intercepts the encryption keys.
- *Timing attacks:* Repeatedly measuring exact execution times of cryptographic operations.
- *Brute force attack:* Trying all keys until correct key is identified.
- *Rubber hose cryptanalysis:* Includes beating, threatening, and extorting to get the secret key.
- *Implementation attacks:* Regardless of the construction of the algorithm the implementation is usually going create the insecurities. A great example of this appears in the WEP that uses the RC4 algorithm. The RC4 algorithm works fine for its intended purpose. RC4 was meant to be a one-time pad. A one-time pad

is where the key is used for one message and then discarded and never used again. The problem with RC4 was when it was implemented in WEP is that the key is reused over and over again, which made that algorithm's implementation vulnerable to attack.

One-Way Functions

At this point we have discussed two of the three components of the CIA triad for crypto. We have covered confidentiality and we have covered authenticity. What we need to discuss now is how to ensure the integrity of the message. As mentioned before, one-way functions are important to cryptography. Public key cryptography or asymmetrical cryptography is just one example of a one-way function.

Another example of a one-way function is message hashing. Hashing is a way of verifying integrity of the information. Hash functions allow you to create an electronic fingerprint for the contents of that file. The most common algorithms for creating hashes are Message Digest 5 (MD5) or Secure Hash Algorithm (SHA). Electronic fingerprints or hashes have to be unique. This uniqueness is necessary because two documents that are very similar need to create completely different hashes to help protect the files from forgery. If an attacker were to modify any one bit in a file, the electronic fingerprint is going to have to change by at least 50 percent of its bits. This stops an attacker from looking at two similar electronic fingerprints and determining that similar hash values mean that the files are two similar files. One of the most common places to see MD5 values is when you are downloading utilities from hacker Web sites.

MD5 checksums (Figure 3.54) provide integrity. When you download a file you can make sure that it hasn't been modified by generating an MD5 sum for the file on your local machine and comparing this MD5 to the MD5 posted on the site. MD5 checksums also provide a way to protect you from downloading Trojaned versions of utilities. MD5 checksums are not 100 percent foolproof. The problem is usually Web administrators who keep these hash values stored in the same directory as the file that you are downloading. If a hacker breaks into the Web site they could modify the download file and then they could also modify the corresponding checksum so that the compromised file will look as if it were a legitimate file. The MD5 algorithm is going to generate a 128-bit electronic fingerprint. The SHA algorithm is going to generate a slightly larger 160-bit fingerprint. Hashes are important because those checksums are used as the first part of setting up digital signatures.

.: Archive Search Results for: wireless

#	Rank	File Name	MD5 Checksum
1	Full Match	9907-exploits/ATT_DoS.txt	16dcd9165b23bf5d2e952fa134284b43
DoS attack on AT&T Wireless text-messaging service			
2	Full Match	advisories/linux-security/linux-security.1-9.txt	61dfd39ef48fbea8f6afa7dbfb9027df
Linux Security Week June 26 - In this issue: The default configuration of wu-ftpd is vulnerable to remote users gaining root access, Simple Object Access Protocol (SOAP), Network Intrusion Detection Using Snort, Updates for Mandrake bind, cdrecord, dump, fdutils, kdesu, xemacs, and xlockmore, Remote users can cause a FreeBSD system to panic and reboot via bugs in the processing of IP options in the FreeBSD IP stack, Remote vulnerabilities exist with all Zope-2.0 releases, NetBSD: libdes vulnerability, RedHat: 2.2.16 Kernel Released, Bastille Linux Review, and Intel admits wireless security concerns. Homepage: http://www.linuxsecurity.com. By Benjamin Thomas			

Figure 3.54 MD5 checksums.

Digital Signatures

The goal of a digital signature is to authenticate the sender to the receiver and also to verify that the message has not been modified. What you end up with is a block of data attached to your message and that is going to be the digital signature. Each user of digital signatures is going to have a public–private key pair. The public key is going to be published and available to everyone and in many cases it is called a digital certificate. The private key is held by the individual and the public key is published as a certificate and it can be published at a number of different places. What is a digital signature?

We know a digital signature starts with the electronic fingerprint, or hash. The process begins by running the contents of the message through a hashing algorithm such as MD5.

Once that task is done, the hash is encrypted with the sender's private key. The encrypted hash is then appended to the end of the message. This is shown in Figure 3.55. The message is then sent across the Internet to the receiver. Anyone can read the message while it is in transit. The goal of the digital signature is nonrepudiation and not confidentiality. The receiver receives the message and extracts the encrypted hash from the rest of the message. The receiver then processes the message through a hash algorithm as well. This generates the MD5 checksum of the message.

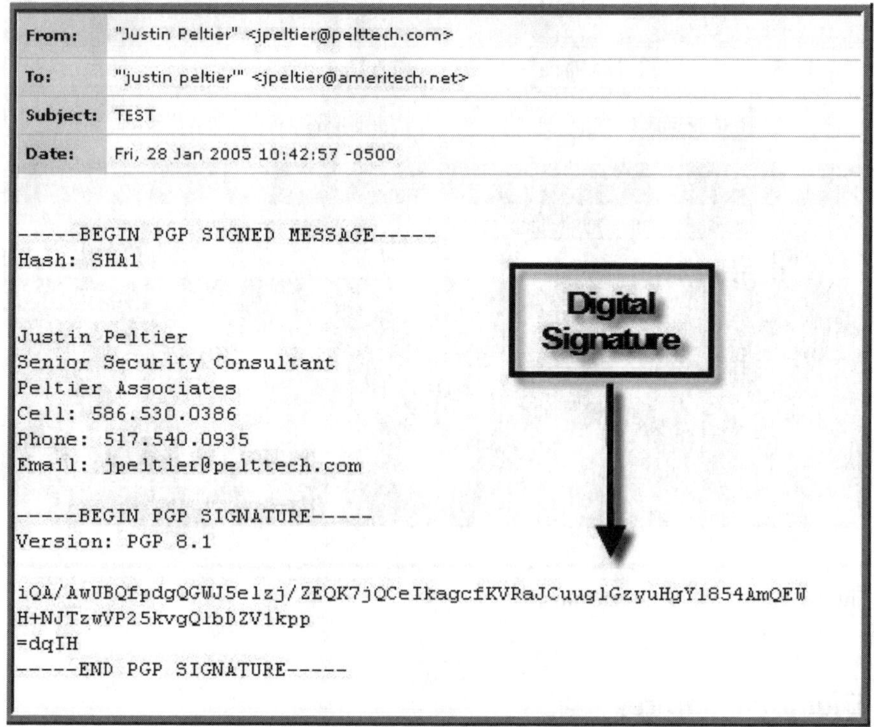

From: "Justin Peltier" <jpeltier@pelttech.com>
To: "'justin peltier'" <jpeltier@ameritech.net>
Subject: TEST
Date: Fri, 28 Jan 2005 10:42:57 -0500
-----BEGIN PGP SIGNED MESSAGE-----
Hash: SHA1
Digital Signature
Justin Peltier
Senior Security Consultant
Peltier Associates
Cell: 586.530.0386
Phone: 517.540.0935
Email: jpeltier@pelttech.com
-----BEGIN PGP SIGNATURE-----
Version: PGP 8.1
iQA/AwUBQfpdgQGWJ5elzj/ZEQK7jQCeIkagcfKVRaJCuuglGzyuHgY1854AmQEW
H+NJTzwVP25kvgQlbDZV1kpp
=dqIH
-----END PGP SIGNATURE-----

Figure 3.55 Digital signatures.

Once the checksum is created, the receiver then uses the sender's public key to decrypt the encrypted hash that was attached to the message. Once the hash is decrypted the receiver compares the sender's hash value with the receiver's hash value. If the hash values are the same the message is assured to have been written by the sender and not modified in transit.

Classic Cryptographic Systems

There are many different systems for encrypting information. The first type of encryption system that we will look at is the classical substitution cipher.

Substitution Ciphers

If you ever pulled a secret decoder ring out of a box of your morning cereal, then you possessed a classical substitution cipher (Figure 3.56). A classical substitution cipher will replace one letter from the plaintext

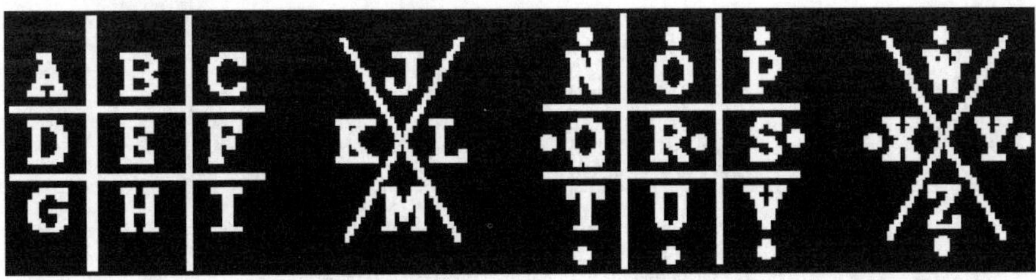

Figure 3.56 Substitution ciphers.

message with another character to make the message encrypted. One of the first cryptosystems used an algorithm known as the Caesar cipher. The Caesar cipher substituted characters by shifting the alphabet three spaces off a certain letter. For example, if we pick the letter "A" the cipher would move it forward three characters to the letter "D". We could then substitute all the letters "A" in our original message with the letter "D".

Here is an example of our original message:

This is a plaintext message

Once we have processed the messages through the Caesar cipher using "C" as our key, the encrypted message becomes:

Wklv lv d sodlqwhaw phvvdjh

Transposition Ciphers

As opposed to classical substitution ciphers our algorithm could use a transposition or permutation cipher. This cipher does not change one letter for another, rather it changes the sequence of the letters in the message. A simple way to perform this operation is to write all the letters of a word in reverse order.

Here is an example of the original message:

This is a plaintext message

Once we have processed the message through our transposition cipher we would end up with a message like this:

sihT si a txetnialp egassem

ABCDEFGHIJKLMNOPQRSTUVWXYZ
BCDEFGHIJKLMNOPQRSTUVWXYZA
CDEFGHIJKLMNOPQRSTUVWXYZAB
DEFGHIJKLMNOPQRSTUVWXYZABC
EFGHIJKLMNOPQRSTUVWXYZABCD
FGHIJKLMNOPQRSTUVWXYZABCDE
GHIJKLMNOPQRSTUVWXYZABCDEF
HIJKLMNOPQRSTUVWXYZABCDEFG
IJKLMNOPQRSTUVWXYZABCDEFGH
JKLMNOPQRSTUVWXYZABCDEFGHI
KLMNOPQRSTUVWXYZABCDEFGHIJ
LMNOPQRSTUVWXYZABCDEFGHIJK
MNOPQRSTUVWXYZABCDEFGHIJKL
NOPQRSTUVWXYZABCDEFGHIJKLM
OPQRSTUVWXYZABCDEFGHIJKLMN
PQRSTUVWXYZABCDEFGHIJKLMNO
QRSTUVWXYZABCDEFGHIJKLMNOP
RSTUVWXYZABCDEFGHIJKLMNOPQ
STUVWXYZABCDEFGHIJKLMNOPQR
TUVWXYZABCDEFGHIJKLMNOPQRS
UVWXYZABCDEFGHIJKLMNOPQRST
VWXYZABCDEFGHIJKLMNOPQRSTU
WXYZABCDEFGHIJKLMNOPQRSTUV
XYZABCDEFGHIJKLMNOPQRSTUVW
YZABCDEFGHIJKLMNOPQRSTUVWX
ZABCDEFGHIJKLMNOPQRSTUVWXY

Figure 3.57 Poly-alphabetic ciphers.

Poly-Alphabetic Cipher

There are many other encryption systems available. Another type of cipher is the poly-alphabetic cipher (Figure 3.57). The Caesar cipher that we discussed before is also an example of a poly-alphabetic cipher in that the message was switched from one alphabet (the one starting with the letter "A") to a new alphabet (the one starting with the letter "D"). Another cipher is the running key cipher.

Running Key Cipher

With a running key cipher all communications come from a pre-agreed-upon set of characters. For example, if I gave you the encrypted message 1234, it probably would not seem like a very well-encrypted message. But if we previously agreed that 1 would mean building one, two meant floor two, three meant room three, and four meant room four, and a message was written on the whiteboard of room four, we would have a secret message.

Sca**m**mers ar**e** taking advantag**e** of recen**t** news that **M**icrosoft is asking us**e**rs to verify th**a**t **t**hey have a legiti**m**ate copy of W**i**n**d**ows, a security firm said Friday.

According to Webse**n**se Secur**i**ty Labs, e-mails bearin**g** t**h**e spoofed address of securi**t**y@microsoft.com **a**nd wi**t**h **t**he **h**eading "Microsoft Windows Updat**e**" ask recipients to update and/or validate **b**oth the Windows' se**ri**al number and the customer's cre**d**it card information on a bo**g**us W**e**b site.

Figure 3.58 Concealment.

Concealment

Concealment is another type of encryption system. If you skip every third word in a message there may a secret message hidden in it. In the example in Figure 3.58 the boldface letters create a hidden message.

Steganography

Steganography is not exactly a form of cryptography; it is actually hiding in plain sight. The advantage of steganogaphy is that no one can tell that a secret message is being sent. With cryptography, any time a message is sent someone could look at the message with a packet sniffer and determine that the message is encrypted. With steganography, the same person with a packet sniffer would only see a photo or a music file go by. Steganography hides hidden messages in pictures or music files. Steganography works because the photo in the example is made up of magnetic ones and zeros. Every byte creates a single pixel of the picture. Each byte is made up of eight ones and zeros. Of the eight bits that make up a single byte, there is one bit which is called the least-significant bit. This bit is just thrown away and not paid any attention to. You can actually take those least-significant bits and switch them to ones and zeros to make your hidden message. When a network sniffer or eavesdropper sees the photo the stegoed bits are ignored for graphic- and sound-rendering purposes. Changing these least-significant bits does not affect the way that picture looks or the music file sounds but it allows a hidden message from the configuration of those ones and zeros in the picture or in the sound file. This technology is currently being used in more organizations and the fear is that terrorist organizations are using similar technology. There was an Internet rumor spreading around rapidly in 2002 that terrorists

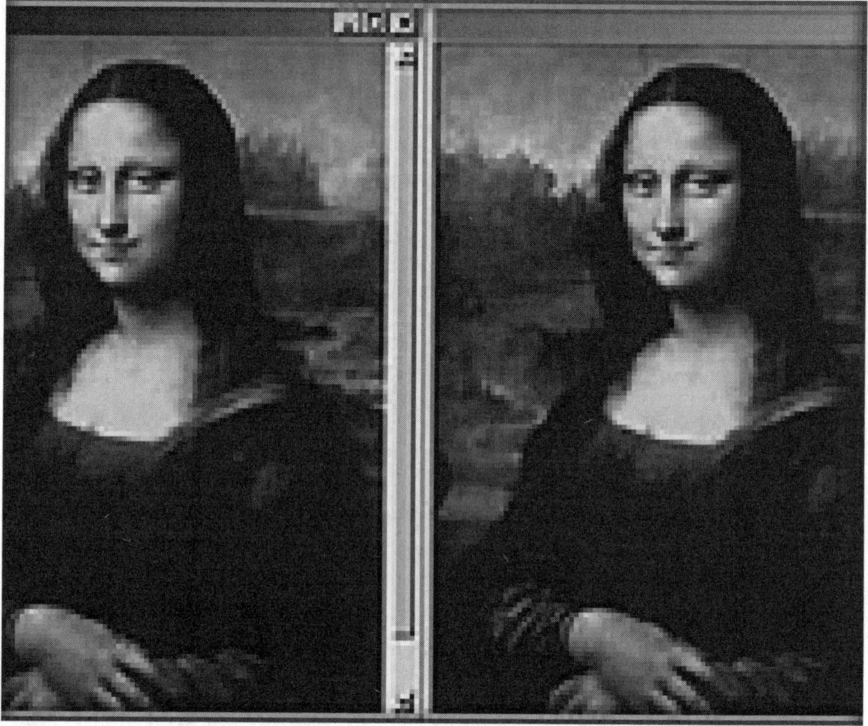

Figure 3.59 Steganography.

were posting hidden messages in steganographed picture files on Internet auction sites. After some research, the rumor was found to be false. In Figure 3.59 one of the pictures contains a hidden message. Can you spot it?

Codes

Do you remember your days of using pig Latin to speak in messages in front of your parents? Pig Latin was an example of a code. A code is just a generic term for agreeing on a system to hide messages.

Encryption Machines

There are also encryption machines (Figure 3.60). The machine that was most popular was called the enigma machine. The enigma machine had numerous rotors and switches that were attached to a typewriter keyboard. When the wheels and switches were turned by the Nazis in World War II

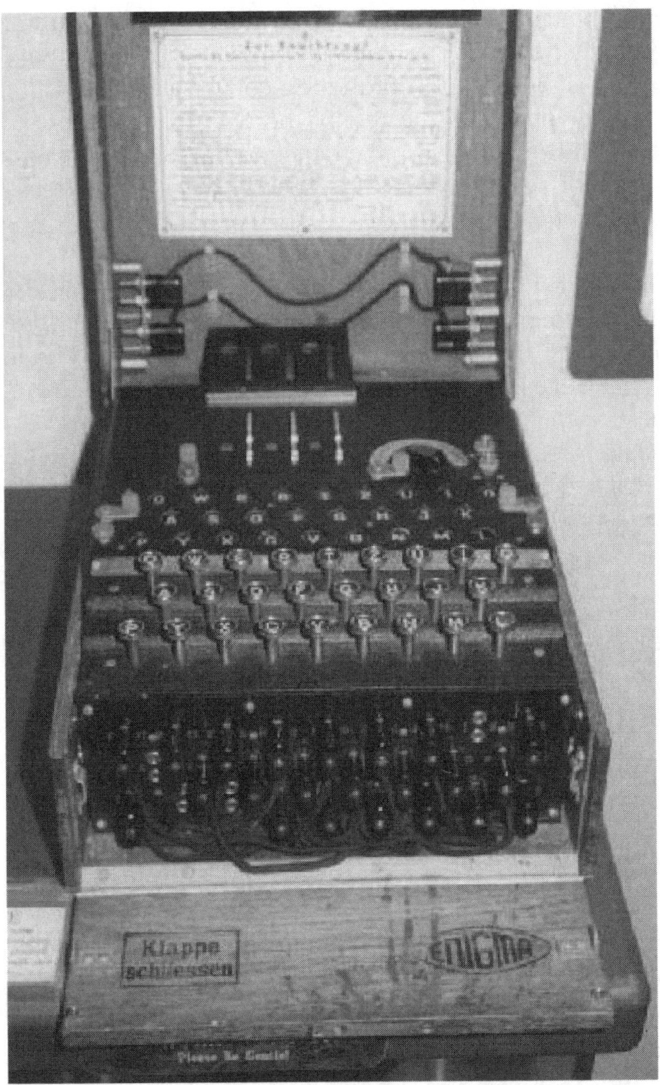

Figure 3.60 Encryption machines.

it would change the keys pressed on the typewriter keyboard to another character on the paper.

Secure Sockets Layer (SSL)

SSL uses both public key and private key cryptography; because of this SSL is known as a hybrid algorithm. SSL begins by using public key cryptography which is slower but more secure to perform an exchange of a session key that uses a symmetric or private key algorithm. The initial key exchange is the only part of the SSL conversation that is protected by public key encryption. All the rest of the data that will be transmitted is done with a private key or symmetric algorithm. SSL is a way of trying to get a balance of security versus the speed. The steps of establishing an SSL connection are:

1. The client begins by sending the server a Client Hello message. This hello message contains the SSL version supported by the client and the cipher suites the client can understand. These cipher suites can have many cryptographic systems and as such the cryptographic strength can vary. The client also sends along the longest key length it can support as well. The following is a list of commonly supported cipher suites along with the corresponding hexadecimal values used in negotiations.

```
SSL2_RC4_128_WITH_MD5 (0x010080)
SSL2_RC2_CBC_128_CBC_WITH_MD5 (0x030080)
SSL2_DES_192_EDE3_CBC_WITH_MD5 (0x0700c0)
SSL2_DES_64_CBC_WITH_MD5 (0x060040)
SSL2_RC4_128_EXPORT40_WITH_MD5 (0x020080)
SSL2_RC2_CBC_128_CBC_WIT_MD5 (0x040080)
TLS_DHE_RS_WITH_AES_256_CBC_SHA (0x000039)
TLS_DHE_DSS_WITH_AES_256_CBC_SHA (0x000038)
TLS_RSA_WITH_AES_256_CBC_SHA (0x000035)
TLS_DHE_RSA_WITH_AES_128_CBC_SHA (0x000033)
TLS_DHE_DSS_WITH_AES_128_CBC_SHA (0x000032)
TLS_RSA_WITH_RC4_128_MD5 (0x000004)
TLS_RSA_WITH_RC4_128_SHA (0x000005)
TLS_RSA_WITH_AES_128_CBC_SHA (0x00002f)
TLS_DHE_RSA_WITH_3DES_EDE_CBC_SHA (0x000016)
TLS_DHE_DSS_WITH_3DES_EDE_CBC_SHA (0x000013)
SSL_RSA_FIPS_WITH_3DES_EDE_CBC_SHA (0x00feff)
TLS_RSA_WITH_3DES_EDE_CBC_SHA (0x00000a)
TLS_DHE_RSA_WITH_DES_CBC_SHA (0x000015)
TLS_DHE_DSS_WITH_DES_CBC_SHA (0x000012)
SSL_RSA_FIPS_WITH_DES_CBC_SHA (0x00fefe)
TLS_RSA_WITH_DES_CBC_SHA (0x000009)
```

```
TLS_RSA_EXPORT1024_WITH_RC4_56_SHA (0x000064)
TLS_RSA_EXPORT1024_WITH_DES_CBC_SHA (0x000062)
TLS_RSA_EXPORT_WITH_RC4_40_MD5 (0x000003)
TLS_RSA_EXPORT_WITH_RC2_CBC_40_MD5 (0x000006)
```

1. Each of these cipher suites has a number of different components. For example, a very common cipher suite is TLS_RSA_WITH_DES_CBC_SHA, where TLS is the protocol version (as opposed to SSL), RSA is the algorithm that will be used to encrypt the session key exchange, DES_CBC is the encryption algorithm (using a 56-bit key in Cipher Block Chaining mode) that will be used to encrypt the bulk data transfer, and SHA is the hash function (which will produce a 160-bit message digest that is used to verify the integrity of the message).
2. The server returns the client hello with one of its own. This server hello nominates the SSL version and the full cipher suite from the options sent by the client in step one.
3. The server sends its digital certificate to the client.
4. The client's browser checks to see if the Certificate Authority (CA) that signed the digital certificate is in the browser's trusted list. Most common CAs are listed in the browser by default and even a few not so common ones. In Firefox this list can be seen by selecting Tools -> Options -> Advanced -> Manage Certificates -> Authorities. There should be a number of Certificate Authorities listed there.
5. The client then verifies the integrity of the digital certificate by first computing a hash of the digital certificate and comparing it to the value of the hash that was included in the certificate. This second hash is created by decrypting the server's digital certificate hash with the public key from the certificate authority. If these hashes match than the client accepts the certificate for further inspection.
6. The next inspection the client does is to check the date of the certificate to see if it is valid and also to verify the URL (i.e., https://www.peltierassociates.com) matches the URL on the certificate. Here the server sends a Server Done message to tell the client that this part of the SSL negotiation is complete.
7. The client extracts the server's public key from the certificate. This is the primary reason for the exchange of all the certificate information.
8. The client creates a session key (symmetric). In the cipher suite listed above this would be where the communication will switch from using RSA for encryption to DES with cipher block chaining.

9. The client encrypts the session key (created in step 8) with the server's public key and sends it to the server with a cipher suite message that tells the server that all future communication should be done with the new session key.
10. The client now sends a Finished message to the server to see if the server can decrypt the message.
11. The server decrypts the session with its private key (the public key of this pair was used to encrypt the session key in step 9). The server then sends a cipher suite message to the client that all future communication will be encrypted using the session key.
12. Finally the server sends its own Finished message to the client. If the client can read the message the negotiation was successful.

If any of these checks in steps 4 to 6 above fails, a single pop-up window is displayed inside the client's browser asking the client if he wishes to continue with the SSL session. This is how an SSL session is established and also how most Internet traffic is secured.

Message Authentication Codes

Message authentication codes are very similar to digital signatures. The difference between MACs and digital signatures is how the information is encrypted. A digital signature uses public key cryptography; a message authentication code uses private key cryptography but it performs the same function. Because a MAC uses private key cryptography the MAC does not authenticate a single person, but rather a MAC authenticates all parties to a conversation. This differs from a digital signature that authenticates an individual. The steps for creating a MAC are the same as the steps for creating a digital signature. You start by creating the message, then you use an MD5sum or SHAsum and you create your hash, and next a session key to encrypt the MAC. The session key has already been pre-exchanged and you use that to encrypt the message authentication code.

Public Key Infrastructure

PKI are the structures necessary for public key cryptography to be effective. There are many different components of PKI and not all components listed here are necessary in every organization. Many organizations have internal certificate authorities where you have to be on their own local area network in order to access their PKI.

Certificate Authority (CA)

A certification authority is the part of the PKI infrastructure that is responsible for publishing the public keys so users can access the public keys to verify the private keys. This physical device may or may not be separate from the registration authority.

Registration Authority (RA)

The registration authority is responsible for enrolling and generating certificates or the public–private key pair for users. This is a process to enroll a user and also the process to publish her certificate publicly.

Certificate Repository

A certificate repository is a part of the CA. This is where the CA holds all public keys.

Certificate Revocation System

Certificates that have been compromised or are expired are added to the certificate revocation list. This is a never-ending list of all certificates that were issued by the certification authority which are no longer valid. In larger organizations the CRLs can be very large and the transfer of the CRL can slow down the entire public key encryption process.

IPSEC

IPSEC is a standard for securing based communication. IPSEC is security on top of standard IP. IPSEC has the functionality to encrypt and authenticate IP-only data. This means that it is not possible to put other network protocols inside an IPSEC packet. IPSEC functions at layer 3, the network layer of the OSI model. IPSEC allows for many simultaneous tunnels from a single device. There are two primary security components when it comes to the IPSEC tunnel: AH and ESP. AH are authentication headers. This replaces the original IP header which just has source and destination with a new header that supports authentication of both parties to make sure that you are actually communicating with the other person. This header contains a Security Associate (SA) and a Security Parameter Index (SPI). These fields are used to authenticate one IPSEC device to the other. Encapsulated Secure Payload (ESP) is what does the encryption inside of

Threat Likelihood	Impact		
	Low (10)	*Medium* (50)	*High* (100)
High (1.0)	**Low** 10 × 1.0 = 10	**Medium** 50 × 1.0 = 50	**High** 100 × 1.0 = 100
Medium (0.5)	**Low** 10 × 0.5 = 5	**Medium** 50 × 0.5 = 25	**Medium** 100 × 0.5 = 50
Low (0.1)	**Low** 10 × 0.1 = 1	**Low** 50 × 0.1 = 5	**Low** 100 × 0.1 = 10

Risk Scale: High (>50 to 100); Medium (>10 to 50); Low (1 to 10)[8]

Figure 3.61 Risk table for NIST Special Publication 800-26.

IPSEC. ESP encrypts the data portion of packets and protects the information in transit over the network.

Project Management for Information Security Managers

You need to know how to implement security program and that means knowing how to prioritize risks.

Figure 3.61 is taken from that 800-26 NIST document again and it just shows you how to put together a threat table so you can classify risks into high, low, and medium risks. A risk table like this is used to help determine which risks are going to have the greatest likelihood to happen to your organization and the greatest devastation on your organization itself. Once you understand the risks to your organization, an information security manager needs to be able to put together an action plan to help mitigate these risks. These concepts are especially critical because many organizations do not fully embrace security and this allows information security tasks to be delayed constantly. One of the most reliable mechanisms for ensuring that information security functions are completed in a timely fashion is to assign a person to be responsible for performing a task or implementing a control. If no one is assigned the responsibility for the tasks completion, it very unlikely the task will ever be performed.

If an information security manager is going to truly get control implemented and tasks accomplished, the information security manager is going to need "people skills" to communicate the need for security. These communications should be both oral and written to gain the necessary support from senior management to ensure the success of the information security program. A typical information security manager may have to communicate the security plan to senior management, the information

POLICIES				
Description	**Findings**	**Recommendation**	**Assigned Person**	**Anticipated Completion**
INFORMATION CONTROL AND CLASSIFICATION	Currently Customer references a data classification scheme in its IT Policy and Procedures; however, that is the only evidence that the Customer assesses the criticality and sensitivity of the information contained within its computer systems.	• The Information Classification schema does not need to be complex or complicated. • Consultant suggests one that includes: • **Public – Information in the public domain or authorized for public dissemination;** • **Internal Use Only – Information not specifically authorized for public dissemination. Information not otherwise classified will default to this category;** • **Non-public Personal Customer – Information which is protected by statute and will result in regulatory impact if disclosed to unauthorized parties;** • **Restricted – Information that will have severe detrimental impact to the safety and soundness of the Bank if disclosed to unauthorized parties.** • Each computer system or application should be graded according to the information it contains. When a system contains more than one level of information the more restrictive will apply.		

Figure 3.62 Project Management Chart.

steering committee, the department heads (or data owners), the user community, and also the information security staff. Each of these groups speak a different language—for the information security manager to be truly effective in communicating the security plan, he must be able to speak the language of each department (see Figure 3.62).

Baselines

Baselines are a minimum set of controls that will be installed on a system that does not meet the requirements for a high sensitivity level. In many organizations the information classification scheme has a sensitivity level of "internal use" and this level applies to all systems that do not meet higher sensitivity criteria. A baseline would be appropriate to use for the "garden variety" systems that do not house more sensitive information. There are many sources for recommended baseline controls. There are government sites such as http://csrc.nist.gov or http://www.nsa.gov/snac/. There are security research organizations like http://www.sans.org and http://www.cisecurity.org. There are also vendor recommended control lists from manufacturers like Cisco (http://www.cisco.com) and Microsoft (http://www.microsoft.com).

The baselines provide a level of security to be applied to most devices and also establish a best practice guideline that an information security manager can follow. It always sounds more appealing to management after an incident has happened to say, "I configured the system using the National Institute for Standards in Technology guidelines" (Figure 3.63).

Example Baseline

Security Policy					
1.1	3.1	***Information security policy***			
1.1.1	3.1.1	**Information security policy document**	Whether there exists an Information security policy, which is approved by the management, published and communicated as appropriate to all employees. Whether it states the management commitment and sets out the organizational approach to managing information security.		
1.1.2	3.1.2	**Review and evaluation**	Whether the Security policy has an owner, who is responsible for its maintenance and review according to a defined review process. Whether the process ensures that a review takes place in response to any changes affecting the basis of the original assessment; example: significant security incidents, new vulnerabilities or changes to organizational or technical infrastructure.		

Figure 3.63 Example baseline.

Wireless

Wireless technology has been one of the most major advancements in networking in the past five years. Wireless networking comes in many different forms—from the traditional wireless network (known as 802.11) to the synchronization of wireless devices to laptops (known as Bluetooth) to the systems that allow users in cars or on foot to determine where in the world; they are better known as Global Positioning System or GPS. While all of these technologies have major advantages, each has an associated security risk. And while all of these risks are fun topics to discuss, we will focus here on 802.11 networking or wireless networking.

There are many different terms used to describe wireless networking. Lately, you can hear many of the following the following terms spewing forth from just about any technologist's mouth:

WLAN—This acronym is shorthand for Wireless Local Area Network

802.11x or 802.11(a,b,g)—This is the name(s) of the IEEE (Institute of Electrical and Electronis Engineers) standard for wireless networking

WiFi—This acronym is shorthand for Wireless Fidelity

How It Works

Regardless of which term is used, we are still talking about allowing computers on our network to communicate with each other without using traditional network cabling. Now you might be wondering exactly how do these computers communicate if there is no direct cable linking the networking together. With wireless networks the information is sent using a radio signal. The big advantage of using these radio signals, as opposed to traditional network cabling, is its simplicity. You can connect computers anywhere in your home or office without being tied to a particular network drop or network jack. Because the computers connect to the network using a radio signal, the computers and network devices can be more than 100 feet apart. The radios used in wireless networks are not so different from the radios used in other technologies, such as your kid's walkie-talkies. Both radios have the ability to transmit and receive. They both have the ability to convert 1s and 0s into radio waves and then back into 1s and 0s. There are some major differences between wireless networks and your kid's walkie-talkies. These are:

- Wireless network radios that work with the 802.11b and 802.11g standards transmit at 2.4 GHz, while those that comply with the 802.11a standard transmit at 5 GHz. Normal walkie-talkies normally operate at 49 MHz. The higher frequency allows higher data rates.
- Wireless network radios use much more efficient coding techniques that also contribute to the much higher data rates. For 802.11a and 802.11g, the technique is known as orthogonal frequency-division multiplexing (OFDM). For 802.11b, it is called Complementary Code Keying (CCK).
- The radios used for wireless networking have the ability to change frequencies. 802.11b network cards can transmit directly on any of three bands, or they can split the available radio bandwidth into dozens of channels and frequency hop rapidly between them. The advantage of frequency hopping is that it is much more immune to interference and can allow dozens of wireless network cards to talk simultaneously without interfering with each other.

Because they are transmitting at much higher frequencies than your kid's Walkie-Talkie, and because of the encoding techniques, wireless network radios can handle a lot more data per second. 802.11b can handle up to 11 megabits per second (although 5.5 megabits per second is more typical, and 802.11b may fall back as low as 1 or 2 megabits per second if there is a lot of interference). 802.11a and 802.11g can handle up to 54 megabits per second (although 28 megabits per second is more typical).

The Alphabet Soup

You might be wondering where the funny 802.11 nomenclature comes from. The Institute of Electrical and Electronics Engineers (IEEE) creates standards and the standards are uniquely numbered. The 802.11 standard covers wireless networks. The a, b, and g notations identify different flavors of the 802.11 standard:

- 802.11b was the first version to reach the marketplace. It is the slowest and least expensive of the three. As mentioned previously, 802.11b transmits at 2.4 GHz and can handle up to 11 megabits per second. The use of 802.11b is still widespread despite many newer standards that have emerged. In many cases, when someone is referring to a wireless network, they mean an 802.11b network.
- 802.11a was next. It operates at 5 GHz and can handle up to 54 megabits per second. 802.11a adoption was much slower and less widespread than 802.11b networks. Because many organizations installed 802.11b networks when the first became available on the market, it was felt that a complete "forklift" upgrade would not be a financially wise idea. So, despite the higher speed, many organizations chose to ignore 802.11a networks.
- 802.11g is a mix of both worlds. Its radio operates in 2.4Ghz space (giving it the cost advantage of 802.11b), but has the 54 megabits per second speed of 802.11a. This is perhaps the most common type of wireless network in use today. All 802.11g networks are backward compliant with 802.11b (due to the use of the same radio frequency) and this allowed for many organizations to upgrade the wireless network without discarding all of the older 802.11b components.

Securing Wireless—The Early Days

Because we have covered the basics of wireless networks, we can now move into more discussion of the cryptosystems used by wireless networks. The first cryptosystem used to protect the confidentiality of wireless networks was WEP. WEP stands for Wired Equivalent Privacy (not wireless encryption protocol, as is often stated), and it is an encryption system for the data that 802.11 sends through the air. WEP has two variations: an older 64-bit encryption (really 40-bit) and the slightly more recent 128-bit encryption (really 104-bit). The 40-bit encryption was the original standard because it could easily be exported outside the United States, but was found to be easily broken. The 128-bit encryption is slightly more secure and is what most people use if they enable WEP on their access points. In most cases, a casual end-user will not be able to access the wireless network that is using WEP unless you are provided the WEP key. Whether at home or on the road, you need to know the WEP key, and then enter it into the wireless network card's configuration, to gain access to the network. The security risk here is that the WEP key used to authenticate the laptop or PDA to the network and is stored locally on these devices. If a laptop or PDA with a WEP key is stolen the thief will be able to authenticate to the wireless network and access network resources as if he was a legitimate network user.

In addition to the security risk of an encryption key being stolen, the WEP cryptosystem itself can be defeated. It has been widely publicized that an attacker can defeat the encryption of WEP and discover the encryption key by resorting to stealing a device. This is due to the construction of WEP. When WEP is active in a wireless LAN, each wireless network packet is encrypted separately with an RC4 cipher stream generated by a 64-bit RC4 key. To understand what this means we need to dig deeper into exactly what RC4 is.

RC4 and the One-Time Pad

Ronald Rivest, of RSA, developed the RC4 encryption algorithm and, since this algorithm has been released to the public, much of the structure is a mystery. This has not stopped RC4 from being a popular algorithm that is used and implemented by many programmers in applications from SSL (secure sockets layer, a way to secure Web traffic) to the previously mentioned WEP encryption. But, because the code of RC4 has not been released, most of the following is a bit of rumored speculation. It has been stated that RC4 was originally designed to be a one-time pad. A one-time pad is the only theoretically unbreakable cipher. A one-time pad is a private (secret) key, also known as a symmetric cipher, where the key size is equal to the plaintext size. Because of this, the key is never re-utilized. And, as the key is never re-utilized (used only once), there is no basis for mathematical cryptanalysis.

An example of a very poor one-time pad would be if you were to encrypt a letter to a friend using a substitution cipher and using J.K. Rowling's *Harry Potter and The Prisoner of Azkaban* as a key. Your friend could decrypt your letter using an identical copy of *Harry Potter and The*

Prisoner of Azkaban. No one else would be able to decrypt your message unless they had a copy of the book you were using as a key.

This is actually a very poor one-time pad because books do not have random or pseudo-random text. A message encrypted using a book as a one-time pad would actually not be difficult to defeat. For a one-time pad to be truly unbreakable, the key must be generated with effective randomness. In the past this has been done by having someone manually pull a lettered ball from a bingo hopper or it was based on a playing card pulled from a shuffled deck. Today this is done through a pseudo-random number generator. This pseudo-random number is generated through pseudo-random program code that will create a string of bits. While these bits are not truly random, they will appear random to the casual observer. This pseudo-random generator is also known as the key stream generator; the output of the generator can also be known as the key stream. One-time pad ciphers are sometimes called Vernam ciphers.

WEP's Implementation of RC4

As stated before, WEP encrypts each wireless network packet with an RC4 cipher stream generated by a 64-bit RC4 key. This key is composed of a 24-bit initialization vector (IV) and a 40-bit WEP key. Initialization vectors are very important whenever two messages are encrypted using the same key. In general, encrypting two messages with the same key will yield the same ciphertext result. This makes recovering both messages simple. Thus, if the same encryption key needs to be re-used, a few random bytes, which can be written into the start of the encrypted file, are prepended to the key. This then changes the key from the first message and the second message to be two different keys.

The IV is used to make the key appear more random. The IV is chosen by the sender and can be changed periodically so every packet will not be encrypted with the same cipher stream. The IV is sent in the clear with each packet. To attempt to verify the integrity of the message encrypted message, an additional 4-byte Integrity Check Value (ICV) also called the Cyclic Redundancy Check (CRC) is computed on the original packet and appended to the end. The ICV (be careful not to confuse this with the IV) is also encrypted with the RC4 cipher stream. Figure 3.64 shows what this looks like.

WEP has been widely criticized for a number of weaknesses. These include:

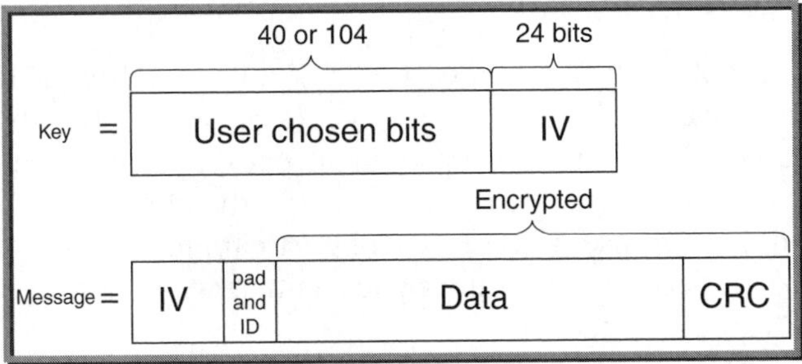

Figure 3.64 WEP encrypted packet.

Weakness: Key Management and Key Size

Key management is not specified in the WEP standard and, therefore, is one of its weaknesses, because without interoperable key management, keys will tend to be long-lived and of poor quality. Most wireless networks that use WEP have one single WEP key shared between every node on the network. Access points (wireless hubs) and client stations must be programmed with the same WEP key. Since synchronizing the change of keys is tedious and difficult, keys are seldom changed.

In addition, the size of the key—40 bits—has been cited as a weakness of WEP. When the standard was written in 1997, 40-bit keys were considered reasonable for some applications. Because the goal was to protect against "casual eavesdropping," it seemed sufficient at the time. The United States did not tightly control exports of 40-bit encryption, and the IEEE wanted to ensure exportability of wireless devices.

The 802.11 standard does not specify any WEP key sizes other than 40 bits. Most vendors have implemented a de facto standard by simply extending the key size to 104 bits, resulting in excellent interoperability. You will often see this called a "128-bit" WEP key, because it sounds better than a 104-bit key, but that is not a fair comparison. This is why you enter 13 characters (or 26 hexadecimal digits) instead of 16 characters when you set up a long WEP key. In either case, 40 bits or 104 bits, the RC4 encryption key includes a 24-bit IV. Obviously, 104-bit keys are more resistant to brute-force attacks than 40-bit keys. For example, if it were to take on average of one week for a brute-force attacker to find a 40-bit key, that attacker would not be able to find a 104-bit key in a billion years—it is actually much, much longer than that. Brute-force attacks on 104-bit keys are not considered the primary weakness of WEP.

Help! My IV Is Too Small

WEP's IV size of 24 bits provides for 16.7 million different RC4 cipher streams for a given WEP key, for any key size. Remember that the RC4 cipher stream is XOR-ed with the original packet to give the encrypted packet that is transmitted, and the IV is sent in the clear with each packet. The problem is IV re-use. If the RC4 cipher stream for a given IV is found, an attacker can decrypt subsequent packets that were encrypted with the same IV or can forge packets.

Because there are only 16 million IV values, how the IV is chosen makes a big difference in the attacks based on IV. Unfortunately, WEP does not specify how the IV is chosen or how often the IV is changed. Some implementations start the IV at zero and increase it incrementally for each packet, rolling over back to zero after 16 million packets have been sent. Some implementations choose IVs randomly. That may sound like a good idea, but it really isn't. With a randomly chosen IV, there is a 50 percent chance of re-use after less than 5,000 packets.

Additionally, there are many methods for discovering the cipher stream for a particular IV. For example, given two encrypted packets with the same IV, the XOR of the original packets can be found by XORing the encrypted packets. If the victim is on the Internet, the attacker can simply ping the victim or send an e-mail message. If the attacker is able to send the victim packets and observe and analyze those encrypted packets, he can deduce the cipher stream.

The ICV and Its Weakness

The WEP ICV is based on CRC-32, an algorithm for detecting noise and common errors in transmission. CRC-32 is an excellent checksum for detecting errors, but an awful choice for a cryptographic hash. Better-designed encryption systems use algorithms such as MD5 or SHA-1 for their ICVs. However, these algorithms have newly discovered vulnerabilities in them as well, especially with SHA-1. It still currently stands that both SHA-1 and MD5 are the best commonly used choices.

The CRC-32 ICV is a linear function of the message, meaning that an attacker can modify an encrypted message and easily fix the ICV so the message appears authentic. Being able to modify encrypted packets provides for a nearly limitless number of very simple attacks. For example, an attacker can easily make the victim's wireless access point decrypt packets for him by simply capturing an encrypted packet stream, modifying the destination address of each packet to be the attacker's wired IP address, fixing up the CRC-32, and retransmiting the packets over the air to the access point. The access point will happily decrypt the packets and forward them to the attacker. (The attack is slightly more complex than that, but to keep this short, we've skipped some of the details.)

The biggest problem with IV- and ICV-based attacks is they are independent of key size, meaning that even huge keys all look the same. These types of attacks will take the same amount of effort.

RC4

RC4 in its implementation in WEP has been found to have weak keys. Having a weak key means there is more correlation between the key and the output than there should be for good security. Remember back to the previous discussion of pseudo-random code, with weak keys the pseudo-random is not random enough and a relationship between the keystream and the key exists. Determining which packets were encrypted with weak keys is easy because the first three bytes of the key are taken from the IV that is sent unencrypted in each packet. This weakness can be exploited by a passive attack. All the attacker needs to do is be within a hundred feet or so of the access point. This is the common attack done with utilities such as Airsnort and Kismet.

Out of the 16 million IV values available, about 9,000 are "interesting" to the most popular attack tool, Airsnort, meaning they indicate the presence of weak keys. The attacker captures "interesting packets," filtering for IVs that suggest weak keys. After that attacker gathers enough interesting packets, he analyzes them and only has to try a small number of keys to gain access to the network. Because all original IP packets start with a known value, it is easy to know when you have the right key. To determine a 104-bit WEP key, you have to capture between 2,000 and 4,000 interesting packets. On a fairly busy network that generates one million packets per day, a few hundred interesting packets might be captured. That would mean that a week or two of capturing would be required to determine the key. In some more recent testing it is possible that gathering enough packets can take place in closer to ten hours if the wireless network is sufficiently busy.

The best defense against this type of attack is not to use weak IV values. Many vendors are now implementing new algorithms that simply do not choose weak IVs. However, if just one station on the network uses weak keys, the attack can still succeed.

The Problems With Message Authentication

Besides the problems mentioned above, there are other security problems with wireless networks. Remembering that cryptography only protects the confidentiality of wireless packets, we still have issues with the other primary information security goals—authenticity and availability. While the availability issues may never be solved, there have been many attempts to further secure the authentication components of wireless networks.

The original 802.11 standard defines two forms of authentication: Open System (no authentication) and Shared Key authentication. These are used to authenticate the client to the access point. Please note the client referred to here is the laptop or PDA device and not the wireless network user. The idea was that authentication would be better than no authentication because the user has to prove knowledge of the shared WEP key, in effect authenticating himself through the use of a trusted device. In fact, the exact opposite is true: If you turn on authentication, you actually reduce the total security of your network and make it easier to guess your WEP key.

Shared Key authentication involves demonstrating the knowledge of the shared WEP key by encrypting a challenge. The challenge is issued from the Wireless Access Point (WAP) and sent to the client. The client then encrypts this challenge with the WEP key and returns the now encrypted challenge to the access point. The problem is that a monitoring attacker using a network sniffer can observe the challenge and the encrypted response. From those he can determine the RC4 stream used to encrypt the response and use that stream to encrypt any challenge he receives in the future. The attacker does this by reversing the XORing process previously discussed. So by monitoring a successful authentication, the attacker can later forge an authentication. The only advantage of Shared Key authentication is that it reduces the ability of an attacker to create a denial-of-service attack by sending garbage packets (encrypted with the wrong WEP key) into the network. However, there are still many other types of DOS attacks that can be done against a wireless network.

Open system gives you better network security. This is a pretty significant statement considering that open authentication allows for anyone to send anything onto the wireless network without authentication first. The advantage of doing this, however, is at least the encryption key will not be exposed to an attacker. In most cases, the attacker will need to have the WEP key in order for the access point to be able to have the packet decrypted correctly on the network, but he can still send whatever he would like. Most network managers should turn off Shared Key authentication and depend on newer mechanisms for authentication, such as 802.1x, to handle the task of properly authenticating wireless users.

Another Standard 802.1x

As discussed earlier, 802.11's optional WEP, all wireless access points (WAP), and wireless clients on the wireless network must use the same encryption key. Each sending station encrypts the body of each frame with a WEP key before transmission, and the receiving station decrypts it using an identical key upon reception. This process somewhat reduces the risk of someone passively monitoring, sniffing the wireless packet by encrypting it.

A major underlying problem with the existing 802.11 standard is that the keys are cumbersome to change. If you do not update the WEP keys often, an unauthorized person with a sniffing tool, such as AirSnort or WEPcrack, can monitor your network for less than a day and decode the encrypted messages. In order to use different keys, you must manually configure each access point and radio NIC with new common keys.

Products based on the 802.11 standard alone offer system administrators no effective method to update the keys. This might not be too much concern with a few users, but the job of renewing keys on larger networks can be a monumental task. As a result, companies either do not use WEP at all or maintain the same keys for weeks, months, and even years. Both cases significantly heighten the wireless LAN's vulnerability to eavesdroppers.

The 802.1x Function

Please do not confuse the authentication mechanism that we are discussing here (802.1x) with the standards mentioned above (802.11 a,b,g). While these terms are both IEEE standards, they are actually completely different. In fact, 802.1x can be used without a wireless network and can run on a traditional (wired) Ethernet network. The use of IEEE 802.1x offers an effective framework for authenticating and controlling user traffic to a protected network, as well as dynamically varying encryption keys. 802.1x ties a protocol called EAP (Extensible Authentication Protocol) to both the wired and wireless LAN media and supports multiple authentication methods, such as token cards, Kerberos, one-time passwords, certificates, and public key authentication. For more specific details on EAP, please read the following sections or refer to the IETF's RFC 2284.

Before we can really delve deeper into 802.1x we need to dissect EAP a bit.

The Relationship between EAP and 802.1x

EAP was originally designed for enterprises that wanted to do more for security than simply employing usernames and passwords for access. This desire gave birth to a new authentication protocol called the Extensible Authentication Protocol (EAP), which was designed to supplement PPP. PPP, or Point to Point Protoco,l was and is commonly used to authenticate remote users to the corporate or other remote network. In fact, many of you may still you PPP if you make a dial-up connection to the Internet.

EAP sits inside of PPP's authentication protocol and provides a generalized framework for several different authentication methods. Commonly supported authentication methods include:

- **EAP-MD5** lets a RADIUS server authenticate LAN stations by verifying an MD5 hash of each user's password. This is a simple and reasonable choice for trusted Ethernets where there is low risk of outsider sniffing or active attack. However, EAP-MD5 is not suitable for public Ethernets or wireless LANs because outsiders can easily sniff station identities and password hashes, or masquerade as access points to trick stations into authenticating with them instead of the real deal.
- **Cisco's Lightweight EAP (LEAP)** goes a notch beyond EAP-MD5 by requiring mutual authentication and delivering keys used for WLAN encryption. Mutual authentication reduces the risk of access point masquerading—a type of Man-in-the-Middle (MitM) attack. However, station identities and passwords remain vulnerable to attackers armed with sniffers and dictionary attack tools. LEAP is mostly attractive to organizations that use Cisco access points and cards and want to modestly raise the security bar.
- **EAP with Transport Layer Security (EAP-TLS)** is the only standard secure option for wireless LANs at this time. EAP-TLS requires the station and RADIUS server to both prove their identities via public key cryptography (i.e., digital certificates or smart cards). This exchange is secured by an encrypted TLS tunnel, making EAP-TLS very resistant to dictionary or other MitM attacks. However, the station's identity—the name bound to the certificate—can still be sniffed by outsiders. EAP-TLS is most attractive to large enterprises that use only Windows XP/2000/2003 with deployed certificates.
- **EAP with Tunneled TLS (EAP-TTLS) and Protected EAP (PEAP)** are Internet Drafts that have been proposed to simplify 802.1X deployment. Both require certificate-based RADIUS server authentication, but support an extensible set of user authentication methods. Organizations that have not yet issued certificates to every station and don't want to just for 802.1X can, instead, use Windows logins and passwords. RADIUS servers that support EAP-TTLS and PEAP can check LAN access requests with Windows Domain Controllers, Active Directories, and other existing user databases. From a sniffing perspective, these

options are just as strong as EAP-TLS. However, user passwords are still more likely to be guessed, shared, or disclosed through social engineering than client-side certificates.

EAP is supposed to head off proprietary authentication systems and let everything from passwords to challenge-response tokens and public-key infrastructure certificates work smoothly.

With a standardized EAP, interoperability and compatibility of authentication methods becomes simpler. For example, when you dial a RAS (remote-access server) and use EAP as part of your PPP connection, the RAS doesn't need to know any of the details about your authentication system. Only you and the authentication server have to be coordinated. By supporting EAP authentication a RAS server gets out of the business of acting as middle man, and just packages and repackages EAP packets to hand off to a RADIUS server that will do the actual authentication. For more on RADIUS please refer to the IETF's RFC 2865.

More on 802.1x

With 802.1x, the initial communications begin with an unauthenticated supplicant (this is the 802.1x term for the client) attempting to connect with an authenticator (this is the 802.1x term for the WAP). The access point responds by enabling a port for passing only EAP (authentication) packets from the client to an authentication server located on the wired side of the access point. The access point blocks all other traffic, such as HTTP, DHCP, and POP3 packets, until the access point can verify the client's identity using an authentication server (almost always RADIUS). However, there are cases where this authentication can take place from an internal database inside the access point. Once authenticated, the access point opens the client's port for other types of traffic. All of the authentication takes place at the Data Link layer of the OSI model and because of this the client (supplicant) does not even need to have acquired a network (IP) address as of yet. To see how this works please see the diagrams following.

Figure 3.65 shows the pre-authentication state of an 802.1x network. The only traffic that will be relayed through the access point will be the authentication traffic. All other traffic will be dropped at the access point (authenticator) and will never make it onto the corporate network.

Once the supplicant (client) has been authenticated it is free to send packets to the internal network. This looks like Figure 3.66.

These are the specific steps that are taken when the client authenticates to the 802.1x network.

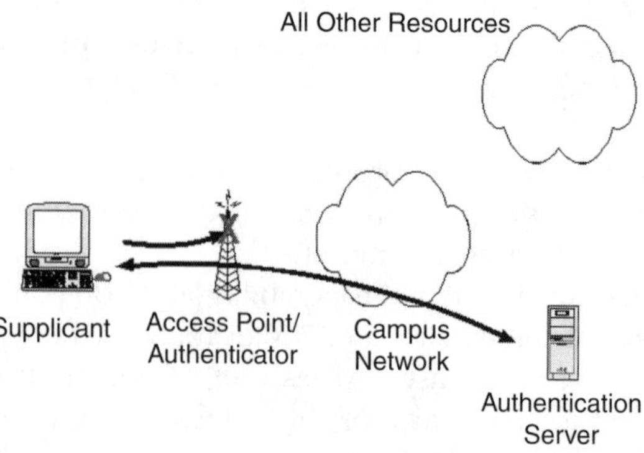

Figure 3.65 Pre-authentication state.

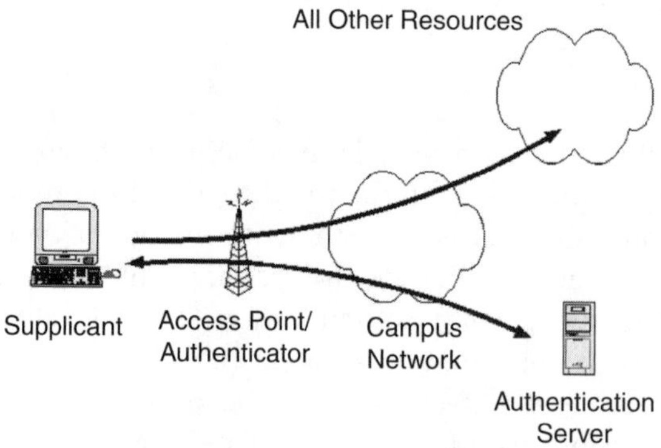

Figure 3.66 Post-authentication state.

1. The client sends an EAP-start message. This begins a series of message exchanges to authenticate the client; think of this as a group of travelers entering the airport and the group's leader (client) asking the ticket agent (access point) which gate the flight is departing from
2. The access point replies with an EAP-request identity message. In the case of the airport, the gatekeeper will ask the travelers for their itinerary and drivers license.
3. The client sends an EAP-response packet containing the identity to the authentication server. The leader in our example will provide their itinerary and drivers license, and the gatekeeper checks the itineraries and identification cards into the airline's computer system

(authentication server) who determines whether the group has a flight at the airport and if so where it is located.

4. The authentication server uses a specific authentication algorithm to verify the client's identity. This could be through the use of digital certificates or other EAP authentication type. In the case of our example, this process simply involves verifying the validity of the traveler's drivers' license and ensuring that the picture on the license matches the traveler. In our example, we'll assume the travelers are authorized.
5. The authentication server will either send an accept or reject message to the access point. So the airline's computer prints out a boarding pass to let the group enter.
6. The access point sends an EAP-success packet (or reject packet) to the client. The gatekeeper informs the travelers that the group can enter the secured area and head to the flight's gate. Of course, the gatekeeper would not let the group in if the airline's computer or security had rejected the group's admittance.
7. If the authentication server accepts the client, then the access point will transition the client's port to an authorized state and forward additional traffic.

The basic 802.1x protocol provides effective authentication regardless of whether you implement WEP or no encryption at all. Most of major wireless network vendors, however, are offering proprietary versions of a security fix to the problems with WEP by adding in dynamic key management, often called Temporal Key Integrity Protocol (TKIP), using 802.1x as a delivery mechanism. If configured to implement dynamic key exchange, the 802.1x authentication server can return session keys to the access point along with the accept message. The access point uses the session keys to build, sign, and encrypt an EAP key message that is immediately sent to the client after sending the success message. The client can then use the contents of the key message to define applicable encryption keys. In typical 802.1x implementations, the client can automatically change encryption keys as often as necessary (in most cases, the default is five minutes) to minimize the possibility of eavesdroppers having enough time to crack the key in current use.

Imagine, as we discussed above, an attacker is using Airsnort or some other WEP defeating utility and is attempting to uncover our WEP key and get unauthorized access to the network. He is going to have to capture between 2,000 and 4,000 interesting packets which means that he will need several hundred thousand packets, or up to several million total packets, to be able to decrypt the WEP key. This will take a minimum of hours and, before the attacker can even capture all of the packets necessary, our WEP key will have changed and will keep changing every five minutes.

802.1x Doesn't Work Alone

It's important to note that 802.1x doesn't provide the actual authentication mechanisms. When utilizing 802.1x, you need to choose an EAP type, such as Transport Layer Security (EAP-TLS) or EAP Tunneled Transport Layer Security (EAP-TTLS), which defines how the authentication takes place. There are many EAP types. Please see the previous section for details.

The important fact to know at this point is that the software supporting the specific EAP type resides on the authentication server and within the operating system or application software on the client devices. The access point acts as a "pass through" for 802.1x messages, which means that you can specify any EAP type without needing to upgrade an 802.1x-compliant access point. As a result, you can update the EAP authentication type as newer types become available and your requirements for security change.

802.1x – Making Wireless Better

The use of 802.1x is well on its way to becoming an industry standard, and you would be wise to include it as the basis for your wireless LAN security solution. Windows XP implements 802.1x natively, and some vendors support 802.1x in their 802.11 access points. Wireless LAN implementations of 802.1x fall outside the scope of the 802.11 standard; however, the 802.11i committee is specifying the use of 802.1x to eventually become part of the 802.11 standard.

802.1x's Partner TKIP

Temporal Key Integrity Protocol (TKIP) is a recent security feature offered by various vendors to correct the weak WEP problem. It was developed by some of the same researchers who found the weaknesses in how RC4 was implemented. TKIP corrects these weaknesses and more.

TKIP still uses RC4 as the encryption algorithm, but it removes the weak key problem and forces a new key to be generated every 10,000 packets or 10KB or every five minutes, depending on the source. In addition, it fixes the security vulnerability with IV's being sent in cleartext by hashing the initialization vector (IV) values. This makes TKIP much more secure than WEP. This means that IVs are now encrypted and are not as easy to sniff out of the air. Because the first three characters of the secret key are based on the three-character IV, the hashing of this value is a must. This further thwarts the effectiveness of utilities such as Airsnort and Kismet.

Also included in TKIP is a stronger and more secure method of verifying the integrity of the data. Remember back to the discussion of WEP, where we showed that the ICV value of WEP was created with CRC-32. While this was fine for integrity, it was very weak with security. With TKIP this is further secured by replacing the old ICV with a new integrity check called the Message Integrity Check, MIC, or Michael. This part of TKIP closes a hole that would allow a hacker to inject data into a packet so the hacker can more easily deduce the streaming key used to encrypt the data. This makes it more difficult for an attacker to modify a packet with the wireless network being aware of the modification.

With the new Message Integrity Check, this prevents the type of exploit where the attacker modifies a packet to get further encryption key information. By verifying that the packet was not altered, and by dumping any packet that appears to be, the hacker will not be able to easily determine the key information. In addition, hashing the IVs creates yet another obstacle to any hacker who somehow deduces the key stream. The hacker would have to determine the correct value of the hashed IVs and this would be significantly more complicated than generating the old CRC-32 check.

However, and even with all this extra security, TKIP is designed like the current version of WEP. This similarity allows TKIP to be backwardly compatible with most hardware devices. This also means that consumers merely have to update their firmware or software to bring their wireless networks up to the new security offerings, such as the previously discussed (802.1x, EAP, and TKIP).

Many security professionals believe that while these new security measures are important, it's only temporary and will be improved upon again. Most treat TKIP like a simple bandage to patch the hemorrhaging artery of WEP security. This is because TKIP, by itself, still operates under the condition that a hacker only has to crack one "password" in order to gain access to the wireless network. This is where TKIP's friends, 802.1x and EAP, come back to help us out. However, in the rare circumstance where TKIP is used alone, the single level of WEP based open authentication can allow the encryption to still be crackable. It seems pretty farfetched that many organizations will over deploy a wireless network in this configuration, but it's possible. The next level of security for a wireless network will go beyond just TKIP and include a multifaceted security scheme using stronger encryption and multiple means of authentication (802.1x). This requires a hacker to have to attack the WLAN from several points, thus making gaining unauthorized access by just simple encryption cracking much more difficult.

Most of the security improvements mentioned above will be included with the new 802.11i standard.

Back to the Alphabet Soup One Last Time—802.11i

The security features that we have mentioned previously in the sections about TKIP, 802.1x, and EAP were all part of an interim standard known at WPA or WiFi Protected Access. The Wi-Fi organization, online at http://www.wi-fi.org, created a standard that would allow for interoperability throughout 802.1x, EAP, and TKIP implementations. Most of these security features were slated to be incorporated into the IETF's new wireless network security standard 802.11i. You might be wondering if the IETF was already going to make the standard, why did the Wi-Fi group jump in. The reason for that is the length of time it would take the IETF committees to approve the 802.11i standard. In fact, 802.11i did not become a full standard until July 29, 2004. This took well over a year from concept to final standard. However the Wi-Fi organization was able to pull WPA together in a matter of months.

Most of the security features of WPA are included with 802.11i, and 802.11i goes even one step beyond with support for a completely new encryption scheme—AES or the Advanced Encryption Standard.

Before we get into AES, and what it is, we should probably first discuss WPA a bit more. WPA allowed for devices to become WPA-certified and support two levels of certification: (1) WPA personal, which allowed EAP authentication to take place in an internal database in the wireless access point, and (2) WPA enterprise, which required the use of an external (RADUIS) authentication server for EAP authentication. WPA personal was often called WPA-PSK for Pre-Shared Key. In fact, the Microsoft EAP authentication still refers to it in that way. Pre-Shared Key allowed for the EAP authentication to use the internal database on the wireless access point.

Currently, the WiFi organization has created a second standard, aptly called WPA2, that encompasses the new AES algorithm into the security features as well. As we just mentioned, WPA2 is the second generation of WPA security, providing enterprise and consumer Wi-Fi users with a high level of assurance that only authorized users can access their wireless networks. WPA2 is based on the final IEEE 802.11i amendment to the 802.11 standard and a key element is that WPA2 is eligible for FIPS 140-2 compliance.

Wireless Summary

Wireless networks are not going anywhere and the popularity of wireless networks is increasing rapidly. We have wireless networks for data, wireless networks for voice, and short range wireless to synch devices, like our Palm Pilots, and to use hands-free headsets for our calls without having a wire attach our ears to the phone. Wireless is practical—it makes networking easier. Wireless appears to be economical because of the reduction in costs for physical cabling and installation. But wireless data travels through an unsecured public medium—the air. Because of the medium, wireless data transfers can be a security risk. All the vulnerabilities that exist in the wired network segment are magnified when wireless networking is implemented. A major part of the reason for this is because most information technology people see wireless as a way to extend the local area network (LAN). Wireless networking may often be called WLANs for Wireless LANs, but wireless should be treated just like any other remote connection into your organization. Because information technology people think that wireless is just another way to extend the LAN, one of the largest problems with wireless is that of architecture. From a security standpoint, the best place to install a Wireless Access Point (WAP) is on your DMZ. The DMZ is a tertiary interface off of the firewall that has a level of trust between that of the trusted (inside) and untrusted (the Internet). This will allow access control to be applied on traffic both leaving and entering the wireless LAN segment.

Buffer Overflows versus Application Security

When it comes to application security, following a system developing life cycle helps to make sure that security is a native part of your applications when you are developing them. A standard component of most good SDLCs is the use of Computer Aided Software Engineering (CASE) tools. In addition to the standard methodology used with the SDLC, CASE provides a development environment that includes prototyping, testing and reviews and, in most cases, object oriented development. While these controls are key for helping to develop secure application, mistakes can still be made. The more complex the application, the greater the likelihood that a coding error will be made at some point. The biggest risk to the security of the application is if the coding error leads to a buffer overflow. A buffer overflow is an attack that uses a flaw in either input validation, data validation, or error checking mechanisms. If a well-developed application has any of these security mechanisms in place, the buffer overflow attack should be stopped. Buffer overflows are caused by both error in programming and an error in programming techniques. When a buffer overflow is possible, an attacker can send more data through the vulnerable application's input field directly to the memory buffer. If too much data is written to the memory buffer, then a buffer overflow occurs and several things can happen. The most simplistic buffer overflow attack will simply create a denial-of-service condition; another attack will create increased privilege for a user or application; and the most dangerous buffer overflow attacks will create a remote code execution environment. Once an attacker reaches this level of buffer overflow, the attacker can effectively do anything he wishes to the compromised computer.

Virtual Private Networks (VPNs)

The most secure mechanism for remote access to a network is to use Virtual Private Network (VPN) technology. VPNs use encryption (primarily IPSEC standard encryption, but SSL is becoming more popular) to create an environment that allows the remote user to appear as if he is on the local area network. There are two primary types of VPNs. The first type of VPN is a site-to-site VPN. This typically happens when a company has at least two offices that are in different geographical locations. The site-to-site VPN will tie the two networks together over the Internet, but through the use of encryption it will appear to users and devices on the networks that the Internet is not there at all. The second type of VPN is the client-to-site VPN. This configuration is popular and is often used with teleworkers and telecommuters. The VPN will allow the remote users to access the corporate network from any Internet connection and the data will be protected from eavesdropping by the aforementioned encryption.

Web Server Security versus Internet Security

There is a difference between Web server security and Internet security. A typical firewall provides Internet security. The typical firewall is usually going to ask one question of traffic destined for the corporate Web server: "Are you on the right port for Web traffic?" As long as traffic is destined for TCP port 80 on the Web server, a firewall is going to allow it. As a Web security device, it is actually going to ask a second question. The second question is more than just making sure the traffic is on the appropriate port—the Web security device asks, "Is this request a request for a permitted Web page, a request that is actually a buffer overflow, or is this some other sort of attack?" Some firewall manufacturers are starting to build this technology into their firewalls—it can be called either intrusion prevention or deep packet inspection. In either case, the firewall is actually looking into the data portion of the packet to attempt to distinguish legitimate traffic from Web server attacks. Web server and Web application are the most often attacked applications because of their need to be available to the entire Internet (see Figures 3.67 and 3.68). There are many different types of Web server attacks; the following are just a few examples:

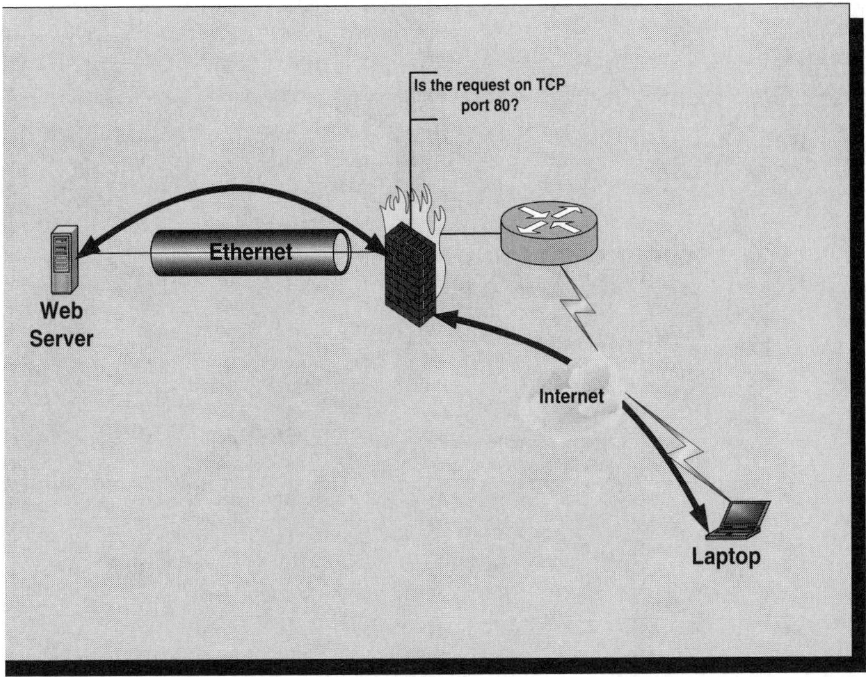

Figure 3.67 Firewall inspection.

- Browser Hi-Jacking
- Cookie Theft
- Server & Client Compromise
- Denial of Service
- Abuse of the Web Application
- User Privacy Invasion

With so many different attacks available for the attacker, Web applications often create the greatest security risk for an organization.

Security Testing

We have discussed models, risks, threats, and controls in this section. The best way to actually determine which model to use, risks to mitigate, threats to plan for, and controls to implement is through the process of security testing. There are many different types of security testing from risk analysis through penetration testing. Each type of security test has its own positives and negatives. It is important for the information security

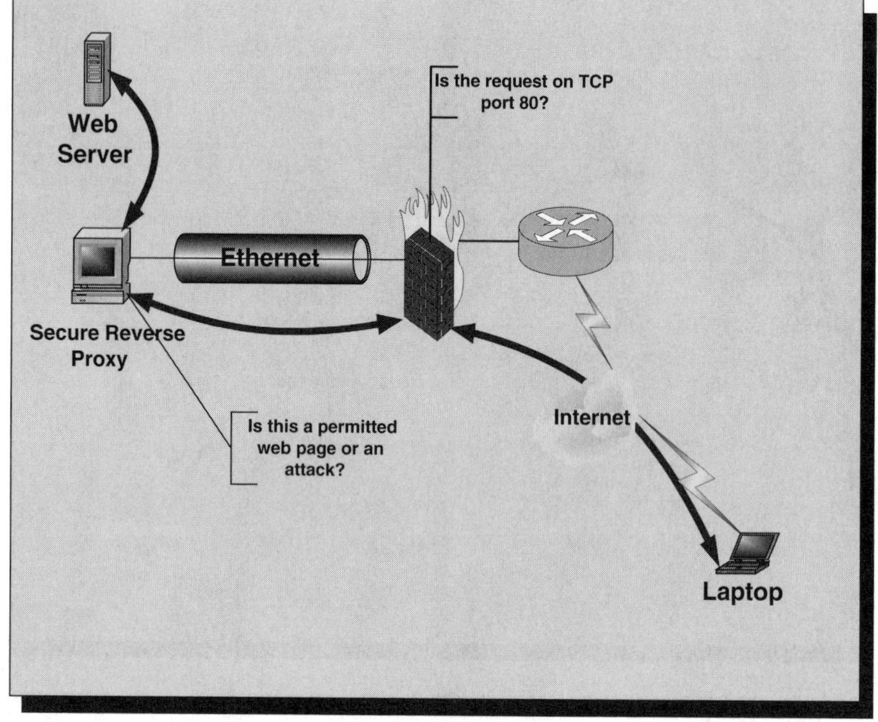

Figure 3.68 Web security inspection.

manager to be able to determine which type of security test is needed for his organization.

Vulnerability Assessment

A vulnerability assessment typically is going to be a technical probe into your system to see if there are any controls that are lacking; usually it is going to be one of the last elements of your security life cycle. A vulnerability assessment is going to attempt to search the entire security domain for an organization and attempt to uncover all security weaknesses.

Vulnerability Assessment

A vulnerability assessment typically is going to be a technical probe into your system to see if there are any controls that are lacking; usually it is going to be one of the last elements of your security life cycle.

Penetration Testing

Penetration testing is like a vulnerability assessment that didn't go to a liberal arts college. It went to technical school; it's very narrowly focused. The goal of a penetration test is to break in. Once you have broken in, you have been successful and the penetration test is complete. A vulnerability assessment is usually much more structured and repeatable. A penetration test is usually just a kind of break-in to the system. Typically you will employ white-hat hackers and they will tell you how tough it was to break in to the system and some things that an attacker would see to fix on your system.

Risk Assessment

Risk assessment is going to look at the impact on the organization and you talked about that quite a bit over the last couple of domains with my dad. Vulnerability assessment versus penetration test: vulnerability assessment is broadly comprehensive. It can look at things such as policy and procedure problems. It can look at things such as administrative controls. A penetration test is going to be very technically focused. The goal is to break into the system. You can do things such as social engineering; it's part of a penetration test regularly where you are trying to break in through the people. Vulnerability assessment versus risk assessment: vulnerability assessment tends to be technical and risk assessment tends to be nontechnical.

Hybrid Approach to Security Testing

There are hybrid approaches. You can do a combination of risk assessment with vulnerability assessment. You can also do a combination of vulnerability assessment and penetration test where you look for the vulnerabilities and then you see if you can actually compromise; you can actually bundle those different approaches together.

Summary

Information security program management is the largest of the five functional areas of the CISM exam. In this section we covered some of the basics of information security and models such as the OSI model. The next section covered some of the common threats to information security and finally we concluded with controls that can help mitigate some of the risks to information security. The information security program management function area covered most of the technical components of the CISM including firewalls, IDS systems, and cryptography.

What Was Covered in This Chapter

- The OSI model
- The TCP/IP model
- The CIA triad
- Information security threats
- Sources for threat information
- Hackers, crackers, and phreaks
- Attacking methodology
- Denial-of-service
- Distributed denial-of-service
- Social engineering
- Information security controls
- Access control
- Mandatory access control
- Discretionary access control
- Rule-based access control
- Role-based access control
- Single sign-on
- One-time passwords
- Password selection
- RADIUS
- 802.1x authentication
- Firewalls
- Packet filter firewalls
- Stateful inspection firewalls
- Proxy firewalls
- Cryptography
- Subdomain isolation techniques
- VLANs
- Web server security
- Wireless
- Application security
- Security testing

Questions

1. Which of the following is not a responsibility of the data or systems owner?
   A. To identify, describe, and designate the sensitivity of their applications systems
   B. To ensure that appropriate security control requirements are included in specifications
   C. To assess security requirements by evaluating application assets, threats, and vulnerabilities
   D. To develop industry best practices

Answer D

2. Which of the following attacks would compromise the integrity of system information?
   A. Denial-of-service
   B. Smurf
   C. SQL Injection
   D. Fraggle

Answer C

3. A policy for the physical component of the information technology infrastructure could work with all of the following except:
   A. Firewalls
   B. ID badges
   C. Cameras
   D. Security guards

Answer A

4. Which of the following is not an example of the platform component of information technology infrastructure?
   A. Switch security
   B. Operating system security
   C. Application security
   D. Anti-virus

Answer A

5. Which of the following is an example of the network component of information technology infrastructure?
   A. Switch security
   B. Operating system security
   C. Application security
   D. Anti-virus

Answer A

6. When implementing a security control, an information security manager needs to be especially aware of:
   A. Change control management
   B. What the organization's competition is doing
   C. A promotion to production procedure
   D. The impact on the end-user community

Answer D

7. Which of the following is often a disadvantage of using a closed system?
   A. Lack of end user support.
   B. Lack of product functionality.
   C. The source code cannot be verified.
   D. The source code is provided by the Internet community at large.

Answer C

8. Which of the following is an advantage of an open system?
   A. End-user support.
   B. The source code can be verified.
   C. Difficulty in management.
   D. All users are always permitted to access the system.

Answer B

9. What would be a disadvantage of deploying a proxy-based firewall?
   A. Proxy-based firewalls may not support custom applications.
   B. Proxy-based firewalls inspect to only the network layer of the OSI model.
   C. Proxy-based firewalls cannot block unwanted traffic.
   D. Proxy-based firewalls do not provide network address translation.

Answer A

10. Which of the following is true of a stateful inspection firewall?
    A. Stateful inspection firewalls protect through all layers of the OSI model.
    B. Stateful inspection firewalls support more custom applications than other firewalls.
    C. Stateful inspection firewalls are faster then other firewalls.
    D. Stateful inspection firewalls do not provide network address translation.

Answer B

11. Which of the following is true regarding a packet filter firewall?
    A. Packet filter firewalls provide more protection than other firewalls.
    B. Packet filter firewalls provide protection through the entire OSI model.
    C. Packet filter firewalls do not provide network address translation.
    D. Packet filter firewalls provide less protection than other firewalls.

Answer D

12. Which of the following would be an advantage to deploying public key (asymmetric) as opposed to private key (symmetric) encryption technologies?
    A. Public key is more scalable.
    B. Public key encryption is faster.
    C. Public key requires less infrastructure.
    D. Private key is easier on the end-user community.

Answer A

13. Digital signatures encrypt the message hash with which of the following keys?
    A. Sender's public key
    B. Sender's private key
    C. Receiver's public key
    D. Receiver's private key

Answer B

14. What term is best defined as a model used to determine the security and functionality of a proposed project?
    A. Prototype
    B. Checkpoint
    C. Journaling
    D. Service level agreement

Answer A

15. What is an advantage in performing a vulnerability assessment over a penetration test?
    A. Penetration tests test the entire network.
    B. Vulnerability assessments compromise a system or network.
    C. Vulnerability assessments are a structured repeatable test.
    D. Vulnerability assessments are faster to conduct than penetration testing.

Answer C

16. What advantage does discretionary access control have over mandatory access control?
    A. Mandatory access control is easier to implement.
    B. Discretionary access control uses extensive labeling.
    C. Discretionary access control has less administrative overhead.
    D. Discretionary access control is determined by policy.

Answer C

17. Which of the following technologies protects the confidentiality of information by embedding the message into an image or music file?
    A. Public key cryptography
    B. Private key cryptography
    C. Digital signatures
    D. Steganography

Answer D

18. Which of the following algorithms is a public key algorithm?
    A. DES
    B. AES
    C. RC4
    D. RSA

Answer D

19. Two-factor authentication can be established by combining something you have, you are, and which of the following terms?
    A. You know.
    B. You read.
    C. You touch.
    D. You need.

Answer A

20. Which of the following can be a security concern with host-based single-sign-on implementations?
    A. Passwords are often stored in plaintext.
    B. Passwords are often transmitted in plaintext.
    C. The authentication host can be a single point of failure.
    D. Lack of scalability.

Answer C

21. A Message Authentication Code (MAC) is a message digest encrypted with which of the following keys?
    A. The sender's public key
    B. The session key

C. The receiver's public key
D. The server's public key

Answer B

22. Message hashes provide which of the following principles of information security management?
    A. Integrity
    B. Confidentiality
    C. Availability
    D. Authentication

Answer A

23. Which of the following terms is best defined as a project to identify the threats that exist over key information and information technology?
    A. Vulnerability assessment
    B. Penetration test
    C. Threat analysis
    D. System development life cycle

Answer C

24. Key escrow is an example of which of the following security principles?
    A. Split knowledge
    B. Two-factor authentication
    C. Need to know
    D. Least privilege

Answer A

25. Which of the following algorithms is an example of a one-time pad?
    A. DES
    B. AES
    C. RSA
    D. RC4

Answer D

26. A one-time pad differs from other symmetric key algorithms in that:
    A. A new key is never exchanged.
    B. The key is used for one message and then discarded.
    C. The length of the key can be longer than for other algorithms.
    D. The key dynamically regenerates.

Answer B

27. Which of the following terms relates to increasing the integrity of information on a system?
    A. Fault tolerance
    B. Fail over
    C. Checkpoint
    D. Host-based intrusion detection

Answer D

28. Which of the following processes comes at the end of the system development life cycle?
    A. Accreditation
    B. Logical configuration
    C. Development
    D. Certification

Answer A

29. Public key cryptographic algorithms can be used for encryption and
    A. Message authentication codes
    B. Digital signatures
    C. Message hashing
    D. Message integrity checks

Answer B

30. What is the first step in the system development life cycle?
    A. Perform a business impact analysis.
    B. Perform a penetration test.
    C. Perform a vulnerability assessment.
    D. Perform a risk analysis.

Answer D

31. When should security become involved in the systems development life cycle?
    A. Prior to implementation
    B. Prior to all audits
    C. During requirements development
    D. During development

Answer C

32. To implement the results of a risk assessment, the information security manger should assign responsibilities and
    A. Define an implementation schedule.
    B. Define an vulnerability matrix.
    C. Define a system development life cycle.

D. Define a matrix for prototyping.

Answer A

33. When comparing the security of wireless networks with traditional or cabled networking:
    A. Wired networking provides more points for potential eavesdropping.
    B. Eavesdropping is not possible on a wireless network.
    C. Wired networking provides some protection from eavesdropping.
    D. Eavesdropping is not possible on a wireless network.

Answer C

34. In order to determine the metrics for your network you will need to begin with a measurement of current network conditions. This is called a
    A. Threat assessment
    B. Baseline
    C. Risk assessment
    D. Prototype

Answer B

35. Which of the following can be a disadvantage of using a centralized access control system?
    A. Lack of consistent administration.
    B. Lack of resource control.
    C. Difficulty in synchronizing account information.
    D. It can create a single point of failure.

Answer D

36. A formal acceptance, by management, of a third-party review of the security controls of a system, network, or application is:
    A. Certification
    B. Authentication
    C. Accreditation
    D. Classification

Answer C

37. Prior to development, to determine possible exposure points to a new application in your organization the information security manager would perform a
    A. Vulnerability assessment
    B. Business impact analysis

C. Risk assessment
D. Penetration test

Answer C

38. Which of the following technologies or standards would apply to authenticating a wireless network connection?
A. Wired equivalent privacy
B. 802.11b
C. 802.11a
D. 802.1x

Answer D

39. Wired Equivalent Privacy (WEP) is a control that increases which of the basic principles of information security management?
A. Confidentiality
B. Integrity
C. Availability
D. Authenticity

Answer A

40. Service-level agreements with a managed service provider provide minimum requirements and are included in a
A. Contract
B. Policy
C. Procedure
D. Standard

Answer A

41. For e-mail messages with the greatest sensitivity which of the following technologies would have to be employed to provide confidentiality, integrity, and authenticity?
A. Digital signatures
B. Message digests
C. Private key encryption
D. Digital signatures and encryption

Answer D

42. Which of the following technologies provide a mechanism for storing a digital certificate?
A. Magnetic cards
B. Smart cards
C. Stream cipher
D. Block cipher

Answer B

43. Which layer of the OSI model would be responsible for ensuring reliable end-to-end delivery of a message?
    A. Physical
    B. Application
    C. Session
    D. Transport

Answer D

44. At what layer of the OSI model would a proxy-based firewall exist?
    A. Physical
    B. Application
    C. Session
    D. Transport

Answer B

45. Message Digest version five (MD5) is an algorithm that is used to ensure message:
    A. Integrity
    B. Authenticity
    C. Confidentiality
    D. Fault tolerance

Answer A

46. Creating a message digest is often the first step in creating a
    A. Packet
    B. Digital signature
    C. Public key
    D. Private key

Answer B

47. An attacker who is attempting to defeat an access control system often starts by performing which of the common types of attacks?
    A. Brute force attack
    B. Denial-of-service attack
    C. Distributed denial-of-service attack
    D. Dictionary attack

Answer D

48. Temporal Key Integrity Protocol (TKIP) is a component of Wi-Fi Protected Access (WPA). What is the major advantage of using TKIP?
    A. TKIP ensures data integrity.
    B. TKIP allows data encryption keys to be changed at regular time intervals.

C. TKIP provides protection against wireless denial-of-service attacks.
D. TKIP increases the signal strength of wireless networks.

Answer B

49. An e-mail with a large attachment designed to slow down the response time for the e-mail server is a representation of what type of malicious code?
    A. Trojan horse
    B. Worm
    C. E-mail bomb
    D. Logic bomb

Answer C

50. What type of malicious code is a code fragment that attaches to a file and often replicates through the sharing of files on a network?
    A. Virus
    B. Worm
    C. E-mail bomb
    D. Logic bomb

Answer A

51. What type of malicious code is typically a complete file that infects only one place on a single system and replicates through the network without file sharing?
    A. Virus
    B. Worm
    C. E-mail bomb
    D. Logic bomb

Answer B

52. True or false: Private key cryptography requires less processing power than public key cryptography.

Answer True

53. Which of the following IPSEC-related terms will help resolve authentication issues present in Internet Protocol (IP)?
    A. High-level Message Authentication Code (HMAC)
    B. Authentication Headers (AH)
    C. Encapsulated Secure Payload (ESP)
    D. Data Encryption Standard (DES)

Answer B

54. Which of the following IPSEC-related terms will help resolve confidentiality issues present in Internet Protocol (IP)?
    A. High-level Message Authentication Code (HMAC)
    B. Authentication Headers (AH)
    C. Encapsulated Secure Payload (ESP)
    D. Data Encryption Standard (DES)

Answer C

55. Which of the following is true regarding IPSEC?
    A. IPSEC will encapsulate Internet Protocol (IP) traffic only.
    B. IPSEC will support only one concurrent tunnel.
    C. IPSEC operates at the physical layer of the ODI model.
    D. IPSEC requires the use of Public Key Infrastructure (PKI).

Answer A

56. Presenting a fraudulent Internet Protocol (IP) address to attempt to bypass the access control enforced by a stateful inspection firewall is an example of what common type of network attack?
    A. Social engineering
    B. Spoofing
    C. SYN flood
    D. Steganography

Answer B

57. Which of the following positions would be most likely to determine the security policy regarding access of information on a system?
    A. Users
    B. Business process owner
    C. Senior management
    D. Information security manager

Answer B

58. Which of the following groups or organizations is most commonly used to develop baselines for information systems?
    A. Developers
    B. Programmers
    C. Software vendors
    D. Promotion to production staff

Answer C

59. Which type of malicious detection software would detect a polymorphic virus by comparing the function of the application rather than comparing it to known signature?

A. Heuristic scanner
B. Host-based intrusion detection
C. Network-based intrusion detection
D. Gateway anti-virus scanner

Answer A

60. What is a primary difference between Secure Sockets Layer (SSL) and Secure HyperText Transfer Protocol (SHTTP)?
    A. SSL only encrypts Web traffic.
    B. SHTTP does not encrypt the data.
    C. SSL does not encrypt the data.
    D. SSL is a transport-layer protocol.

Answer D

61. Which statement most accurately reflects the encryption used by SSL?
    A. The session key is encrypted using asymmetric key encryption and the bulk data is encrypted with symmetric encryption.
    B. The bulk data transfer is encrypted using asymmetric encryption; the key is exchanged out of band.
    C. SSL uses asymmetric encryption for both session key exchange and bulk data encryption.
    D. SSL does not use encryption.

Answer A

62. If you wanted to ensure the integrity of a message, which of the following technologies would provide the most insurance against tampering?
    A. Logging before and after records
    B. Digital signatures
    C. Asymmetric encryption
    D. Symmetric encryption

Answer B

63. A vendor is recommending implementation of a new technology that will give your application nonrepudiation. Which of the following primary tenants of information security will be addressed with this solution?
    A. Availability and integrity
    B. Confidentiality and integrity
    C. Confidentiality and authenticity
    D. Authenticity and integrity

Answer D

64. Which of the following primary tenants of information security will be addressed by using 802.1x with a wireless network?
    A. Authentication
    B. Availability
    C. Integrity
    D. Confidentiality

Answer A

65. Which of the following technologies is commonly used in conjunction with 802.1x authentication?
    A. Remote Authentication Dial In User Service (RADIUS)
    B. Single Sign On (SSO)
    C. Public Key Infrastructure (PKI)
    D. Intrusion Detection System (IDS)

Answer A

66. Which common type of access control system assigns rights to job functions and not user accounts?
    A. Rule-based access control
    B. Role-based access control
    C. Mandatory access control
    D. Discretionary access control

Answer B

67. Which of the following is an example of security issues that can occur within the system development life cycle?
    A. Lack of senior management support.
    B. Security is not involved in the requirements development.
    C. Vendor interoperability.
    D. Network latency.

Answer B

68. The information security manager needs to be most aware of which of the following issues when implementing new security controls?
    A. Impact on end users
    B. Senior management support
    C. System development life cycle
    D. Annual loss expectancy

Answer A

69. Which of the following security concerns needs to be addressed during the disposal phase of the system development life cycle?
    A. Maintaining integrity of information

B. Maintaining availability of the system
C. Maintaining nonrepudiation of user access
D. Maintaining confidentiality of information

Answer D

70. Change control can be used in many phases on the system development life cycle. At which phase of the system development life cycle would you not use a change control process?
A. Development
B. Installation
C. Disposal
D. Requirements

Answer D

71. Which of the following types of controls would affect direct access to system consoles?
A. Process
B. Platform
C. Physical
D. Network

Answer C

72. Which of the following types of controls would directly affect the security of an operating system?
A. Process
B. Platform
C. Physical
D. Network

Answer B

73. Which of the following technologies would utilize a Public Key Infrastructure (PKI)?
A. Secure HyperText Transfer Protocol (SHTTP)
B. Secure Shell (SSH)
C. Message Authentication Codes (MAC)
D. Digital signatures

Answer D

74. Smart card technology is often used for what information security purpose?
A. Message Integrity
B. Authentication
C. Confidentiality

D. Availability

Answer B

75. Extensible Markup Language (XML) is a language often used with Web application development. XML provides which of the following?
    A. Dynamic content delivery
    B. Dynamic message integrity
    C. Dynamic user authentication
    D. Dynamic client configuration

Answer A

76. An acceptable use policy would be an example of which type of control?
    A. Process
    B. Platform
    C. Physical
    D. Network

Answer A

77. Which type of attack against access control systems uses a list of common words?
    A. A brute force attack
    B. A denial-of-service attack
    C. A dictionary attack
    D. A network spoofing attack

Answer C

78. Which type of information security process assigns a level of sensitivity to data as it is being created, amended, enhanced, stored, or transmitted?
    A. Risk analysis
    B. Risk assessment
    C. Network vulnerability assessment
    D. Information classification

Answer D

79. Which type of device creates a variable, alternating current (AC) field for the purpose of demagnetizing magnetic recording media?
    A. A degausser
    B. A demagnetizer
    C. A deionizer
    D. A deflator

Answer A

80. Which of the following terms frequently refers to a network segment between the Internet and a private network?
    A. A security domain
    B. A zone of control
    C. A DeMilitarized Zone (DMZ)
    D. A security kernel

Answer C

81. Which type of network attack captures sensitive pieces of information, such as passwords, passing through the network?
    A. Spoofing
    B. SYN flood
    C. Sniffing
    D. Steganography

Answer C

82. Which of the following technologies would best secure the data on a laptop or other device that could be stolen?
    A. Data encryption
    B. File deletion
    C. No access to the floppy drive
    D. Steganography

Answer A

83. Which of the following attacks is an example of a passive attack?
    A. Spoofing
    B. SYN flood
    C. Information gathering
    D. Port scanning

Answer C

84. Which of the following common network attacks is an example of a denial-of-service attack?
    A. Spoofing
    B. SYN flood
    C. Sniffing
    D. Port scanning

Answer B

85. Which of the following common network attacks is an example of an active attack?
    A. Information gathering
    B. Traffic analysis

C. Sniffing
D. Port scanning

Answer D

86. Which type of network attack is most likely to present the ability to execute commands on the compromised machine?
    A. Spoofing
    B. SYN flood
    C. Sniffing
    D. Buffer overflow

Answer D

87. Which attack is due to poor programming practices?
    A. Spoofing
    B. SYN flood
    C. Sniffing
    D. Buffer overflow

Answer D

Chapter 4

Information Security Management

Functional Area Overview

The objective of this job practice area is to focus on the tasks and knowledge necessary for the information security manager to effectively manage information security within an organization. It contains a description of various techniques the information security manager can use and the areas on which the information security manager should focus. This functional area comprises 24 percent of the CISM® examination and comprises approximately 48 questions.

Security management is supported by such documents as

- Organization for Economic Co-operation and Development (OECD)
- Institute of Chartered Accountants in England
- ISO/IEC 17799 (ISO 27002)
- British Standard 77 99 (ISO 27001)
- Information Systems Audit and Control (ISACA®), Control Objectives for Information Technology (CobiT®)
- National Institute of Standards and Technology (NIST) Special Publication (SP) 800–55, 800–26 and 800–12

An effective information security management process requires senior management commitment and support. Management must demonstrate a commitment to security. Management shows this commitment by clearly approving and supporting formal security policies, monitoring and measuring organizational performance in implementing the security policies, and by supporting security awareness and training for all staff throughout the organization. This may require special management-level training, inasmuch as security is not necessarily a part of management expertise.

As we discussed in Chapter 1 on governance, security policies and procedures must reflect business objectives, be reviewed regularly, and use a risk-based approach to identify sensitive and critical information resources. Using the information discussed in the risk management chapter we know that there should be a clear understanding of threats and risks, how the risks may affect the functioning of the organization and the fulfillment of the organization's mission, and the integration of security into the operations of the enterprise. Once the risks and the potential for harm are understood, appropriate measures are taken to mitigate such risks and ensure that any residual risks remaining are at an acceptable level.

The development of the information systems security policy, which provides the framework for designing and developing appropriate management, operational, and technical controls, is the responsibility of the top level of management within an organization. Implementation of the policy can be delegated to the appropriate level. The policy contributes to the protection of information assets. Its objective is to protect the information capital against all types of risks, accidental or intentional. An existing and enforced information systems security policy is of paramount importance for an organization's survival and development. The policy should ensure systems conformity with laws and regulations, integrity of the data, confidentiality, and availability.

All employees of an organization and, where relevant, third-party users should receive appropriate training and regular updates on the importance of security in organizational policies and procedures. This includes security requirements, legal responsibilities, and business controls, as well as training in the correct use of information processing facilities, for example, log-on procedures and use of software packages. For new employees, this should occur before access to information or services is granted.

In order to assess the effectiveness of an organization's security programs on a continuous basis, information security managers must have an understanding of the organization's monitoring activities in assessing the effectiveness of security programs and controls established. For example, many of these issues relate to compliance with applicable laws and regulations requiring organizational due diligence to security and privacy of sensitive information, particularly as it relates to specific industries (e.g., banking and financial institutions, healthcare). Other reviews relate to organizational compliance with security policies and procedures established by the organization as a security "baseline" in reducing risk to acceptable levels for established information security programs. As information resources change while in a production state, the security baseline should be maintained. All changes must be recertified by the appropriate level of management.

In this chapter you will learn about the following information security management tasks. How to ...

1. Ensure that the rules of use for information systems comply with the enterprise's information security policies.
2. Ensure that the administrative procedures for information systems comply with the enterprise's information security policies.
3. Ensure that services provided by other enterprises including outsourced providers are consistent with established information security policies.
4. Use metrics to measure, monitor, and report on the effectiveness and efficiency of information security controls and the compliance with information security policies.
5. Ensure that information security is not compromised throughout the change management process.
6. Ensure that vulnerability assessments are performed to evaluate effectiveness of existing controls.
7. Ensure that noncompliance issues and other variances are resolved in a timely manner.
8. Ensure the development and delivery of the activities that can influence culture and behavior of staff including information security education and awareness.

CISM Mapping

When the information security risk management functional areas are mapped to ISO 17799 and the domains from the CISSP® common body of knowledge, it shows just how many different areas of knowledge from which we are going to be drawing information (see Table 4.1). The information security risk management section is restricted to the risk analysis, assessment, mitigation, and vulnerability assessment.

Introduction

Ensuring that the rules of use for information systems comply with the enterprise's information security policies is imperative in every well-managed organization. These rules of use must comply with the organization's

Table 4.1 Mapping CISM Governance to ISO 17799 and CISSP Domains

Information Security Program Management *ISO 27002 Section*	*CISSP® Domain*
6. Asset Management	1. Access Control
10. Access Control	3. Security Management
11. Systems Acquisition, Development and Maintenance	4. Applications Security
13. Compliance	7. Operations Security

information security policies. These are standard minimum rules of use that the organization has defined as necessary to protect its critical information. Safe network use can often include several rules including:

- Sharing files on the network
- Correct use of the operating system (e.g., UNIX, Linux, Windows, etc.)
- Peer-to-peer software (e.g., Kazaa, Morpheus, etc.)
- Copyright infringement
- Account password safety

The information security manager should ensure that operating procedures comply with the enterprise's information security policies. The information security manager can achieve this goal efficiently through the organization's change management process. Considering security implications during the change management process will help ensure that modifications to the information systems are made in compliance with the information security policies and that security vulnerabilities are not mistakenly introduced into the environment.

Other common rules of use include:

- Internet rules of use
- Electronic mail rules of use
- Application rules of use
- Network rules of use

The information security manager should be involved in the development of these rules of use to ensure that they comply with the organization's information security policies.

Information Systems Compliance

File sharing is the practice of making files available for other users to download over the Internet and smaller networks. Usually file sharing follows the peer-to-peer (P2P) model, where the files are stored on and served by personal computers of the users. Most people who engage in file sharing are also downloading files that other users share. Sometimes these two activities are linked together. P2P file sharing is distinct from file trading in that downloading files from a P2P network does not require uploading, although some networks either provide incentives for uploading such as credits or force the sharing of files being currently downloaded.

A peer-to-peer (or P2P) computer network (Table 4.2) is a network that relies primarily on the computing power and bandwidth of the participants in the network rather than concentrating it in a relatively low number of servers. P2P networks are typically used for connecting nodes via largely ad hoc connections. Such networks are useful for many purposes. Sharing content files containing audio, video, data, or anything in digital format is very common, and real-time data, such as telephony traffic, is also passed using P2P technology.*

A pure peer-to-peer network does not function in a client/server environment; it identifies equal peer nodes that simultaneously function as both "clients" and "servers" to the other nodes on the network. This model of network arrangement differs from the client/server model where

Table 4.2 Peer-to-Peer Examples

Pure peer-to-peer:	*Hybrid peer-to-peer:*
• Peers act as clients and server	• Has a central server that keeps information on peers and responds to requests for that information.
• There is no central server managing the network	• Peers are responsible for hosting the information (as the central server does not store the information), for letting the central server know what resources they want to share, and for downloading its shareable resources to peers that request it.
• There is no central router	• Route terminals are used addresses, which are referenced by a set of indices to obtain an absolute address.

* Marling Engle. Vulnerabilities of P2P systems and a critical look at their solutions, May 2006.

communication is usually to and from a central server. A typical example for a non-peer-to-peer file transfer is an FTP server where the client and server programs are quite distinct, and the clients initiate the downloads or uploads and the servers react to and satisfy these requests.

Administrative Procedures

Documented procedures should be prepared for system activities associated with information processing and telecommunications. These procedures would include media handling, system start-up and shut-down procedures, backup requirements, system and equipment maintenance, data center access and control, contingency plans, and employee safety.

The objective of procedure development is to establish the process to ensure the correct and secure operation of the information technology infrastructure. Roles and responsibilities should be established giving consideration to segregation of duties, where appropriate, to reduce the risk of negligent or deliberate system misuse.

We discussed policy development in Chapter 1 on governance. Procedure writing is different from policy writing in that it is not useful to have teams develop the procedures. Procedures will not have to be approved by a management team. So the process is quicker, but will require some work.

Unlike the policy development process, the use of a team to develop procedures will actually slow the process down. Many security professionals reach this stage of the information security program and believe that the bulk of their work is complete and now it will be up to the Subject Matter Experts (SME) to write the procedures. This is probably not going to work. The SMEs are usually the same groups of people required now to provide documentation for the work they perform. They are busy with their day-to-day functions and are already hard pressed to find the time to worry about existing paperwork let alone adding the requirement that they write procedures.

When developing procedures use a technical writer to gather the relevant information from the SME and put that information into one of the procedure formats. Ask him to bring any written procedures he may have created on the subject and any other visual aid (perhaps a flowchart or an information flow model; see Figure 4.1).

Schedule the meeting for 45 minutes. This should be long enough to get the information necessary, but not so long as to affect the SME's busy schedule. Remember to treat the SME with respect and to listen to what she has to say, but keep her on track. After you have gathered all of the

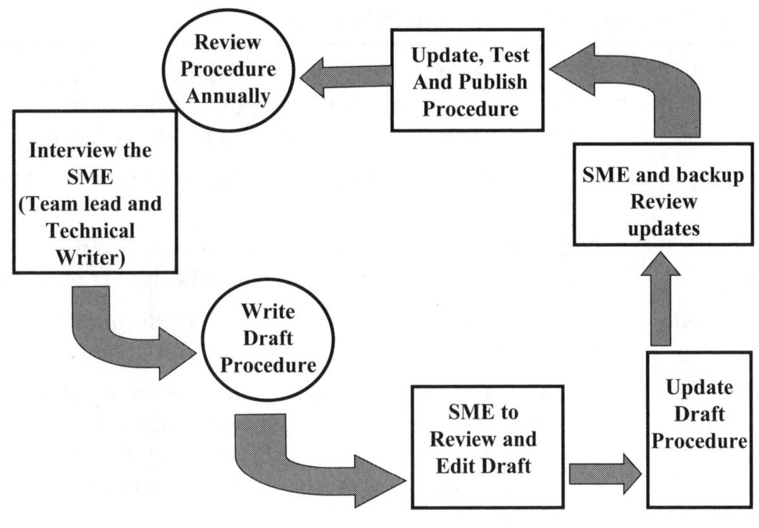

Figure 4.1 Procedure writing flow model.

Table 4.3 Procedure Writing Steps

Steps	*Description*
1.	The material just discussed will be put into procedure format.
2.	A draft procedure will be sent to the SME for review and content editing.
3.	The technical writer will update the procedure based on the SME's remarks.
4.	The updated procedure will be sent to the SME and the SME backup for a final review.
5.	Any additional updates will be incorporated into the procedure.
6.	The procedure will be tested (either with the backup or some other person).
7.	If the procedure provides the proper results, it will be published in the appropriate procedure document.

information you can about the subject, inform the SME as to what the next steps will be (Table 4.3).

When putting the SME's words into a procedure, it will be necessary to ensure that the procedure is developed properly. There are procedure writing requirements just as we have examined in the policy and standards

Table 4.4 Procedure Development Checklist

Title	Establish what the topic of the procedure is going to be. Try to avoid being cute with your choice of words. Remember you are writing for a business environment.
Intent	Discuss what the procedure is attempting to accomplish in general terms.
Scope	Briefly describe the process that the procedure is going to cover. (i.e., Implementing a UNIX userID request).
Responsibilities	Identify who is to perform what steps in the procedure. Use job functions rather than individual names.
Sequence of Events	It is very important to understand the timing and conditions for performing the tasks identified in the procedure. Some tasks are not executed at a specific time, but must be performed when a specific condition is met.
Approvals	Identify any necessary approvals and when these approvals must be met. Approvals will be obtained prior to the execution of the procedure process.
Prerequisites	List any preconditions that must be met before starting the procedure process.
Definitions	Remember the audience. It will be beneficial to include a discussion of any terms and acronyms that are included in the body of the procedure.
Equipment Required	Identify all equipment, tools, documents and anything else the individual executing the procedure will need to perform the tasks.
Warnings	Some tasks, if operated in an improper sequence, could cause severe damage to the enterprise. Identify those key tasks and review the importance of understanding exactly when the task is to be executed and under what set of circumstances.
Precautions	Identify all steps to be taken to avoid problems or dangers (i.e., "Unplug before performing maintenance.")
Procedure Body	These are the actual steps to be performed in the execution of the procedure.

development process. For some reason, requirements seem to come in tens. So let us examine the ten requirements for procedure writing (see Table 4.4).

1. *Write to the Audience:* Procedures are created and implemented with the sole intention to be read and used by the user community. Always keep the audience in mind when writing procedures. When you interview the SME you will get a flavor for the language that is used in that area. Write the procedure to reflect this level of technology. However, when writing procedures to support Business Continuity Planning (BCP) activities, the audience has changed. Instead of the SME, the audience may be someone filling in for the SME. So before any procedure can be written, it will be necessary to know who the audience is and what their level of knowledge of the subject at hand is.
   Every department has its own language; therefore the procedures must be developed using the terms that they are used to. If you write procedures using the wrong "language," the procedure may as well be written in Sanskrit. The intended audience will not be able to understand it, or they will find it difficult to follow.
2. *Organize the Material:* The procedures must be written in a logical and flowing manner so that the reader can understand the meaning. If the text is not properly planned, the possibility is great that the intended audience will not clearly understand what is expected of them. The procedure must be broken up into easily digestable bits of information. Don't expect the user to read a long and involved passage and then successfully execute the appropriate processes. The television program *Friends* gave us a perfect example of what can go wrong if procedures are not properly followed or if they are designed incorrectly. The character Rachel was creating a trifle dessert from a recipe. She started with sponge cake, then custard, then fruit, then sponge cake, and then the pages stuck together. She finished the trifle with a layer of ground meat and then potatoes. She had combined the trifle recipe with one for shepherd's pie. If the procedure is created in a convoluted manner, this could happen to your organization.
3. *Read and Edit the Materials*: Do not just run the spellchecker and assume that the editing is complete. Before handing over the material to the editor, proofread what has been written and see if it makes sense to you. If you are unable to understand what you have written, then it will probably be harder for others to understand. After the technical writer has developed the draft procedure, have the document proofed for grammar and spelling. Once that is complete, have someone in the group read through the procedure to see if it follows a logical sequence. Once these steps have been completed, then the procedure is ready for the SME to review.

4. *Find Subject Experts:* The first step in any procedure development process is to either know the subject or to find someone who does and use his knowledge to write the procedure. The subject expert may not understand the procedure writing process, so it may be necessary for you to sit with him and take notes on how the process works and then write the procedure. Make sure that one of the editors is the subject expert. However, the subject expert should not be the person to test the procedure. The expert knows the topic so well that he might assume information that is not present in the procedure.
5. *Use Clear Familiar Words:* The procedure's intended audience will not be pleased if they are confronted with a document filled with words, expressions, and acronyms with which they are unfamiliar. It will be important to have a definition section in some procedures. This should be done up front and provide the reader with whatever is necessary to complete the process at hand.
   Employees have different roles and these roles support the activities of the other roles and responsibilities. To establish a level of understanding through this book, let us examine typical roles found in an organization and what they are responsible for with regard to risk analysis and risk management
6. *Keep Sentences Short and Simple:* Remember the KISS (Keep It Simple Sweetie) principle. Long sentences increase the level of frustration of the user and decrease the level of understanding. An appropriate average sentence length for procedures is between 10 and 15 words. Unless you are a writer of the caliber of James Joyce, it would be wise to keep the sentences to the 15-word maximum level. Typically, procedures are better if the sentences are brief and often they do not have to be correct syntaxwise. Phrases such as "Hit Enter" or "Toggle switch" are sufficient when writing procedures.
7. *Use Illustrations to Support the Topic:* "A picture is worth a thousand words" may be a cliché, but it is true. Whenever applicable, break up the text with a graphic that depicts what is being discussed. These graphics can be pictures, charts (flow, pie, bar, etc.), tables, or diagrams. These will help the user to visualize the subject and can provide the material necessary for a clear understanding of the process.
   Illustrations include the use of screen prints. This will help the users if they are interacting with a computer system. By providing a picture of the screen, the user will be able to visualize what the process looks like and what is expected as a response.

8. *Use an Active Voice:* In the active voice, the sentences stress what has to occur. It will identify who is responsible for what action. For example, a passive voice might read as follows, "All tape drives are to be cleaned by the tape operators." An active voice might read as follows, "The tape operators are responsible for cleaning the tape drives on each shift." The active voice identifies who is responsible and for what they are responsible.
9. *Ensure Grammar and Punctuation Are Correct:* The number one deadly sin is not taking care of this key element. Too many times materials have been sent out for content review and the text is filled with errors of grammar and punctuation. It is hard enough to get a critique of the subject; by presenting the reviewer with error-filled material, they will correct the form and forget to comment on the substance. If this is not your strong suit, find someone that can do these edits.
10. *Use a Conversational Style:* This does not mean that the text should be full of slang and idioms; it should just be presented in an informal style. Most people communicate better when they are speaking than when they are writing. It could be that many individuals write to impress the reader as opposed to writing to express an idea. One very easy way around this problem is to write as if you are talking to the intended audience. However, if you have a tendency to speak like William F. Buckley, Jr., then you might want to have someone else review the material. Even though a conversational style is preferred, this form does not relieve you of the responsibility of being precise.

Not every procedure will require all of the elements found in the procedure development checklist. Some may even require additional steps. As with any checklist, this is only a series of thought starters. The list that will be used by you may have additional items, or fewer.

Operation procedures, and the documented procedures for system activities, should be treated as formal documents and changes must go through a review and authorization process.

A key component in the administrative procedures process is to implement a change management process that will help ensure that modifications to the information technology infrastructure are controlled and approved. The ability to track and approve changes to the production environment will go a long way in establishing an effective internal control structure.

Change management is the process of controlling changes to the infrastructure or any portion of services offered, in a controlled manner,

Table 4.5 Change Management Phases

Change Management Phase	*Task Descriptions*
Initiation	Request of change is made formally
Assessment	Analyze request Develop the implementation strategy Determine implementation specifications Estimate cost for implementation Review security implications Record change request Submit change request for approval
Authorization	Owner reviews Assessment findings and issues approval
Implementation	Develop changes based on specifications Create code to add or subtract functionality Submit program code to Quality Assurance for testing and Owner approval Submit approved changes to Production Control to move into production Make version changes Link to Production Report changes to management

ensuring approved changes with a minimum disruption to the processing environment and user community. See Table 4.5.

The change management process uses the concept of separation of duties to ensure that changes to the production environment meet quality and security needs and requirements (see Table 4.6). If two elements of a transaction are processed by different individuals, each person provides a check over the other. Separation of duties also acts as a deterrent to

Table 4.6 Define Separation and Segregation of Duties

Separation of duties	Its objective is to ensure that duties (roles) are assigned to individuals in a manner so that no one individual can control a process from start to finish.
Segregation of duties	A method of working whereby tasks are apportioned between different members of staff in order to reduce the scope for error and fraud.

fraud or concealment because collusion with another individual is required to complete the fraudulent act. Separating responsibility for program or system change from testing and updating the production environment is a critical control element.

The change control process ensures that adequate testing is performed on all changes. The procedures also require that the developer create an effective rollback or disaster recovery plan. Change control also ensures that changes are traceable and auditable and requires that all documentation be completed prior to closing out the request form.

Effective change control can uncover when there might be a modification to production rules, proxies, or system parameters. The review and testing process provides the opportunity to avoid potential hardware failures. Because there is a peer review of the code portion to this process, the possibility of malicious code is reduced.

Ensure Services Outsourced Are Consistent

When establishing a relationship with a third party, the organization should ensure that security controls and service levels are documented in the language of the contract. As we discussed in Chapter 1 on governance, one of the key Tier 1 policies that is used to support security needs and requirements is the procurement and contracts policy.

> *Procurement and Contracts:* This policy establishes the way in which the organization conducts its business with outside firms. This policy addresses those items that must be included in any contract and this includes language that discusses the need for third parties to comply with organizations policies, procedures, and standards.

This policy is probably one of the most important for information security and other organization policies and standards. We can only write policies and establish standards and procedures for employees; all third parties must be handled contractually. It is very important that the contract language reference any policies, standards, and procedures that are deemed appropriate.

Too often policies contain language that "the policy applies to all employees, contractors, consultants, per diem, and other third parties." Just because this language appears in a policy does not make it effective. Third parties must be handled contractually. It will be necessary for the security professional to work with the procurement group and legal staff

Table 4.7 Outsourcing Definitions

Key Terms	*Definition*
Outsource	To obtain goods or services from an outside (third party) provider
Service level agreement (SLA)	Performance objectives reached by negotiation between the user and the provider of a service, or between an outsourcer and an organization
Contract	A binding agreement between two or more parties that is enforceable by law
Proposal	A formal description of the creation, modification or termination of a contract. A proposal may serve as the information flow model for future agreements and may be accepted or rejected by the entity or entities that receive it.

to ensure that purchase orders and contracts have the necessary language. It would be wise to include a confidentiality or nondisclosure agreement.

Service delivery by a third party should include the agreed upon security arrangements, service definitions, and aspects of service management. When developing outsourcing arrangements (Table 4.7), it will be necessary to plan the migration plan of information and services, and that security is maintained during the transition period.

The contract should also address the issues of business continuity plans and disaster recovery plans and the right to review and monitor their effectiveness.

Outsourcing is no reason to vary from the established information security policies and standards. During proposal and evaluation the information security manager must be part of the assessment team. It is imperative that the information security manager be part of the decision-making process.

The organization should monitor the provisions of the contract on a regular basis. This process should include reviews, assessments, and formal audits to ensure adherence to security terms and conditions. The reporting and resolutions of security incidents should also be examined to ensure that they are being properly managed.

The responsibility for managing the relationship with a third party must be assigned to a designated entity. The organization should ensure that the third party has assigned the responsibility for checking for compliance and enforcement of the agreed-upon requirements.

In the outsourcing environment, the contracting organization should maintain overall control of all security aspects for sensitive information and mission-critical systems and applications. The contracting organization should be a member of the third-party's change management process.

It remains the responsibility of the contracting organization to manage the changes to the provision of the service level agreements, including maintaining and improving existing security policies, procedures, and controls.

Measure, Monitor, and Report Effectiveness and Efficiency of the Controls and Compliance Policies

The foundation of strong upper-level management support is critical, not only for the success of the security program, but also for the implementation of a program to measure the effectiveness of the security program. This support establishes a focus on security within the highest levels of the organization (see Table 4.8). Without a solid foundation (i.e., proactive support of those persons in positions that control IT resources), the effectiveness of the security program can fail when pressured by politics and budget limitations.

Table 4.8 Roles and Responsibilities for Security Program Assessment

Roles and Responsibilities in Measuring Security Program Effectiveness	
Senior Management	• Demonstrate support for IS program • Ensure program has adequate resources (Human and financial) • Actively promote IS program • Approve policies, standards and procedures
Chief Information Security Officer	• Report to Senior Management of the state of the IS program at least annually • Implement program to measure IS effectiveness • Provide sufficient resources to complete the assessment • Communicate program goals and objectives to management and employees
Business Managers/ Resource Owners	• Participate in the assessment process • Ensure staff is aware of the program • Provide sufficient resources to complete the assessment • Support implementation of corrective measures resulting from assessment

The second component of an effective security program is practical security policies and procedures backed by the authority necessary to enforce compliance. Practical security policies and procedures are defined as those that are attainable and provide meaningful security through appropriate controls. The ability to measure the effectiveness of the program will be affected if there are no procedures in place.

The third component is developing and establishing quantifiable performance metrics that are designed to capture and provide meaningful performance data. To provide meaningful data, quantifiable security metrics must be based on information security performance goals and objectives, and be easily obtainable and feasible to measure. They must also be repeatable, provide relevant performance trends over time, and be useful for tracking performance and directing resources.

Finally, the measurement of the security program itself must emphasize consistent periodic analysis of the data available. The results of this analysis are used to apply lessons learned, improve the effectiveness of existing security controls, and plan future controls to meet new security requirements as they occur. Accurate data collection must be a priority with stakeholders and users if the collected data is to be meaningful to the management and improvement of the overall security program.

The success of an information security program implementation should be judged by the degree to which meaningful results are produced. A comprehensive security analysis program should provide substantive justification for decisions that directly affect the security posture of an organization. These decisions include budget and personnel requests and allocation of available resources. An assessment of the security program should be able to provide a precise basis for preparation of required security performance-related reports.

The information security program is a dynamic changing process and requires continuous monitoring to ensure the objectives of the program are meeting the mission or business objectives of the organization. It is important to use the results of the monitoring to effect change. As part of the monitoring process, it will be necessary to conduct regular vulnerability assessments to test the controls and safeguards. We briefly discuss vulnerability assessments shortly. The topic is covered in more detail in Chapter 5 on incidence response.

During the design and implementation of the security program the information security manager should ensure that Key Performance Indicators (KPI) are defined and that the mechanism to measure progress against those indicators is implemented. This way the information security manager can assess the success or failure of various security components and whether they are cost justifiable.

Table 4.9 Key Security Management Terms

Security Term	*Definition*
Key Performance Indicators (KPI)	Also Key Success Indicators (KSI), help an organization define and measure progress toward organizational goals.
Surveillance	Close observation of a person or group (usually by the police).
Monitoring	The act of overseeing the progress of a process to ensure that the rights and well-being of the organization are protected, that the data are accurate, complete, and that the conduct of the staff is in compliance with the policies, applicable regulatory requirements and with standards of conduct.

Whatever KPIs are selected, they must reflect the organization's goals, they must be key to its success, and they must be quantifiable (measurable). KPIs usually are long-term considerations. The definition of what they are and how they are measured does not change often. The goals for a particular KPI may change as the organization's goals change, or as it get closer to achieving a goal. See Table 4.9 for a listing of key security management terms.

Ensure That Information Security Is Not Compromised Throughout the Change Management Process

Information security must be part of the change management process because requesters and owners do not always understand security implications of the requested changes. The role of the security administrator is to analyze and assess the impact of all changes to the production environment.

Formal management responsibilities and procedures must be in place to ensure satisfactory control of all changes to equipment, software, or procedures. When changes are made, an audit log containing all relevant information must be retained.

Inadequate change control is a common cause of system, application, or security failures. Unauthorized or poorly tested changes to the production environment can affect competitive advantage, customer confidence, and return on investment.

Changes to the production environment should only be made when there is a valid business reason to do so. Updating the production system

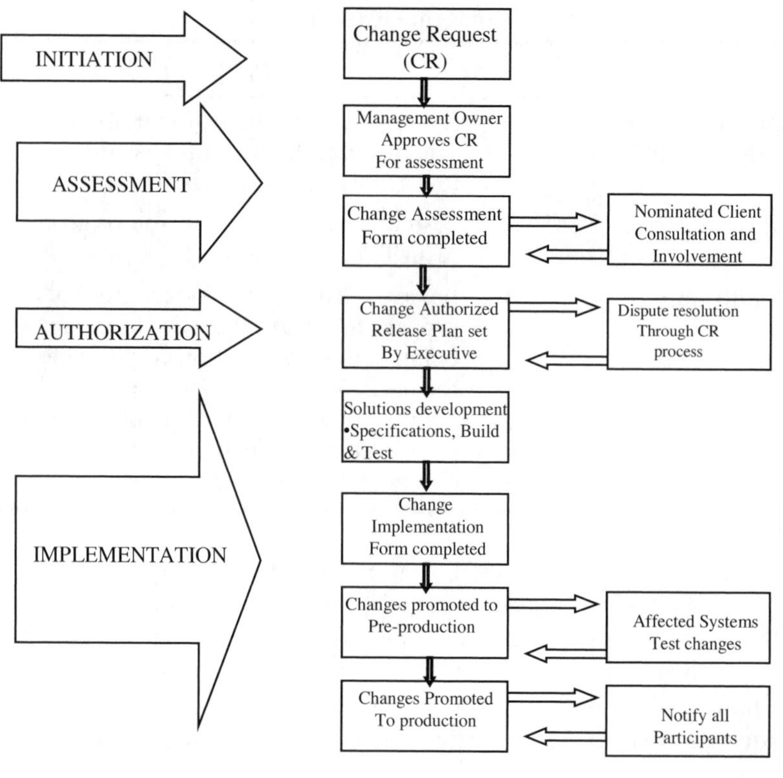

Figure 4.2 Change management visual model.

to apply the latest version or patch may not always be in the best interest of the organization. All changes, even patches and new releases, must go through change control to assess their impact on the user community.

The change management process was discussed in detail in Section 4.3 of this chapter. Figure 4.2 is a quick reference for the change management process.

The information security manager should understand the change and configuration management activities used by the organization so that security implications can be considered and addressed. Each organization may have a different process for change and configuration management as well as those responsible for various tasks. The information security manager should understand these processes so that security implications can be managed early in the process, before changes are made to production.

Perform Vulnerability Assessments to Evaluate Effectiveness of Existing Controls

The Network Vulnerability Assessment (NVA) is a part of the ongoing information security life cycle. As with any business process, the information security life cycle starts with a risk analysis. Management is charged with showing that "due diligence" is performed during decision-making processes for any enterprise. A formal risk analysis provides the documentation that due diligence is performed.

Once the decision to move forward has been made, the organization must conduct a risk assessment to identify threats, prioritize those threats to establish a risk level, and then identify controls to help mitigate high-level risks. Once controls have been selected, the organization will have to do a cost-benefit analysis to determine whether to implement the controls.

Risk mitigation is a systematic methodology used by senior management to reduce mission risk. Risk mitigation can be achieved through any of the following options.

- *Risk Assumption:* To accept the potential risk and continue operating or to implement controls to lower the risk to an acceptable level
- *Risk Avoidance:* To avoid the risk by eliminating the risk cause or consequences (such as forgoing certain functions of the system or shutting down the system when risks are identified)
- *Risk Limitation:* To limit the risk by implementing controls that minimize the adverse impact of a threat's exercising a vulnerability (such as use of avoidance, assurance, detective, or recovery controls)
- *Risk Planning:* To manage risk by developing a risk mitigation plan that prioritizes, implements, and maintains controls
- *Risk Transference:* To transfer the risk by using other options to compensate for the loss, such as purchasing insurance

Once the controls or safeguards have been implemented, it is appropriate to conduct an assessment to determine if the controls are working. In the information security profession this is where the NVA comes into play. The information security team will be assessing existing controls, safeguards, and processes that are part of the infrastructure. This process, the assessment, will ensure that controls are effective and that they will remain so. Table 4.10 gives a listing of risk management terms.

There are two major goals of a network vulnerability assessment. The first goal of a technical vulnerability assessment is to test everything

Table 4.10 Risk Management Terms

Term	*Definition*
Risk Management	The total to identify, control and minimize impact of uncertain events. The objective of risk management is to reduce risk to an acceptable level. Support of this process by senior management is a demonstration of their due diligence.
Risk Analysis	Is a technique used to identify and assess factors that may jeopardize the success of a project or achieving a goal. Another term for this process is a Project Impact Analysis (PIA). Risk analysis is used to determine if there is a business need to begin a project.
Risk Assessment	Organizations use risk assessment to determine what threats exist to a specific asset and the associated risk level (probability of threat occurrence and impact) of that threat. The threat prioritization (establishing the risk level) provides the organization with the information needed to select appropriate controls measures, safeguards or counter measures to lower the risk to an acceptable level.
Risk Mitigation	Is the process in which an organization implements controls and safeguards to prevent identified risks from ever occurring, while at the same time implementing a means of recovery should the risk become a reality in spite of all efforts.
Vulnerability Assessment and Controls Evaluation	Systematic examination of a critical infrastructure, the interconnected systems on which it relies, its information, or product to determine the adequacy of security measures, identify security deficiencies, evaluate security alternatives, and verify the adequacy of such measures after implementation.

possible. Often it is useful to think in "new-age" terms and consider the NVA a holistic NVA. The reason that it is important to test the entire security domain is somewhat obvious. An intruder only needs one hole to break into the network; it really does not matter if that hole lies in the primary firewall or through a modem connected to an executive's desktop computer. But there are some factors that will limit how deep you can make the network vulnerability assessment. The two factors that most often get in the way of a complete NVA are time and cost. The time you spend running your network vulnerability assessment is generally time that you are not spending on your other job functions, and this can cost your company money or affect your company in other ways. Also, the cost of the network vulnerability assessment may limit the tools that you will have at your disposal for the testing period. If your organization has a somewhat meager budget for the technical areas of a network vulnerability assessment, don't worry too much. There are a number of great tools that are completely free, that will allow you to run a very respectable NVA without spending a fortune collecting tools.

The second goal of a technical network vulnerability assessment is to generate a clear concise report that will be read and used by your management or your customers. One of the most common rookie mistakes in running a network vulnerability assessment is to run a NVA tool with all the default options, have it generate a default report, and then print out thousands of pages with every vulnerability inside a client's domain, starting from huge vulnerabilities such as a non-password-protected telnet session on the company's primary Internet router, down to very small vulnerabilities such as a workstation responding to ping. This method delivers a lot of pages for the customer to read over, and a very thick binder that will look impressive sitting on a shelf of the CSO's office for years to come. The question lies in the value of this type of vulnerability assessment.

In a perfect world the actual goal of a network vulnerability assessment is to produce useful results. A handy thing to remember is that useful to one type of individual is not as useful to other types of people. For example, a CEO is going to care little of the details of a potential security hole involving malformed ICMP packets, but this type of information is going to be very useful for the technician who may be charged with the task of fixing the problem. The CEO is more likely to be concerned with how the entire security system is doing compared to evaluation criteria or industry standards.

To help produce useful results, the amount of data given in a final report must be readable by the audience desired for each segment. Typically, a NVA report will begin with a one-page summary detailing how the security of the customer is doing in general. This is intended for senior management types to read. Following this section of the report is the general opinion section. This section is intended to be for line managers who will want more level of detail than senior management, but not as much as the company technicians who will be more interested in the next section of the report.

The next section of the report has the specific vulnerability findings from the assessment. In this area vulnerabilities are listed by name with a description of the vulnerability, why this vulnerability is important to fix, the areas of the enterprise that could be affected by this vulnerability, and finally the steps needed to fix the hole from a high level of detail.

After the three aforementioned sections, the next section details what you did as part of the NVA and what you would have liked to do.

The first component describes how you would typically run a network vulnerability assessment and the steps involved. The second component shows what deviations from your normal testing policy you followed at the customer's wishes. This is where you can get even with the customer who just wanted to have you come in and run a single tool and leave. It also stops future would-be vulnerability assessment runners from coming in and stating that they run a much more complete vulnerability assessment and can provide more value than the vulnerability assessment that you had run.

Vulnerabilities are documented problems or errors that can be used maliciously to make the system perform in an unintended way. There are undocumented vulnerabilities in all systems, but trying to test for the unknown will be a very daunting task. This is where the largest amount of attacks are going to be coming from, as illustrated in Figure 4.3.

In Figure 4.3 there are four different stages in the vulnerability life cycle. The first phase, vulnerability discovered, is where someone uncovers the vulnerability. Often this happens through a Web site posting, where someone has an idea that might produce a hole and asks for comment on the potential feasibility. The next step in the discovery phase is where

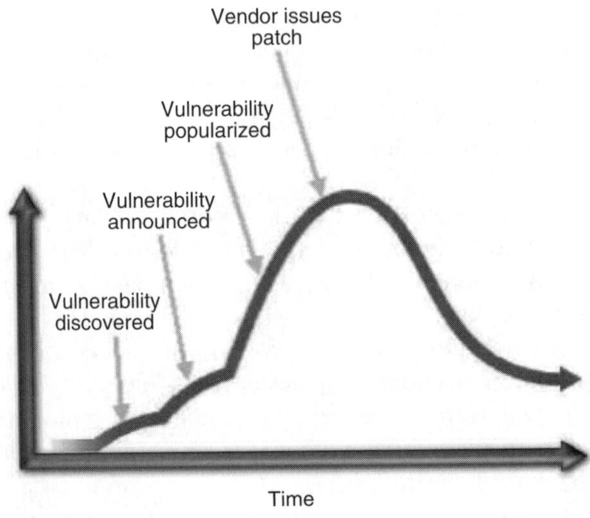

Figure 4.3 Vulnerability life cycle.

a "proof of concept" script is written. At this stage the script is only created to answer the question posted to the newsgroup or Web site. At this stage very few people are making use of the newfound vulnerability. The only people who would know of the new vulnerability's existence would be friends of the person who submitted the idea or regular readers of the Web site where it was initially posted. If the script that was written to answer the original question is successful the next phase begins.

The second phase, vulnerability announced, is where Web sites that specialize in announcing new vulnerabilities post a warning about the new hole discovered. In this phase more attackers are checking for the exploit and testing many systems on the Internet. Because many people subscribe to e-mail announcements from these places, such as Security Focus, the general knowledge of the exploit has gone up considerably.

The next phase, vulnerability popularized, occurs when a very easy-to-use script is written or a point-and-click tool is created. At this point general knowledge of the vulnerability has spread to include almost anyone who would have an interest. This is where the group of Internet malcontents generally referred to as "script kiddies" would be out running the script or tool against very large numbers of Internet hosts. If the vulnerability is big enough to reach popular news outlets it will happen during this phase.

The final phase of the vulnerability life cycle occurs when the vendor affected by the vulnerability, or security device vendor, releases a fix to protect against the automated attacks. It is important to note that once the vulnerability has a patch to protect against it, the attacks do not completely stop. Just think of one of the recent well-publicized vulnerabilities such as Code Red. Although most large companies have patched their systems long ago, some systems on the Internet are still vulnerable. And as long as some systems are still vulnerable, attackers are going to continue to look to see if the target system is vulnerable.

There are two primary classes of vulnerabilities; hard and soft. Hard vulnerabilities are mistakes made by the company who wrote the software and have left open a hole for potential exploit. These types of vulnerabilities are often referred to as "bugs" and often are fixed with service packs and hotfixes. However, it is difficult to keep up to date with the near-constant patching and hotfixing of all the systems in a complex enterprise. A major security vendor observed some time ago that on a Windows NT system almost daily a new vulnerability was being discovered. This often leads to missed service patches and vulnerabilities being left open, even after the fix has been released. The reason for this large number of vulnerabilities lies in system complexity. Although system complexity leads to an easier-to-use system, it increases both the number of lines of code necessary, and also the number of services running on a system. Most vendors do an exceptional job checking for errors in coding, however, the raw number of lines of code that needs to be checked is absolutely enormous. The numbers of lines of code in popular operating systems are listed in Table 4.11.

The second type of vulnerability, soft, can in no way be blamed on the software manufacturer. Soft vulnerabilities are often misconfigurations by network and security administrators. In this tumultuous economic environment, capital resources may not be available to send administrators to training on the very products that they must support. This can lead to mistakes in both the setup and maintenance of devices, as well as configurations that do not support the company's information security policies. When performing a technical network vulnerability assessment you must look for both kinds of vulnerabilities. Also, it may be of note, that soft vulnerabilities may be the result of a network or security device being "hacked". Once a penetrator gets into a system, he may modify the operational parameters in any way he wishes. As a rule of thumb, if you ever see profanity in the configuration files of a system, it might be wise to look deeper for evidence of a penetration. The most notable exception seems to be in the title of the security configuration policy itself; where it is not uncommon to see titles such as "last <*expletive deleted*> try".

There are additional types of soft vulnerabilities such as:

- A lack of general security policies
- General security policies that go against industry best practices
- A lack of security system procedures
- A lack of configuration or change management
- Logging not enabled

The information security manager should know that threats to the organization's information resources are being reported on a daily basis. These vulnerabilities are often identified within software and hardware that previously were unknown. The information security manager should be aware of vulnerability reporting sources so that the security program can be modified to address any vulnerability that may be presented. These sources are discussed in Chapter 5 on incident response.

Having this knowledge enables the information security manager to modify the security program, as necessary, ensuring that information resources are continually protected per the business needs of the organization.

Table 4.11 Vulnerability Assessment Terms

Vulnerability Assessment Terms	*Definitions*
Vulnerability Assessment	Systematic examination of a critical infrastructure, the interconnected systems on which it relies, its information, or product to determine the adequacy of security measures, identify security deficiencies, evaluate security alternatives, and verify the adequacy of such measures after implementation.
Penetration Test	The portion of security testing in which the evaluators attempt to circumvent the security features of a system. The evaluators may be assumed to use all system design and implementation documentation that may include listings of system source code, manuals, and circuit diagrams. The evaluators work under the same constraints applied to ordinary users.
Remediation	Cleanup or other methods used to remove or contain vulnerabilities.
Cracker	Is an individual who attempts to access computer systems without authorization. These people are often malicious, as opposed to hackers, and have many means at their disposal for breaking into a system.
Hacker	A slang term for a computer enthusiast. Among professional programmers, the term hacker implies an amateur or a programmer who lacks formal training. Depending on how it used, the term can be either complimentary or derogatory, although it is developing an increasingly derogatory connotation. The pejorative sense of hacker is becoming more prominent largely because the popular press has co-opted the term to refer to individuals who gain unauthorized access to computer systems for the purpose of stealing and corrupting data. Hackers, themselves, maintain that the proper term for such individuals is cracker.
Phreaker	A Phreaker exploits the omission of security controls in your system that occurred during installation or repair. The Phreaker steals from your system without the need to change any of your parameters. The only tools required to be a very good phreaker are patience and social engineering skills.

Ensure That Noncompliance Issues and Other Variances Are Resolved in a Timely Manner

Noncompliance issues usually result in risks to the organization, so it is important that specific processes are implemented to address these issues in a timely manner. The level of severity will dictate the approach that should be employed. As discussed in the risk assessment process, it will serve the organization well to establish a process to prioritize the noncompliance issues to ensure the higher-priority items are addressed first.

Typically, noncompliance issues are uncovered through many different mechanisms including:

- Regular monitoring
- Security reviews and assessments
- Change management process
- Vulnerability assessments
- Audit activity

The implementation, operation, use, and management of the information processing environment are subject to statutory, regulatory, and contractual requirements. All relevant requirements and the organization's approach to meet them should be explicitly defined, documented, and kept current for each system, application, platform, infrastructure component, and organization.

It is important that senior management be aware of the specific requirements. It is the role of the CISO to implement specific controls and identify individual responsibilities to meet these requirements. These roles and responsibilities must be documented.

Intellectual property rights must be properly addressed by the management team and compliance controls implemented by the CISO (see Tables 4.12 and 4.13). Intellectual property rights include software copyright, trademarks, patents, source code, licenses, and documentation.

As we discussed in the governance chapter, the rights and requirements for compliance and intellectual property ownership are generally spelled out in the terms of employment portion of the Tier 1 employment policy. This policy will include a discussion of ownership of all materials created while employed by the organization. Additionally, the filing for patents will also be documented.

Controls must be put in place to allow management to approve employee use of information-processing facilities. Any use of organization-provided resources for nonbusiness or unauthorized purpose, without management approval, should be regarded as improper use and a violation of the

Table 4.12 Compliance Terms

Compliance Term	*Definitions*	
Fiduciary Duty	An obligation to act in the best interest of another party. For instance, a corporation's board member has a fiduciary duty to the shareholders, a trustee has a fiduciary duty to the trust's beneficiaries, and an attorney has a fiduciary duty to a client.	
Due Care	The care that a reasonable person would exercise under the circumstances.	
Due Diligence	Is a measure of prudence, activity, or assessment, as is properly to be expected from, and ordinarily exercised by, a reasonable and prudent person under the particular circumstances; not measured by any absolute standard but depends on the relative facts of the special case.	
Duty of Loyalty	Decisions must be made in the best interest of the organization.	
	Conflict of Interest	Individuals must divulge any interest in outside relationships that may conflict with the enterprise's interests.
	Duty of Fairness	When presented with a conflict of interest, the individual has an obligation to act in the best interest of all parties.
	Corporate Opportunity	When presented with "material inside information" (advanced notice on mergers, acquisitions, patents, etc.) the individual will not use this information for personal gain.
	Confidentiality	All matters involving the corporation share be kept in confidence until they are made public.

employee's terms of employment. If any unauthorized activity is identified by monitoring or other means, it should be brought to the attention of the proper authority for review and possible disciplinary action.

It is important to seek legal counsel before implementing monitoring procedures. All users should be aware of the precise scope of their permitted access and of the monitoring in place to detect unauthorized

Table 4.13 Intellectual Property Terms

Intellectual Property Terms	*Definitions*	
Copyright	A person's right to prevent others from copying works that he or she has written, authored or otherwise created. Copyright is in effect for the lifetime of the author plus 95 years.	
	Public Domain	Refers to created materials which either by law are not protected by copyright or patent, or their protection under the law has lapsed.
	Fair Use Doctrine	Section 107 of the Copyright Act establishes the "fair use" doctrine which provides for specific exemptions from copyright liability. An example of this is the use of certain excerpts of a written work for educational purposes.
Patents	Grant inventors limited property rights to exclude others from duplicating, using, or selling. *Protect Results of Science, Technology & Engineering*	
Trade Secret	Trade Secrets: Information that Provides a Competitive Advantage. *Protect Ideas.*	
Trademarks	A word, name, symbol, etc. used to identify goods & to distinguish them from those of others. *Protect representation of products & services*	

use. The level of authorization is determined by business need and must be approved by the appropriate management personnel.

At log-on a warning message should be presented on the computer screen indicating that:

- The system is for authorized use only.
- Activities will be monitored.
- By completing the log-on the user agrees to the monitoring.

The legality of monitoring the usage varies from country to country and may require management to advise employees, contractors, and any other users of such monitoring or to obtain their agreement. Where the

Table 4.14 Compliance and Audit Terms

Compliance Terms	*Definitions*
Certification	Comprehensive evaluation of the technical and non-technical security features of an information system and other safeguards, made in support of the approval/accreditation process, to establish the extent to which a particular design and implementation meet a set of specified security requirements.
Compliance Audit	Review of controls and safeguards to determine whether the entity is complying with specific procedures or rules.
Accreditation	A formal declaration by a designated approving authority that a particular information system, professional or other employee or contractor, or organization is approved to perform certain duties and to operate in a specific security mode, using a prescribed set of safeguards.

system being entered is used for public access, such as a public Web server, and is subject to security monitoring, the warning banner should be displayed.

Managers should ensure that all security policies, standards, and procedures within their area of responsibility are carried out correctly to achieve compliance (Table 4.14). It is important to conduct regular reviews of employee compliance levels. The result of reviews and corresponding corrective actions should be recorded and maintained. The information should be used to update the information security program.

Technical compliance checking should be performed by experienced personnel, or by an automated software package. The reports generated should be reviewed by technical specialists. Any technical compliance check should be carried out by competent authorized persons and under the supervision of management.

Technical compliance checking involves the examination of operational systems to ensure that hardware and software controls have been correctly implemented and maintained. Compliance checking covers such activities as penetration testing and vulnerability assessments.

Information Security Awareness and Education

An effective information security program cannot be implemented without implementing an employee awareness and training program to address policy, procedures, and tools. Learning consists of three key elements as shown in Table 4.15.

The following address the elements that make up a successful information security awareness program. We address the role organization personnel play in the information security program and how to use this information to your benefit. We discuss how to establish awareness program scope, how to segment the audience, and how to ensure content is effective in getting the message to the user community

Introduction

Development of information security policies, standards, procedures, and guidelines is only the beginning of an effective information security program. A strong security architecture will be rendered less effective if there is not a process in place to make certain that the employees are made aware of their rights and responsibilities with regard to organization information assets.

All too often security professionals implement the "perfect" security program, and then are surprised that it fails because they forgot to sell their product to their constituents. In order to be successful, the information security professional must find a way to sell this product to the customers.

For years I have heard information security professionals discuss their jobs in terms of overhead, as if this is some evil thing. Nearly every employee within an enterprise is overhead. Even the CEO, CFO, CTO, and CIO are all overhead. However, they have learned what we need to learn, and that is that we all add value to the bottom line of the enterprise.

Table 4.15 Training Terms

Training Terms	*Definitions*
Awareness	The process which is used to stimulate, motivate and remind the audience what is expected of them.
Training	Is the process that teaches a skill or the use of a required tool.
Education	Is the specialized, in-depth schooling required to support the tools or as a career development process.

Our task, just like the big "C"s is to ensure that the business objectives or mission of the enterprise is met. What the information security professional has failed to do is to sell the services of information security.

Key Security Requirements

The information security triad of confidentiality, integrity, and availability drive the security program. Management, however, is concerned that information reflects the real status of the organization and that they can have confidence that the information available to them can be used to make informed business decisions. An effective information security program endeavors to ensure that the organization's information and its processing resources are available when authorized users need them.

The goal of confidentiality extends beyond just keeping the bad guys out; it also ensures that those with a business need have access to the resources they need to perform their jobs. Confidentiality ensures that controls and reporting mechanisms are in place to detect problems or possible intrusions with speed and accuracy.

An effective security program must take into account the business objectives or mission of the organization and ensure that these goals are met as safely and securely as possible. Understanding the customer's needs must be the first step in establishing an effective information security program. The awareness program must reinforce these objectives and will make the program more acceptable to the employee base.

As important as a set of written policies, standards, and procedures is in defining the architecture of the security program and the infrastructure that supports it, the true fact of the matter is that most employees will not have the time or desire to read these documents. The objective of the awareness program is to take the message to the people.

The information security program has five key elements that must be presented to the audience. These include:

- A process to take the message to the user community to reinforce the concept that information security is an important part of the business process
- Identification of the individuals who are responsible for the implementation of the security program
- The ability to determine the sensitivity of information and the criticality of applications, systems, and business processes
- The business reasons why basic security concepts such as separation of duties, need-to-know, and least privilege must be implemented

- That senior management supports the goals and objectives of the information security program

Believe in What You Are Doing

Before you can begin to put together a program to sell information security to your fellow employees, you must first sell the product to yourself. Many information security professionals hear either directly or indirectly that the role they are performing is overhead and that it inhibits the other employees from meeting their assigned objectives. The part about overhead is true, but so are the vast majority of employees. The "C" level employees (CEO, CFO, CTO, CISO, etc.) are all overhead. However, they have a charter that establishes their legitimacy and describes how they support the business objectives or mission of the organization.

You will need to have a charter published, but more important, you will have to persuade yourself that what you do adds value to the organization. Whenever I am teaching a class on information security issues I always give the attendees a homework problem. The exercise is to come up with four things that you, as a security professional, do to help your enterprise meet its business objectives or mission. These four items should be expressed in nonsecurity, nontechnical, nonaudit terms. Use the language of the business unit managers to express your four value-added statements.

When creating your value-added statements, do not state that you "add users to the system using ACF2." Instead, sell your services by stating that you ensure that authorized users are given access to information resources in a timely and efficient manner. Tell your audience what it is that you do that enables them to do their job.

Just as you have to prepare to sell your job and its duties to management and fellow employees, so must you be prepared to sell the services that you provide. Again these services must be presented to the user community in the language they understand. Security requirements or audit requirements are not part of the business process and they do not exist. There are only business objectives or mission requirements. So when we present our services, we must use the terms that management uses.

> *Risk Analysis:* Risk analysis is a technique used to identify and assess factors that may jeopardize the success of a project or achieving a goal. This process is also known as project impact analysis. This process will include a cost-benefit analysis and typically incorporates the features and benefits of the asset or process under review.

Risk Assessment: Organizations use risk assessment to determine what threats exist to a specific asset and the associated risk level of that threat. The threat prioritization (establishing the risk level) provides the organization with the information needed to prioritize where to implement appropriate controls measures, safeguards, or countermeasures to lower the risk to an acceptable level.

Policies: Management establishes its goals and objectives for protecting the assets of the enterprise by implementing policies. Policies are used to introduce the concepts of what is expected of all employees when using enterprise assets and to what noncompliance can lead. The messages of the policies are also included in the contract language so that third parties are aware of their responsibilities.

With policies implemented along with an awareness program, the enterprise then can seek relief in the courts, if necessary, to protect its assets. Policies establish the behavior expected of all personnel granted access to that asset.

Procedures: These are probably the easiest security measures to explain return on investment. Procedures are the step-by-step process used to complete a task. They provide users with the information needed to complete a task and ensure management that the tasks are being completed in a uniform and approved manner. Procedures improve efficiencies in employee workflow and assist in the prevention of misuse and fraud.

Standards: Remember Y2K, that historical event that caused many of us a lot of extra work? It was lack of standards or the ignoring of standards that made management spend so much money to retrofit the fixes. Standards are a way of ensuring that programs and systems will work together and that when there is a need to do error searching, the people looking through old code will be better able to understand what is out there.

By establishing standards the enterprise limits rogue applications, systems, platforms, hardware, or software. There is less time spent in supporting nonstandard activities or products. When a new application or system is moved into production, the existing systems and applications will not have to make modifications to handle nonstandard information or data. Standards are a cost-savings process that supports the efficient running of the enterprise.

Business Continuity Planning: Since the events of September 11, 2001, most organizations have seen the need to implement an enterprisewide continuity plan. Management has always been charged with a fiduciary responsibility to protect the assets of the enterprise. BCP is a process that allows management to show that they have exercised due diligence with respect to the information processing resources and assets. By having a plan and testing the plan, the enterprise is showing to employees, stakeholders, and interested third parties that the continued operation of the enterprise has been addressed and is taken seriously.

Although these are only examples of how to sell your information security services, they do provide you with the idea of how this can and should be done. To be successful, the information security professional must step into the role of the businessperson. Security is a portion of the entire business process and must use the words and objectives of the business units to be successful. Our goal is not just to have security endure, but we want it to prevail. To do this we must become an active voice in the business or mission of our organizations.

Program Goals

Employees want to know what is expected of them and whom to turn to for assistance. The ongoing information security awareness program will provide those answers to the user community. The employees need to understand the security program is supported, approved, and directed by senior management.

Another key goal of an awareness program is to ensure that all personnel get the message. The process should begin with new employee orientation and continue through the final exit interview. In between there should be at least annual mandatory refresher classes and sessions.

Contract personnel need to be made aware of the information security program goals and objectives, but be cautious when considering whether to include third parties in regular employee training and awareness sessions. Normally, your organization would want the contract house to conduct the awareness training for its personnel. At least, hold separate awareness sessions for contract personnel. Be sure to work with the purchasing and legal departments to ensure that the language of the contracts specifies adherence to the security program.

All too often the programs fail because there is little or no followup. There is usually the "big splash" kickoff and then not much else. Over the years management and employees have been trained how to respond to the big event, and that is to do nothing.

In the 1970s management and employees were introduced to a concept termed "Quality of Work Life (QWL)". This bold new concept was to address how employees felt about the job, their bosses, and fellow employees. Management would then take steps to improve the work atmosphere. In the 1980s we were introduced to "Total Quality Management (TQM)" where we discovered that employees were our most important asset and that they needed to be empowered. In the 1990s we were trained in the "Learning Organization" and were introduced to the concept of the "Ladder of Inference". What management and employees learned from these concepts was that the best way to deal with any new program is to wait. Expend the least amount of energy as possible and there is a good chance that it will go away or die due to inaction.

The employees know that inaction or indifference is the best tool to use when confronted with a new initiative. To be successful it will be necessary to map out a strategy to keep the message in front of the user community on a regular basis. When mapping out your program, you might want to consider incorporating special dates into the calendar of events. For an information security program consider doing something on these dates:

- May 10: International Emergency Response Day
- September 8: Computer Virus Awareness Day
- November 30: International Computer Security Day

However, keeping the message in front of the user community is not enough. The message must make the issues of information security come alive and become important to all who see the message. This can be accomplished in part by finding ways to tie the message in with the goals and objectives of each department. Every department has different needs and objectives. The message you bring must address those needs.

Find ways to make the message important to the employees. When discussing controls, identify how they help protect the employee. For example, when requiring employees to wear identification badges, many security programs tell employees that this requirement has been implemented to meet security objectives. What employees should be told is that the badges ensure that only authorized persons have access to the workplace. The goal of this security measure is to protect the employee in the workplace by ensuring that only authorized personnel have access. When presenting controls, present the message to the employees in a manner that shows them the benefit.

Finally, the security program is meant to reduce losses associated with the intentional or accidental disclosure, modification, or destruction of information or the denial of services from the systems or applications. This can be accomplished by raising the consciousness of the user community in the ways to protect information and the processing resources. By ensuring that these goals are met, the organization will be able to improve employee efficiency and productivity.

Segmenting the Audience

To be successful, the awareness program should take into account the needs and current levels of training and understanding of the employees and audience. Typically there are the following key ways to establish an effective segmentation of the user audience:

- Current level of computer usage
- What the audience really wants to learn
- How receptive the audience is to the security program
- How to gain acceptance
- Who might be a possible ally

Current Level of Computer Usage

To assess the current level of sophistication in computer usage, it will be necessary to ask questions of the audience. Although sophisticated workstations may be found in employees' work areas, their understanding of what these devices can do may be very limited. Ask questions as to what the tasks are and how the tools available are used to support these tasks. It may come as a surprise to find out that the newest and most powerful system on the floor is being used as a glorified 3270 terminal.

Be an effective listener. Listen to what the users are saying and scale the awareness sessions to meet their needs. In the awareness field, one size or presentation does not fit all.

What Does the Audience Really Want to Learn?

One way to get the audience open to listening to the security message is to provide them with awareness training on topics that are in the news. My team and I would watch for news shows such as *Dateline* or *48 Hours* or the evening news to run a segment on some current issue. We would purchase a copy of that segment and make it available to the departments for their staff meetings. We did this initially with phone card theft and cell phone cloning. Although these issues were not actually part of the information security program, we were able to tie a brief information security message into the presentation.

In today's environment the concern over identity theft is a perfect lead-in to the issues surrounding information security. So take the time to find out what the concerns are of the user community and tap into those needs to present your message.

Determine How Receptive the Audience Is

Identify the level of receptiveness to the security program. Find out what elements are being accepted and which ones are meeting resistance. Examine the areas of noncompliance and try to find ways to either alter the requirement or find a better way to present its objectives. Do not change fundamental information security precepts just to gain unanimous acceptance; this is an unattainable goal. Make the program meet the greater good of the organization and then attack the pockets of resistance to lessen the impact.

One method of determining levels of receptiveness is to conduct a "walkabout". A walkabout is conducted after normal working hours and looks for certain key indicators:

- Offices locked
- Desks and cabinets locked
- Workstations secured
- Information secured
- Recording media (diskettes, tapes, CDs, USB drives, etc.) secured

Seek Out Ways to Gain Acceptance

Work with the supervisors and managers to understand what their organization's needs are and how the program can help them. Remember, it is their program. It will be necessary for you to learn to speak their language and understand their specific needs. No single awareness program will work for every single business unit or department. You must be willing to make alterations to the program and show a willingness to accept suggestions.

The best way to gain acceptance is to ensure that the employees and managers are partners in the security process. Never submit a new control or policy to management without sitting down with them individually to discuss and review the change. By knowing what each department or business unit does, you will be able to present the change to the manager and discuss how it will help him meet the goals and objectives.

It will also be important to know the peak activity periods of the various departments and what the managers' chief concerns are with regard to meeting objectives. When meeting with the managers, be sure to listen to their concerns and be prepared to ask for their suggestions on how to improve the program. When I was starting out in the security business, I ran into managers who had "an issue" that they wanted resolved. When I came back with the resolution, I often found that they had "another issue." After working this process a couple of iterations, I found that the best way to prevent "additional issues" was to be prepared for the "issues" list. I would answer item number one and, if presented, item two. If the manager went to a third item, I would ask if there were any additional "issues." This would allow me to get all of the items out and then move forward.

Possible Allies

Find out which managers support the objectives of the security program and those who have the respect of their peers. Look beyond the physical security and audit departments. Seek out the business managers that have a vested interest in seeing the program succeed. Use their support to springboard the program to acceptance.

When discussing the security program, avoid referring to it as "my program." Senior management has identified the need for a security program and has tapped you as their messenger and catalyst to move the program forward. So when presenting the program to user groups, employees, and managers, refer to the program as "their program" or as "our program." Make them feel that they are the key stakeholders in this process.

In a presentation used to introduce the security program to the organization, it may be beneficial to have the CEO or president introduce the subject through a video and say something such as the following.

> Just as steps have been taken to ensure the safety of the employees in the workplace, the organization is now asking that the employees work with us to protect our second most important asset: information. If the organization fails to protect its information from unauthorized access, modification, disclosure, or destruction, then the organization faces the prospect of loss of customer confidence, competitive advantage, and possibly jobs. All employees must accept the need and responsibility to protect our intellectual property and processing resources.

Involve the user community and accept their comments whenever possible. Make the information security program their program. Use what they identify as important as a key to the awareness program. By having the users involved, then the program truly becomes theirs and they will be more willing to accept and internalize the process.

Program Development

As we discussed above, the awareness presentation will vary based on the needs of the audience. Not everyone needs the same degree or type of information to do her job. An awareness program that distinguishes between groups of people and presents only information that is relevant to that particular audience will have the best results.

The job category is one way to segment the awareness audience and will provide the presenter with guidelines as to type and duration of presentation. A standard presentation should typically last no longer than 45 minutes and should consist of a combination of live discussion and videotape or movie information. This form and length of presentation is fine for employees and line supervision.

Business unit managers have two or more departments or groups reporting to them and have less time. Schedule an individual 20-minute meeting with these managers and have two or three pages of materials to use to support your discussion. Stress the objectives of the program and how the program can be used by the business unit to meet its objectives.

Senior management (including officers and directors) will have about 15 minutes available for the presentation. Have a one-page summary for them and discuss how the program supports them in their fiduciary duty and how it helps them meet their due diligence obligation.

Contractors and other third parties will need their own awareness sessions which typically follow the format of employees and line supervision presentations. Whenever possible, segregate third parties from the awareness training of regular full-time employees. This will help to ensure that the message for third parties is consistent and that there is no confusion as to their job status.

Once the audience has been segmented, it will be necessary to establish the roles that the users will be expected to assume. These roles may include managers acting as the information owners, service providers (either internal or external) acting as custodians of the intellectual property, and general users.

For any message that is to be delivered, be sure to employ the KISS (Keep It Simple, Sweetie) practice. You will have other opportunities to present material to the user community. Don't try to present all the information security goals and objectives in one session. Remember you have only about 30 minutes of attendee attention.

Inform the audience but try to stay away from commandments or directives. Discuss the goals and objectives using real-world scenarios. Use anecdotes to reinforce the concept that problems can happen here and that they do. A good story will be remembered long after the session is over. Quoting policies, procedures, standards, or guidelines will turn off the audience quickly. Policies and procedures are boring; if employees want more information, give them a reference card to help them find the resource.

Try to avoid telling employees that something is being implemented to "be in compliance with audit requirements." This is at best a cop-out and fails to explain in business terms why something is needed. The awareness session presents management's beliefs and objectives for the use and protection of the organization's information resources.

Methods to Convey the Message

How do people learn and where do people obtain their information? If you can answer these questions then your awareness program will have a better chance for success. Depending on what needs to be accomplished in the learning process, the manner in which the message is to be conveyed may be different. If we were implementing a training program we would be able to select from these basic methods of training:

- Buy a book and read about the subject.
- Watch a video on the subject.
- Ask someone to demonstrate the process.

For most employees, the last method is preferred for training. Most people like the hands-on approach and want to have someone there to answer questions.

With an awareness program the process is a little different. In awareness we want to raise consciousness about an issue. Awareness is to stimulate and motivate the audience about an issue or objective. It will be necessary to tap into the method most used by our audience to receive information. According to the *USA Today*, over 90 percent of the people obtain their news and information from television or radio. To make an awareness program work, it will be necessary to use this delivery model.

Knowing how people learn will help us in implementing an effective security awareness program. Neural-linguistic programming is the study of how people learn. This process has identified three basic ways in which people learn. These are:

1. Auditory: These people have to hear something in order to grasp it.
2. Mechanical: This learning type must write down the element to be learned. Those taking notes during meetings are typically mechanical learners.

3. Visual: This type of learner, which 90 percent of our audience is, needs to see a picture or diagram to understand what is being discussed. People who learn via this method normally have white-boards in their offices and use them often.

Because so many of our employees use the television as their primary source for gathering information, it is important to use videos and other visual stimuli to reinforce the message. Visual models can include posters, pictures, and videos. The use of videos serves several purposes.

With the advent of the news magazine format so popular on television today, our employees have become conditioned to accept the information presented as factual. This allows us to use the media to present them with the messages we consider important. Because the audience accepts material presented in this format, the use of videos allows us to bring in an "informed" outsider to present the message. Many times our message fails because the audience knows the messenger. Being a fellow worker, our credibility may be questioned. A video provides an "expert" on the subject.

There are a number of organizations that offer computer and information security videos. As we discussed above, consider having a senior executive videotape a message that can be run at the beginning of the awareness session. However, be very careful when considering developing your own 20-minute security video. Costs for creating a quality in-house video of 20 minutes can exceed $100,000.

An effective awareness program will also take advantage of brochures, newsletters, or booklets. In all cases the effectiveness of the medium will depend on how well it is created and how succinct the message is. One major problem with newsletters is finding enough material to complete the pages each time you want to go to press. One way to present a high quality newsletter is to look for vendors that provide such services. Typically, the vendor supplies the textual material for the newsletter and the company can put its logo and masthead on the newsletter with space for a small column of specific information.

Many organizations are decentralizing the information security responsibility and requiring each business unit to establish an information security coordinator. One of the tasks of this individual is to present the awareness sessions to their specific organization. An effective method of getting a consistent message out using this format is to "train the trainers."

The security awareness presentation is typically created by the central information security group and then regional training sessions are held to present the message and tools to the unit coordinators. During this half-day session, the key concepts are reinforced and the coordinators work with the security team to customize the session for their needs. This method helps ensure that the message presented meets the overall need of the organization and that the business unit feels that the message is directed towards their requirements.

Presentation Keys

Although every organization has its own style and method for training, it might help to review some important issues when creating an awareness program. When creating your awareness program, remember that the topic of information security is very broad. Try not to get overwhelmed with the prospect of providing information on every facet of the information security program in one meeting. The old adage of, "How do you eat an elephant? One bite at a time," must be adhered to.

Prioritize the message to the user community. This will require that there be a risk assessment performed on the information security infrastructure that will provide the organization with a prioritized list of security issues. Select the most pressing issue from this list or a topic that the Information Security Steering Committee has identified as vital.

The information security awareness program is an continuous process and you will have many opportunities to present the security messages. Identify where to begin, present the message, reinforce the message, and then build to the next objective. Keep the awareness sessions as brief as possible. It is normally recommended to keep the sessions to no more than 50 minutes. There are a number of reasons for under an hour: biology (you can only hold coffee for so long), attention spans, and productivity issues.

Start your session with an attention-grabbing piece such as the chief executive's video message or even an ice-breaker "personality test." One that I use, shown in Figure 4.4, is a quite simple one to start some sessions.

Tailor the presentation to the vocabulary and skill set of the audience. Know who you are talking to and provide them with information they can use and understand. This is not to have the appearance of a doctoral dissertation.

The awareness session must take into account the audience and the culture of the organization. Understand their needs, knowledge, and what the jobs of the attendees are. Knowing what the attendees do for a living will assist the presenter in striking a relationship with them.

Stress the positive and business side of security. Just as we discussed in selling security, you will have to sell them the concept that security is good for them. I often use the following analogy when discussing this issue. At the end of World War II, some GIs found that people living in areas of Europe lived for years beyond what Americans did. One of the factors in this long life was their eating of yogurt. So these GIs decided

Personality Test		
Using word association techniques, write down the first response that comes into your head when you hear each of the following words:		
Term		***Meaning***
Dog		How you view your own personality
Cat		How you view your partner's personality
Rat		How you view your boss' personality
Ocean		How you view your own life
Coffee		How you view your **LOVE** life

Figure 4.4 Sample ice-breaker.

to introduce yogurt to the American culture. One major problem, plain yogurt has a nasty taste. To be successful, the GIs had to find a way to make it palatable to the American taste. So they added fruit to the bottom of the cup and Americans could then stir up their good-tasting yogurt.

Information security is plain yogurt. To most of our employees it leaves a bad taste in their mouths. You are going to have to find a way to make the message palatable to the user community. This is done by understanding their needs and adjusting the message to meet their issues. Reinforce the message by providing booklets, brochures, or trinkets with the message or slogan.

Presentation Format

See Table 4.16 for a training presentation format.

Effective Communication

An effective information security program will depend on how well the message is communicated to the audience. Although many of us are

Table 4.16 Training Presentation Format

Step	*Activity*
Introduction	Start with an introduction of the topic and how the security program will support them in the completion of their tasks and jobs. This is where the senior management video would also be presented.
Message	Follow the introduction with the message. Typically this would either be a live presentation (see Effective Communication Tips) or the information security video.
Compliance Issues	Discuss any methods that will be employed to monitor compliance to the security objectives and provide the audience with the rationale for such compliance checking.
Questions & Answers	Provide the audience with about ten minutes for questions and answers. Ensure that every question is recorded and the answer is provided during the session (which is best) or where the answer will be posted. Use the Q & A from one session as input or background for your newsletter follow up.
Reinforce	Give then some item that will reinforce the message to them when they are back in their work areas.

confident in the importance of the message we will be presenting, often times the message is missed because of other factors. To be as effective as possible, it might be helpful to identify potential barriers to effective communication.

- *Image:* Dress as the audience is dressed, only a little better. Many organizations have converted to business casual dress, however, when you are presenting, it is important to exhibit the proper respect and professionalism to your audience. I once worked for a company that was headquartered in the Pacific Northwest. I had just finished 22 years with a global manufacturer located in the Midwest and they had just begun business casual. I was shocked at the attire of my fellow employees. I believe it is known as "grunge-rock chic." When we went to do work at the client site, I required the salesperson to inform us as to how the clients dressed. I had to make sure we abandoned our avant-garde look and became more traditional. I went to a meeting one time and did not recognize my own employee; he "cleaned up real nice."
- *Prepare:* Nothing will turn an audience off quicker than a presenter who stumbles around for materials or loses his or her place. Make certain that all audio-visuals are working properly (get there early and test everything).
- *Present:* Do not read your presentation. Use bullet points or brief phrases from which to speak. With any luck your audience will know how to read. Avoid reading verbatim the presentation slides. Speak to the audience as if you are having a conversation with them.
- *Jargon:* As information security professionals, we speak a very strange language. Many of us have also come from the information systems environment and this will compound the problem. I strongly recommend that you practice the presentation in front of a select focus group.
- *Audience:* Know your audience and speak to them in terms they will understand. Each and every department has its own language. Do your homework and learn what terms are important to them and use them correctly in your presentation.
- *TLAs:* A TLA is a Three-Letter Acronym (TLA) for three-letter acronyms. The next time you attend a meeting, keep a running score of the TLAs and FLAs (four-letter acronyms) that are bandied about. Say what you mean and keep the TLAs to a minimum and define them before using them

- *Idioms:* Be careful with language. Our organizations have many different ethnic groups and slang terms may be misunderstood or even offensive. Be mindful of those in your audience and select your terms wisely.
- *Priorities:* As security professionals, we feel that security is the organization's most important objective. However, purchasing, accounting, payroll, human resources, and other departments have other priorities.
- *Schedule:* Just as every department has a unique language and priorities, they also have deadlines. Schedule your presentations around their busy periods. Try to become part of a regular staff meeting if possible.
- *Time:* Keep the awareness sessions brief and businesslike. At Gettysburg, Edward Everett was the featured speaker and spoke for nearly two hours. President Lincoln spoke second and in less than five minutes and the world remembers his Gettysburg Address. Remember it is quality not quantity that will make a successful presentation.

Information security is an important part of doing business today. The message of employee responsibilities must be presented to them on a regular basis. To have a chance for success, a good presenter will be clear, concise, and brief. Know your audience and play to their needs and concerns. By doing your homework, the audience will be more open to receive the message. If they accept the message as being meaningful, then the objectives of information security will become incorporated into the business process.

When to Do Awareness

Any awareness session must be scheduled around the work patterns of the audience. Take into account busy periods of the various departments and make certain that the sessions do not affect these peak periods.

The best times for scheduling awareness sessions are in the morning on a Tuesday, Wednesday, or Thursday of a regular work week. First thing Monday morning will affect those getting back and starting the week's work. Having a session on Friday afternoon will not be as productive as you would like. The bodies may be in the room, but the minds and souls have already departed. This timeframe will result in the onset of the "stunned owl" syndrome. This is a process where the words no longer go in one ear and out the other. At this point the words hit the audience in the forehead and fall to the floor.

The physiological clock of humans is at its lowest productivity level right after lunch. If you turn out the lights to show a movie, make sure to turn up the volume so it can be heard over the snoring. Try to avoid the after-lunch time period.

Also, schedule sessions during off-shift hours. Second- and third-shift employees should have the opportunity to receive the message during work hours just as do those on day shift. I once did a presentation to the third-shift employees after their regular shift. I was assured by their management that an hour of overtime was all they needed to stay awake. Well, one young lady dozed off as soon as the lights went out and she did not wake up until I went over to tell her everyone had gone home.

Presentation Styles

As we discussed briefly before, each group of employees requires a different timeframe and approach to security awareness presentations. We review the requirements here.

Senior Management

Although most other sessions will last no more than 50 minutes, senior management has less time, even for issues as important as information security. Prepare a special brief, concise presentation and have available in-depth supporting documentation.

Unlike typical presentations, senior management does not want a video and personality test. They may not even want presentation slides. They generally prefer that the presenter sit with them for a few minutes and discuss the issues and how the security program will support their objectives.

Quickly explain the purpose of the program, identify any problem areas, and what solutions you propose. Suggest to them an action plan. Do not go to them with a problem for which you have no solution. Do not ask them to choose a solution from several you present because they might do just that and it might not be what is needed. You are the expert here and they are expecting you to come to them with your informed opinion on how the organization should move forward.

They are expecting a sound rational approach to information security. They will be interested in the overall cost of implementing the program and how this program benchmarks against others in the same industry or business.

Managers

These individuals are focused on getting their jobs done. They will not be interested in anything that appears to slow down their already tight schedules. To win them over, it will be necessary to demonstrate how the new controls will improve performance processes. As has been stressed throughout this section, the goal of security is to assist management in meeting business objectives or the overall mission.

Stress how the new processes will give the employees the tools they need (such as access to information and systems) in a timely and efficient manner. Show them the problem resolution process and who to call if there are any problems with implementation of the new process.

Line Supervisors and Employees

The employees are going to be skeptical. As we have discussed above, they have been through so many company initiatives that they have been trained to wait and hope the process will pass over. The compliance-checking concept will assist in getting the message to them that information security is here to stay.

Identify what is expected of them and how it will assist them in gaining access to the information and other resources they need to complete their assigned tasks. Point out that by protecting access to information, they can have a reasonable level of assurance (remember to avoid using absolutes) that their information assets will be protected from unauthorized access, modification, disclosure, or destruction.

The Message

The message to be presented will be based on whether your organization has an effective information security program in place and how active it is. For those organizations just activating the program, it will be necessary to convince management and employees of its importance. For organizations with an existing out-dated program, the key will be convincing management that there is a need for change.

The employees need to know that information is an important enterprise asset and is the property of the organization. All employees have a responsibility to ensure that this asset, like all other company assets, is properly protected and is used to support management-approved activities. The awareness program will allow employees to be made aware of the possible threats and what they can do to combat them.

The scope of the program must be made clear to the audience. Is the program limited to only computer-held data or does the program reach to all information, wherever it is found and however it is generated? The awareness process must ensure that employees know the total scope of the program. It must enlist their support in protecting this vital asset because the mission and business of the enterprise depend on it.

Summary

Information security is more than just policies, procedures, standards, and guidelines. It is more than just responses to audit comments or industry requirements. It is a business process that requires a cultural change for most employees.

Before anyone can be required to be compliant with a security measure, they must first be made aware of the need and the process. This is an ongoing process that begins during new employee orientation and continues through the post-employment exit interview. It must be conducted at least on an annual basis and include regular reminders.

Information security management does not require huge budgets. It does require some time and proper project management. The message must be kept in front of the user community and different vehicles of delivery should be used. Use your contacts in the industry to bring in speakers to support your program and use videos whenever possible.

Before you can sell your security program to any of the employees, you must sell it to yourself. The information security program must be the voice of reason and logic. Start small and expand. By the time the employees realize there is a security program, it will already be part of the culture.

What Was Covered in This Chapter

- Information security policies, standards, and procedures
- Managing implementation of the security program
- Managing third-party access and services
- Methods to measure security program acceptance
- Due diligence activities and reviews
- Vulnerability assessment requirements
- Risk management issues
- Change management requirements
- Awareness, training, and education

Questions

1. The change management procedure most likely to cause concern to the information security manager is when:
   A. Fallback processes are tested the weekend immediately prior to when the changes are made.
   B. Users are notified via electronic mail of major scheduled system changes.
   C. Manual process is used by operations for comparing program versions.
   D. Development managers have final authority for releasing new programs into production.

Answer D

2. Which of the following would indicate that an automated production scheduling system has inadequate security controls?
   A. Control statements are frequently changed to point to test libraries.
   B. Failure of a process will automatically initiate the resetting of parameters.
   C. Developers have read access to both production and test schedules.
   D. Scheduling personnel have the ability to initiate an emergency override.

Answer A

3. When a trading partner who has access to the corporate internal network refuses to follow corporate security policies, the information security manager should initiate which of the following?
   A. Revoke their access.
   B. Provide minimal access.
   C. Send a breach of contract letter.
   D. Contact the partner's external auditors.

Answer B

4. Which of the following is most important in writing good information security policies?
   A. Easy to read and understand
   B. Allows for flexible interpretation
   C. Describes technical vulnerability issues
   D. Changes whenever operating systems are upgraded

Answer A

5. Which of the following would be the best approach when conducting a security awareness campaign?
   A. Provide technical details on exploits.
   B. Target system administrators and the help desk.
   C. Provide customized messages for different groups.
   D. Target senior managers and business process owners.

Answer C

6. Performance objectives reached by consensus between the user and the provider of a service, or between an outsourcer and an organization are discussed is a(n):
   A. Outsource
   B. Contract
   C. Service level agreement
   D. Controlled by security administration

Answer C

7. The act of overseeing the progress of a process to ensure that the rights and well-being of an enterprise are protected; that the data is accurate, complete, and verifiable; and that the conduct of the staff is in compliance with the policies, with applicable regulatory requirements, and with standards of the field is termed:
   A. Surveillance
   B. Monitoring
   C. Service level agreement
   D. Level of trust that is granted to system users

Answer B

8. Cleanup or other methods used to remove or contain vulnerabilities:
   A. Remediation
   B. Penetration testing
   C. Vulnerability assessment
   D. Hard to do

Answer A

9. An individual who attempts to access computer systems without authorization. These people are often malicious, as opposed to hackers, and have many means at their disposal for breaking into a system:
   A. Phreaker
   B. Placker
   C. Employee
   D. Cracker

Answer D

10. An obligation to act in the best interest of another party. For instance, a corporation's board member has a _________ to the shareholders, a trustee has a _______ to the trust's beneficiaries, and an attorney has a _________ to a client:
    A. Due diligence
    B. Required by law
    C. Prudent person concept
    D. Fiduciary duty

Answer D

11. Access to, knowledge of, or possession of information based on need to perform assigned job duties:
    A. Need to know
    B. Least privilege
    C. Classified
    D. Job rotation

Answer A

12. The process of identifying and defining all items in a system, recording and reporting the status of these items and requests for change, and verifying the completeness and correctness of these items:
    A. Configuration management
    B. Change management
    C. Service level agreement
    D. Business impact analysis

Answer A

13. Comprehensive evaluation of the technical and nontechnical security features of an information system and other safeguards, made in support of the approval/accreditation process, to establish the extent to which a particular design and implementation meet a set of specified security requirements:
    A. Certification
    B. Compliance audit
    C. Accreditation
    D. Nonrepudiation

Answer A

14. A binding agreement between two or more persons that is enforceable by law:
    A. Contract
    B. Service level agreement

C. Outsource
D. Proposal

Answer A

15. Process of controlling modifications to the infrastructure or any aspect of services, in a controlled manner, enabling approved changes with minimum disruption:
    A. Rotation of assignments
    B. Separation of duties
    C. Change management
    D. Service level agreements

Answer C

16. File sharing is the practice of making files available for other users to download over the Internet and smaller networks. The file sharing model, where the files are stored on and served by personal computers of the users is called:
    A. Kazaa
    B. Morpheus
    C. Peer-to-peer
    D. Hybrid

Answer C

17. Every department has its own language therefore the procedures must be developed using the terms that they are used to. If you write procedures using the wrong "language," the procedure may as well be written in Sanskrit. The intended audience will not be able to understand it, or they will find in difficult to follow. The individual(s) that will provide the information for the procedure body are typically:
    A. Socially Awkward Males (SAM)
    B. Subject Matter Experts (SME)
    C. Business Approval Team (BAT)
    D. Technical Writing Expert (TWP)

Answer B

18. A key component in the administrative procedures process is to implement a process that will help ensure that modifications to the information technology infrastructure are controlled and approved. The ability to track and approve changes to the production environment will go a long way in establishing an effective internal control structure. This process is called:
    A. Service level agreement
    B. Due diligence

C. Copyright compliance
D. Change management

Answer D

19. A method of working whereby tasks are apportioned between different members of staff in order to reduce the scope for error and fraud:
A. Segregation of duties
B. Challenge response
C. Rotation of duties
D. Checks and balances

Answer A

20. The policy that establishes the way in which the organization conducts its business with outside firms is termed what? This policy includes language that discusses the need for third parties to comply with organization policies, procedures, and standards.
A. Terms of employment
B. Procurement and contracts
C. Service level agreements
D. Nondisclosure agreement

Answer B

21. Performance objectives reached by negotiation between the user and the provider of a service, or between an outsourcer and an organization. These can be internal as well as external.
A. Terms of employment
B. Procurement and contracts
C. Service level agreements
D. Nondisclosure agreement

Answer C

22. During the design and implementation of the security program the information security manager should ensure that Key Performance Indicators (KPI) are defined and that the mechanism to measure progress against those indicators is implemented. This way the information security manager can assess the success or failure of various security components and whether they are cost justifiable.
A. Design requirements
B. Assessment variables
C. Penetration testing criteria
D. Key success indicators

Answer D

23. Changes to the production environment should only be made when there is a valid business reason to do so. Updating the production system to apply the latest version or patch may not always be in the best interest of the organization. All changes, even patches and new releases, must go through what process to assess their impact on the user community?
    A. Change management
    B. Peer review of code
    C. Structured walk-through
    D. Quality assurance testing

Answer A

24. The systematic examination of a critical infrastructure, the interconnected systems on which it relies, its information, or product to determine the adequacy of security measures, identify security deficiencies, evaluate security alternatives, and verify the adequacy of such measures after implementation is termed:
    A. Risk mitigation
    B. Penetration testing
    C. Vulnerability assessment
    D. Risk assessment

Answer C

25. The portion of security testing in which the evaluators attempt to circumvent the security features of a system. The evaluators may be assumed to use all system design and implementation documentation which may include listings of system source code, manuals, and circuit diagrams. The evaluators work under the same constraints applied to ordinary users.
    A. Risk mitigation
    B. Penetration testing
    C. Vulnerability assessment
    D. Risk assessment

Answer B

26. A slang term for a computer enthusiast. Among professional programmers, the term implies an amateur or a programmer who lacks formal training. Depending on how it is used, the term can be either complimentary or derogatory, although it is developing an increasingly derogatory connotation. The pejorative sense of this activity is becoming more prominent largely because the popular press has co-opted the term to refer to individuals who gain

unauthorized access to computer systems for the purpose of stealing and corrupting data.

A. Hacker
B. Cracker
C. Phreaker
D. Spaminator

Answer A

27. This is a measure of prudence, activity, or assessment, as is properly to be expected from, and ordinarily exercised by, a reasonable and prudent person under the particular circumstances; not measured by any absolute standard but depending on the relative facts of the special case,
    A. Fiduciary duty
    B. Due care
    C. Due diligence
    D. Duty of loyalty

Answer C

28. Section 107 of the Copyright Act establishes this doctrine provides for specific exemptions from copyright liability. An example of this is the use of certain excerpts of a written work for educational purposes. This doctrine is called:
    A. Public domain
    B. Fair use
    C. Patent pending
    D. Trademark usage

Answer B

29. Comprehensive evaluation of the technical and nontechnical security features of an information system and other safeguards, made in support of the approval process, to establish the extent to which a particular design and implementation meet a set of specified security requirements.
    A. Accreditation
    B. Compliance audit
    C. Vulnerability assessment
    D. Certification

Answer D

30. To be successful, the awareness program should take into account the needs and current levels of training and understanding of the

employees and audience. Typically there are five key ways to perform this activity:

- Current level of computer usage
- What the audience really wants to learn
- How receptive the audience is to the security program
- How to gain acceptance
- Who might be a possible ally.

This security awareness process is called:

A. Divide and conquer
B. Audience participation
C. Audience segmentation
D. Stunned owl syndrome

Answer C

Chapter 5

Response Management

Functional Area Overview

The response management functional area deals with processes and solutions for responding to an incident. This functional area comprises 13 percent of the CISM® examination and comprises approximately 26 questions.

In this chapter you will learn about the following terms:

- Business continuity planning
- Disaster recovery planning
- Incident response
- Computer forensics
- Post-event reviews

CISM Mapping

When the response management functional area is mapped over to ISO 17799 and the domains from the CISSP® common body of knowledge, it covers a number of different areas (see Table 5.1). This functional area is not as large as other functional areas, but it still encompasses a number of different solutions and disciplines.

Table 5.1 Response Management

ISO 17799 Section	*CISSP Domain*
4. Information security organization	3. Security management
7. Physical and environmental security	8. Business continuity planning
8. Computer and network management	9. Law, investigations, and ethics
9. System access control	10. Physical security
10. Systems development and maintenance	
11. Business continuity planning	

Introduction

This functional area is different from the other functional areas in that this functional area occurs when the controls that we have covered up to this point fail. Response management is, at its most basic, about what to do when the controls have failed. The focus of this section is on planning and responding to security incidents.

Threat Source Information

In Chapter 3 we discussed threats to information security systems and in each of the function areas we discussed controls. In every organization there will be a time when a control fails or a new threat emerges that does not have a corresponding control. The result of this failure of control will lead to an incident or a disaster. A disaster as defined by the *Disaster Recovery Journal* is "A sudden, unplanned calamitous event that brings about great damage or loss. Any event that creates an inability on the organization's part to provide critical business functions for some undetermined period of time." An incident is defined by the *DRJ* as "A disruption in service that lasts less than 24 hours." It is important for the information security manager to stay up to date on the latest threats that can lead to either a disaster or an incident. Also in Chapter 3 we discussed sources for understanding the latest threats.

Because the number of threats increases every year and information security budgets do not necessarily increase with the number of threats, it is necessary to prioritize which threats have the greatest potential for damage to your organization. First you need to prioritize the threats based on which threats are most likely to affect the organization in terms of frequency and likelihood. Once you have determined the likelihood, the second phase is to determine the impact on your organization if that threat were to hit your organization. There are a number of different sources that can be used to determine the likelihood that your organization is to be hit. These sources of information can include security research organizations, vendors, and government sites. Some examples of security research organizations include:

- BugTraq from http://www.securityfocus.com. This service includes both archive and mailing list functionality to provide frequent updates to the information security manager.
- Internet Storm Center is available at http://isc.sans.org. This is one of the most comprehensive sources of attack information on the Internet. The information about attacks is updated very frequently and this information can be used as an advanced warning system. The front page of the Internet Storm Center can be seen in Figure 5.1.

Some examples of vendor-provided attack information include:

- Symantec's Security Response Center available at http://securityresponse.symantec.com. This site is much like the Internet Storm Center listed above.

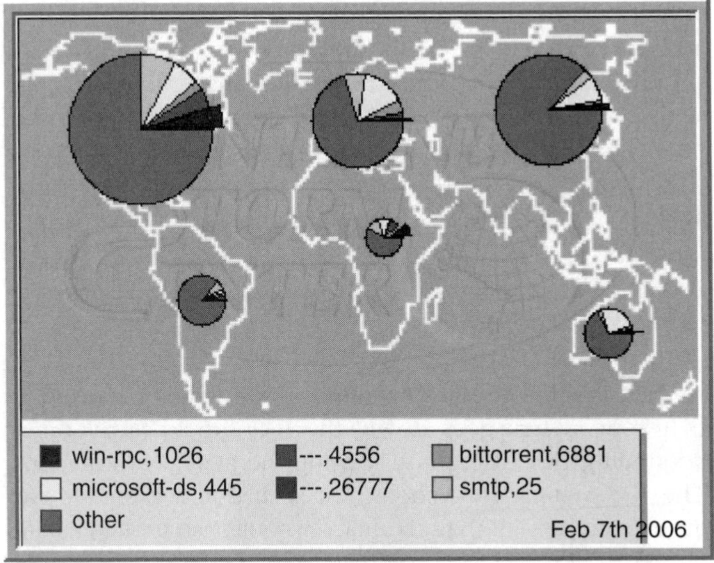

Figure 5.1 Internet Storm Center.

- Microsoft's Security Bulletin Center available at http://www.microsoft.com/technet/security/default.mspx. This site provides Microsoft specific security information.

Some examples of government-provided attack information include:

- The National Vulnerability Database available at http://nvd.nist.gov/. Although this does not provide statistics for current attack levels as the security research organizations do, it does provide a definitive database of current vulnerabilities.

The Role of Intrusion Detection and Anti-Virus Systems

Also in Chapter 3 we discussed the control that is intrusion detection or intrusion prevention systems as well as anti-virus systems. These systems will provide actual information about the number and types of attacks that are attempted against your organization. These systems provide some of the hardest data in terms of actual attacks that your organization will see. However, there is a bit of a trade-off, in that as an information security manager you cannot plan for attacks that have already commenced. This is why the combination of the sites listed above with real-time data of intrusion detection systems and anti-virus systems can provide a much better overall picture of current security concerns.

Because we covered, in detail, the components of an IDS system in Chapter 3 on information security program management, we only briefly cover the most critical functions that an IDS should have. As an information security manager, you should be familiar with intrusion detection policies (how to create and edit the IDS policies) and also the properties of your IDS system.

IDS Properties

- An IDS should be a fault-tolerant system which means in the event that your system goes down, the IDS should have some way of continuing processing and logging the attack information.
- The IDS system itself should be secure and it should not create an exposure point that an attacker could use to gain unauthorized access to your network.
- IDS systems such as anti-virus systems should be continuously running. This means that there is no way to bypass processing of

the specific security. As soon as the IDS device is booted the IDS software should be running. In addition a key component of an IDS system is that it can be modified to adapt to new exploits.

- Also an IDS should not impose access overhead.
- Furthermore, an IDS should be able to detect any anomalies from the baseline of your organization's normal processing environment.
- An IDS should have audit logs that can be backed up or spooled off to another device which will store log information in the event of a failure of the IDS.
- Lastly, an IDS should be able to identify the motivation for attack and the corresponding skill level of an attacker.

Business Continuity Planning and Disaster Recovery Planning

It is the middle of the night and you are sleeping soundly. You realize that you are being rudely awakened by the playing of "Whip It" by Devo coming from your cell phone. A quick check of the bedside clock lets you know that it is currently 3:30 AM. It is with this knowledge that you ponder the merits of downloading the new ringtone and wonder aloud if you have made the correct choice. Your night continues to get worse when you answer your cell phone to find out that your company's Web site has been defaced by an attacker and it is now your responsibility to "fix it." After some groggy reflection you remember that your disaster recovery plan has no provision for a cracker breaking into your network and you get the wonderful feeling that you are once again a high-wire acrobat operating without a net.

This is a true emergency and often in this type of situation, calamitous mistakes can be made. What is necessary here is an Incident Response (IR) process. Of course, the best course of action would have been to have anticipated and planned for this, months in advance. In many cases you may have done the "planning," but the budgeting was left to someone else and it never really made it into the procedures manual. I often had a situation where I had the plan worked out, but my management team had no interest in my plan. If we had performed any prior planning we would be dealing with Incident Management as opposed to Incident Response. Because any or all of the reasons for not having an existing plan in place can be true, let's stop affixing the blame and start fixing the problem.

The Planning

In the example above, it would have been a better situation if we had been prepared in advance. In most cases the process for planning should look something like the diagram shown in Figure 5.2.

In Chapter 2 on risk management we detailed the processes for appropriate steps to take to manage and help create an acceptable level of risk. Because we have already spent an entire chapter covering these concepts we do not rehash them here. We begin our process by discussing business continuity planning.

Business Continuity Planning and Disaster Recovery Planning

Two terms that are often seen together are Business Continuity Planning (BCP) and Disaster Recovery Planning (DRP). Although these terms are related they are not the same (see Figure 5.3). Business continuity planning is the process for planning for continuity of business operations for the entire enterprise in an event of a disaster or similar incident. A small

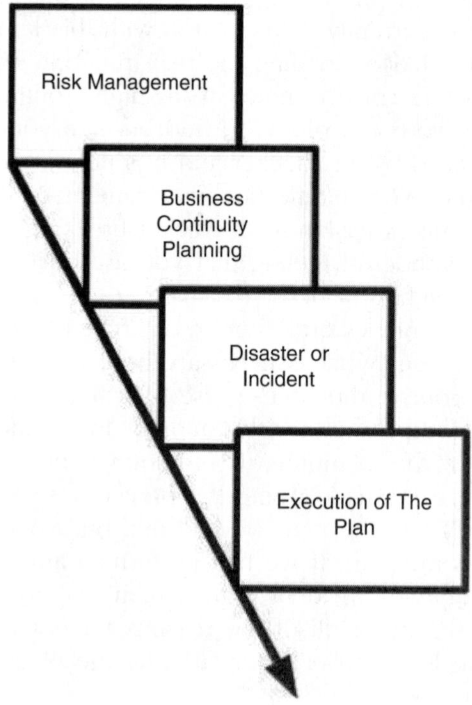

Figure 5.2 Planning process.

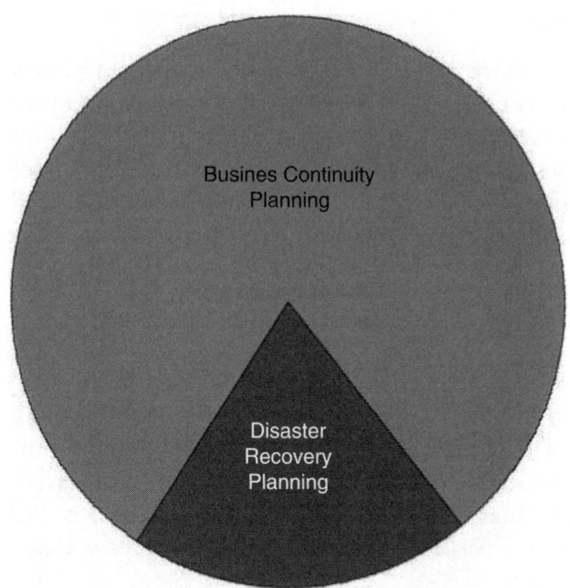

Figure 5.3 Relationship of BCP to DRP.

portion of the overall BCP is the disaster recovery plan. In fact the BCP is often made up of several individual plans that we look at in the next section. The portion of the BCP that covers the recovery of the information technology infrastructure is called the disaster recovery plan. It can be said that the role of the DRP is the process for bringing up the data center after a disaster. When we discuss business continuity planning we are talking about planning for the entire corporate structure and this means that business continuity planning is not an IT function (this should be performed for all areas of the enterprise and not just IT). IT does have a portion of the BCP just as does every other business unit and the information processing portion of a corporate business continuity plan is called the disaster recovery plan. Let's take a deeper look into what all of this means.

The goal of the business continuity plan is to assist the organization to continue functioning though normal operations are disrupted. It includes action to take before, during, and after a disaster has occurred. Advance planning and preparations are necessary to minimize loss and to ensure the availability of critical information resources during the disaster. The mantra of the business continuity planner is, "It's always better to have a plan and not need it than need the plan and not have it."

BCP Resources

There are also many resources to assist in business continuity planning including various national standards, organizations, and publications such as the *Disaster Recovery Journal*, and vendors such as SunGuard. In our opinion the best freely available resource is the NIST Special Publication 800-34 available from http://csrc.nist.gov/publications. The definitions and terms in the following sections are taken from this resource.

Stages of BCP

Because of the fluid and changing environments in most organizations, it is important to incorporate business continuity planning into the Systems Development Life Cycle (SDLC). Creating business continuity plans is not as simple as just sitting down and writing a plan from start to finish. There are several steps that are necessary in most organizations. Figure 5.4 shows a common process for BCP and each of these stages is described in depth later in this chapter.

Reasons for BCP

BCP allows an organization to maintain business operations, save time, cut down on mistakes, lessen stress, and provide for costing information in the event of a disaster. The greatest reason for contingency planning is to keep the revenue flowing for your organization in the event of a disaster, to meet contractual obligations, or for customer satisfaction. The primary goal of BCP is to minimize short- and long-term loss of business by allowing you to have the necessary materials available to recover your business processes. A great secondary reason for BCP is the byproduct of the BCP process: you will have identified your critical resources, assets, and dependent systems. BCP may not take place overnight, in almost all cases it will not, and BCP can take several years. Although BCP is often a necessary process, BCP may have failed in your organization in the past. This is to say that the creation of the BCP has failed and not that the business was not able to continue.

Most often the reason that BCP fails is that BCP does not get full senior management support. Because of the length of time it takes to develop a BCP the costs can be quite high. Due to the costs, BCP is often done in response to some outside force (such as a high-profile disaster such as a hurricane, tsunami, or bombing). For the BCP process to gain senior management support, you as an information security manager have to perform a risk analysis or risk assessment. The risk analysis or risk assessment process will provide the metrics to help senior management

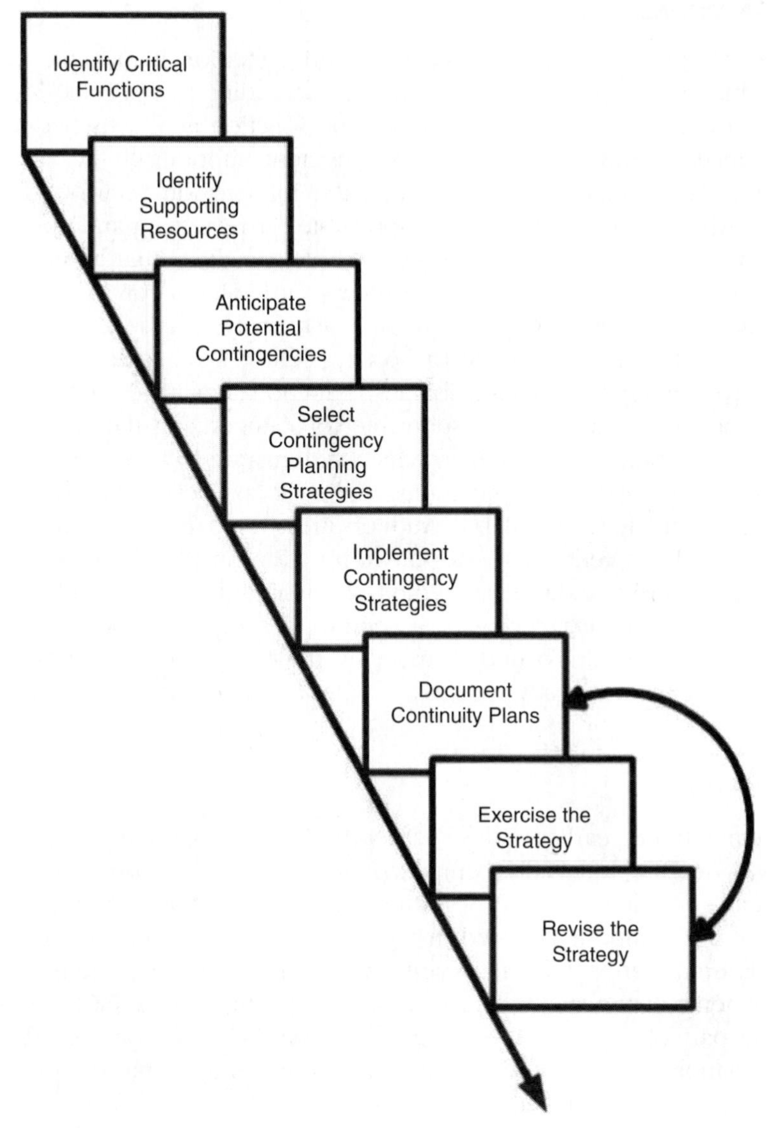

Figure 5.4 BCP processes.

understand the benefits of creating a continuity plan from a business standpoint. The risk assessment process is truly a business process not only because you may have legal or other requirements, but also because a BCP can prove to your customers and clients that you have a plan in place to continue to meet your contractual obligations.

BCP Responsibilities

For a BCP process to be successful, executive (senior) management must perform two functions. The first function, according to NIST 800-34, is to create a policy regarding BCP. The second function is directly tied to this first function, and it is to provide consistent support of the planning process. These functions may include the Information Security Steering Committee. This group (ISSC) is responsible for reviewing and approving the plan and ensuring that it's tested at least on an annual basis. This is a common part of a due diligence process for having a contingency plan. The ISSC may review the result of the risk analysis and determine that creating a BCP is going to be too costly. Senior management is not the only group with BCP responsibilities. Functional managers (department heads or data owners) are responsible for categorizing the criticality of systems, prioritizing the order in which systems are to be recovered, and are also responsible for integrating the BCP process into the System Development Life Cycle (SDLC). Auditors are often part of the BCP process as well. Auditors generally perform two functions in the BCP process. The first is to ensure due diligence in the tasks assigned to senior and function management and also to provide a neutral party or referee when the BCP plan is to be tested. To understand why the BCP process in most cases will be lengthy and costly we look in detail at the components of a BCP.

Types of Plans

As we mentioned earlier in this chapter the BCP is not a one-piece discrete entity. The BCP is usually composed of many smaller plans that when taken as a whole create the BCP. Not every organization is going to need each of the components listed in Figure 5.5 and many organizations will use different terms and acronyms to describe the components. Some components may actually be created as addendums to the BCP and may not be part of the BCP itself. Figure 5.5 shows these components and their relationship to the overall BCP. The terms and definitions are taken from the NIST Special Publication 800-34.

Business Continuity Plan (BCP)

The BCP focuses on sustaining an organization's **business functions** during and after a disruption. An example of a business function may be an organization's payroll process or consumer information process. A BCP may be written for a specific business process or may address all key business processes. IT systems are considered in the BCP in terms of their support to the business processes. In some cases, the BCP may not address

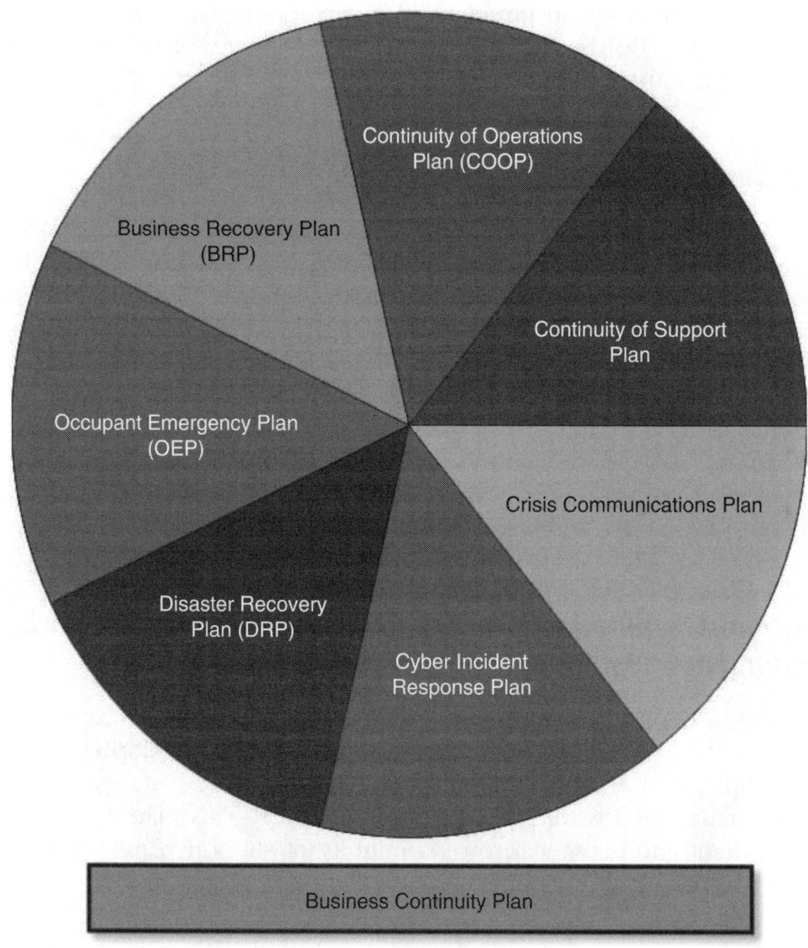

Figure 5.5 BCP components.

long-term recovery of processes and return to normal operations, solely covering interim business continuity requirements. A disaster recovery plan, business resumption plan, and occupant emergency plan may be appended to the BCP. Responsibilities and priorities set in the BCP should be coordinated with those in the Continuity Of Operations Plan (COOP) to eliminate possible conflicts.

Business Recovery Plan (BRP), also Business Resumption Plan

The BRP addresses the restoration of business processes after an emergency, but unlike the BCP, lacks procedures to ensure continuity of critical processes throughout an emergency or disruption. Development of the BRP should be coordinated with the disaster recovery plan and BCP. The BRP may be appended to the BCP.

Continuity of Operations Plan (COOP)

The COOP focuses on restoring an organization's (usually a headquarters element) essential functions at an alternate site and performing those functions for up to 30 days before returning to normal operations. Because a COOP addresses headquarters-level issues, it is developed and executed independently from the BCP. Because the COOP emphasizes the recovery of an organization's operational capability at an alternate site, the plan does not necessarily include IT operations. In addition, minor disruptions that do not require relocation to an alternate site are typically not addressed. However, COOP may include the BCP, BRP, and disaster recovery plan as appendices.

Continuity of Support Plan/IT Contingency Plan/Network Contingency Plan

Continuity of support planning may be synonymous with IT contingency planning. Because an IT contingency plan should be developed for each major application and general support system, multiple contingency plans may be maintained within the organization's BCP. This plan contains the development and maintenance of continuity of support plans for general support systems and contingency plans for major applications.

Crisis Communications Plan

Organizations should prepare their internal and external communications procedures prior to a disaster. A crisis communications plan is often developed by the organization responsible for public outreach. The crisis communication plan procedures should be coordinated with all other plans to ensure that only approved statements are released to the public. Plan procedures should be included as an appendix to the BCP. The communications plan typically designates specific individuals as the only authority for answering questions from the public regarding disaster response. It may also include procedures for disseminating status reports to personnel and to the public. Templates for press releases are included in the plan.

Cyber Incident Response Plan

The cyber incident response plan establishes procedures to address cyber attacks against an organization's IT system(s). These procedures are designed to enable security personnel to identify, mitigate, and recover from malicious computer incidents, such as unauthorized access to a system or data, denial-of-service, or unauthorized changes to system hardware, software, or data (e.g., malicious logic, such as a virus, worm, or Trojan horse). This plan may be included among the appendices of the BCP.

Disaster Recovery Plan (DRP)

As suggested by its name, the DRP applies to major, usually catastrophic, events that deny access to the normal facility for an extended period. Frequently, DRP refers to an IT-focused plan designed to restore operability of the target system, application, or computer facility at an alternate site after an emergency. The DRP scope may overlap that of an IT contingency plan; however, the DRP is narrower in scope and does not address minor disruptions that do not require relocation. Depending on the organization's needs, several DRPs may be appended to the BCP.

Occupant Emergency Plan (OEP)

The OEP provides the response procedures for occupants of a facility in the event of a situation posing a potential threat to the health and safety of personnel, the environment, or property. Such events would include a fire, hurricane, criminal attack, or a medical emergency. OEPs are developed at the facility level, specific to the geographic location and structural design of the building. The facility OEP may be appended to the BCP, but is executed separately. See Figure 5.6 for a plan summary.

Business Impact Analysis (BIA)

A BCP cannot read, "Bring up all systems simultaneously." It would be impossible to do this. As such it is critical to bring up systems in order of criticality. In order to determine which systems are most critical a Business Impact Analysis (BIA) is performed. A BIA is often the first step of BCP once senior management has defined the policy regarding the support of the BCP.

It might seem as if rating the criticality of systems should be a simple task, but often the process can be quite difficult. The reasons for difficulty in performing a BIA start with no person or business unit wanting to admit

Plan	Purpose	Scope
Business Continuity Plan (BCP)	Provide procedures for sustaining essential business operations while recovering from a significant disruption	Addresses business processes; IT addressed based only on its support for business process
Business Recovery (or Resumption) Plan (BRP)	Provide procedures for recovering business operations immediately following a disaster	Addresses business processes; not IT-focused; IT addressed based only on its support for business process
Continuity of Operations Plan (COOP)	Provide procedures and capabilities to sustain an organization's essential, strategic functions at an alternate site for up to 30 days	Addresses the subset of an organization's missions that are deemed most critical; usually written at headquarters level; not IT-focused
Continuity of Support Plan/IT Contingency Plan	Provide procedures and capabilities for recovering a major application or general support system	Same as IT contingency plan; addresses IT system disruptions; not business process focused
Crisis Communications Plan	Provides procedures for disseminating status reports to personnel and the public	Addresses communications with personnel and the public; not IT focused
Cyber Incident Response Plan	Provide strategies to detect, respond to, and limit consequences of malicious cyber incident	Focuses on information security responses to incidents affecting systems and/or networks
Disaster Recovery Plan (DRP)	Provide detailed procedures to facilitate recovery of capabilities at an alternate site	Often IT-focused; limited to major disruptions with long-term effects
Occupant Emergency Plan (OEP)	Provide coordinated procedures for minimizing loss of life or injury and protecting property damage in response to a physical threat	Focuses on personnel and property particular to the specific facility; not business process or IT system functionality based

Figure 5.6 BCP plans summary.

the lack of critical systems. In many cases functional managers or individuals may feel that if none of their systems is rated the highest in criticality, they may become expendable. Office politics may play a very real role in tainting the outcome of a BIA. This is why the final responsibility of determining the criticality of systems should lie with the ISSC or senior management.

Beside political issues there are other reasons that a BIA can be complex. System complexity can make it difficult to define all resources in an organization and thus make it difficult to define a criticality level. Also, system dependencies can affect the criticality of a system. For example, a financial organization may have customer account information rated as most critical and all other systems are rated far lower. These lower systems could include systems such as the interface to the credit reporting bureaus, which may be rated at the least critical level. However, the interface to the credit reporting bureaus may be a crucial part of the business process for creating new lines of credit and loans for customers.

Without this least critical system (credit bureau reporting) the most critical system (customer account access) may not function. In the world of BCP this secondary and less critical process would be known as a dependency of the more critical process.

Another factor in determining the criticality of a system as part of a BIA may be time dependencies. For example, the payroll system in most companies is only utilized for a few days during the month. If an organization pays employees on the 15th and the 30th of each month, the payroll system would be critical on those days. Any other time during the month the payroll system may receive a much lower rating in the BIA process. These time-dependent critical systems may be end of month, end of quarter, or end of year critical.

To recap, here are some of the most common issues in performing a business impact analysis:

- Politics of critical systems
- System complexity
- Dependent systems
- Time dependencies

Performing a BIA

As you might have guessed from the previous section, it is often necessary to begin with an inventory of devices, systems, software, and applications before beginning the business impact analysis. The inventory process by itself can often be time consuming and expensive, but we have come across a few utilities that have saved us some time in performing the inventory. Pay utilities such as Network Asset Tracker from MIS Utilities and DesignXpert Visio Edition from NetFormX are great for searching out network devices that might be forgotten or unknown by the current IT support staff. There are also open source utilities such as AutoScan from http://autoscan.free.fr/. Utilities for inventorying the software installed on systems can be obtained from the Business Software Alliance at http://www.bsa.org/usa/antipiracy/Free-Software-Audit-Tools.cfm.

Once the inventory is complete it is time to proceed with the core of the BIA process. There are many different methods that can be used. There are software-based packages that allow for functional managers to use an intranet site and these packages work well for very large organizations. In most cases the expense of the entire BCP process will require a less-expensive BIA option and this is usually a paper-based questionnaire process. In almost all cases the questionnaire will not be overly time consuming and will be less expensive than most software options. Figure 5.7 is an example of a questionnaire from NIST 800-34. Surprisingly, most BIA questionnaires are very similar in structure to this figure.

Preliminary System Information

Organization:	Date BIA Completed:
System Name:	BIA POC:
System Manager Point of Contact (POC):	
System Description: *{Discussion of the system purpose and architecture, including system diagrams}*	
A. Identify System POCs	**Role**
Internal {Identify the individuals, positions, or offices *within* your organization that depend on or support the system; also specify their relationship to the system}	
▪ ▪	▪ ▪
External {Identify the individuals, positions, or offices *outside* your organization that depend on or support the system; also specify their relationship to the system}	
▪ ▪	▪ ▪
B. Identify System Resources *{Identify the specific hardware, software, and other resources that comprise the system; include quantity and type}*	
Hardware ▪ ▪	
Software ▪ ▪	
Other resources ▪ ▪	
C. Identify critical roles {List the roles identified in Section A that are deemed critical}	
▪ ▪ ▪ ▪	

Figure 5.7 Business Impact Analysis questionnaire.

D. Link critical roles to critical resources {Identify the IT resources needed to accomplish the roles listed in Section C}

Critical Role	Critical Resources
	▪ ▪
	▪ ▪
	▪ ▪

E. Identify outage impacts and allowable outage times {Characterize the impact on critical roles if a critical resource is unavailable; also, identify the maximum acceptable period that the resource could be unavailable before unacceptable impacts resulted}

Resource	Outage Impact	Allowable Outage Time
	▪ ▪	▪ ▪
	▪ ▪	▪ ▪
	▪ ▪	▪ ▪

F. Prioritize resource recovery {List the priority associated with recovering a specific resource, based on the outage impacts and allowable outage times provided in Section E. Use quantitative or qualitative scale (e.g., high/medium/low, 1-5, A/B/C)}

Resource	Recovery Priority

Figure 5.7 (Continued)

Business Impact Analysis Results

The results of the BIA should be the overall criticality of the system and also the Maximum Tolerable Outage (MTO) or Recovery Time Objective (RTO). The concept of the MTO or RTO is critical for the overall BCP process. The MTO is defined as the maximum amount of time that a system or process can be offline before the business can no longer recover. An RTO is the same except that the RTO is expressed as a timeframe for recovery of a system. The usage of MTO is mostly being replaced with the RTO objective standard. Both of these terms can be explained in the following scenario.

If the payroll system of Acme Bank is affected by a disaster, most employees will continue coming to work if the paychecks are a few days late. Once the paychecks are more than ten days late, most employees will stop coming in to work and in most cases this means the business will fail even if the IT infrastructure is recovered. This ten-day period from when paychecks are supposed to be sent out would be the maximum tolerable outage: MTO. Expressing this as a recovery point objective would be to say that the payroll system would have to be recovered within ten days of the normal pay time during the event of a disaster.

Although the MTO and RTO are almost always calculated in days, the scale for criticality of a system or process can use many different labels. Some organizations will classify the BIA rating with either a low, medium, or high scale. Other organizations use an A to F rating, and the most common appears to be a 1 to 5 rating scale. We use the 1 to 5 rating scale in the future examples in the chapter. Using the 1 to 5 scale, applications that rate as either a 1 or 2 will be the highest priority to return to processing. An application that is rated a 3 in criticality will be returned to processing as soon as convenient. Applications that rate as a 4 or 5 in criticality will not be returned to processing as part of the disaster recovery plan, but will return to processing as part of the business resumption plan. Level 4 and 5 applications will only return to processing as business operations move to the permanent processing location and not at the disaster recovery site. See Figure 5.8.

The chart in Table 5.2 shows business processes, functional owner, criticality for the organization and to the department, as well as the maximum tolerable outage time for Acme Bank.

Reasons for BIA

As stated above, business impact analysis is the first step in BCP after senior management defines a BCP policy. Performing a BIA has many benefits for the rest of the BCP process. The BIA will ensure that

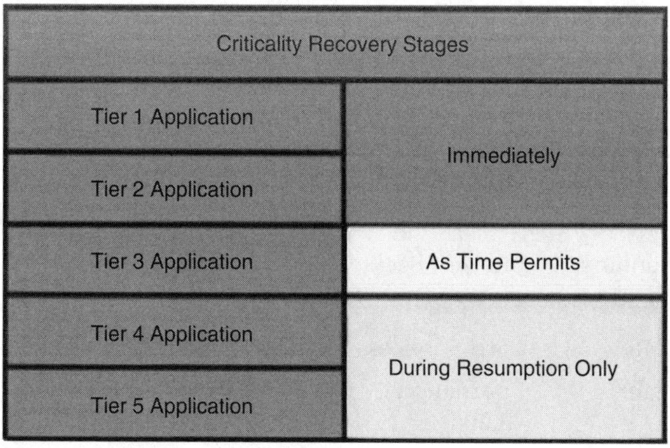

Figure 5.8 Criticality recovery locations.

application processing will resume based on the business plan of your organization. This means that a BIA will relate security objectives to the organization mission. In addition a BIA quantifies how much to spend on security measures to assist in both risk mitigation before the disaster or incident and also controls to allow recovery of application processing within the recovery time objective. Because the BIA provides you with an understanding of what is critical and a timeframe to restore processing, the BIA provides long-term planning and guidance for the rest of the BCP process. To summarize the goals of a BIA are to understand economic and operational impacts, determine recovery timeframes, identify a most appropriate strategy cost-justified to a recovery plan, and include BCP in normal business decision-making processes.

Finding Resources and Dependencies

The BIA focuses on restoring business processes. These processes run on top of IT systems. At this point it is necessary to find all of these resources and assign the same level of criticality to the support devices as the level of the process that runs of top of the infrastructure. In some organizations this process is all part of the BIA. In fact, this is the way I prefer to perform the process, but I do know that several organizations will create two steps in this process. If your organization uses the two-step process the result of this phase will be a matrix similar to that in Table 5.3.

Table 5.2 Sample BIA Results

Process	*Department*	*Criticality* Overall	*Criticality* Dept.	*Maximum Tolerable Downtime (Business days)*
Branch Operations	Operations	1	1	0.5
General Ledger	Accounting	1	1	0.5
Internet Banking	Internet Backing	1	1	0.5
Mortgage Servicing	Mortgage	2	1	0.5
ATM Card Reissue	Card Services	1	2	1
Wire Transfer	International Banking	3	2	1
Notifications	Collections	3	2	2
Loan Services	Loan Services	3	1	2
Mortgage Origination	Mortgage	2	1	2
Benefits	Human Resources	2	2	5
Charge Card Issue	Card Services	3	2	5
Loan Approval	Loan Services	3	2	5
Merchant Services	Small Business Services	3	1	5
Payroll	Accounting	1	1	5
Payroll	Human Resources	1	1	5
Terminations	Human Resources	3	3	5

Alternate Sites

Once you have performed the BIA it is time to look for the most major component of the BCP. A decision needs to be made as to which type of contingency plan your organization is going to create. This process is going to be affected primarily by which type of alternate site your organization is going to choose. There are several different types of alternate sites and there are strengths and weaknesses to each. As an information security manager you should understand the differences between the types of sites. The following site information is taken from NIST 800-34.

Table 5.3 Resource Dependencies

	Computer Applications			
Process	*Mainframe Name*	*Server Name*	*LAN*	*Local Software*
Accounts Payable	MF1			
ATM Card Reissue	MF2			
Benefits		SuperServer1		MSOffice
Branch Operations	MF1			MSOffice
Branch Support				MSOffice Publisher
Card Reissues	MF1	SuperServer2		
Charge Card Issue	MF1	SuperServer2		
Corporate banking				MSOffice
Credit Administration	MF1	SuperServer1	Client	MSOffice
Disputed Charges		SuperServer3		
Collections	MF1			
Financial Statements	MF3			
Fixed Assets	MF4			
General Ledger	MF1			
Internal Communications				MSOffice Publisher
Internet Banking		SuperServer1		
Loan Approval			PartnerNet	MSOffice
Loan Collection	MF1		Client	MSOffice
Loan Services	MF1			MSOffice
Merchant Services	MF1	SuperServer2		
Mortgage Origination			PartnerNet	
Mortgage Servicing	MF1		Extranet	MSOffice
Payroll		SuperServer3		MSOffice
Payroll		SuperServer3		MSOffice
Recovery	MF1		Client	
Recruitment		SuperServer3	Client	MSOffice
Terminations	MF1			
Wire Transfer				

Cold Sites

Cold sites typically consist of a facility with adequate space and infrastructure (electric power, telecommunications connections, and environmental controls) to support the IT system. The space may have raised floors and other attributes suited for IT operations. The site does not contain IT equipment and usually does not contain office automation equipment, such as telephones, facsimile machines, or copiers. The organization using the cold site is responsible for providing and installing the necessary equipment and telecommunications capabilities. A cold site is basically a shell with a raised floor and power.

Warm Sites

Warm sites are partially equipped office spaces that contain some or all of the system hardware, software, telecommunications, and power sources. The warm site is maintained in an operational status ready to receive the relocated system. The site may need to be prepared before receiving the system and recovery personnel. In many cases, a warm site may serve as a normal operational facility for another system or function, and in the event of contingency plan activation, the normal activities are displaced temporarily to accommodate the disrupted system.

Hot Sites

Hot sites are office spaces appropriately sized to support system requirements and configured with the necessary system hardware, supporting infrastructure, and support personnel. Hot sites are typically staffed 24 hours a day, seven days a week. Hot site personnel begin to prepare for the system arrival as soon as they are notified that the contingency plan has been activated.

Mobile Sites

Mobile sites are self-contained, transportable shells custom-fitted with specific telecommunications and IT equipment necessary to meet system requirements. These are available for lease through commercial vendors. The facility often is contained in a tractor-trailer and may be driven to and set up at the desired alternate location. In most cases, to be a viable recovery solution, mobile sites should be designed in advance with the vendor, and an SLA should be signed between the two parties. This is necessary because the time required to configure the mobile site can be extensive, and without prior coordination, the time to deliver the mobile site may exceed the system's allowable outage time.

Mirrored Sites

Mirrored sites are fully redundant facilities with full, real-time information mirroring. Mirrored sites are identical to the primary site in all technical respects. These sites provide the highest degree of availability because the data is processed and stored at the primary and alternate site simultaneously. These sites typically are designed, built, operated, and maintained by the organization.

Reciprocal Agreements

Reciprocal agreements are very rare to see functioning in business. A reciprocal agreement is an agreement between two organizations that contractually obligate the organization not experiencing the disaster to provide processing facilities to the organization experiencing the disaster. In most cases the agreements do not function because of the disruptive nature of co-locating the processing on the other organization's applications. In theory reciprocal agreements are very advantageous because of the low cost and high amount of equipment, but because of the aforementioned disruptions to normal operations most organizations would choose another offsite facility.

There are obvious cost and ready-time differences among the five options. The mirrored site is the most expensive choice, but it ensures virtually 100-percent availability. Cold sites are the least expensive to maintain; however, it may require substantial time to acquire and install necessary equipment. Partially equipped sites, such as warm sites, fall in the middle of the spectrum. In many cases, mobile sites may be delivered to the desired location within 24 hours. However, the time necessary for installation can increase this response time. The selection of fixed-site locations should account for the time and mode of transportation necessary to move personnel there. In addition, the fixed site should be in a geographic area that is unlikely to be negatively affected by the same disaster event (e.g., weather-related impacts or power grid failure) as the organization's primary site. As sites are evaluated, the information security manager should ensure that the system's security, management, operational, and technical controls are compatible with the prospective site. Such controls may include firewalls and physical access controls, data remanance controls, and security clearance level of the site and staff

Table 5.4 Off Site Comparison

Site	*Cost*	*Hardware Equipment*	*Tele-communications*	*Setup Time*	*Location*
Cold Site	Low	None	None	Long	Fixed
Warm Site	Medium	Partial	Partial/Full	Medium	Fixed
Hot Site	Medium/ High	Full	Full	Short	Fixed
Mobile Site	High	Dependent	Dependent	Dependent	Not Fixed
Mirrored Site	High	Full	Full	None	Fixed

supporting the site. The chart in Table 5.4 summarizes the differences among site locations.

Implementation and Writing

Once the alternate location has been decided, it is time to implement the plan and begin plan writing. The writing of the plan should include information about equipment location, equipment purchase, vendor contacts, and service level agreements. The implementation of the plan should include the data backup strategy and any other redundancy necessary for the plan to be successful. Once the plan is written, it should be presented to the ISSC for approval. Once the plan is approved, strict version tracking should occur. Version tracking will stop two groups from enacting different versions of the BCP in the event of a disaster. Once a version of the plan is accepted by the ISSC, it is time to move onto the next phase: training.

Team Training

All teams need to be trained on the BCP or BCP components that they will be working with in the event of a disaster. It is also important to use cross-training so that groups of employees can perform more than one function during the disaster. Cross-training is critical because in the event of a disaster or penetration, you may not be at full staff. It is a sad truth that some disasters may leave employees unavailable to enact the BCP. It is important to spread responsibilities and knowledge to multiple people to provide redundancy in the event that a team or team leader is not available. It is also critical that one person is not overly burdened, because it is very difficult for one person to be in two or three places at once. This means that an employee can only be assigned to one team and cannot perform mutually exclusive tasks in terms of time. Team members may need additional training and experience in order to perform the necessary tasks of the BCP.

Testing the Plan

Once the plan is written it is time to perform the initial test. BCP plans are living documents that need to be constantly updated as systems are installed, business units merge, and other organizational changes occur. The plan needs an initial test because in many cases the author of the BCP plan components is a Subject Matter Expert (SME). As an SME it is possible to miss steps because of in-depth knowledge of the process.

A few years ago a client asked me to write a network contingency plan. In this plan one of the steps that I had written was, "Drive to the tape backup facility and get the tape backup tapes." Once the plan was written we tested the plan with a table-top walkthrough. This test required that everybody who was involved in the disaster recovery was around the room and everybody worked from a copy of the plan. The goal of this type of test is for the team members to look at the plan and see if they could perform their tasks from only the instructions listed in the plan. A team member asked a really brilliant question once they read the "Drive to the tape backup facility and get the tape backup tapes" line. The question was, "Where is the facility?"

It was a good question, and that type of information is needed in the disaster recovery plan. Another step that was missing from the NCP was how to call ahead to the facility to let them know to have the tapes ready. The last piece that was missing from just this one stage was how were the team members to get to the tape storage facility in the event that their vehicle was damaged in the incident. All of these steps were easy for me to miss because I was very familiar with the concept and simply did these tasks without thinking. This is just one example of why the subject matter expert should not exclusively write the plans, because it is so easy to miss those details.

Exercising and Testing the BCP/DRP

There are many different kinds of tests of the BCP, from full interruption testing, which should not be done during peak processing time, to table-top walkthroughs, which can be done just about anytime. Before beginning any type of testing the information security manager should compile a list of test objectives. This list will provide you with a mechanism to see how well your plan performs. Testing is crucial to ensure that all team members have the necessary training to perform their tasks. Also, frequent testing will provide experience for the BCP process, so the tasks will not be completely new to the team members when a disaster happens. Here are some common types of BCP tests:

- *Table-top testing:* A reading of the plan with all team members
- *Simulation:* A mock disaster scenario that may be very detailed or high level depending on the goals of the test
- *Technical recovery testing:* Attempting to recover backup copies of the data
- *Alternate site recovery testing:* Testing the move to the alternate site
- *Test of supplier facilities and services:* Checking for compliance with contractual service level agreements
- *Full-interruption testing:* A full cut-over of production processing to alternate sites or devices

Testing or exercising the plan proves the feasibility of the recovery process, verifies compatibility for the backup facilities, and ensures adequacy of test team procedures. It trains the team members, validates lines of coordination and communications, provides mechanisms for maintaining and updating the plan, and promotes management confidence, selling the concept and success of the plan. What should not occur as part of the test is to disrupt essential work or business processes.

Each organization should appoint someone to be a referee. This person is going to be an independent reviewer and will ensure that team members are not cheating during the test. The basic goal of the referee is to stop team members from using those resources that should not be available.

Once the test of the plan is completed it is necessary to use project management skills so the follow-up after the test of the business continuity plan is done. This will help lead to constant plan improvement.

When testing the plan, it is important to respect mistakes and problems, learn from the results, ensure multiple versions of the plan do not exist, and we want very definitely to have version control.

Improve the Plan

The result of the evaluation should be a list of things that should be fixed and it is very rare that there should be no areas for improvement. In fact as an information security manager if you exercise the plan and there are no things that you need to improve upon you did not test the plan hard enough. If there are no areas for improvement after the test, it is recommended to test the plan again under a more difficult scenario. Once areas for improvement are found the tasks should be assigned to someone, a timeline for completion should be established, and a review of the completed tasks should occur.

Updating the Plan

As we discussed above, a BCP is a living document. It is necessary to keep up with the changing needs and changing structure of the organization. The updating of the BCP should be part of the SDLC. When a system is upgraded or when a new system is rolled out, standard practice should be to ensure that the disaster recovery and business continuity plan gets modified to include the new systems.

Three Phases of BCP

In disaster response there are three phases (Figure 5.9). They are response, recovery, and restoration. The response phase requires creation of an emergency response plan and a crisis communications plan. The two key elements involved in the response phase are to stabilize the environment and to protect the people. Once these objectives are achieved then it is time to begin the initial portions of the business continuity plan. As there are many components of a BCP there are also many teams involved in the business continuity process. Common examples of teams are taken from NIST 800-34 and are listed in Table 5.5.

Once an incident has happened it is still not a disaster until it is declared. Before a disaster can be declared the Crisis Management Team (CMT) needs to be assembled. The CMT is typically made up of senior executives, the PR staff, and the HR staff. Once the CMT is in place the damage assessment team can proceed to determine if the incident is truly a disaster. No recovery plans are implemented until the assessment team has evaluated the site and reported back to the crisis management team.

Once the site has been assessed the crisis management team will declare a disaster (if it is warranted). Once the declaration has occurred some processes will happen concurrently. This begins with the implementation of your recovery strategy. This will start with the process to restore processing to your Tier 1 and Tier 2 applications, systems, and business processes. Remember we determined the Tier 1 and Tier 2 applications from the business impact analysis. At the same time as the recovery team is beginning to enact the plan, the offsite storage team would be heading out to the storage facility to locate the tape backups of your organization's data. Also, the salvage team will go into the disaster site and salvage whatever equipment is salvageable. The salvaging of equipment is for the

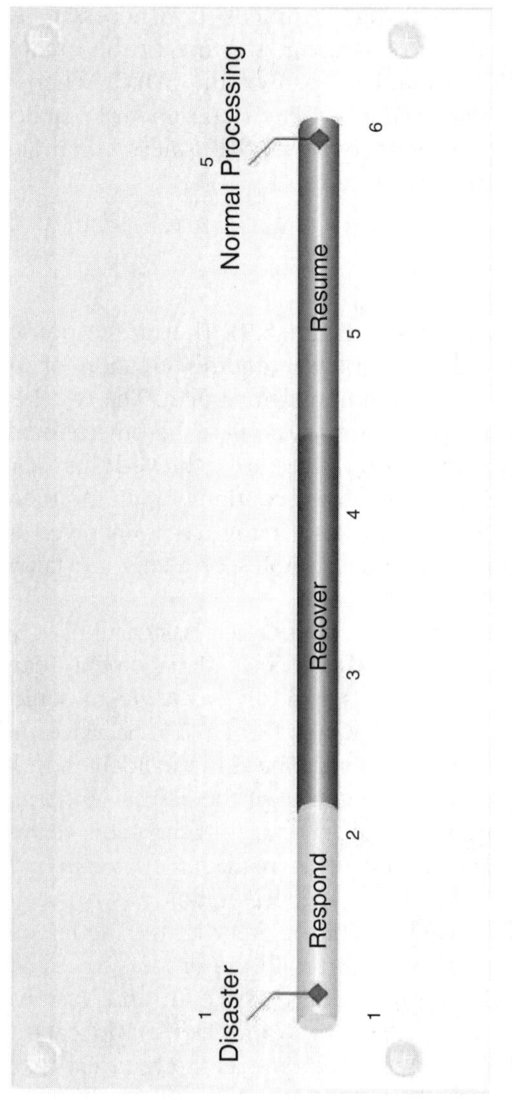

Figure 5.9 Disaster response.

Table 5.5 Business Continuity Teams

• Senior Management Official	• Alternate Site Recovery Coordination Team
• Management Team	• Original Site Restoration/Salvage Coordination Team
• Damage Assessment Team	• Test Team
• Operating System Administration Team	• Administrative Support Team
• Systems Software Team	• Transportation and Relocation Team
• Server Recovery Team (e.g., client server, Web server)	• Media Relations Team
• LAN/WAN Recovery Team	• Legal Affairs Team
• Database Recovery Team	• Physical/Personnel Security Team
• Network Operations Recovery Team	• Procurement Team (equipment and supplies)
• Application Recovery Team(s)	
• Telecommunications Team	
• Hardware Salvage Team	

resumption level of the plan. The salvage team will work with the restoration team for the resumption in your final environment.

Remember that most disaster facilities are only temporary and even in the case of complete loss of the main processing location, it will not be possible to stay in the disaster facility for long. The resumption phase of the plan is all about getting the processing to occur in the primary site, whether it is a new location or the old location. The restoration team will start by bringing up Tier 3 to 5 applications for processing in the permanent site. Once those applications are running, Tier 1 and 2 applications will be running in a parallel processing mode. Once the parallel processing is running appropriately, the cut-over will take place to move all of the processing to the primary processing facility. Once all processing is back at the primary site the disaster is over.

Incident Response

In the previous sections we discussed planning for and responding to a disaster. In this section we focus on responding to an incident. An incident is less severe than a disaster and typically an incident will create an outage of 24 hours or less. One of the most common examples of an incident is an attacker gaining unauthorized access to a system that belongs to your organization. Another common example is a malicious code (virus or worm) outbreak on your organization's network. Incident response is the process for responding to this type of event. As with BCP, an incident response plan is always better to have and not need than need and not have.

Incident response is a rapidly evolving field. Because of this there are no well-established national standards for incident response. The two most commonly referenced documents for incident response are the National Institute of Standards and Technology (NIST) Special Publication 800-86 and Spafford and Carrier's paper "Digital Investigative Framework," as presented at the Digital Forensic Research Workshop of August 2004, and is available at http://www.digital-evidence.org/papers/index.html. Figure 5.10 shows the incident response process.

Discovery

There are many ways that incidents can be discovered. More often than not you are going to get information about your incident through accidental discovery. Accidental discovery occurs when an anomalous event is detected. Some examples of accidental discovery would be the 75 cent accounting error in the Cuckoo's Egg and the case of the hacker who was detected because he was using an assistant's account to log into the system at 2:00 AM. Intrusion detection systems, intrusion prevention systems, and audit logs can all provide other methods for discovering malicious code or an attacker.

Notification

As an information security professional the only responsibility after an event has been discovered is to report the event to senior management. The responsibility of how to investigate the incident belongs to management and not the information security professional. When it comes to notifying senior management you want to let them know immediately and the best way is to use out-of-band notification. It is not a good idea to send e-mails to their Blackberries or to send e-mails to their corporate accounts because these communications can be intercepted by the attacker or disgruntled employee. The best way to notify management is in a face-to-face meeting. For any future discussions of the ongoing investigation, it is to use out-of-band communications.

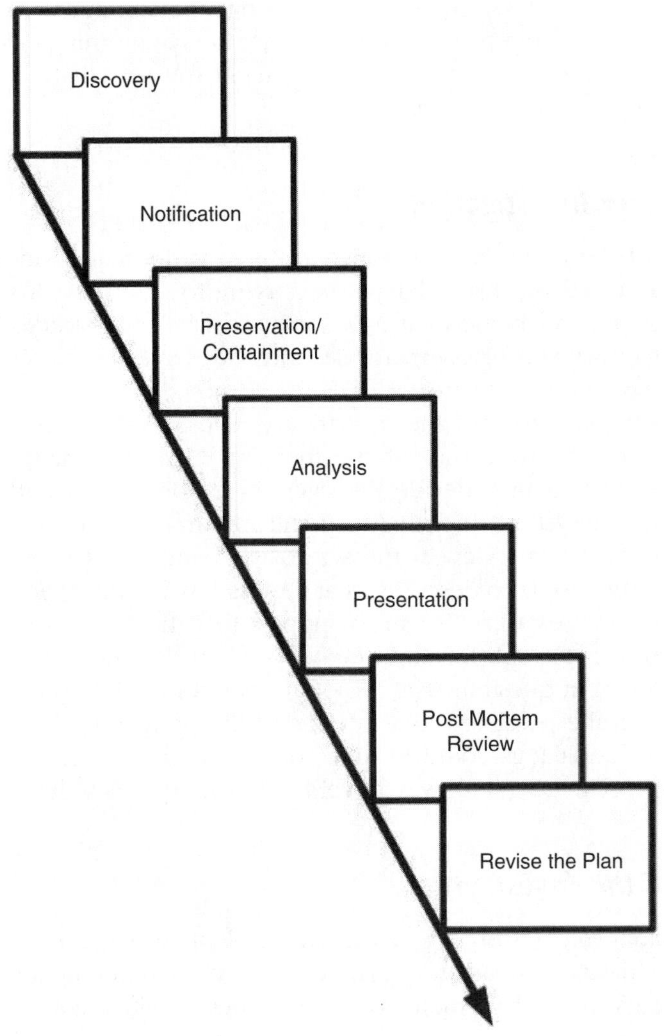

Figure 5.10 Incident response process.

This may seem very intuitive to you as an information security person but you need to impress upon management the sensitivity of investigative materials. In one of the last investigations I ran at my former company, I was investigating my boss for potential theft. I was called into the office of my boss's boss and asked to run an investigation on my boss. We did a very good job keeping her in the dark up until the boss's boss got my final output report. He then put the report on his secretary's desk on a Thursday, because he forgot that she had Friday off from work. This meant that the copy of the output report from my investigation sat on her desk for three days. There was not a single person in that 400-person company that had not read the findings by Monday morning. This is why you may need to impress upon management the sensitivity of incident and investigation information.

Preliminary Investigation

The goal of the preliminary investigation is to verify that an incident has actually occurred. At this point you are trying to determine if the report is truly a computer crime or if it is someone who is mistaken. We have two great bogeymen of computer security. We have the hacker and we have the virus.

The best place to start the preliminary investigation is to review the complaint or information about the incident. Once you have reviewed the complaint you may decide the event is a nonincident and is just a mistake. If you believe that this may still be an event, the next step in the process is to interview witnesses to the event. This process is just simply asking people to describe what they saw when the event occurred. If the interview responses seem to support that the event is an incident the next step is to look for audit log records on devices that are not the primary device in question. The reason to look for audit logs or alternates is because of the possible forensic value of the primary system. Alternate locations of audit logs could include routers, firewalls, and servers. The audit records can go a long way to verify that an event is truly an incident.

Goals of the Investigation

Senior management should provide the incident response manager with the goals for the investigation. There are several different investigative requirements. The requirements would help define which course of action should be taken. Here are some common goals and courses of action:

- *Do nothing:* This is the least expensive option and is often taken by organizations without regulatory requirements to investigate incidents.
- *Conduct surveillance:* This is a more expensive option, but still a relatively inexpensive option. In this course of action the investigation will focus on interviewing people and monitoring for future incidents.
- *Eliminate security holes:* A quick and sometimes costly option is to plug the hole that allowed the incident to occur. Once the hole is plugged the investigation is over.

- *Criminal investigation:* This is the most expensive option. The goal of this investigation is for the attacker to be prosecuted in a criminal court.
- *Civil investigation:* This is the second most expensive option. Evidence is gathered using strict processes, but not as strict as if a criminal investigation were the primary goal. The end goal of a civil investigation is to recover monetary losses for the offending attacker in a civil court.

There are a few different reasons for deciding which goal for the investigation is necessary. One reason could be to limit business loss due to interruption of processing. Another reason would be to save the good name of the organization. Yet another reason could be reduction of liability if you have some kind of legal or regulatory compliance. As mentioned before, an information security manager has one responsibility once you believe an event has occurred: that responsibility is to notify senior management. They are the ones who give you the criteria for the investigation and the green light to proceed. These decisions are not the information security manager's responsibility.

Disclosure

Some incidents need to be disclosed to customers, law enforcement, an oversight board, or a government agency. If your company is affected by legislation such as California's SB-1386 or Gramm–Leech–Bliley, it might be necessary to notify everyone whose personal information was compromised. The good news about disclosure as an information security professional is that the decision to disclose is not yours. As an information security manager, you need to be able to advise senior management about disclosure. In most cases the legal department may have the final call if disclosure is required because of different legal and regulatory compliance issues. As an information security manager you should never make a direct disclosure to the media about a security incident even if it is required by law. Typically this disclosure should be performed by the public relations person.

Conducting Surveillance

Because I really don't think we need to discuss what the "do nothing" option for the goal of an investigation requires, we start with the next least expensive option: conducting surveillance. The most common ways to perform surveillance are to conduct either electronic surveillance or physical surveillance. Surveillance in either form occurs when you have identified a suspect and you look for changes in patterns. Surveillance is different from monitoring because monitoring applies to everyone, whereas surveillance applies just to those suspected of involvement in the incident.

Electronic Surveillance

Electronic surveillance is becoming more popular. These techniques are used by parents to oversee what children are doing on the Internet, what spouses are doing on the Internet, and also to see what employees are doing with corporate resources. Electronic surveillance techniques can take many forms. Some of the most common examples would be firewall log files, system audit logs, keystroke loggers, and also surveillance utilities. Although all of these measures can be effective, the most feature rich are the surveillance utilities. There are many examples of surveillance utilities and an example of the most popular pay utility is eBlaster from SpectorSoft. There are several free versions of surveillance utilities that include software packages such as Beast, Guptachar, BackOrafice, and Virtual Network Computing (VNC). The level of stealth that an electronic surveillance utility has will affect the effectiveness of the utility. Figure 5.11 shows an example of an electronic surveillance utility that is among the stealthiest of currently available utilities.

There can be many different goals for electronic surveillance. The most common goals are to detect a change in use of a system or other resources. For example, a disgruntled employee may be accessing resources that he does not need to access for his normal job function. The other common goal of electronic surveillance is to gather evidence of an ongoing computer crime. An example of this would be if an employee were e-mailing company secrets to a competitor.

Physical Surveillance

Physical surveillance monitors the suspect and not the system used by the suspect. Physical surveillance entails monitoring the suspect for lifestyle changes. For example, a suspect may start driving a new expensive car, wearing designer clothes, and taking expensive vacations. If the suspect is living beyond his current level of income, it should be a clue that perhaps the suspect is the perpetrator.

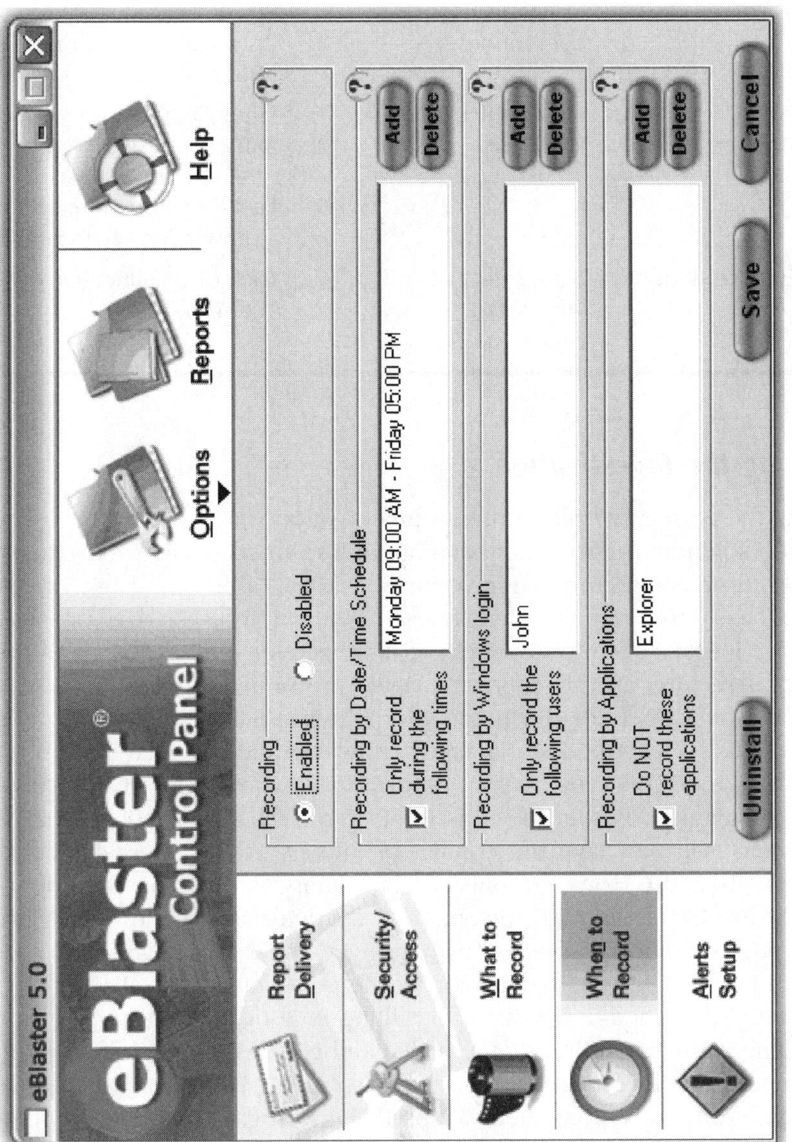

Figure 5.11 eBlaster.

Table 5.6 Investigative Groups

Group	*Strengths*	*Weaknesses*
Internal Security Team	1. Understanding of the systems and personnel	1. May be suspect or perpetrator 2. Potential conflict of Interest
External Consultants	1. No conflict of Interest	1. High Costs 2. Difficult to find highly trained consultants 3. Lack of prior intimate knowledge of systems
Law Enforcement	1. No conflict of Interest 2. Less cost	1. Lack of investigative control

Running the Investigation

Finding the correct people to run an investigation is a tough process. The common solutions are to either have internal security, outside consultants, or law enforcement run the investigation. See Table 5.6. Each of the choices has strengths and weaknesses in the investigative process. Although internal security teams have a far greater understanding of the security, structure, and personnel involved in the investigation, they may be either the suspect or the perpetrator. Knowledge of the systems is a definite plus for internal security teams, however, the potential for conflict can raise major concerns. If you choose not to use an internal security team, you may choose outside consultants to run the investigation. Outside consultants will not have the conflict of interest as the internal security team members do. However, outside consultants do not have the knowledge of local systems and personnel as the internal security teams do. There is an additional concern with using outside consultants and that concern is the skill and qualification of the consultant team. It is difficult to find highly trained and skilled consulting investigators. Once a quality consulting team can be found, the price can be quite high. The last option for running the investigation is law enforcement. Different jurisdictions have different law enforcement teams that investigate computer crimes. Some of the different law enforcement organizations are:

- State Police
- County Police
- Federal Bureau of Investigation (FBI)

- Department of Justice (DOJ)
- Royal Canadian Mounted Police (RCMP)

Information about the groups for U.S.-based computer crime can be found at http://www.usdoj.gov/criminal/cybercrime/fedcode.htm. If law enforcement is investigating your computer crime the conflict of interest that was present in the use of internal security teams is definitely removed. In addition, there is little or no cost associated with law enforcement investigating the crime.

The trade-off to using law enforcement to investigate the computer crime is the lack of investigative control. This can afffect an organization in two ways. The first is law enforcement cannot choose to ignore any laws that may be broken by your own organization. This may affect an organization that is using stolen (unlicensed) software on machines or if the organization is otherwise engaged in criminal activities. The second way that lack of investigative control can affect an organization is that it is much harder to control what information is released to the public when law enforcement is running the investigation. There have been some issues in the past with law enforcement seizing machines as evidence in a computer crime and not returning the systems for very long periods of time. In most environments today, law enforcement is more willing to work with the organization in regard to seizing critical systems for analysis.

Factors of Investigation

The number one factor when it comes to running an investigation is cost. Cost is the number one factor. Money is what it's going to come down to when it comes to investigations. So you guys got an understanding of what the biggest factor is going to be? It's cost, yeah. Cost may encompass legal and regulatory issues that might include fines or financial penalties. Secondary issues to the investigation will be issues of privacy, evidence search and seizure, and information dissemination. Information about an investigation can be leaked to the media outlets. Remember the testimony of Barry Bonds in front of the grand jury regarding BALCO. That was supposed to be sealed and the information should never have been revealed to anyone outside of people present in the courtroom. Barry Bonds' testimony ran on the front page of the *San Francisco Chronicle* on December 3, 2004. So you may have some leaks with the information when you are utilizing outside departments or consultants. This leads to a loss of investigative control. Loss of investigative control may be amplified when law enforcement is involved.

Most Likely Suspects—Insiders, Outsiders, and Collaboration

When it comes to who should be a suspect, keep in mind that it is slightly more likely to be an insider. Past trends have reported that it was significantly more likely to be an insider than an outsider, but the statistics of 2005 show that the numbers are about even (see Figure 5.12). The general rule of thumb is that more attacks are attempted by outsiders, but more successful attacks are originated from inside users. If all evidence in your computer crime investigation is pointing to an outsider, look for the insider who's tipping off the outsider as to how to actually make the attack successful. This is the collaboration process. The greatest source of this information is the annual joint CSI/FBI Computer Crime and Security Survey. This study is available for free at http://www.gosci.com.

Table 1: How Many Incidents? From the Outside? From the Inside?

How many incidents, by % of respondents	1–5	6–10	>10	Don't know
2005	43	19	9	28
2004	47	20	12	22
2003	38	20	16	26
2002	42	20	15	23
2001	33	24	11	31
2000	33	23	13	31
1999	34	22	14	29
How many incidents from the outside, by % of respondents	**1–5**	**6–10**	**>10**	**Don't know**
2005	47	10	8	35
2004	52	9	9	30
2003	46	10	13	31
2002	49	14	9	27
2001	41	14	7	39
2000	39	11	8	42
1999	43	8	9	39
How many incidents from the inside, by % of respondents	**1–5**	**6–10**	**>10**	**Don't know**
2005	46	7	3	44
2004	52	6	8	34
2003	45	11	12	33
2002	42	13	9	35
2001	40	12	7	41
2000	38	16	9	37
1999	37	16	12	35

CSI/FBI 2005 Computer Crime and Security Survey
Source: Computer Security Institute

2005: 453 Respondents

Figure 5.12 CSI/FBI survey results.

Suspects/Witnesses/Interview

When it comes to talking to witnesses, you'll have to determine who is going to be conducting the interview. There are a number of great resource books to help with the interview and interrogation process. One of my personal favorites is *The Principles of Kinesic Interview and Interrogation Technique* by Stan Walters (CRC Press LLC, Boca Raton, FL, 2003). This book is great for assisting the interviewer in how to read and categorize body language from either a witness or a suspect. There are other resources that may prove equally handy to have. One is the book, *Influence: Science and Practice* by Robert B. Cialdini (HarperCollins Publishers, New York, 1993). This book defines the six principles of persuasion:

1. *Reciprocation:* By first giving a little, the target is more likely to comply.
2. *Social Validation:* If they think it's what "everyone else" is doing, they are more likely to comply.
3. *Commitment/Consistency:* First, get their buy-in to the general cause.
4. *Friendship/Liking:* Establish quickly a sense of familiarity with the target.
5. *Scarcity:* Get them buying-in impulsively to giving up the information.
6. *Authority:* Establish credibility quickly with claims of authority.

Understanding these techniques is also handy for performing social engineering. In the confines of conducting an interview or interrogating a suspect these techniques can be used to help establish rapport with the suspect and also to get the suspect to reveal critical information. Another resource is both a book and also a training course. These resources use the Reid Technique for determining nontruthful response from a suspect or a witness. The book resource is titled *Essentials of the Reid Technique: Criminal Interrogations and Confessions* and it is written by Joseph P. Buckley (Jones and Bartlett Publishers, Boston, 2005). As mentioned before, there is also a training course that accompanies the book. The Reid technique uses Neural-Linguistic Programming (NLP) to assess the level of truth from a suspect or witness. There is also a training class on NLP offered by Brad Smith from CIR Consulting. The last interview and interrogation resource we mention is a system called the Micro Expression Training Tool. This program was developed by Paul Ekman and as opposed to using kinesic (body language) or NLP (brain patterns), it uses small facial expressions to determine if a facial expression matches the content of the discussion.

Regardless of which interview and interrogation system you use, it is a good rule of thumb to treat suspects and witnesses differently. You will want to be much firmer when it comes to questioning someone who you believe may have committed the crime versus someone who reported the event happening. It is important to note that there is also a very high statistical probability that the person reporting the incident was the person causing the incident, so this may affect your case.

We have a large consulting company that we work with and they have found that 70 percent of reported laptop thefts can be recovered by an intense interrogation process of the person declaring the lost laptop. Out of all the laptops that were reported stolen they can get seven out of ten back by simply talking to the person about how the laptop went missing. During the interview the interviewer never becomes confrontational. The interviewer simply asks questions to find the holes in the person reporting the stolen laptop's story. By simply asking questions the interviewer eventually gets the reporting person to admit that he or she actually still has the laptop.

Freezing the Environment

When it comes to actually seizing a system for doing the forensic type of investigation, you are going to have to make sure that you have good information about the system. This would include information about details on the configuration of the system. You would need to know if any change is made that it will not overwrite critical data. Also you need to know if there is hard drive encryption in place, because if you shut down a system with hard drive encryption and you don't know the key to get back into the hard drive, you are not going to be able to get the information off that system. This is why you'll need to talk to system security experts to find out what type of security mechanisms can be in place inside that system before seizure commences.

Team Members

Who's going to be involved? Who are the team members for doing an investigation? Typically you're going to have a lead investigator. This is going to be like the conductor for the symphony. This is going to be the person who's going to be responsible for coordinating all of the tasks. Some of the people who will usually be involved will be somebody from information security, somebody from the legal department, somebody from IT if you have a separate IT and information security department, and someone from human resources. The lead investigator need not be a technical person because the primary responsibilities of the lead investigator are to coordinate the investigation and to make sure policies and procedures are followed.

Post-Incident Access

During the investigation it is important to decide if the suspect will continue to have access to either his system or the target of attack system. If your suspect continues to have access you have to be cognizant that he may be destroying evidence on that system or he may have put in some type of logic bomb that is waiting to destroy the evidence on your target system. Once you've made all those determinations you may go after him with a search warrant or a writ of possession. This determination is usually made by the ISSC with assistance from the legal department.

Seizing the System

D-day occurs when you are actually going to seize the system. There are two cardinal rules of this system seizure process. The first rule is, "Do no harm." This means that any process that you will use in this phase of the investigation must not destroy the data on the target system. The second rule is, "Ponder and deliberate before you move." This means that before you perform an action you should evaluate alternatives and prepare for consequences. The first order of business for the seizure phase is limit access to the target system. The reason for this is to ensure that there is very little likelihood that the evidence is going to be damaged or modified in any way. You want to protect the evidence, remembering your mantra of do no harm. As an information security manager you will need to use controls to secure the area. Common controls would be a sign-in/sign-out sheet, an evidence log, and perhaps physical controls to stop physical access to the secure space.

If you remember the first rule—do no harm—you will not want to touch the keyboard or mouse to clear the screensaver. You will want to leave that system in the same state as you found it. To provide assurance that your processes will not modify data, a common control is to videotape the process or take photographs of the process. This will provide photographic evidence that will show exactly what you did to the system.

Once physical access has been secured, the next step is to begin the documentation (see Figure 5.13). In many cases you will begin the documentation with a sketch of the secured area. This should include all

Evidence Collection Worksheet

Original Media Access Worksheet

TO DOCUMENT EACH ACCESS TO ORIGINAL MEDIA	Date:	Time:
	Accessed by:	
	Computer ID:	
Location of Computer:		
BIOS SETTINGS		
Access Date:	System Date:	
Access Time:	System Time:	
BIOS Set to Boot to CD ROM	YES	NO
BIOS Settings Modified to Boot to CD ROM	YES	NO
SEARCH		
Following files extensions were searched for:		

JPG	JPEG	GIF	BMP	OTHER:
PNG	AVI	MPEG	MPG	

Following text and/or file names were searched for:		
During search the following directories were examined:		
Search revealed following:		
Results documented to media	YES	NO
Computer Seized	YES	NO
Special Notes:		Time Ended

Figure 5.13 Evidence worksheet.

physical connections to the system. These connections should be backed up with photographic evidence. Any physical cable or connection to the target system needs to be documented. In addition to the connection documentation you will want to document all potential avenues of entry

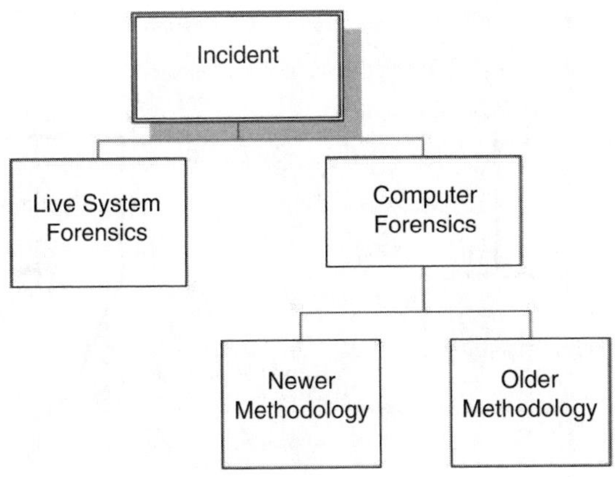

Figure 5.14 Live system forensics and traditional forensics.

into the secure area. Also you will want to capture the contents of the monitor, even if it is just the screensaver so you can show the state of that system when you approached it. It has been suggested to me to not use digital cameras because the media (pictures) can be altered by programs such as Photoshop and photographic evidence should be film cameras instead. Because of these concerns there are cached digital forensics cameras that create an MD5 hash of the picture as soon as the picture is taken. This will depend on the rules of your local jurisdiction and to be safe, you need to know the laws of your local area when you are running this type of investigation.

Forensic Processes

There are two types of computer forensics that can be done (see Figure 5.14). The types are live system forensics and the more common computer forensics processes. In most cases the computer forensic process is used, but live system forensics is becoming more common.

Live system forensics is most often used when the investigation is targeting inappropriate files. The files could be stolen software, critical company secrets, illegal images, or source code for malicious programs. Live system forensics occurs on the target system and not on a separate forensic machine. The live system methodology was introduced in a forensic first responder guide that is available at www.linux-forensics.com/forensics/knoppixManual.pdf.

The common computer forensic process has two methodologies (see Figure 5.15). One is an older methodology and the other is a newer methodology. Each methodology has its advantages and disadvantages.

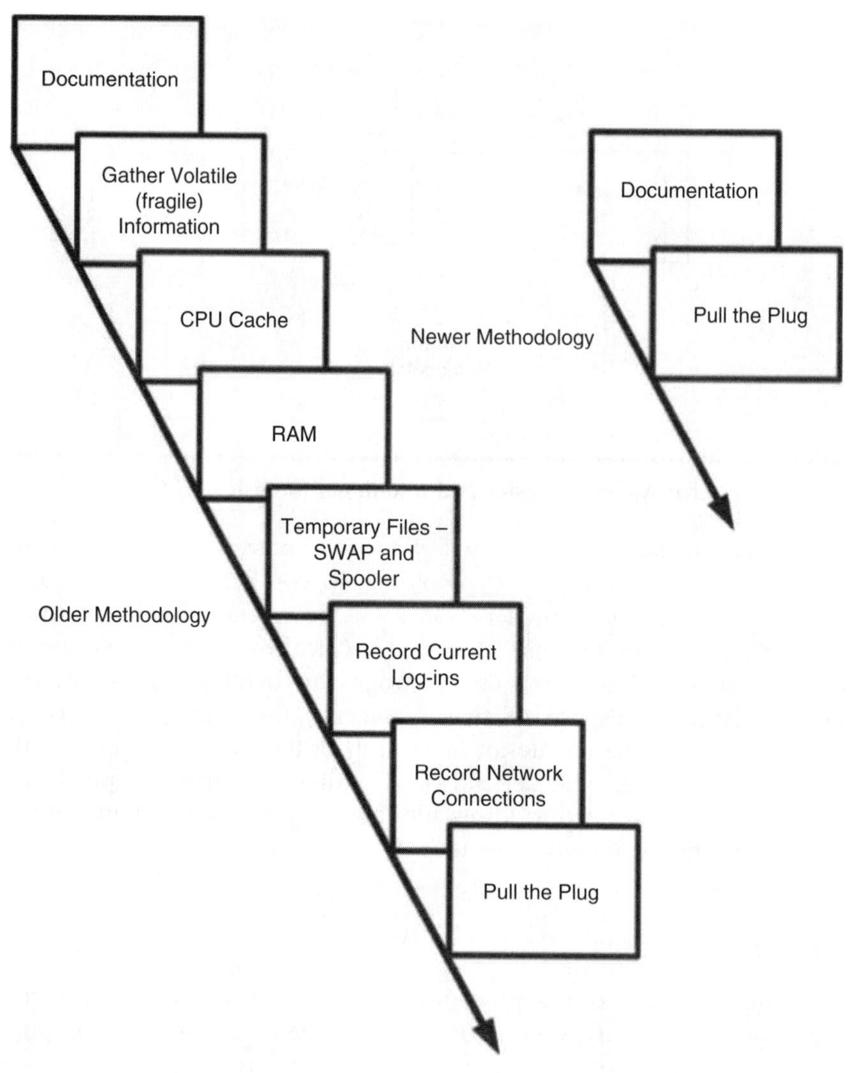

Figure 5.15 Forensic methodology comparison.

So after we've captured the contents of the system, there are two different next steps that can be taken. If you are using the older forensic methodology, you would be recovering evidence that would disappear when the system was powered off. This evidence can be called either volatile evidence or fragile evidence. Typically the evidence is recovered in order of volatility. The most volatile source of storage on a system is the CPU cache. The CPU cache is a very small area of very fast storage, which can be dumped to a file on a Linux system. Information resident in the CPU cache usually is only present for seconds. The next most volatile source of storage in a system is RAM. The contents of RAM can be dumped to a file as well. Data can be present in RAM for significantly longer than it can be present in the CPU cache, but the lifespan in memory (RAM) is short too. Many viruses and worms are present only in RAM and never exist on the hard drive.

The next most volatile area of storage is the SWAP file or virtual memory. This is actually a file that is present on the hard drive, so it is not truly volatile, but the process of pulling the plug may make the SWAP file unreadable by some forensics utilities. In equal order of volatility are spooler queues or temp files. These files are not truly volatile either and can usually be recovered using common computer forensics techniques. The last volatile information sources to gather are the current log-ins to the target system and the network connection table. These sources of information are volatile and they will definitely disappear once the plug is pulled. The advantage to using this methodology is that you will be able to gather evidence that will be lost forever when the plug is pulled. The disadvantage is the number of modifications that will be made to the target system. With this methodology once you dump the contents of the CPU cache, the contents of RAM changes. Once you dump the RAM contents, the SWAP file changes. This may call into question the validity of the evidence collected.

In the newer methodology these volatile sources of information are lost. In the newer methodology once we have finished documenting the system, we pull the plug. This will preserve the contents of the hard drive in the most pristine state possible. The drawback is that we will never be able to see the contents of the volatile sources of storage. Using either methodology we always pull the plug and not shut the system down gracefully. Pulling the plug will ensure that the OS will not modify the contents of system files while the shutdown process is running. It is common for an OS to change hundreds of files while the shutdown process is running. The pulling of the plug may present a problem in recovering the data from file systems that use heavy journaling. Both Solaris® and IRIX® are known to have this problem. As an investigator if you encounter these systems it is a good idea to consult with an expert as to the best practice for these systems.

Inventory Internal Devices

Once you've unplugged the system the next step is to document the internal contents. This can be done by taking a photograph of the system and driver and also recording the serial number of the drive or drives.

This information should be documented on an evidence worksheet like the one in Figure 5.16.

Forensic Processing—Imaging

This is just a quick reminder that this process is for traditional forensics and not for live system forensics. Once the documentation of the drive has been completed it is time to make a forensic backup of the suspect drive. This backup is a bit-stream image. A bit-stream image creates a backup of more than just the files on the drive. A bit-stream image will also create a backup of file fragments, free space, and disk space that has never been written to. What a bit-stream image will do is create a complete image of everything on a hard drive to another hard drive. There are several ways to perform a bit-stream image. There are hardware devices that will perform the bit-stream backup at the push of a button. The most common hardware forensic image device is the ImageMASSter Solo Professional 2 available from http://www.abcusinc.com/ICS-ImageMASSterSolo2ProPlus.html. There are also pay software programs that can perform a bit-stream backup such as EnCase® from Guidance Software, and Forensic ToolKit™ from AccessData.

The most common option is to use free utilities to perform the bit-stream backup. In most cases the free utility for the bit-stream will be "*dd*" from a bootable Linux CD. There are several choices for bootable CDs. Almost all of these CDs are going to be what is known as a Linux "live-CD." You do not have to be a Linux expert, or even Linux familiar to be able to use this tool in an emergency. All it will require is following some instructions. What is perhaps the most common distribution is called Knoppix. In order to get your own Knoppix CD you will have to download the Knoppix file from the Knoppix Web site (see Web site name below). This file will come in the *.iso* format. These files can be opened with most common CD-creating utilities such as Roxio or Nero. Once you have the *.iso* file downloaded to your system, simply opening the *.iso* file with your CD-creating software will prompt you to insert a blank CD into the CD burner. From this point the software will create a new CD for you. Once this CD is created, you can reboot your system (with the CD in the CD-ROM drive) and it will begin loading your new Linux system. To summarize, the steps necessary to create a "live CD" are:

1. Download the *.iso* image file.
2. Burn it to a CD.
3. Insert the CD into the compromised system.

Many "live CD" distributions are customized for different purposes. We have created a pretty decent list of "live CD" distributions and posted

EVIDENCE CHAIN OF CUSTODY FORM – FOR FORENSIC IMAGES ONLY

Case #:	Page: of

HARD DRIVE/COMPUTER DETAILS

Item #:	Description:	
Manufacturer:	Model #:	Serial #:

IMAGE DETAILS

Date/Time Image Created:	Created By:	Method Used:	Image Name:	HASH:	Drive Used To Store Image:

Figure: 5.16 Evidence worksheet.

them at http://www.pelttech.com/security/knoppix.htm. Here are some of the common "live CD" distributions that can be used for IR/Forensics:

- Knoppix: Available from http://www.knopper.net/knoppix/index-en.html. This was the first popular "live CD" distribution and most other distributions are derived from this distribution. It is still my favorite choice for performing IR.
- Penguin Sleuth: Available from http://www.linux-forensics.com. This distribution is customized for forensic usage, but it lacks native USB support and it is a bit dated. This distribution will not recognize some newer graphics adapter cards and will load only a text-based screen. It does include many of the common computer forensic utilities and it is still widely used.
- Helix: Available from http://www.e-fense.com/helix/. This distribution is also customized for forensic usage and it is being updated regularly. The most current version (Version 1.6-07-28-2005) of Helix was released July 28, 2005. It also includes many common forensics tools and also includes tools for use in a Windows® environment.

Because all of these software CDs are available free the only cost to you is that of a blank CD.

Once you have created the bootable CD, it is time to perform the bit-stream backup. This process should start by inserting your Knoppix CD into the CD drive and powering up your forensic system. When the system is booted to the CD you should see a "Knoppix:" prompt if you are using Knoppix or Penguin Sleuth. If you are using Helix you should see a GUI menu interface for booting the system (see Figure 5.17).

If you see the "Knoppix:" prompt you need to disable the swap feature of the Knoppix system. This will stop the CD from creating a temporary file on the hard drive of the compromised system's drive and thereby modifying the potential evidence. It is also a good idea to boot into the command line only mode. At the "Knoppix:" prompt, you should type `knoppix 2 noswap`.

When Knoppix is done booting you should have a prompt on the system. From here you will need to type the following commands. (These steps assume that you are using an external USB drive to hold the images and the compromised server's driver is using an IDE drive. The steps would be similar if the drives were another type, but the drive names would change. It is also assumed that the image hard drive is formatted with a Linux file system (e.g., ext2 or ext3.))

The first step is to create a directory called images. This is done by:

```
mkdir /images
```

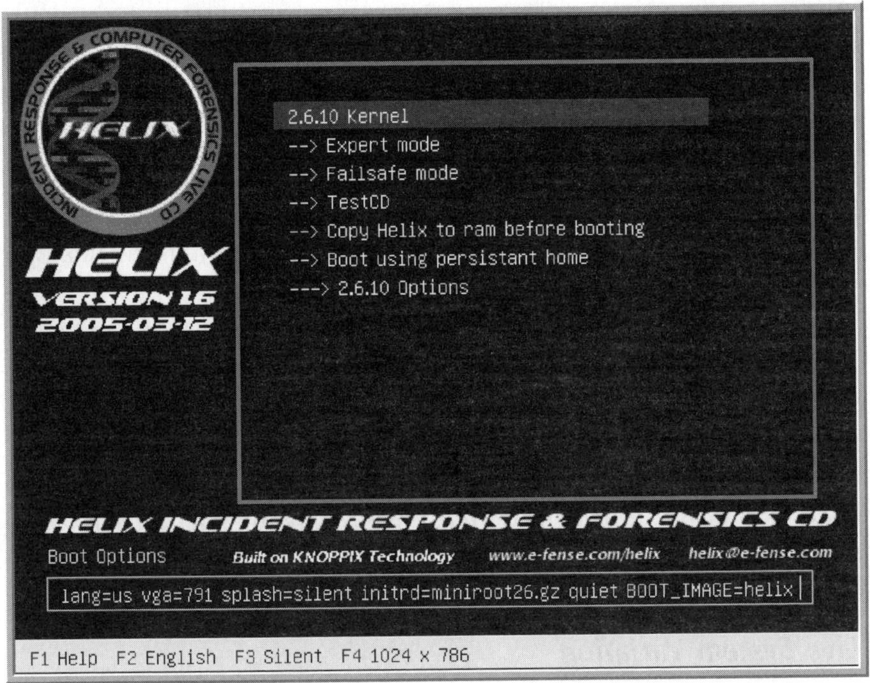

Figure 5.17 Helix boot screen.

Then mount the suspect hard drive read only. This is done by:

```
mount -ro /dev/hda1 /mnt/hda1
```

Then mount your image drive read/write. This is done by:

```
mount -rw /dev/uba1 /images
```

We now need to authenticate the original file system. The command for this is:

```
md5sum /dev/hda1 > /images/dateorig.txt
```

This will create the MD5 of the suspect hard drive. You can see the contents of this file by typing:

```
cat /images/dateorig.txt
```

We now need to perform a bit stream backup. This will copy the entire suspect hard drive including unallocated space, slack space, and truly unallocated space as well as all files and fragments. We will use the dd command for this. To start type the following.

```
dd if=/dev/hda1 of=/images/date.img
```

To see the status press "ALT + F2". This will move you to a new virtual terminal. You can type a command here without interrupting the process running on the first virtual terminal.

Then `cd /images`

Then `ls -l` (Notice the file size changing.)

To move back to the first screen press "ALT + F1". Once the drive has been successfully backed up we will now need to authenticate the new image to ensure that the drive image was copied exactly. To do this, type the following.

```
md5sum /images/date.img > /images/dateimage.txt
```

We need to compare our MD5sums to make sure that the backup is exactly the same. To do this type:

```
cat /images/dateorig.txt
cat /images/dateimage.txt
```

These commands should yield the same values. If they do, you have successfully created a forensic backup of the compromised system.

Live System Variation

Live system forensics are used when the traditional forensics process is either not needed, or the time to process is too great, or the cost is too high. One of the greatest attributes to live system forensics is the reduced cost. This does not mean committing to a huge budget or expensive software tools, but it does require a toolkit. The first thing you are going to need for your toolkit is a big hard drive. The drive that I am currently using is a Western Digital 300-GB IDE drive. These drives are pretty easy to find for less than $100, but in an emergency the price should not be more than $150 to $200.

The second piece of your toolkit is going to be some way to attach this drive. There are several options available here:

1. You can try to mount the drive using the internal IDE interface of your compromised Web server.
2. You can purchase an external USB drive when you are making your initial purchase.
3. You can purchase an external USB adapter kit.

For me, the third option is the one that I choose regularly. I just keep my eyes open for Internet specials on external USB mounting kits and buy a handful when the price is low. The average price for these kits is $16 to $26. These adapters are just plain handy to have around. It stops you from having to open up the compromised Web server and the costs are far less than purchasing an already USB-mounted drive.

The last piece necessary for your toolkit is going to be some sort of bootable CD that will provide you with the software necessary to perform local system forensics.

Some other handy tools to have are paperclips. You can use a paperclip to manually eject a CD drive to insert your bootable "live CD." Once you have pulled the plug on the target system, it is the best time to attach your external USB drive to the target system. Once you have the CD in and the USB drive attached go ahead and restore power to the machine. You will want to interrupt the boot process so that you can enter the system's BIOS configuration and record the system time. This is often done by pressing a specific key during the boot process. The most common keys are <F1>, <Del>, or <Esc>. Once you are in the BIOS, it is also a good idea to list any difference between the compromised system's time and the actual time. This can all be recorded on the Evidence Intake sheet as shown in Figure 5.13. Once the system is powered up the forensic image process is identical to the process listed above.

Forensic Processing—Imaging

After you have created the forensics of the suspect system it is time to see if the image has any data of evidentiary value in it (see Figure 5.18). There are several utilities that can be used to process the image, both pay and open source utilities. The pay utilities are the same as the pay utilities that can be used for creating the bit-stream backup. Popular examples of pay forensic processing utilities include EnCase® from Guidance Software and Forensic ToolKit™ from AccessData. The most common open source utility for forensic processing is Autopsy. Forensic processing can include recovering deleted files; searching for file fragments; uncovering hidden, encrypted, or password-protected files; searching for image files, e-mails, or inappropriate software; and reconstructing log files.

If the forensic processing does not yield any results, backup tapes are another good source of potential evidence. In some cases, if these sources do not produce any evidence you may wish to boot the system to the original OS such as Windows XP™. This may give more possible information than the forensic processing, but usually it does not. The practice of booting to the original OS is not used often because the booting process can change hundreds of files. Once the forensic processing is done it is time to prepare the report.

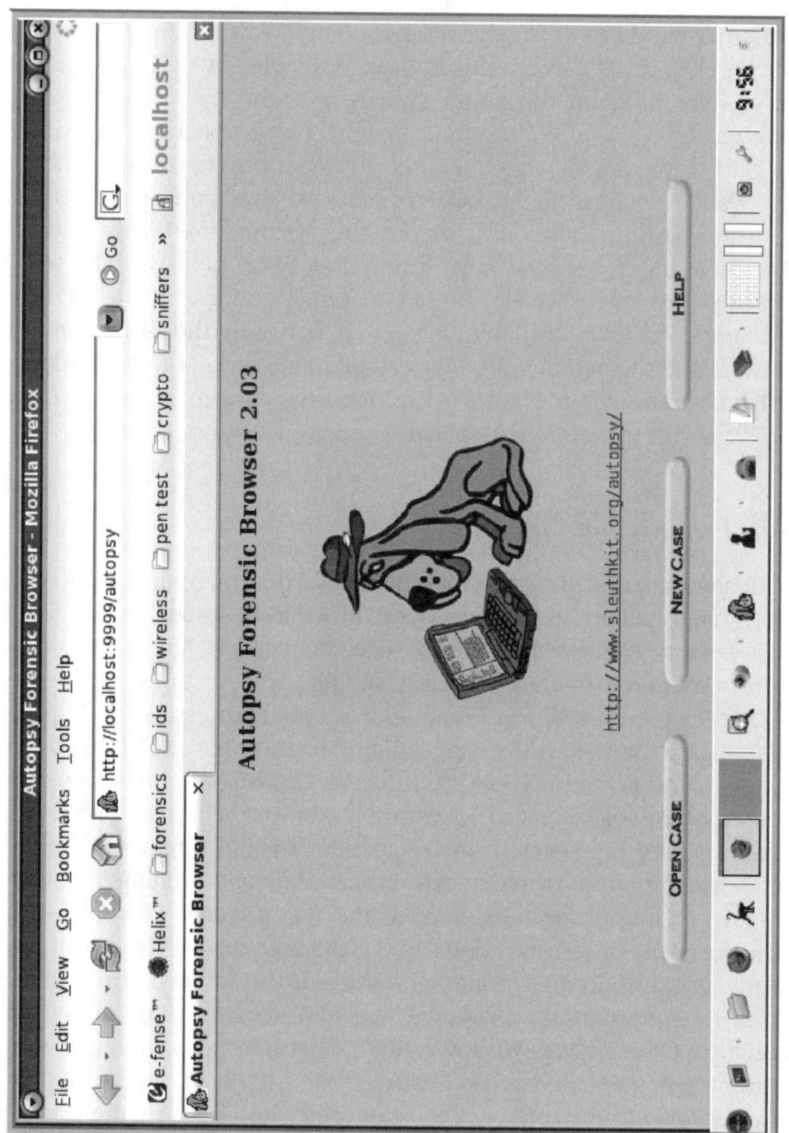

Figure 5.18 Forensic image processing.

Forensic Reporting

Most forensic processing utilities include a built-in reporting module. Forensic reporting is often difficult for technicians because forensic reporting should be brief and this is counter to how most technicians write. As technicians, we often include a large amount of background information to explain a concept. For forensic reporting no background information should be included and only the necessary summaries of facts and evidence uncovered.

Criminal and Civil Courts

Criminal courts are often the most difficult courts to have computer-related evidence accepted at trial. The greatest questioning of the validity of evidence will happen in criminal courts. In criminal courts the goal is to punish the offender and the victim is society. In a criminal trial the defendant is found either guilty or not guilty. Crimes can be either misdemeanors or felonies. Misdemeanor crimes are typically crimes that have a maximum penalty of jail time of less than one year. Felony crimes typically have jail terms of greater than one year. The standard of proof in a criminal court is reasonable doubt. In civil court the standard of proof is preponderance of evidence. The questioning of computer-related evidence in civil court is less than that of criminal court. In civil court the defendant is found either liable or not liable. The punishments in civil courts are not incarceration, but are monetary fines. With computer crimes, civil courts are where the victim can recover monies lost to the crime.

Types of Evidence

There are many different forms of evidence that can be used in a computer crime trial:

- *Direct:* Oral testimony by witness
- *Real:* Tangible objects, physical evidence
- *Documentary:* Printed business records, manuals, printouts
- *Demonstrative:* Used to aid a jury (models, illustrations)

Each type of evidence can have different forms. Some examples include:

- *Best:* Least susceptible to tampering or alteration
- *Secondary:* Less reliable in proving guilt or innocence
- *Direct:* Proves a fact without additional information

- *Conclusive:* Irrefutable and cannot be contradicted
- *Circumstantial:* Proves a fact that can be used to deduce another fact
- *Corroborative:* Used to help prove an idea or point
- *Opinion:* Can only be introduced by an expert witness

Exclusionary Rule

For evidence to be introduced in a court it must be legally obtained. This means that the gathering of the evidence was not a crime in and of itself. So we can't steal a laptop from someone's home to process the hard drive in that laptop for evidence of a crime. In addition to the evidence being legally obtained, evidence must be relevant and reliable. If the evidence is extraneous to the court case, it is not relevant. If the evidence was obtained using poor forensic practices it would not be reliable.

Evidence Life Cycle

There is a normal life cycle of evidence in a computer crime case; see Figure 5.19. The life cycle begins with the collection of the evidence. Once the evidence has been collected the evidence is subjected to forensic processing. Once the forensic processing is done the evidence must be stored and handled in a secure fashion so there can be no tampering with the evidence. After this the evidence is presented to the court and the process ends when the evidence is returned to the victim or the system owner.

Incident Post Mortems

Once the incident is over it is time to perform a postmortem review of the incident response process. Each incident provides great feedback that can be used to improve the incident response for the next incident. Some of the areas of incident response and also security that will typically be part of a postmortem review would be checking the incident response plan for its effectiveness: checking the information dissemination policy to see if information was leaked to the media, to see if the incident reporting policy was sufficient, and to see if people understood the processes when they believed their system had been compromised. As part of the postmortem improvement you may have to put together an electronic monitoring statement which informs users that information on the network is owned by the company and the company has the ability to capture any information without violating the privacy of the users.

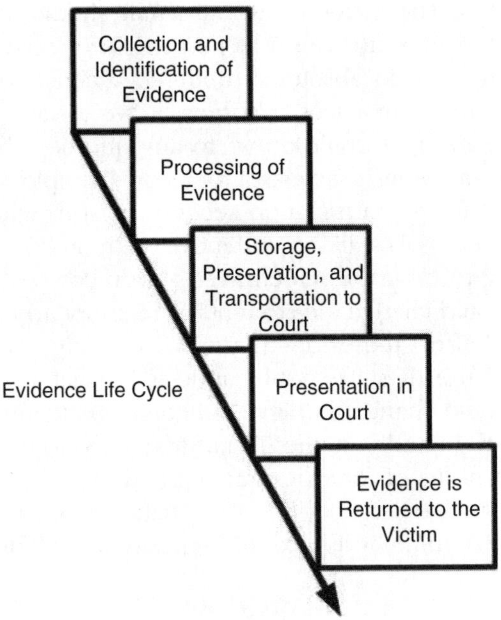

Figure 5.19 Evidence life cycle.

In addition, improvements may have to be made to create an audit trial on more systems and also in building access controls. Another improvement may be to create and implement a warning banner to let people know that the company owns the information and the system they are logging into is monitored, and by completing the log-in they are consenting to the monitoring. These are just some of the common examples of controls that may need to be increased after an incident has occurred. This is by no means a definitive list of controls, and these controls may not apply to your organization. The most important part of the postmortem review process to understand as an information security manager is that the process should exist and that it can improve the incident response plan for the next incident.

Incident Response Training

All security staff needs to be trained to do no harm, the primary mantra of a computer forensic and incident response person. Additional training should focus on training employees on how to recognize an incident and how to report an incident. This training is especially important for the help desk staff and the training should also focus on how to report the incident and also escalation procedures to make sure that adequate response happens. The incident response staff should also be trained to understand that if they are not 100 percent sure what to do, the best course of action is to do absolutely nothing. When I work with people and train them in best practices of forensics, we always explain that you never want to answer, "I don't know" to any question that you could be asked regarding a forensic investigation. For example, one of the very easy inclinations for an information security person, when a system has been compromised, is to walk up and move the mouse or hit the keyboard or do something to clear the screensaver so you can see the system. This simple action would change the contents of memory and also of the SWAP file which could affect the evidentiary value of the compromised system. This means that the IR staff should understand that it is critical to take no action that could change, modify, and contaminate any of the evidence inside the system. In addition, the IR staff may need to be specially trained employees with hours of forensics training and experience. You can have your own computer emergency response team in-house, as long as they get the requisite training and have the requisite knowledge of what to do in the event.

Difficulties with Following the Plan

I find a lot of organizations have good disaster recovery plans in case of a natural disaster. Often a plan is missing that covers what to do in the event of a computer penetration. These two types of plans have completely different objectives. In the case of a natural disaster the primary goal is to return to process as soon as possible. In the case of a computer penetration the primary goal is to preserve as much evidence of the compromise as possible. Because of the completely different set of rules between the two types of plans it is necessary to create two different documents that explain how to enact the plan. This is partly to do with the risk associated with performing an immediate restore from tape backup in the event of a system penetration. This process would be restoring the vulnerability to your system and in addition you will also be destroying any evidence of the crime. An immediate restore from tape backup would negate any chance of figuring out how that system was compromised. The plan for incident response in the event of a system compromise, as well as the data preservation guideline, should be put together with your organization's legal counsel to make sure you are gathering the data legally using sound forensic practices.

Containment

After you believe an incident has occurred, look for the scope and size of the affected system: how far did the incident spread? This is the mantra of containment, which is often illustrated by the defense-in-depth strategy. The defense-in-depth mechanism provides redundancy to your security controls. Defense in depth is where you have a secondary control providing security in the event your primary control fails. A common example of this would be installing the IPTables or TCPWrappers firewall in addition to an enterprise-class software firewall on a UNIX-based system. The defense in depth would continue to protect the organization in the event that the enterprise-class software firewall were compromised. In this case the IPTables or TCPWrappers would continue to filter or block traffic in the event that an attacker had compromised the primary firewall software. This defense should actually be an additional step deeper, when the UNIX OS was hardened to minimize the number of potential security exposure points. All of the redundant controls would minimize the outbreak and also minimize the impact of the penetration. In addition the controls would make the penetration more difficult and would also provide more evidence to determine how the attack occurred.

A common component of incident response is to back-trace the incident. The back-trace process occurs when you are going to try to trace from the compromised computer back to the originating source. Because many attackers use other compromised systems on the Internet as hops to attempt to hide the true source of the attack, it is necessary to identify all the possible paths and means of attack. There is an example case where a large organization was infected with the SQL Slammer worm despite the fact that their organization was protected along its perimeter by gateway anti-virus and firewall products. A primary concern of the incident response team was to determine how the SQL Slammer worm was able to get on the organization's network if none of the routers or firewalls would allow the SQL Slammer attack to traverse them. After a long investigation a determination was made that the SQL development staff was at fault. The SQL development staff took their laptops home at night, and attached the laptops to their home wireless network where the infection occurred. When the SQL developers were done working for the night they suspended their systems as opposed to shutting them down. When they went in to work the next day they resumed their sessions and because SQL Slammer is resident only in memory and the memory was not cleared because of the suspension and not a reboot of the system, they had a SQL Slammer outbreak. The incident response team was able to figure out how the outbreak occurred because all other exposure points had a control that would have blocked the SQL Slammer worm.

Government Facilities to Assist in Planning for a Disaster

As an information security manager you need to understand what government facilities exist when it comes to incident response and natural disasters. An example of such a facility is FEMA, the Federal Emergency Management Agency (www.fema.gov). FEMA can provide statistics about which types of disasters are most likely to happen and also FEMA can provide information about their own planned response which may include details such as the evacuation route. If your area has to be evacuated, they can tell you about city evacuation plans. FEMA can also tell you about natural disaster planning for different areas. Please understand that this information may or may not always be available. The availability of this information can be dependent on the terrorist threat level and also if a disaster is currently occurring. In the event of a disaster information may only be released on a need-to-know basis. However, if you request this information during a period of calm they are usually willing to share the information with you.

Escalation Procedures and Notification

Part of the disaster recovery plan should include both how to escalate the incidents and how people should be notified and in what specific order. Typical groups that will need to be notified in the event of an incident include senior management, the public, shareholders, and the legal department. Any decision to release information should be done in accordance with an information dissemination policy and that should be created in conjunction with public relations, legal counsel, and senior management. Escalation procedures should not just be restricted to escalation with your own organization, but the plan should also have escalation processes for dealing with vendors. This is needed in case you have a vendor employee that is not responding quickly enough or is creating issues that is hindering the response plan. The escalation procedure would provide a mechanism to reach a higher-ranking employee to resolve any issues. This means that not only does the information security manager need to have primary contact information but also escalation numbers so you can contact additional personnel to resolve problems.

Help Desk Training

Help desk personnel are often the first line of defense and also the first group that can notice an incident has occurred. It is imperative that help desk teams are trained to differentiate between a normal help desk request and social engineering attacks. Part of the training for help desk teams should include verifying the information of employees. Help desk teams also need to be trained to resist the pressure attacks that a social engineer may attempt to use against them. This means that help desk teams need to be trained in the company's escalation process and they should understand when to refer requests to a manager.

Summary

Response management is the smallest of the five functional areas of the CISM exam. In this section we covered business continuity planning and the component plans of the BCP. We also discussed incident response and computer forensics. All of the concepts in this chapter are evolving concepts that are changing rapidly. These areas are some of the newest in information security and as such most of the concepts will continue to evolve and mature.

What Was Covered in This Chapter

- Business continuity planning
- The difference between a disaster and an incident
- Threat and attack information sources
- Business impact analysis
- Network inventories
- Maximum tolerable outages
- Recovery time objectives
- Recovery point objectives
- Alternate processing sites
- Training for BCP
- Testing the BCP
- Writing the BCP
- The three phases of BCP: respond, recover, and resume
- BCP teams
- Incident response
- Discovery
- Notification
- Preliminary investigation
- Investigation goals
- Disclosure
- Physical and electronic surveillance
- Factors of investigation

- Likely suspects
- Interview and interrogation techniques
- Preservation and containment
- Incident response team members
- Seizing the system
- Analysis
- Live systems forensics
- Computer forensics
- Forensic methodologies
- Creating forensic images
- Forensic reporting
- Presentation
- Criminal and civil courts
- Types of evidence
- Exclusionary rule
- Evidence life cycle
- Postmortem reviews
- Incident response training
- Defense in depth
- Government facilities to assist in planning for a disaster
- Escalation procedures
- Help desk training

Questions

1. Which of the following is not a responsibility of the data or systems owner?
   A, To identify, describe, and designate the sensitivity of their applications systems
   B. To ensure that appropriate security control requirements are included in specifications
   C. To assess security requirements by evaluating application assets, threats, and vulnerabilities
   D. To develop industry best practices

Answer D

2. Which of the following attacks would compromise the integrity of system information?
   A. Denial-of-service
   B. Smurf
   C. SQL Injection
   D. Fraggle

Answer C

3. A policy for the physical component of the information technology infrastructure could work with all of the following except
   A. Firewalls
   B. ID badges
   C. Cameras
   D. Security guards

Answer A

4. Which of the following is not an example of the platform component of information technology infrastructure?
   A. Switch security
   B. Operating system security
   C. Application security
   D. Anti-virus

Answer A

5. Which of the following is an example of the network component of information technology infrastructure?
   A. Switch security
   B. Operating system security
   C. Application security
   D. Anti-virus

Answer A

6. When implementing a security control, an information security manager needs to be especially aware of:
   A. Change control management
   B. What the organization's competition is doing
   C. A promotion to production procedure
   D. The impact on the end-user community

Answer D

7. Which of the following is often a disadvantage of using a closed system?
   A. Lack of end-user support
   B. Lack of product functionality
   C. The source code cannot be verified
   D. The source code is provided by the Internet community at large

Answer C

8. Which of the following is an advantage of an open system?
   A. End-user support
   B. The source code can be verified

C. Difficulty in management
D. All users are always permitted to access the system

Answer B

9. What would be a disadvantage of deploying a proxy-based firewall?
   A. Proxy-based firewalls may not support custom applications
   B. Proxy-based firewalls inspect only to the network layer of the OSI model
   C. Proxy-based firewalls cannot block unwanted traffic
   D. Proxy-based firewalls do not provide network address translation

Answer A

10. Which of the following is true of a stateful inspection firewall?
   A. Stateful inspection firewalls protect through all layers of the OSI model
   B. Stateful inspection firewalls support more custom applications than other firewalls
   C. Stateful inspection firewalls are faster then other firewalls
   D. Stateful inspection firewalls do not provide network address translation

Answer B

11. Which of the following is true regarding a packet filter firewall?
   A. Packet filter firewalls provide more protection than other firewalls
   B. Packet filter firewalls provide protection through the entire OSI model
   C. Packet filter firewalls do not provide network address translation
   D. Packet filter firewalls provide less protection than other firewalls

Answer D

12. Which of the following would be an advantage to deploying public key (asymmetric) as opposed to private key (symmetric) encryption technologies?
   A. Public key is more scalable
   B. Public key encryption is faster
   C. Public key requires less infrastructure
   D. Private key is easier on the end-user community

Answer A

13. Digital signatures encrypt the message hash with which of the following keys?
   A. Sender's public key
   B. Sender's private key

C. Receiver's public key
D. Receiver's private key

Answer B

14. What term is best defined as a model used to determine the security and functionality of a proposed project?
    A. Prototype
    B. Checkpoint
    C. Journaling
    D. Service level agreement

Answer A

15. What is an advantage in performing a vulnerability assessment over a penetration test?
    A. Penetration tests test the entire network
    B. Vulnerability assessments compromise a system or network
    C. Vulnerability assessments are a structured repeatable test
    D. Vulnerability assessments are faster to conduct than penetration testing

Answer C

16. What advantage does discretionary access control have over mandatory access control?
    A. Mandatory access control is easier to implement
    B. Discretionary access control uses extensive labeling
    C. Discretionary access control has less administrative overhead
    D. Discretionary access control is determined by policy

Answer C

17. Which of the following technologies protects the confidentiality of information by embedding the message into an image or music file?
    A. Public key cryptography
    B. Private key cryptography
    C. Digital signatures
    D. Steganography

Answer D

18. Which of the following algorithms is a public key algorithm?
    A. DES
    B. AES
    C. RC4
    D. RSA

Answer D

19. Two-factor authentication can be established by combining something you have, you are, and which of the following terms?
    A. You know
    B. You read
    C. You touch
    D. You need

Answer A

20. Which of the following can be a security concern with host-based single-sign-on implementations?
    A. Passwords are often stored in plaintext
    B. Passwords are often transmitted in plaintext
    C. The authentication host can be a single point of failure
    D. Lack of scalability

Answer C

21. A Message Authentication Code (MAC) is a message digest encrypted with which of the following keys?
    A. The sender's public key
    B. The session key
    C. The receiver's public key
    D. The server's public key

Answer B

22. Message hashes provide which of the following principles of information security management?
    A. Integrity
    B. Confidentiality
    C. Availability
    D. Authentication

Answer A

23. Which of the following terms is best defined as a project to identify the threats that exist over key information and information technology?
    A. Vulnerability assessment
    B. Penetration test
    C. Threat analysis
    D. System development life cycle

Answer C

24. Key escrow is an example of which of the following security principles?

A. Split knowledge
B. Two-factor authentication
C. Need to know
D. Least privilege

Answer A

25. Which of the following algorithms is an example of a one-time pad?
    A. DES
    B. AES
    C. RSA
    D. RC4

Answer D

26. A one-time pad differs from other symmetric key algorithms in that:
    A. A new key is never exchanged
    B. The key is used for one message and then discarded
    C. The length of the key can be longer than for other algorithms
    D. The key dynamically regenerates

Answer B

27. Which of the following terms relates to increasing the integrity of information on a system?
    A. Fault tolerance
    B. Failover
    C. Checkpoint
    D. Host-based intrusion detection

Answer D

28. Which of the following processes comes at the end of the system development life cycle?
    A. Accreditation
    B. Logical configuration
    C. Development
    D. Certification

Answer A

29. Public key cryptographic algorithms can be used for encryption and
    A. Message authentication codes
    B. Digital signatures
    C. Message hashing
    D. Message integrity checks

Answer B

30. What is the first step in the system development life cycle?
    A. Perform a business impact analysis
    B. Perform a penetration test
    C. Perform a vulnerability assessment
    D. Perform a risk analysis

Answer D

31. When should security become involved in the systems development life cycle?
    A. Prior to implementation
    B. Prior to all audits
    C. During requirements development
    D. During development

Answer C

32. To implement the results of a risk assessment, the information security manger should assign responsibilities and
    A. Define an implementation schedule
    B. Define a vulnerability matrix
    C. Define a system development life cycle
    D. Define a matrix for prototyping

Answer A

33. When comparing the security of wireless networks with traditional or cabled networking:
    A. Wired networking provides more points for potential eavesdropping
    B. Eavesdropping is not possible on a wireless network
    C. Wired networking provides some protection from eavesdropping
    D. Eavesdropping is not possible on a wireless network

Answer C

34. In order to determine the metrics for your network you will need to begin with a measurement of current network conditions. This is called a
    A. Threat assessment
    B. Baseline
    C. Risk assessment
    D. Prototype

Answer B

35. Which of the following can be a disadvantage of using a centralized access control system?
    A. Lack of consistent administration
    B. Lack of resource control
    C. Difficulty in synchronizing account information
    D. It can create a single point of failure

Answer D

36. A formal acceptance, by management, of a third-party review of the security controls of a system, network, or application is:
    A. Certification
    B. Authentication
    C. Accreditation
    D. Classification

Answer C

37. Prior to development, to determine possible exposure points to a new application in your organization the information security manager would perform a:
    A. Vulnerability assessment
    B. Business impact analysis
    C. Risk assessment
    D. Penetration test

Answer C

38. Which of the following technologies or standards would apply to authenticating a wireless network connection?
    A. Wired equivalent privacy
    B. 802.11b
    C. 802.11a
    D. 802.1x

Answer D

39. Wired Equivalent Privacy (WEP) is a control that increases which of the basic principles of information security management?
    A. Confidentiality
    B. Integrity
    C. Availability
    D. Authenticity

Answer A

40. Service level agreements with a managed service provider provide minimum requirements and are included in a:
    A. Contract
    B. Policy
    C. Procedure
    D. Standard

Answer A

41. For e-mail messages with the greatest sensitivity which of the following technologies would have to be employed to provide confidentiality, integrity, and authenticity?
    A. Digital signatures
    B. Message digests
    C. Private key encryption
    D. Digital signatures and encryption

Answer D

42. Which of the following technologies provides a mechanism for storing a digital certificate?
    A. Magnetic cards
    B. Smart cards
    C. Stream cipher
    D. Block cipher

Answer B

43. Which layer of the OSI model would be responsible for ensuring reliable end-to-end delivery of a message?
    A. Physical
    B. Application
    C. Session
    D. Transport

Answer D

44. At what layer of the OSI model would a proxy-based firewall exist?
    A. Physical
    B. Application
    C. Session
    D. Transport

Answer B

45. Message Digest version five (MD5) is an algorithm that is used to ensure message:
    A. Integrity

B. Authenticity
C. Confidentiality
D. Fault Tolerance

Answer A

46. Creating a message digest is often the first step in creating a:
    A. Packet
    B. Digital signature
    C. Public key
    D. Private key

Answer B

47. An attacker who is attempting to defeat an access control system often starts by performing which of the common types of attacks?
    A. Brute force attack
    B. Denial-of-service attack
    C. Distributed denial-of-service attack
    D. Dictionary attack

Answer D

48. Temporal Key Integrity Protocol (TKIP) is a component of Wi-Fi Protected Access (WPA). What is the major advantage with using TKIP?
    A. TKIP ensures data integrity
    B. TKIP allows data encryption keys to be changed at regular time intervals
    C. TKIP provides protection against wireless denial-of-service attacks
    D. TKIP increases the signal strength of wireless networks

Answer B

49. An e-mail with a large attachment designed to slow down the response time for the e-mail server is a representation of what type of malicious code?
    A. Trojan horse
    B. Worm
    C. E-mail bomb
    D. Logic bomb

Answer C

50. What type of malicious code is a code fragment that attaches to a file and often replicates through the sharing of files on a network?
    A. Virus

B. Worm
C. E-mail bomb
D. Logic bomb

Answer A

51. What type of malicious code is typically a complete file that infects only one place on a single system and replicates through the network without file sharing?
A. Virus
B. Worm
C. E-mail bomb
D. Logic bomb

Answer B

52. True or False: Private key cryptography requires less processing power than public key cryptography.

Answer True

53. Which of the following IPsec-related terms will help resolve authentication issues present in Internet Protocol (IP)?
A. High-level Message Authentication Code (HMAC)
B. Authentication Headers (AH)
C. Encapsulated Secure Payload (ESP)
D. Data Encryption Standard (DES)

Answer B

54. Which of the following IPsec-related terms will help resolve confidentiality issues present in Internet Protocol (IP)?
A. High-level Message Authentication Code (HMAC)
B. Authentication Headers (AH)
C. Encapsulated Secure Payload (ESP)
D. Data Encryption Standard (DES)

Answer C

55. Which of the following is true regarding IPSEC?
A. IPSEC will encapsulate Internet Protocol (IP) traffic only
B. IPSEC will support only one concurrent tunnel
C. IPSEC operates at the physical layer of the ODI model
D. IPSEC requires the use of Public Key Infrastructure (PKI)

Answer A

56. Presenting a fraudulent Internet Protocol (IP) address to attempt to bypass the access control enforced by a stateful inspection firewall is an example of what common type of network attack?
    A. Social engineering
    B. Spoofing
    C. SYN flood
    D. Steganography

Answer B

57. Which of the following positions would be most likely to determine the security policy regarding access of information on a system?
    A. Users
    B. Business process owner
    C. Senior management
    D. Information security manager

Answer B

58. Which of the following groups or organizations is most commonly used to develop baselines for information systems?
    A. Developers
    B. Programmers
    C. Software vendors
    D. Promotion to production staff

Answer C

59. Which type of malicious detection software would detect a polymorphic virus by comparing the function of the application rather than comparing it to a known signature?
    A. Heuristic scanner
    B. Host-based intrusion detection
    C. Network-based intrusion detection
    D. Gateway anti-virus scanner

Answer A

60. What is a primary difference between Secure Sockets Layer (SSL) and Secure HyperText Transfer Protocol (SHTTP)?
    A. SSL only encrypts Web traffic
    B. SHTTP does not encrypt the data
    C. SSL does not encrypt the data
    D. SSL is a transport layer protocol

Answer D

61. Which statement most accurately reflects the encryption used by SSL?
    A. The session key is encrypted using asymmetric key encryption and the bulk data is encrypted with symmetric encryption
    B. The bulk data transfer is encrypted using asymmetric encryption; the key is exchanged out of band
    C. SSL uses asymmetric encryption for both session key exchange and bulk data encryption
    D. SSL does not use encryption

Answer A

62. If you wanted to ensure the integrity of the message, which of the following technologies would provide the most insurance against tampering?
    A. Logging before and after records
    B. Digital signatures
    C. Asymmetric encryption
    D. Symmetric encryption

Answer B

63. A vendor is recommending implementation of a new technology that will give your application nonrepudiation. Which of the following primary tenets of information security will be addressed with this solution?
    A. Availability and integrity
    B. Confidentiality and integrity
    C. Confidentiality and authenticity
    D. Authenticity and integrity

Answer D

64. Which of the following primary tenets of information security will be addressed by using 802.1x with a wireless network?
    A. Authentication
    B. Availability
    C. Integrity
    D. Confidentiality

Answer A

65. Which of the following technologies are commonly used in conjunction with 802.1x authentication?
    A. Remote Authentication Dial In User Service (RADIUS)
    B. Single Sign On (SSO)
    C. Public Key Infrastructure (PKI)

D. Intrusion Detection System (IDS)

Answer A

66. Which common type of access control system assigns rights to job functions and not user accounts?
    A. Rule-based access control
    B. Role-based access control
    C. Mandatory access control
    D. Discretionary access control

Answer B

67. Which of the following is an example of security issues that can occur within the system development life cycle?
    A. Lack of senior management support
    B. Security is not involved in the requirements development
    C. Vendor interoperability
    D. Network latency

Answer B

68. The information security manager needs to be most aware of which of the following issues when implementing new security controls?
    A. Impact on end users
    B. Senior management support
    C. System development life cycle
    D. Annual loss expectancy

Answer A

69. Which of the following security concerns needs to be addressed during the disposal phase of the system development life cycle?
    A. Maintaining integrity of information
    B. Maintaining availability of the system
    C. Maintaining nonrepudiation of user access
    D. Maintaining confidentiality of information

Answer D

70. Change control can be used in many phases on the system development life cycle. At which phase of the system development life cycle would you not use a change control process?
    A. Development
    B. Installation
    C. Disposal
    D. Requirements

Answer D

71. Which of the following types of controls would affect direct access to system consoles?
    A. Process
    B. Platform
    C. Physical
    D. Network

Answer C

72. Which of the following types of controls would directly affect the security of an operating system?
    A. Process
    B. Platform
    C. Physical
    D. Network

Answer B

73. Which of the following technologies would utilize a Public Key Infrastructure (PKI)?
    A. Secure HyperText Transfer Protocol (SHTTP)
    B. Secure SHell (SSH)
    C. Message Authentication Codes (MAC)
    D. Digital signatures

Answer D

74. Smart card technology is often used for what information security purpose?
    A. Message integrity
    B. Authentication
    C. Confidentiality
    D. Availability

Answer B

75. Extensible Markup Language (XML) is a language often used with Web application development. XML provides which of the following?
    A. Dynamic content delivery
    B. Dynamic message integrity
    C. Dynamic user authentication
    D. Dynamic client configuration

Answer A

76. An acceptable use policy would be an example of which type of control?
    A. Process

B. Platform
C. Physical
D. Network

Answer A

77. Which type of attack against access control systems uses a list of common words?
A. A brute force attack
B. A denial-of-service attack
C. A dictionary attack
D. A network spoofing attack

Answer C

78. Which type of information security process assigns a level of sensitivity to data as it is being created, amended, enhanced, stored, or transmitted?
A. Risk analysis
B. Risk assessment
C. Network vulnerability assessment
D. Information classification

Answer D

79. Which type of device creates a variable, alternating current (AC) field for the purpose of demagnetizing magnetic recording media?
A. A degausser
B. A demagnetizer
C. A deionizer
D. A deflator

Answer A

80. Which of the following terms frequently refers to a network segment between the Internet and a private network?
A. A security domain
B. A zone of control
C. A DeMilitarized Zone (DMZ)
D. A security kernel

Answer C

81. Which type of network attack captures sensitive pieces of information, such as passwords, passing through the network?
A. Spoofing
B. SYN flood
C. Sniffing

D. Steganography

Answer C

82. Which of the following technologies would best secure the data on a laptop or other device that could be stolen?
    A. Data encryption
    B. File deletion
    C. No access to the floppy drive
    D. Steganography

Answer A

83. Which of the following attacks is an example of a passive attack?
    A. Spoofing
    B. SYN flood
    C. Information gathering
    D. Port scanning

Answer C

84. Which of the following common network attacks is an example of a denial-of-service attack?
    A. Spoofing
    B. SYN flood
    C. Sniffing
    D. Port scanning

Answer B

85. Which of the following common network attacks is an example of an active attack?
    A. Information gathering
    B. Traffic analysis
    C. Sniffing
    D. Port scanning

Answer D

86. Which type of network attack is most likely to present the ability to execute commands on the compromised machine?
    A. Spoofing
    B. SYN flood
    C. Sniffing
    D. Buffer overflow

Answer D

87. Which attack is due to poor programming practices?
    A. Spoofing
    B. SYN flood
    C. Sniffing
    D. Buffer overflow

Answer D

Index

B

C

D

E

F

G

H

I

J

K

L

M

N

O

Q

R

S

T

U

V

W

X

Z